Limiting institutions?

MANCHESTER
UNIVERSITY PRESS

Limiting institutions?

The challenge of Eurasian security governance

*edited by James Sperling, Sean Kay
and S. Victor Papacosma*

Manchester University Press

Manchester and New York

distributed exclusively in the USA by Palgrave

Published by Manchester University Press
Oxford Road, Manchester M13 9NR, UK
and Room 400, 175 Fifth Avenue, New York, NY 10010, USA
www.manchesteruniversitypress.co.uk

Distributed exclusively in the USA by
Palgrave, 175 Fifth Avenue, New York,
NY 10010, USA

Distributed exclusively in Canada by
UBC Press, University of British Columbia, 2029 West Mall,
Vancouver, BC, Canada V6T 1Z2

British Library Cataloguing-in-Publication Data
A catalogue record for this book is available from the British Library

Library of Congress Cataloging-in-Publication Data applied for

ISBN 0 7190 6604 2 *hardback*
     0 7190 6605 0 *paperback*

First published 2003

11   10   09   08   07   06   05   04   03   10   9   8   6   5   4   3   2   1

Typeset in Photina
by Action Publishing Technology Ltd, Gloucester
Printed in Great Britain
by Bell & Bain Ltd, Glasgow

To Joy, Anna-Marie and Evie

Contents

IV   Conclusion

Contributors

Douglas Blum is Associate Professor of Political Science at Providence College.

David P. Calleo is University Professor, Dean Acheson Professor of European Studies and Director of European Studies at the Paul Nitze School of Advanced International Studies, the Johns Hopkins University.

Jaewoo Choo is Research Fellow, Northeast Asia Team, Korea International Trade Association (Seoul, Korea).

Geoffery Cockerham is a PhD candidate in the Department of Political Science, University of Arizona.

P. Terrence Hopmann is Professor of Political Science and Research Director of the Program on Global Security of the Thomas J. Watson Institute for International Studies, Brown University.

Stuart Horsman is a Research Analyst at the UK Foreign and Commonwealth Office.

Stuart Kaufman is Associate Professor of Political Science at the University of Kentucky.

Sean Kay is Associate Professor of Political Science at Ohio Wesleyan University and non-resident fellow at the Eisenhower Institute, Washington, DC.

Panagiota Manoli is Secretary of the Parliamentary Assembly of the BSEC (PABSEC) Economic, Commercial, Technological and Environmental Affairs Committee, PABSEC International Secretariat, Istanbul, Turkey.

S. Victor Papacosma is Professor of History and Director of the Lemnitzer Center for NATO and EU Studies, Kent State University.

Simon Serfaty is Professor and Eminent Scholar in International Studies at Old Dominion University (ODU), Norfolk, Virginia, and Director of European Studies at the Center for Strategic and International Studies (CSIS).

James Sperling is Professor of Political Science at the University of Akron.

Joshua B. Spero, Assistant Professor of Political Science at Fitchburg State College, served from 1994 to 2000 as the senior civilian strategic planner on Euro-Atlantic and NATO security issues for the Joint Chiefs of Staff.

John P. Willerton is Associate Professor of Political Science at the University of Arizona.

Phil Williams is Professor of International Security in the Graduate School of Public and International Affairs, University of Pittsburgh, and was formerly Director of the Ridgeway Center, University of Pittsburgh.

Preface and acknowledgements

The unification of Germany and the dissolution of the Soviet Union nullified the oft-remarked upon geopolitical and strategic certitude that had evolved after 1945. The dissolution of the Soviet Union, in particular, erased the geopolitical demarcation of the eastern boundary of the 'West' and the southern boundary separating greater Europe from the Middle East. Similarly, the Soviet-American competition had produced a *de facto* distinction between the geopolitics of Asia and the geopolitics of Europe. Eurasia, as a geopolitical designation, lost the currency it had enjoyed in the early twentieth century owing to the consolidation of the internal and external Soviet imperium, the post-civil war consolidation of China, and the Atlantic orientation of postwar American foreign policy.

Eurasia remains a rather ill-defined geostrategic space in two respects. First, any line of demarcation along its southern periphery can be as easily claimed as a part of the northern periphery of the Middle East. Second, the accent placed on the Asian or the European in Eurasia will perforce reflect an individual's mental map, which is in turn shaped by idiosyncratic variables (intellectual habit and national origin) and substantive ones (the nature of the security threat examined and the membership of the regional institution(s) engaged in the critical task of security governance). It is our hope that *Limiting Institutions?* makes a contribution to the debate over the source and nature of the security threats facing the European security order in the early twenty-first century and the role formal institutions can play in the task of regional (and by extension global) security governance, however Eurasia is eventually delimited.

The chapters in this book took final shape after draft papers were presented at an international conference sponsored by the Lyman L. Lemnitzer Center for NATO and European Union Studies at Kent State University. The conference, 'Limiting Institutions? The Challenge of Eurasian Security', was held on 28–29 September 2001. We initially planned to address the emerging need for new research and analysis of the Eurasian region, particularly the requirements of security governance, when our discussions to hold the conference began the preceding September. It became quickly evident that the meeting's significance heightened in the aftermath of 11 September 2001, but we also had to consider cancelling the conference owing to the widespread (and understandable) reticence to board an airplane so soon after the attack on the Pentagon and the destruction of the Twin Towers of the World Trade Center. When we asked the conference participants whether we should postpone or even cancel the event entirely, they all agreed the conference needed to go forward as scheduled. *Limiting Institutions?* is the product of that meeting.

Mention must be made of individuals, other than the authors, who contributed to the conference's success. Lawrence S. Kaplan, director emeritus of the Lemnitzer Center, who has vigorously maintained his productive relationship with it, offered a characteristically stimulating luncheon address, 'Reflections on the Lemnitzer Center's Relevance to the History of the Atlantic Alliance'. Participants also benefited greatly from the insightful and timely observations delivered by Ambassador Charles Dunbar (retired) in his evening presentation, 'US Policy in Eurasia and Beyond'. Thanks are also owed to a number of individuals who served as panel chairs and discussants, including Andrew Barnes, Boleslaw Boczek, Patrick Clawson, Joseph H. Danks, Hanna Freij, Jonathan Helmreich, John Logue, Steven Oluic, Argyrios Pisiotis and Mark R. Rubin.

S. Victor Papacosma would like to express his gratitude to the staff from the Lemnitzer Center and Kent State University's Center for International and Comparative Programs, who provided important administrative services in the organisation of the conference: Alan Coe, Sandy Baker, Judith Carroll and John Gannon. Sean Kay would like to thank his departmental secretary, Pam Laucher, for her help and Bill Louthan. James Sperling would like to thank his long-suffering research assistant, Keery Walker, for her cheerful disposition and occasional willingness to do what is asked of her.

The editors dedicate this book to their wives, Joy Sperling, Anna-Marie Kay and Evie Papacosma, who have gracefully endured the academic and other eccentricities of their American spouses.

James Sperling
Sean Kay
S. Victor Papacosma

Abbreviations and acronyms

ASBP	Aral Sea Basin Program
ASOC	Air Sovereignty Operations Centres
BSC	Black Sea–Caucasus Cooperation
BSCC	Black Sea–Caucasus–Caspian Political Forum
BSEC	Black Sea Economic Cooperation
BVO	Basin Management Authority
CAC	Central Asian Cooperation Organisation
CAEC	Central Asian Economic Community
CAEU	Central Asia Economic Union
CENTCOM	Central Command
Centrasbat	Central Asian Peacekeeping Battalion
CFSP	Common Foreign and Security Policy
CIS	Commonwealth of Independent States
CPC	Conflict Prevention Center
CSBM	confidence- and security-building measure
CSCE	Conference on Security and Cooperation in Europe
DRMS	Defense Resource Management Studies Program
EEU	Eurasian Economic Union
EMU	European Monetary Union
ESDI	European Security and Defence Identity
ESDP	European Security and Defence Policy
EUCOM	European Command
FSU	former Soviet Union
GDP	gross domestic product
GNP	gross national product
GUAM	Georgia, Ukraine, Azerbaijan and Moldova grouping
GUUAM	Georgia, Ukraine, Uzbekistan, Azerbaijan and Moldova grouping
HCNM	High Commissioner on National Minorities

HEP	hydroelectric production
ICAS	Interstate Council on Problems of the Aral Sea Basin
ICWC	Interstate Commission on Water Coordination
IFAS	International Fund for the Aral Sea
IFOR	Implementation Force
IGC	intergovernmental conference
IMF	International Monetary Fund
IMRO	Internal Macedonian Revolutionary Organisation
KFOR	Kosovo Implementation Force
LTTE	Liberation Tigers of Tamil Eelam
NATO	North Atlantic Treaty Organisation
NGO	non-governmental organisation
NLA	National Liberation Army
ODIHR	Office of Democratic Institutions and Human Rights
OSCE	Organisation for Security and Cooperation in Europe
PfP	Partnership for Peace
PIMS	Partnership for Peace Information Management System
PTA	preferential trading arrangement
RAI	Regional Airspace Initiative
REACT	Rapid Expert Assistance and Cooperation Teams
SACEUR	Supreme Allied Commander Europe
SCO	Shanghai Cooperation Organisation
SDS	Serbian Democratic Party
SFOR	Stabilisation Force
SHAPE	Supreme Headquarters Allied Powers Europe
SSR	Soviet Socialist Republic
TRACECA	Transport Corridor Europe Caucasus Asia
UNDP	United Nations Development Program
UNPREDEP	United Nations Preventive Deployment Force
WARMAP	Water Resources Management and Agricultural Production
WEU	Western European Union
WMD	weapons of mass destruction
WTO	World Trade Organisation

I
Introduction

1

Eurasian security governance: new threats, institutional adaptations

James Sperling

Halford Mackinder developed the geostrategic formulation recognising that international politics encompasses the globe. His simple formulation, which guided early twentieth-century policy-makers and theorists in North America and continental Europe alike, held that the state that controls the Eurasian heartland controls the periphery, and the state that controls the periphery controls the world.[1] More so than in the first decade of the twentieth century, the European system has ceased to be 'European' – the great powers are no longer solely European in the cultural or geographical sense. The end of the Cold War eradicated the *cordon sanitaire* provided by the Soviet empire that largely protected the prosperous western half of Europe from the dysfunctional social, ideological or religious, political and economic systems of Eurasia. Paradoxically, the North Atlantic Treaty Organisation (NATO), the institution that best served the security interests of the West in its competition with the Soviet Union, is now relatively ill-equipped to defend against or resolve the threats emanating from Eurasia to the Atlantic system of security governance, which had emerged over the course of the postwar period and is now facing a difficult transition to the post-Cold War environment.

The changing nature of the security agenda and security dilemmas facing the states of Europe and North America make the transatlantic community increasingly vulnerable to threats originating outside its immediate geographic ambit, a point brought home to the United States on September 11 2001. The openness of the European states to external influences, the free movement of peoples and goods, and domestic political liberalism have made these states soft targets. The international system described by Mackinder remains operative in the still-important military sense: states remain defined by their territoriality and the existential threat posed to them by a direct military attack by another state. At the same time, however, the European states are less concerned about territoriality (and the threat of war) and more concerned with sustaining the western system of security governance and extending it as far eastward into Eurasia as necessary. The western European states and the United States wish to reproduce in Eurasia their norms of statecraft, particularly the prohibitory norm against the use of weapons of mass destruction, as well as to impose dispute- and conflict-resolution mechanisms of western design. To put it benignly, the Americans and western Europeans hope to manufacture the conditions necessary to project the security community created in the Atlantic area in the postwar period into the eastern periphery of Eurasia.[2]

A question arises as to whether this system of security governance, which is being progressively extended from western to eastern Europe, can be eventually projected farther into Eurasia. The concern is not simply that the 'Great Game' of diplomacy played out by Great Britain and Tsarist Russia in the nineteenth century will be replicated as a triangular competition between the United States, Russia and China. Central Asia and the Balkans, in particular, have regained a lost geostrategic or geoeconomic significance in the twenty-first century. These areas' importance is linked to their pivotal geographical position as a nexus between the Atlantic security zone and the Middle East and Asia and as potential buffers or transit points between the Islamic Middle East and Christian Europe. Central Asia will play an especially critical role as an alternative source of energy supply for Europe and Northeast Asia, will either help repair or deepen the environmental distress occasioned by climatic change, will serve either as a sanctuary for terrorism against the West or as a staging ground for its eradication, and may become transformed into a region defined by weak state structures and ethnic irredentism or by strong states with democratic institutions.

Perhaps as important, the evolution of Islam in this region – whether it will assume a relatively non-intrusive secular role as in Turkey or a radical variant of Islamic fundamentalism as in the Taliban's Afghanistan – will have important implications for the security of Europe's southern flank, the prospect for deep and secure economic ties between Eurasia and Europe, and the geostrategic relationships between Eurasia's greater and lesser powers. Three important policy-relevant questions with theoretical implications are of interest: what are the nature of the security threats posed to Europe that originate in Eurasia? Can the 'West' incorporate Eurasia into the western system of security governance? Will the future system of security governance be cooperative or will it evolve into a competitive system of balancing and shifting alliances? *Limiting Institutions?* focuses on the security dilemmas facing the states of Eurasia, the sources and kinds of threats posed to the European political space by Eurasia, and the role that international institutions are playing and may play in the creation of a sustainable system of security governance encompassing the Eurasian land mass.

Security governance in Eurasia

Security governance is the policy problem confronting the great Eurasian powers in the contemporary international system. The postwar security system encompassing the Eurasian landmass was governed by the stable crisis produced by the bipolar distribution of power and the alliance system it spawned. Conflicts between the two superpowers, the United States and Soviet Union, were played out in the deadly logic of nuclear deterrence, limited wars along the periphery of Asia, and proxy wars in Africa and Latin America. The ideological Manichaeism and structural rigidity of the postwar period have now yielded to structural fluidity and ill-defined civilisational disputations.

The postwar system of countervailing power created by NATO and the Warsaw Pact unraveled with the latter's dissolution and the progressive transformation of NATO from a military alliance with an Atlantic perspective into a pan-European political organisation with an increasingly residual military role. The challenge of security governance for the West reflects neither the transformation of NATO into a political organisation nor the nascent emergence of a Euro-American security community extending eastward and encompassing the Russian Federation. The challenge *is* located in the absence of and difficulty of constructing an effective system of governance encompassing the whole of Eurasia.

Security governance has received increasing attention since 1989.[3] Its rising conceptual salience is derived in large measure from the challenges presented by the 'new' security agenda. Security governance has been defined as 'an international system of rule, dependent on the acceptance of a majority of states (or at least the major powers) that are affected, which through regulatory mechanisms (both formal and informal), governs activities across a range of security and security-related issue areas'.[4] This definition of security governance is largely consistent with that of those analysts who insist that: institutions are mechanisms employed by states to further their own goals;[5] states are the primary actors in international relations and some states are more equal than others;[6] power relationships are not only material but normative;[7] and states are constrained by institutions with respect to proscribed and prescribed behaviour.[8] This broad conceptual definition of security governance allows scholars to investigate the role institutions play from any number of methodological perspectives. As importantly, it allows us to ask if the necessary conditions exist in Eurasia for the successful eastward extension of the Atlantic security community into Eurasia or if the dynamics of the Eurasian state system are incompatible with it. It leaves open the possibility that the system can be extended into Eurasia as well as the prospect that the Eurasian state system will embrace the logic of anarchy and manifest its by-products, the balancing of power and perfidious alliance partners.

5

Both Robert O. Keohane and Robert Jervis have addressed the requirements of security governance in the contemporary international system.[9] Jervis has argued that the western system of security governance produced a security community that was contingent upon five necessary and sufficient conditions. The first two concern beliefs about war and the cost of waging it. The first requires national elites generally to eschew wars of conquest, and war as an instrument of statecraft, at least with one another; the second that the costs of waging such a war outweigh any conceivable benefits, material or other. The second two conditions are the embrace of political and economic liberalism. The first requires national elites to accept that the best path to national prosperity is peaceful economic intercourse rather than conquest or empire, in order to eliminate the rationale for war and economic closure. The second calls for the existence of domestic democratic governance, in order that the domestic practice of compromise, negotiation and rule of law characterises relations between states. The final condition stipulates that states be satsified with the territorial status quo, a condition that mitigates the security dilemma.[10]

All five conditions are met in the Atlantic security community; they are lacking in most of Eurasia. Keohane recognises this problem in his discussion of the barriers to global governance.[11] Keohane's expressed scepticism about constructing a system of global governance is instructive in the context of extending the Atlantic system of security governance. He identified three barriers to global governance that can usefully be adapted to the problem of security governance in Eurasia. The first is the cultural, religious and civilisational heterogeneity of Eurasia, which probably prohibits the wholesale adoption of the European norms and principles that animate the existing Atlantic system of security governance. European norms are as likely to be particular as they are universal. The second and related barrier is the absence of a consensus about beliefs and norms, which would make the likelihood of extending the Atlantic system of security governance into Eurasia virtually non-existent.[12] The third barrier to a Eurasian system of security governance is the absence of an institutional fabric that is both thick enough to meet the challenge of governance and consistent with indigenous (rather than European) norms and beliefs about the practice of statecraft and even national governance.

Both Jervis and Keohane expressed concern about the sustainability of the western systems of governance and the prospects for their eventual globalisation. Jervis asked the question, 'What are the implications of the existence of the security community for international politics in the rest of the world?' That query is not the one addressed in this book. Instead, we pose an alternative question, 'What are the implications of an anarchical Eurasia for the Atlantic security community?' The problem facing the states of Eurasia is a simple one: will the efforts to extend or impose western values and institutional forms into Central and East Asia produce a convergence or divergence of behaviour around the pre-existing European norm, some normative compromise between the Occident and Orient, or a lapse into the corrosive competition inherent to international anarchy? Will a failed effort to extend the western system of security governance into Eurasia delegitimise it? Will the heterogeneity of the states occupying the geopolitical space of 'Eurasia' push all states towards a renewed embrace of the sovereignty norm and the system of alliances it inevitably engenders?

These questions are important because the evolution of international politics in Eurasia is not peripheral to European security and is central to the successful expansion of the Atlantic security community into eastern Europe, including the Russian Federation. The postwar security order sponsored by the United States was a system of security governance suffused by three norms: democratic governance and conformity with the market, collective defence, and multilateralism.[13] As long as bipolarity characterised the European state system and as long as the requirements of nuclear deterrence and conventional balance dominated the security calculus, there was little debate among elites about the fundamental threat posed to Europe or how to meet that threat. The absorption or participation of the Eurasian states into this institutionalised system of security governance presents an important challenge to continuing systemic stability. The very heterogeneity of this grouping of states – a geopolitical heterogeneity internal to the states of the Atlantic community and a normative heterogeneity between the states of Eurasia and the Atlantic community – raises at least five questions about the institutionalisation of security in Eurasia: why is Eurasia relevant to the security concerns of the Atlantic Community? What are the security dilemmas faced by the states of Eurasia? What relevance does alliance theory have for the evolution of Eurasian security? What are the boundaries of a Eurasian system of security governance and how high are the barriers for assimilating non-European states into a European order? What role can institutions play in creating a Eurasian system of security governance?

Diffusion and the new security agenda

The absence of a Eurasian system of security governance is given special meaning and force owing to the changing nature of the security threats facing the states of prosperous Europe. The long-lived distinctions between the 'high' and 'low' politics of international affairs and between domestic and foreign policy have been increasingly rendered obsolete by the changed context of state action and changing nature of the European state.[14] The 'high' politics of diplomacy and the 'low' politics of commerce had largely obscured the now transparent interdependence between these two fields of action. The line between foreign and domestic policy has become so blurred that the distinction has lost much of its conceptual force. The emergence of new arenas and sources of conflict – weak state structures, ethnic conflict, environmental threats – and new technologies that render state boundaries increasingly porous – particularly cyberspace and the internationalisation of commerce and capital – have broadened the systemic requirements of security.[15] The new security agenda raises two important questions: why have these new security threats risen to prominence in the post-Cold War period? Do the Eurasian states pose a putative threat to the systemic or milieu goals of the Atlantic states, to the integrity of the central and eastern European states and authority structures, or to the societal integrity of those states individually and collectively? Put differently, can the security threats posed by Eurasia to itself and to Europe be treated as the relatively simple problem of identifying state-to-state threats that unequivocally represent a state-centric security calculus where the state is both the subject and object of analysis? The answers to these questions are central to the chapters in Part II of *Limiting Institutions?*.

The most promising conceptual category of response focuses on the altered structure of the European state system and the changing nature of the European state.[16] The emergence of new security threats in Europe suggests that we can no longer conceive of security in terms of a policy choice restricted to specific dyads of states. Threats can no longer be simply dissaggregated into the capabilities and intentions of states; primacy can no longer be attributed to the state as either agent or object.[17] A definition of security restricted to the traditional concern with territorial integrity or the protection of ill-defined but well-understood 'national interests' would exclude threats to the social fabric of domestic or international societies or threats emanating from states with imperfect control over their territory, weakened legitimacy, or persistent interethnic conflicts. Moreover, the growing irrelevance of territoriality and the continuing importance of jurisdicational sovereignty have left states vulnerable to these new categories of threat: national responses are no longer adequate, yet the division of political space into states jealously guarding their sovereignty inhibits collective responses to these diffused threats. The sovereignty norm of the Westphalian system, therefore, has placed a barrier to cooperative outcomes – even in the Atlantic security community.

The key characteristic of the Westphalian state is its 'territoriality'. Described by John H. Herz as a 'hard shell' protecting states and societies from the external environment, territoriality is increasingly irrelevant, not only in Europe but in the newly formed states of Eurasia. States no longer enjoy the luxury of a 'wall of defensibility' that leaves them relatively immune to external penetration. As noted by Wolfram Hanrieder, even though Herz later changed his mind about the demise of the territorial state, 'his argument on the changed meaning and importance of territoriality was clearly valid'.[18] It not only forces us to change our conception of power – shifting attention from the military-strategic to the economic – but should also change our understanding of threat. As the boundaries between the state and the external environment have become increasingly blurred, it leaves open the possibility that the new security threats may operate along channels dissimilar to the traditional threats posed to the territorial state.

The 'interconnectedness' of the post-Westphalian state system, most visible in western Europe, was facilitated and reinforced by the success of the postwar institutions of American design as well as by European economic and political integration.[19] Geography, technological innovations, the convergence around the norms of political and economic openness, and a rising 'dynamic density' of the Atlantic political space have progressively stripped away the prerogatives of sovereignty and eliminated the autonomy once afforded powerful states by territoriality.[20] These elements of the contemporary European state system appear to have linked the states of Europe together irrevocably, are spreading outwards into Eurasia, and now facilitate the transformation of domestic and foreign policy disequilibria in the Eurasian states into security threats for the affluent states of Europe.

The porousness of national boundaries in the contemporary European state system has made it more likely that 'domestic' disturbances – particularly those that are either economic or environmental in origin – are not easily contained within a single state and are easily diffused throughout the European system. The postulated ease with which domestic disturbances are transmitted across national boundaries and the difficulty of defending against those disturbances underline the strength and vulnerability of the contemporary state system: the openness of these states and societies along an ever expanding spectrum of interaction provides greater levels of collective welfare than would otherwise be possible, yet the very transmission belts facilitating that welfare also serve as diffusion mechanisms hindering the ability of the state to inoculate itself against disturbances within the subsystem. The concept of diffusion is highly suggestive in this context.[21]

The different elements of the new security agenda explored in the chapters that follow are spread by at least four readily identifiable diffusion mechanisms: the growing dynamic density of the Eurasian political space; flawed or underdeveloped civil societies or political institutions of democracy; geographic propinquity; and the ubiquitousness of cyberspace. Cyberspace, for example, has helped erase national boundaries and signified the potential irrelevance of geographic space. It still escapes effective state control and provides the perfect instrument for non-state and societal actors seeking to destabilise any particular state or aspect of a society. Geographic propinquity and the absence of effective interstate barriers to migration mean that domestic disturbances anywhere in the Eurasian political space, be it from ethnic strife, environmental degradation, or the criminalisation of national economies or of state structures, could be externalised and initiate destabilising migratory flows.

It is the growing dynamic density of the Eurasian security space in conjunction with the estabished dynamic density of the Atlantic security space that provides the most pervasive and nettlesome mechanisms of diffusion. The dynamic density of the Atlantic security space gives the European state system its distinctive character, particularly the erosion of meaningful national boundaries and the progressive loss of state control over the decisions of individuals, markedly within the sphere of the economy. The very transmission belts of economic prosperity – largely unrestricted capital markets, high levels of trade, and the absence of exchange controls – also provide the mechanisms for facilitating the criminalisation of national economies, for initiating the erosion of the authority and legitimacy of weak states in transition, and for generating exogenous shocks to national economies that states can no longer effectively control, especially as Eurasia becomes integrated into the Atlantic economy. Moreover, the states along the periphery of affluent Europe are plagued by weak civil societies, ineffective or corrupted judiciaries and other democratic structures, and economies that are either criminalised or escape the effective jurisdiction of national authority. Not only are these states hostage to their interdependence with the rest of Europe, but that interdependence has the potential to transform Eurasian disequilibria – domestic or regional – into potential security threats for the states of affluent Europe.

National authorities in the Atlantic area can no longer discharge their responsibilities by simply maintaining territorial integrity and ensuring economic growth. The broadening of the security agenda has increased the tasks and difficulties of governance, while the transformation of the European state has made it increasingly difficult to achieve its security goals. Security threats now require a joint rather than unilateral resolution. Security threats cannot be simply disaggregated into the capabilities and intentions of states; primacy can no longer be attributed to the state as either agent or object. Rather, security threats have acquired a system-wide significance that demands an alternative conceptualisation of the security dilemmas facing states and the institutional responses to them.

The old and new security dilemmas: the Eurasian paradox

Does the traditional security dilemma continue to constrain state choice in the Eurasian context? Yes and no. Unlike the European security space, where there is growing agreement that the dilemma has been resolved and a security community has emerged, the security dilemma continues to plague interstate relations throughout most of Eurasia.[22] Robert Jervis located the security dilemma in the unhappy circumstance that 'many of the means by which a state tries to increase its security decrease the security of others'.[23] Many Eurasian states remain fixated with issues of territorial integrity and face acute territorial challenges (e.g., China and the Xinjiang province or Russia and Chechnya). These states also remain relatively unencumbered by the widespread norm against the use of military force to resolve outstanding territorial disputes among one another (e.g., India and Pakistan); these states remain challenged in many cases by internal threats to legitimacy (e.g., Azerbaijan and Karabagh).

Whereas amity has become the contextual hallmark of interstate relations within a wider Europe, enmity remains the hallmark of a large number of bilateral relationships in Eurasia. This unfavourable external context should therefore lead us to expect significant barriers to cooperation and consequently to the effective institutionalisation of security relations between the Eurasian states. Moreover, the continued (and rational) preoccupation with relative gains calculations by the Eurasian states guarantees that their prime objective will be to ensure that cooperation does not lead to a disadvantageous change in the hierarchy of regional power. These states remain, in Joseph Grieco's felicitous phrase, 'defensively positional' – states are more concerned with their relative power position (however defined) than with assuring the maximum absolute gain derived from cooperation.[24] Thus, the context of state action is not particularly supportive of institutionalised security cooperation or the wholesale embrace of the European system of security governance.

At the same time, this security dilemma has become less intense and inverted along Eurasia's western frontier. Within Europe, the postwar security dilemma of military insecurity has been replaced by the post-Cold War security dilemma of ensuring political and economic stability along its borders. The nations of western Europe fear the negative consequences of political and economic insecurity in eastern Europe and beyond. Consequently, any measures taken by the nations along Europe's eastern periphery that enhance national security, defined broadly in its military or economic dimensions, are viewed as a positive contribution to European security rather than as a threat to it. This new security dilemma, derived from the contest over the allocation of scarce national resources between policies that generate domestic plenty and those that generate external stability, also provides an incentive and possibility for the nations of western Europe to cooperate with their eastern neighbours even at the risk of being exploited: security free-riding by these nations poses a lesser threat to the NATO states than does the re-emergence of authoritarian regimes or economic collapse that could disrupt the reconciliation of the two halves of Europe. This change in the perception of threat is illustrated by: the transformation of NATO into a political alliance encompassing both halves of Europe; the creation of the NATO–Russian Council that may be the first step towards full Russian membership in NATO; the Ukrainian application for NATO membership, which, if accepted, will project the alliance in the Eurasian 'heartland'; and NATO's Partnership for Peace (PfP) programme, which has made critical inroads into ordering civil–military relations and fostering security cooperation along the entire southern Eurasian periphery, from Albania to Tajikistan. For the founding states of the European Union (EU) and NATO, therefore, the concern is not with its neighbours seeking too much security, but with its neighbours being too insecure.

The Eurasian states face both security dilemmas and a policy paradox: the security dilemma identified by Jervis requires each state to guard against any disadvantageous change in the military status quo while pursuing an advantageous change in its position along the regional hierarchy; and policies redressing the new security dilemma, which is preoccupied with fostering states that are domestically secure and economically prosperous, could produce a disadvantageous change in the regional hierarchy of states. In the absence of a system of security governance, particularly the institutionalisation of the norms and rules of European statecraft, Eurasia will remain a source of instability for the Atlantic security community. Stability in Eurasia – as in eastern and southern Europe – remains dependent upon a stable economic and military environment, but in much less favourable circumstances. Unlike eastern and southern Europe, however, it is likely that the transitions to democracy and the market economy will remain generally intractable owing to unfavourable economic, cultural, ethnic and political factors domestically and a competitive military-strategic calculus internationally. Institutions have none the less made inroads into Eurasia, but will they facilitate the transition to the European-sponsored security community, or simply move Eurasia towards a less conflict-riven international society?

Alliance theory and Eurasia: help or hindrance to understanding?

Alliances are perhaps the most 'primitive' form of international institution. They have also been the most important historically. Alliances, as either formal or informal institutions, are regarded as effective mechanisms for regulating disequilibria in the international system.[25] A weak system of security governance in Eurasia could be founded upon a system of alliances. An alliance-based system of security governance, however, suffers from one important disability: military alliances are not particularly well-equipped to address the security challenges currently facing these states. The sources, as opposed to the symptoms, of conflicts arising from ethnic irredentism, weak state structures, energy shortages and environmental dislocations, to name a few, are not easily resolved by military means. A reliance upon alliances, both as a policy instrument and as a conceptual device for ordering inter-state relations, could well prove a dangerous choice in the changed Eurasian security environment.

Alliance theory has provided the framework for understanding not only the evolution of the postwar European security order, but that of the European state system since 1648. The contemporary debate has been largely framed by the question of whether states balance power, interests or threats.[26] There are two ancillary questions driving this debate. The first asks whether states, in forming those alliances, balance or bandwagon.[27] The second revolves around the appropriate assumption to make about state preferences; viz., do states maximise absolute or relative gains? (While this particular debate over preferences is largely spent, it is clear that a system of security governance along the European model would require an external environment that would allow states to maximise absolute rather than relative gains.)[28] The problem of bandwagoning and balancing remains salient in a condition of anarchy. Stephen Walt has provided a relatively uncompli- cated and useful definition of both: '*Balancing* is defined as allying with others against the prevailing threat; *bandwagoning* refers to alignment with the source of danger ... balancing is alignment with the weaker side, band- wagoning is with the stronger.'[29] However, the relative fluidity of the contemporary international system, the evolution of a security community among the states of democratic Europe and North America, and the changed status of the state, particularly the limitations on state autonomy in meeting many of the new security threats, have made this debate potentially less relevant to the problem of security governance.[30]

One insight from the alliance debate that continues to have relevance is the problem of buck-passing and chain-gangs, two byproducts of alliance behaviour in a multipolar system.[31] While contemporary Eurasia cannot be considered multipolar in any meaningful sense, the Eurasian system is more fluid today than at any time since the 1930s. Consequently, the behaviour associated with buck-passing and chain-gangs may remain relevant to the challenges posed by the new security agenda.[32] Buck-passing, as a reformu- lation of the free-rider problem, arises because states 'wish to avoid bearing unncessary costs or because they expect their relative position to be strengthened by standing aloof from the mutual bloodletting'.[33] In the Eurasian setting, buck-passing occurs at two levels: first, the Americans have made a concerted effort to shift the costs of eliminating the underlying causes of the new security threats to the Europeans; and second, the Europeans (and the Americans) have also made an effort to shift the political and financial costs of redressing the structural disabilities of the states in transition to international and regional institutions, particularly NATO, the Organisation for Security and Cooperation in Europe (OSCE) and the EU.

Chain-gangs are more problematic, because they can only arise when states experience 'a high degree of security interdependence within an alliance ... each state feels that its own security is integrally intertwined with the security of its alliance partners. As a result, any state that marches to war inexorably drags its alliance partners with it.'[34] Once again, the parallels between this formulation and the Eurasian state system are inexact, but highly suggestive. If geographic propinquity, the ubquitious- ness of cyberspace, a growing interaction density, ethnic conflict and weak state structures do function as agents of diffusion, then it would follow that the security of the Eurasian states is 'integrally intertwined'. Consequently, if the states of prosperous Europe – the full members of NATO and the EU in particular – wish to control their external environment and minimise the risks posed to the existing system of governance, they cannot allow those states along Europe's periphery to remain outside or excluded from the EU- and NATO-dominated system of security governance. This requirement raises two additional questions: what are the outer boundaries of the European system of security governance? Can the Eurasian states be assimilated into a system of security governance that reflects European norms, values and identities?

Boundaries and assimilation

Extending the western system of security governance into Eurasia raises the problem of identifying the criteria that will demarcate the outer boundary of the future European system of security governance. Within the context of EU or NATO enlargement, the question has turned on whether Europe is defined as having two tiers of states (the assimilated and the unassimilated) or as having two speeds (assimilated but with differentiated membership in the various institutions of economic and military security).[35] Within the context of Eurasia, the question turns on the relevance of the region to the European security order, the precise delination of what geographic space Eurasia occupies, and the limits placed on any institution or group of institutions governing this geopolitical area. NATO has emerged as the key security institution governing and maintaining order in the European geostrategic space; and the EU has emerged as the key economic institution governing and maintaining order in the European geoeconomic space.

Other security institutions explored in *Limiting Institutions?* – the OSCE, the Commonwealth of Independent States (CIS), the Shanghai Cooperation Organisation (SCO), the Black Sea Economic Cooperation (BSEC) and others – may eventually play a more prominent role than NATO or the EU in governing Eurasian security, but each is handicapped by a potentially debilitating heterogentity of membership (OSCE), exclusivity by design (CIS), a volatile membership (Georgia, Ukraine, Uzbekistan, Azerbaijan and Moldova grouping [GUUAM]), disparate interests and expectations for the institution among the member-states (SCO) or a relative lack of legitimacy (BSEC). The overlapping membership of these Eurasian security institutions may contribute to the creation of a single set of norms governing statecraft in the region, but there is no guarantee that those norms will be consistent with those of the Atlantic community. Moreover, the final boundaries of these institutions, including NATO and the EU, remain ill-defined and undetermined. The problem of establishing the appropriate boundaries of each institution (not to mention their appropriate scope and function) complicates the difficult challenge of coping with the 'politics of inclusion' and the requirement of assimilation if a stable and peaceful security order is to evolve in Eurasia.[36] The transition to the politics of inclusion initiated by the end of the Cold War has opened up the European political space and accelerated the growing cultural, political, military-strategic and societal intermingling of Europe and Eurasia. However promising and pleasing this development is from a normative point of view, it does deepen the potential for the external-isation and diffusion of domestic disequilibira and complicates the task of security governance in both Europe and Eurasia.

The politics of inclusion is complicated by the absence of a ready-made geographical boundary like the one the United States (and the Soviet Union) faced in 1947. We are reminded that, in an unconstrained environment, geographic space and institutional size will matter. As club theorists like to point out, clubs are viable only so long as the benefits of membership are not outweighed by its costs. In the context of a system of security governance, the enlargement of any of these institutions can lower their value for any individual state. And unlike previous international systems, which could be effectively governed by the powerful few, the contemporary international system can be effectively disrupted by the weak many.

The boundary conditions of the Eurasian and European systems – geopo-litical, institutional-legal, transactional and cultural – have likewise changed.[37] While there has been a dismantling of the boundary conditions that separated the eastern and western halves of Europe, many of the critical boundary conditions remain in place between Europe and Eurasia, particu-larly civilisational disputations, divergent geostrategic challenges, and the practice of multilateralism within institutional frameworks. Only the trans-actional boundary has been lowered. One consequence of this development has been the need to address the problem of Eurasian security governance. Whereas the Cold War's end revealed the false cultural boundary dividing central, eastern and western Europe, the lowering of the transactional boundary within Eurasia has brought into sharp relief the persistent and divisive cultural boundary between Christian Europe and its Islamic periph-ery. While the changed boundary conditions of the European political space pushed the OSCE, EU and BSEC to practise a 'politics of inclusion', NATO was initially handicapped in this regard since the 'politics of exclusion' was its *raison d'être*. Yet we have the paradoxical outcome that it is NATO that has practised most effectively the 'politics of inclusion' with the institutional innovations of the North Atlantic Cooperation Council, the Euro-Atlantic Political Cooperation, and the PfP programme, as well as the creation of the NATO–Russian Council in 2002. Security institutions of Eurasian origin, particularly the CIS and SCO, clearly practise the politics of exclusion, but even in the case of the SCO, the Chinese have belatedly recognised that its final membership and agenda should remain open.[38] The politics of inclu-sion initiated by the changed boundary conditions of post-Cold War Europe and Eurasia indicates that the progressive and all-inclusive eastward extension of the western system of security governance is all but inevitable. Yet the precise form and content of such a development remain undetermined, and the effort may ultimately fail, particularly as that system is based on European values and norms which are not negotiable and treated as universal rather than as particular.

The role of institutions in alleviating conflict and promoting cooperation

What role can international institutions play in mediating conflict and fostering cooperation? Recent scholarship has focused on issues of institutional design and on the roles that international institutions play in managing conflicts of interest in constrained environments, in fostering cooperation by lowering transaction costs or by promoting confidence-building measures, and in facilitating conflict resolution mechanisms that deter war. Much of the scholarship has also focused on the necessary and sufficient conditions required for international institutions to perform that task.[39] Two alternative theories of international relations, neo-liberal institutionalism and social constructivism, have generated particularly promising propositions for understanding the role of institutions as facilitators of cooperation and conflict management. One variant of neo-liberal institutionalism focuses on the functions performed by institutions to mitigate conflicts of interest and facilitate cooperation, while another has linked the utility of international institutions to categories of strategic interaction. In either case, international institutions allow states to overcome or mitigate the defensive and uncooperative logic of anarchy.[40] Social constructivism, which postulates that identity and normative belief systems shape material interests, view institutions as evidence that states are governed by a normative system and that the requirements for collective identity formation are being met.[41]

In the past, studies of international institutions have generally investigated the patterns of conflict and cooperation in the transatlantic political system that emerged after World War II. This preoccupation with the western security and economic systems left scholars open to the initial charge that they were only looking where institutions appeared to exert some impact on preference formation – namely in the Atlantic area.[42] A second and more fundamental problem with the empirical analyses of institutions has been that Europe in particular has proven an 'easy' case, because a unique set of historical circumstances, the bloodshed and devastation of the two 'world' wars, convinced the Europeans to relax their sovereign prerogatives in the interest of peace and prosperity. More important, the focus on Europe carries with it an inherent European bias with respect to the preference for a multilateralised and institutionalised statecraft as well as the essential content of the norms necessary to govern those states' behaviour. The security dilemmas facing the arc of Eurasian states that stretches from the Balkans to China provide a good empirical test of the proposition that formal or informal institutions and the norm of multilateralism are not particular to Euro-Atlantic states, in either a cultural or a geographic sense, and can be successfully and fruitfully extended into the Eurasian landmass.

The discussion so far has focused on the structural and contextual changes in the European political space which have made it necessary to broaden the definition of security. Systemic stability and the prospect for a peaceful and cooperative pan-European security order are largely contingent upon the successful transition to the market and multiparty democracy in Europe and along its periphery. And those transitions, in turn, are contingent upon a stable economic and military environment.[43]

The precise role of institutions in the post-Cold War security architecture remains contested. This unsettled state of affairs raises the question of institutional choice and design, a matter complicated by the necessity of accommodating an expanded conception of security that extends beyond the traditional concern of assuring territorial integrity and the physical protection of national assets from military threat. The interrelationships between the institutions governing the 'new' and traditional elements of the security calculus, as well as the interaction or interdependencies between them, remain uncharted. Yet it is the management of the institutional interdependence of the EU, NATO, OSCE, BSEC, CIS, GUUAM[44] and SCO, in particular, which may eventually define the contours of the future Eurasian security order and Eurasia's place in the European and North American definition of interest and calculus of action.

There are good reasons to suspect that these security institutions can and do play a prominent and constructive role in Eurasia. First, the provision of multiple fora to resolve outstanding conflicts of interest or to meet common threats will serve the security interests of the European states, at least from a systemic perspective. A closer relationship to NATO, for example, may provide Eurasian states with a reassuring security guarantee (regardless of whether it is debased or not). Likewise, a closer relationship with the EU could enhance these nations' economic prospects by providing privileged access to the largest market in the world. The evolution of the CIS and the BSEC into viable markets could provide alternative routes to economic prosperity and the eradication of poverty, an underlying source of conflict. The SCO, as an institutional form of Eurasian origin, may provide normative and cultural reassurance for the Eurasian states and thereby facilitate cooperation with Europe, or it may serve as a potential counterweight to NATO so long as Russia is denied full membership. Second, the deeper engagement of these institutions could support the normative and belief system presently suffusing the European system of security governance: the importance of democratic governance domestically, the rejection of war as a mechanism for dispute resolution, the legitimacy of existing dispute- and conflict-resolution mechanisms, and the preference for multilateral solutions to common security challenges. Finally, these norms and beliefs generate two other important externalities: they create a common frame of reference for identifying and resolving conflicts of interest; and they create a community of interest and values critical to meeting the external conditions necessary for sustained cooperation and diffuse reciprocity. If these norms and beliefs took root in Eurasia, it would facilitate the extension of the western system of security governance or at least engender its onset.

Conclusion

It would not be unduly optimistic to claim that institutions could perform limited, but regionally restricted, security governance roles in Eurasia; scepticism must none the less be reserved for any claim that a single set of institutions will coalesce into a Eurasian system of security governance in the near future. There are significant barriers to a lock-step eastward enlargement of the Atlantic system of governance or the emergence of a Eurasian system of governance congruous with the European normative and belief system. One barrier is located in the asymmetrical evolution of the European and Eurasian state, namely the transition from a warfare to a welfare state. Another is the context of international politics in Eurasia, which presently compels states to focus on relative rather than absolute gains in the calculation of state policy. A third is located in the inability to foster a collective identity encompassing the European and Eurasian states, which, in turn, will impair international cooperation and institution building.

The European and Eurasian states are at different stages of evolution: the European state has lost or willingly abandoned sovereign prerogatives in the interest of maximising either national welfare or security. This progressive erosion of national sovereignty is the result of two tendencies: the voluntary transfer of sovereignty to international or supranational institutions to resolve outstanding conflicts between states or manage dilemmas of collective action; and the involuntary loss of sovereignty to the market and the subsequent efforts to recapture that sovereignty via multilateral governance. Within Eurasia, many new states jealously guard their decade-old sovereignty, and their less sophisticated national economies are not integral parts of the international economy. Thus, the perceived need for international institutions is correspondingly lower.

A relatively high level of enmity in interstate relations, sharpened by the externalisation of intra-state ethnic conflicts, provides the second barrier to a unified system of security governance. The context of state action has a major impact on the formulation of national preferences, which are not immutable but are linked quite closely to the external constraints facing a state, particularly the level of amity and enmity in the international system.[45] Where there are high levels of enmity, cooperative outcomes are unlikely; where there are high levels of amity, cooperative outcomes are facilitated. An extension of the western system of security governance requires that amity characterise the Eurasian system – the last decade, however, has not pointed in that direction. The barriers to collective identity formation are the most problematic and are derived, in part, from the first two. One solution to the dilemma of collective action – a motor propelling the institutionalised cooperation in the Atlantic community – is located in the process of collective identity formation that has arguably occurred in the Atlantic security system.[46] There are two distinct aspects of interstate relations that vary positively with collective identity formation and the emergence of a security community more generally: the level of economic interdependence and the extent to which there has been a convergence of domestic values. On the first measure, the relatively low level of economic interdependence within Eurasia and between Eurasia and Europe makes collective identity formation, and the wholesale Eurasian adoption of the western system of security governance, less likely. The convergence of Eurasian domestic values around the European norm is also lacking and unlikely. There has been a progressive convergence of domestic values in the states comprising the Atlantic area: they have embraced the twin virtues of the market economy and multiparty democracy as well as a preference for multilateral rather than unilateral solutions to common problems.[47] In Eurasia, there is a wide variety of regime types conjoined to ethnic and religious animosities, and multilateralism remains a relatively alien form of statecraft. As compared to Europe, Eurasia is a highly heterogeneous security space and the prospects for a collective identity are correspondingly low. Moreover, there is neither an effective institutional mechanism for enforcing the convergence of domestic values on a pan-regional basis, nor a certainty that the values underpinning the western system of security governance are either universal or compatible with existing indigeneous belief systems and normative values.

The chapters constituting this volume are generally supportive of this sceptical assessment. Yet, there is also evidence that elements of the western system of security governance have mitigated conflict, shaped expectations and engendered security cooperation in Eurasia. The following chapters provide answers to a common set of questions: what are the boundaries of the European security order and what role does Eurasia play in that order? What are the content of the new security agenda, the nature of the security dilemmas facing the Eurasian states, and the opportunities for externalising regional conflicts? What role can European and indigenous institutions be expected to play in mediating conflict and facilitating security cooperation in this region of the world? *Limiting Institutions?* is divided into four parts. Part II investigates the contemporary security challenges facing Eurasia that may also impinge upon the future stability of the existing European security order; Part III investigates the current roles played by institutions seeking a governance role in Eurasia and the success those institutions have had in fostering security cooperation and mitigating conflict in Eurasia.

Part II examines a broad range of threats to Eurasian stability and the European security order. Douglas Blum, in Chapter 2, investigates the important role played by identity politics in the shaping of the Eurasian security environment. Blum focuses on the potentially combustible mix of contested national identities and weak state structures that have emerged in the successor states of the former Soviet Union. He highlights in particular the negative impact that malformed or contested ethnic and national identities have upon state capacity. His analysis provides three important insights: weak states with contested national identities are unlikely to prove dependable partners within multilateral frameworks; some Eurasian states are unlikely to develop national identities compatible with the western system of security governance; and the delegitimisation of already weak state structures could prove to be a fundamental source of instability and conflict in this region largely beyond the reach of the European powers or European-sponsored institutions. Stuart Kaufman, in Chapter 3, looks at the consequences of ethnic conflict for intra-state and interstate war. His investigation of ethnic conflict in Bosnia, Macedonia and Mountainous Karabagh leads to a number of important conclusions for those wishing to extend the reach of western institutions of security governance. First, ethnic conflict is not only a cause of international insecurity, but may also be the result of security competition between states. Second, an important source of ethnic conflict is how vital interests are constructed, particularly the way in which competing ethnic groups make mutually exclusive claims to the same territory. Third, this construction of vital interests is responsible for the persistence of security dilemmas in Eurasia. His contribution is particularly relevant for those claiming that security institutions like NATO or the OSCE can play a constructive and decisive role in this region.

Weak national identities and ethnic conflict have found expression in transnational terrorism. Phil Williams, in Chapter 4, examines a novel dimension of transnational terrorism, namely, the rising role played by transnational criminal organisations, either as domestic sources of instability and delegitimisation or as an 'off-shore' source of instability for Europe. Williams, who details the elements of the new security paradigm, argues that sources of the terrorist threat to Europe originate along or beyond the European periphery. His analysis, which documents the links between weak state capacity and the phenomenon of transnational terrorism, focuses upon the success enjoyed by organised crime in rolling back the state and weakening the existing system of security governance.

Part II concludes with two chapters investigating two specific security threats, one drawn from the 'new' and the other from the traditional security agenda. Stuart Horsman, in Chapter 5, investigates the prospect for interstate violence arising from environmental conflict, specifically the allocation of riverine water in Central Asia. His chapter underscores the historical importance of water allocation as a source of conflict and war, and argues that water allocation conflicts in the twenty-first century are likely to function as an indirect or contributory cause of regional instability. Horsman provides a sceptical assessment of both the existing institutional solutions to water allocation conflicts amongst the Central Asian states and the potential for conflict between those states and China. Jaewoo Choo then addresses the importance of Caspian Sea oil and natural gas reserves outside the familiar concern with the creation of an integrated transport network augmenting the energy security requirements of western Europe. Instead, he places Caspian Sea oil reserves into the more volatile geopolitical context of Sino-American competition in the region. Choo argues that the Chinese and American competition for Central Asian energy reserves has important implications not only for the energy security of the Occident and Orient, but also for the geopolitical evolution of the Asia-Pacific. He details the interaction of the American response in Central Asia to the September 11 terrorist attacks, the intertwined issues of development, exploitation and transport networks for Caspian Sea oil, and China's desire to reverse the growing American influence in its own backyard.

Part III identifies and examines the key regional institutional actors that have an established security governance role in Eurasia. These chapters address a set of specific questions: what role has each institution sought for itself in the region? How well has each institution achieved its objectives there? What are the limits and relevance of each institution to regional security governance? Sean Kay, in Chapter 7, investigates the traditional preoccupation with security dilemmas, the protection of territorial integrity, alliance formation and the pursuit of geostrategic advantage. He identifies the problems attending alliance formation in the region and the patterns of balancing and bandwagoning that are likely to emerge. Kay's chapter focuses on the confluence of national interests that led to the creation of the CIS, GUUAM and SCO, and concludes that these institutions have largely failed to cultivate cooperative multilateralism or abate the security dilemmas that function as barriers to it.

P. Terrence Hopmann and Joshua B. Spero, in Chapters 8 and 9, investigate the roles played by arguably the two most important regional security organisations, the OSCE and NATO, respectively. The OSCE and NATO's PfP programme assumed the important role of institutionalising western norms on a pan-European basis during the 1990s. Hopmann and Spero question whether the OSCE and NATO will be capable of playing a similar role in Eurasia. Hopmann details the evolving role assumed by the OSCE in Eurasia, the regional institution with the most inclusive membership. The OSCE has been charged with the important task of conflict prevention in Europe and Eurasia. Hopmann assesses the OSCE's performance in the last decade and concludes that the OSCE's record in the region is difficult to ascertain precisely because the institution's success is measured by the immeasurable 'dogs that don't bark'. Spero, who was directly involved in the creation of the PfP programme, details its institutional and political evolution. He places the demand by Eurasian states for membership in PfP within the framework of alliance theory, focuses on how the western model of civil–military relations was institutionalised in this region, suggests that the expansion of PfP into this region has strengthened the NATO-based security order, and demonstrates that it has alleviated the security dilemmas these states would face in its absence.

John Willerton and Geoffrey Cockerham, in Chapter 10, explore the CIS, one of the two quasi-constitutional actors in the region. The CIS, which remains an underdeveloped institution, has the potential to reintegrate the arc of states along the southern border of the Russian Federation into a not unimportant economic actor for Europe. Willerton and Cockerham focus particularly on the CIS's unrealised potential as an instititution central to the tasks of security provision, economic integration and political stability in Eurasia. They address three important questions: will the efforts of the Russian Federation to bind these states into a single institutional framework harm or benefit the security interests of the West? Is the CIS something more (or less) than the institutionalisation of a renewed Russian bid for Eurasian hegemony? Will the CIS evolve into something more than a paper confederation? Panagiota Manoli, in Chapter 11, appraises the potential role of the BSEC as an effective regional security institution. Turkey's sponsorship of the BSEC served the largely unrealised Turkish strategy of 'cooperative hegemony' in the Black Sea region. It was designed as a mechanism that would institutionalise a leadership role for Turkey in the region, enhance Turkey's importance for Europe, and foster cooperation along Europe's southern periphery. Manoli investigates whether the BSEC has performed any or all of these functions. She finds that it has neither provided a regional security umbrella nor constituted an economic bloc. Instead, the institution's continuing *raison d'être* has been the creation and strengthening of a 'diplomatic community' that provides the basis for regional conflict resolution and cooperation across an increasing number of issue areas.

Simon Serfaty, in Chapter 12, looks at the security governance role of the EU, the second quasi-constitutional actor in Eurasia. He charts the evolution of the EU as a prominent facilitator of the transition process in central and eastern Europe as well as the succesor states of the former Soviet Union, and addresses the security ramifications of the EU's projected enlargement, which will, *inter alia*, leave the EU abutting the western boundary of Eurasia. Serfaty raises three important questions: what role can the EU reasonably be expected to play in Eurasian security governance? Will the process of enlargement and the difficulties of security governance along the immediate southern and eastern peripheries of Europe preclude an important role for the EU? How will the process of deepening affect the EU's security and foreign policy ambitions and capabilites? He reaches the pessimistic conclusion that the EU will be a severely constrained actor in Eurasian security governance owing to the immediate challenges of deepening and the eastern enlargement.

In Part IV, David P. Calleo concludes *Limiting Institutions?* with a sweeping overview of the geostrategic developments in Eurasia since 1989 and the consequences of those developments for the evolution of the Atlantic and Pacific systems of security governance. Calleo poses and answers the fundamental question: how should these states arrange their power relationships to guarantee stability and order best in the twenty-first century? He argues for the deliberate construction of a 'self-consciously plural system' that would strike a balanced relationship between the United States, Europe, Russia and China. Yet the establishment of a global Westphalian order, Calleo's preferred solution to the challenge of global peace and stability, faces the significant barrier posed by the unilateralist impulses and unipolar fantasies of American diplomacy.

Notes

1 See Halford Mackinder, 'The Geographical Pivot of History', *Geographical Journal*, 23:4 (1904), pp. 421–44.
2 See Karl W. Deutsch *et al.*, *Political Community and the North Atlantic Area: International Organizations in the Light of Historical Experience* (Princeton, NJ: Princeton University Press, 1953). A good introduction to the current debate is found in Emanuel Adler and Michael Barnett (eds), *Security Communities* (Cambridge: Cambridge University Press, 1998).
3 See James N. Rosenau and Ernst-Otto Czempiel (eds), *Governance Without Government: Order and Change in World Politics* (Cambridge: Cambridge University Press, 1992); James N. Rosenau, *Along the Domestic–Foreign Frontier: Exploring Governance in a Turbulent World* (Cambridge: Cambridge University Press, 1997); Oran R. Young, *Governance in World Affairs* (Ithaca, NY: Cornell University Press, 1999); Robert O. Keohane, 'Governance in a Partially Globalized World', *American Political Science Review*, 95:1 (2001), pp. 1–13; and Mark Webber, 'Security Governance and the "Excluded" States of Central and Eastern Europe', in Andrew Cottey and Derek Averre (eds), *Ten Years after 1989: New Security Challenges in Central and Eastern Europe* (Manchester: Manchester University Press, 2002), pp. 43–67.
4 Cited in Webber, 'Security Governance'.
5 This assumption is central to rational choice theorists. See Barbara Koremenos, Charles Lipson and Duncan Snidal, 'The Rational Design of International Institutions', *International Organization*, 55:4 (2001), pp. 761–99.
6 This assumption is central to realist accounts of international politics. See, *inter alia*, Kenneth Waltz, *Theory of International Politics* (New York: Random House, 1978); and Robert Gilpin *War and Change in World Politics* (Cambridge: Cambridge University Press, 1981).
7 This assumption is central to social constructivist accounts of international politics. See Jeffrey T. Checkel, 'The Constructivist Turn in International Relations

Theory', *World Politics*, 50:2 (1998), pp. 324–48, esp. pp. 325–6; and Ted Hopf, 'The Promise of Constructivism in International Relations Theory', *International Security*, 23:1 (1998), pp. 171–200.

8 This assumption is central to institutionalist accounts of international politics. See Lisa L. Martin and Beth A. Simmons, 'Theories and Empirical Studies of International Institutions', *International Organization*, 52:4 (1998), pp. 729-57; and James G. March and Johan P. Olsen, 'The Institutional Dynamics of International Political Orders', *International Organization*, 52:4 (1998), pp. 943–69.

9 Keohane, 'Governance'; and Robert Jervis, 'Theories of War in an Era of Leading Power Peace', *American Political Science Review*, 96:1 (2002), pp. 1–14.

10 Jervis, 'Theories of War', p. 8. On the last condition, see Randall L. Schweller, 'Neorealism's Status Quo Bias: What Security Dilemma?', *Security Studies*, 5:3 (1996), pp. 90–121; and Mark W. Zacher, 'The Territorial Integrity Norm: International Boundaries and the Use of Force', *International Organization*, 55:2 (2001), pp. 215–50.

11 Keohane, 'Governance'.

12 *Ibid.*, p. 7.

13 See James Sperling and Emil Kirchner, 'The Security Architectures and Institutional Features of Post-1989 Europe', *Journal of European Public Policy*, 42:2 (1997), pp. 155–70.

14 For a statement of this perspective, see Stanley Hoffmann, *World Disorders: Troubled Peace in the Post-Cold War Era* (Lanham, MD: Rowman and Littlefield, 1998), pp. 110–16.

15 See Barry Buzan, Ole Wæver and Jaap de Wilde, *Security: A New Framework for Analysis* (Boulder, CO: Lynne Rienner, 1998); and James Sperling and Emil Kirchner, 'Economic Security and the Problem of Cooperation in Post Cold War Europe', *Review of International Studies*, 24:2 (1998), pp. 221–37.

16 For an early statement of this argument, see Wolfram F. Hanrieder, 'Dissolving International Politics: Reflections on the Nation-State', *American Political Science Review*, 72:4 (1978), pp. 1276–87.

17 See Glenn H. Snyder, 'Alliances, Balance, and Stability', *International Organization*, 45:1 (1991), pp. 121–42, esp. 126–7.

18 John H. Herz, 'The Rise and Demise of the Territorial State', *World Politics*, 9:4 (1957), pp. 473–93; and Hanrieder, 'Dissolving International Politics', pp. 1280–1.

19 On the transition to a post-Westphalian state in Europe, see March and Olsen, 'Institutional Dynamics', pp. 944–7.

20 Dynamic density is defined as the 'quantity, velocity, and diversity of transactions' by John Gerard Ruggie in 'Continuity and Transformation in the World Polity: Toward a Neo-Realist Synthesis', in Robert O. Keohane (ed.), *Neorealism and its Critics* (New York: Columbia University Press, 1986), p. 148.

21 On diffusion, see Benjamin A. Most and Harvey Starr, 'Diffusion, Reinforcement, Geopolitics, and the Spread of War', *American Political Science Review*, 74:4 (1980), pp. 932–46; Randolph M. Siverson and Harvey Starr, 'Opportunity, Willingness, and the Diffusion of War', *American Political Science Review*, 84:1 (March 1990), pp. 47–67; and Gary Goertz, *Contexts of International Politics* (Cambridge: Cambridge University Press, 1994), pp. 75–81.

22 See Jervis, 'Theories of War'; and John Duffield, 'Transatlantic Relations after the Cold War: Theory, Evidence, and the Future', *International Studies Perspectives*, 2:1 (2001), pp. 93–115.

23 Robert Jervis, 'Cooperation under the Security Dilemma', *World Politics*, 30:2 (1978), pp. 167–214.

24 Cited in Duncan Snidal, 'Relative Gains and the Pattern of International Cooperation', *American Political Science Review*, 85:3 (September 1991), p. 722.

25 See Gilpin, *War and Change*; and Richard Rosecrance, *Action and Reaction in World Politics: International Systems in Perspective* (Boston: Little, Brown, 1963).

26 See respectively, Waltz, *Theory of International Politics*; Stephen Walt, *Origins of Alliances* (Ithaca, NY: Cornell University Press, 1987); and Randall L. Schweller, *Deadly Imbalances: Tripolarity and Hitler's Strategy of World Conquest* (New York: Columbia University Press, 1998).

27 For a summary of this set of arguments, see chapter 7 by Sean Kay in this volume.

28 The debate over preferences, which began with the publication of Waltz's *Theory of International Politics*, was (perhaps) resolved by Robert Powell in his 'Absolute and Relative Gains in International Relations Theory', *American Political Science Review*, 85:4 (1991), pp. 1303–20. This debate, whether resolved or not, leaves open the more important question of where preferences come from.

29 Walt, *Origins of Alliances*, pp. 17, 21.

30 For the original formulation, see Deutsch *et al.*, *Political Community*. For overviews of the recent scholarship, see Mary N. Hampton, 'NATO, Germany, and the United States: Creating Positive Identity in Trans-Atlantia', *Security Studies*, 8:2 (1998/99), pp. 235–69; and Jervis, 'Theories of War', pp. 1–14.

31 Thomas J. Christensen and Jack Snyder, 'Chain Gangs and Passed Bucks: Predicting Alliance Patterns in Multipolarity', *International Organization*, 44:2 (1990), pp. 137–69.

32 *Ibid.*, pp. 144–7.

33 *Ibid.*, p. 141.

34 *Ibid.*, p. 140.

35 This specific question is addressed in James Sperling (ed.), *Two Tiers or Two Speeds? The European Security Order and the Enlargement of the European Union and NATO* (Manchester: Manchester University Press, 1999).

36 On the 'politics of inclusion', see Michael Smith, 'The European Union and a Changing Europe: Establishing the Boundaries of Order', *Journal of Common Market Studies*, 34:1 (1996), pp. 5–27; and on the systemic requirement of assimilation, see Kalevi J. Holsti, *Peace and War: Armed Conflicts and International Order, 1648–1989* (Cambridge: Cambridge University Press, 1991).

37 These boundary conditions are identified in Smith, 'European Union'.

38 The institutional beginning of the SCO was the Shanghai Five. When a sixth member was added, it was decided to re-name the organisation the SCO and to keep open its future membership and purpose.

39 For a brief but comprehensive overview of the roles of institutions in global governance generally, see Keohane, 'Governance'; on the importance of institutional design, see Barbara Koremenos, Charles Lipson and Duncan Snidal (eds), *The Rational Design of International Institutions*, special issue of *International Organization*, 55:4 (2001).

40 A strictly functionalist approach to institutions is found in Robert O. Keohane,

After Hegemony: Cooperation and Discord in the World Political Economy (Princeton, NJ: Princeton University Press, 1984), while two representative game-theoretic approaches are found in Arthur Stein, *Why Nations Cooperate* (Ithaca, NY: Cornell University Press, 1993), and Lisa Martin, 'Interests, Power and Multilateralism', *International Organization*, 46:4 (1992), pp. 765–92.

41 Representative are Alexander Wendt, *Social Theory of International Politics* (Cambridge: Cambridge University Press, 1999); Peter Katzenstein (ed.), *The Culture of National Security: Norms and Identity in World Politics* (New York: Columbia University Press, 1996); and Martha Finnemore and Kathryn Sikkink, 'International Norm Dyamics and Political Change', *International Organization*, 52:4 (1998), pp. 887–917.

42 See Susan Strange, '*Cave! Hic Dragones*: A Critique of Regime Analysis', *International Organization*, 36:2 (1982), pp. 479–96.

43 This argument is made in James Sperling, 'Two Tiers or Two Speeds? Constructing a Stable European Security Order', in Sperling, *Two Tiers or Two Speeds?*, pp. 181–98.

44 Uzbekistan formally gave notice in June 2002 of its intention to suspend its membership in GUUAM. Uzbekistan joined the organisation in 1999, two years after it was formed by Georgia, Ukraine, Azerbijan and Moldova in 1997. We have retained GUUAM in the text since the narratives cover the period during which Uzbekistan was a member, although in certain contexts it will also read GUAM.

45 Powell, 'Absolute and Relative Gains'; see also Arnold Wolfers, *Discord and Collaboration: Essays on International Politics* (Baltimore, MD: Johns Hopkins University Press, 1962).

46 Alexander Wendt, 'Collective Identity Formation and the International State', *American Political Science Review*, 88:2 (1994), pp. 384–96, esp. p. 386. This criterion is central to the cooperative form of security governance defined in Webber, 'Security Governance', p. 45; Jervis, 'Theories of War', p. 8; and Keohane, 'Governance', p. 7.

47 On the fragility of collective identity formation, see Mary N. Hampton and James Sperling, 'Positive/Negative Identity: Germany and the Euro-Atlantic Communities', *Journal of European Integration*, 24:4 (2002), pp. 281–302.

II
Security threats

2

Contested national identities and weak state structures in Eurasia

Douglas Blum

Since their very inception, many of the Soviet successor states have been beset by ethnic violence, crime, trafficking – in arms, drugs and people – terrorism, poverty, pollution and migration.[1] Most have also faced deeper problems of legitimacy and ideological drift. To a significant extent these pathologies can be traced back to the delegitimisation of the entire Soviet world view, and the lack of any viable replacement. The existence of an institutional vacuum in the post-Soviet geopolitical space has both contributed to such problems and impeded their successful resolution. The post-Soviet states have been forced to rebuild themselves by establishing basic institutions of governance and administration. At the same time the massive legitimacy problems they face call for nation building, along either inclusive/civic or exclusive/ethnic lines. Moreover, the post-Soviet transition is further complicated by its taking place in the context of globalisation and as such is marked by heightened economic interdependence, technology development and diffusion. A critical question, then, is how the state – understood here in traditional Weberian terms – responds to such challenges, and what the results are for its ability to achieve developmental and political goals while consolidating its own sovereignty.

The literature on globalisation and the state has generally addressed this question from a functional standpoint, considering the competence of centralised states to manage their responsibilities alone. Recent works in this vein have analysed the complex pattern of 'bargains', 'reconfigurations' and 'delegations' of sovereign authority as part of the state's response to globalisation. Less attention has been paid to the role of the state in promoting and defending the reproduction of a favoured national identity. This analytical indifference is puzzling, inasmuch as constructions of national identity are crucial for internal organisation and cohesion as well as for relations with external actors. Consequently the ongoing reproduction of identity is essential for maintaining group boundaries, or the 'self-Other nexus' in Fredrik

Barth's terms.[2] It is precisely the validity of these boundaries which is challenged under globalisation. Central to understanding the role of the state in post-Soviet Eurasian security is the recognition of its embeddedness in the overlapping and contradictory processes of cultural flux, state building and nation building.

This chapter investigates both the state in post-Soviet Eurasia as the primary site of institutionalisation and the state's concerted international action in the sphere of security. This investigation requires a major caveat: state-centric approaches to security impose analytical costs by obscuring substate and transnational actors and processes. In particular, state-centric conceptualisations are inadequate for grasping fully the decentralised aspects of control and organisation, because they overlook the social and discursive dimensions of these processes.[3] While this approach is limited in theoretical depth and analytical scope, it is useful for the specific purpose of highlighting the state in its traditional Weberian form, as a uniquely privileged, central, bureaucratic agent driving regional political dynamics and (potentially) managing shared security dilemmas.[4]

It has already become well-accepted to note that nations are, as Benedict Anderson famously argued, 'imagined communities'.[5] Not only do its members have to imagine their essential commonality with others, but the characteristics and boundaries of the group must be discursively created. Thus while the term 'nation' implies the existence of some group as a pre-existing referent, the group cannot be understood as having a primordial solidarity based on intrinsic characteristics. Rather, national identity consists of the ostensibly shared characteristics which are constructed as being representative of the nation.[6] National identity is rather an intersubjective fiction, because identity formation is not an objective fact based on some manifest material foundation. Thus, its ontological standing is unavoidably flimsy. This in turn makes it essential for national identity to be socially reproduced by its holders.

This 'reproduction' of national identity takes place through an ongoing social discourse which centers on two key markers: historical constitution and normative qualities. The first marker includes claims about who belongs to the group or on what objective social basis the nation coheres; that is, particular ethnic versus all-inclusive civic identity as the basis of citizenship – membership may be defined in terms of specific markers such as language or religion which are more inclusive than ethnicity. Such criteria are more restrictive than a civic identity, which would apply to anyone born within the geographic boundaries of the state. However it is defined, national identity competes with more parochial criteria for membership, such as region, clan or tribe. The obverse of membership inclusion is the delineation of difference and the construction of Others, whether as friends, enemies, or specific value-neutral outsiders.[7]

The second, normative marker concerns the fundamental social values of the group as a whole. Such categorisations of identity go beyond the 'who' of membership to include the 'how' and 'why' of political life: honour, role or purpose, power and so forth. Whether or not such values are actually achieved is of course less important than the shared sense of meaning they impart and the social cohesion this fosters. Indeed, broad social internalisation of officially articulated national identity is crucial for the state's legitimacy, and thus for its exercise of authority and its ability to mobilise willing compliance.[8] It is perhaps most accurate to say that national identity constrains and at the same time enables government action, thus helping to shape the ultimate trajectory of state building and international conduct.[9] This process of national identity formation and active reproduction is clearly evident in the post-Soviet Eurasian states.

Nation building in Eurasia: the fusion of civic and ethnic identities

By 1991 the Soviet practice of ethnicising politics (and promoting ethnic identification along historical-cultural lines) had become deeply entrenched. Thus despite their largely fictitious origins in Stalin's nationalities policy of divide and rule, these constructions provided one important basis for the separatist unrest that brought down the Soviet Union, an irony which has not gone unremarked.[10] Post-Soviet nation building has also continued the practice of officially prescribed historiography. Scholars and cultural elites have dutifully laboured to produce 'homeland myths', as well as myths of ancient origin, glorious descent and intrinsic national character.[11] For the most part ethnic, not religious, identities have been especially salient and highly politicised, leading some observers to refer to the 'ethnification of religion' in former Soviet Eurasia. Inasmuch as religion provides an important source of cultural solidarity, its expression has been officially manipulated and adapted to current social and political needs.[12]

At the same time a curious dualism is evident in the policies of the post-Soviet states. Officially, exclusivist ethnic nationalism is rejected by all (with the partial exception of Armenia); instead tolerance is espoused and the dangers of ethnic extremism are repeatedly stressed in multinational states such as Azerbaijan, Kazakhstan and Russia. Yet in practice, in all of the Eurasian countries except Russia, national identity projects have been pursued predominantly in ethnic terms.[13] For example in Kazakhstan and Azerbaijan, the titular nationality has accrued substantial advantages in political representation and cultural rights, but is tempered somewhat by the official self-image of multinationalism. This very ambivalence, as well as the overriding prominence of ethnic nationalist constructs, comes into play in the choice of foreign policies and institutional affiliations. While ethnic attachments are central to ongoing notions of national purpose, and for designation of Others, civic and even universalist ideas come to the fore as a product of heightened international interaction.

Eurasian identity narratives

What are the nature and significance of prevailing national identities in post-Soviet Eurasia? The evolution of national identity has produced three broad categories of states: those with a well-consolidated national identity; those where national identity remains contested, but where key cleavages are not ethnic; and those where there is significant identity fragmentation along ethnic lines. What follows is a brief overview which delineates the key similarities and differences among the Eurasian states, particularly with regard to the relationship between national identity and foreign policy orientation.

The first group includes Armenia and, at least superficially, Turkmenistan; that is, states with well-consolidated national identities. Clearly at one end of the spectrum is Armenia, which has a nearly homogeneous population and a unified national identity based on common cultural symbols and an image of historical suffering.[14] The war with Azerbaijan has led to a situation in which ethnic identity far outweighs any meaningful civic alternative. Along with Armenia, at least judging from surface appearances, it may be possible to include Turkmenistan in this category. Certainly the official national identity is pronounced, including an ethnicised self-representation replete with various Turkic and Islamic cultural symbols and inventions.[15] However, the Niyazov regime is so closed and so highly authoritarian that it is impossible to gauge accurately whether the apparent consensus over national identity is real, and anecdotal reports suggest it may not be.

The second group to be distinguished consists of Russia, Moldova and Azerbaijan: the national identity discourse in each remains essentially contested, but the key identity cleavages are not drawn along ethnic lines. Chechnya, Transdniestria and Nagorno-Karabakh are obviously glaring exceptions to this rule, but they make up only a small part of each country's total geographic space and identity discourse.

Analysts have stressed the multiplicity of competing narratives within the Russian polity, ranging from liberal-westerniser to unreconstructed neo-Soviet.[16] Between 1991 and 2000, this welter of opposing voices prevented consolidation of an ideological basis for mobilisation. However, Vladimir Putin's emergence signals an effort to rebuild and strengthen the nation-state by invigorating a pragmatic statist discourse. While no definitive answer has emerged in the quest to define a unifying 'Russian idea', the mainstream debate has narrowed significantly as extreme right- and left-wing views have been marginalised.

One prominent theme involves the re-emergence of distancing from the West, along with an exceptionalist self-image as the embodiment of some transcendent truth or goodness, increasingly linked to Christian Orthodoxy.[17] This is often connected with an image of Russia as essentially a Eurasian 'great power'. In contrast, an equally important tendency identifies Russia as fully European, and as such set apart from America with regard to culture and security concerns.[18] Both narratives, however, share a predominantly geopolitical orientation to world politics. Another common feature is an insistence on maintaining preponderant influence in the 'near abroad', which appears to reflect an extension of native geopolitical space in Russian national consciousness.[19]

Moldova has experienced a modern history of incorporation into the Russian empire and later annexation by the Soviet Union (with loss of territory to Ukraine). During perestroika a recrudescence of national identity took place, mainly through the rediscovery of Romanian roots. Since gaining independence, however, there has been a powerful resurgence of Moldovan identity, initially constructed along ethnic lines as Latin and historically Roman, including perhaps above all an assertion of non-Russian cultural particularity. This too changed, however, following the sharp reactions of the sizeable Gagauz and Ukrainian populations, resulting in the articulation of a civic Moldovan identity which has persisted alongside the ethnic variant.[20] The ultimate willingness of Moldovans to allow Gagauz autonomy has resulted in a relatively stable domestic order, aside from the smouldering conflict in Transdniestria.[21] Even here, as Stuart Kaufman has cogently argued, the conflict has been essentially elite-led, in contrast to Nagorno-Karabakh, where extensive and especially vicious ethnic violence has resulted in conflict being mass-led and self-perpetuating.[22]

Finally, Azerbaijan presents a somewhat more ambiguous picture. It boasts a well-established *official* national identity associated with claims of a unique heritage based on an improbable blend of Turkism, Zoroastrianism, moderate Islam, and its historical function as 'bridge' between Asia and Europe along the Silk Road.[23] At the same time there remain strong local allegiances and ethnic distinctions, including submerged tensions between Azeris, Russians, and also Lezgins and Talysh (besides Armenians), as well as stubborn religious cleavages (roughly two thirds of the Islamic population is Shi'ite, one third Sunni).[24] This persistence of parochialism is hardly surprising inasmuch as there has been little historical basis for national identity formation among Azeri elites, who were significantly affected by russification and are still generally lukewarm in their expressions of pan-Turkism.[25] Perhaps the most powerful source of social cohesion and state legitimacy is the war in Nagorno-Karabakh, which has at least generated some degree of collective identity as victim of Armenian aggression[26] – perhaps a slender reed on which to construct a national identity conducive to developmental state building in the future.

The third group of states includes Georgia, Ukraine and Kazakhstan, each of which is characterised by a substantial degree of identity fragmentation along ethnic lines. The most extreme example is Georgia, which provides something of a cautionary tale. Here civil war has been the legacy of virulent strains of ethnic nationalism and a refusal to accommodate difference, a pattern which emerged under Gorbachev and continued into the post-Soviet period. Intense identity fragmentation has resulted among ethnic Georgians, Abkhaz and Ossetians, each now residing within separate territorial enclaves.[27] This unfortunate outcome has been shaped by conscious strategies pursued by elites as well as by the nature of public institutions created to meet political demands.

A similar geographic patchwork quilt of identity formation can be observed in Ukraine, although with relatively greater mutual tolerance. From an ethnic perspective Ukraine includes some 21 million Ukrainophone Ukrainians, 17 million Russophone Ukrainians, and 11 million Russians.[28] These ethnic and linguistic categories generally correspond to distinct discourses of ethnic identity, including Ukrainophile, pan-Slavic and Russophile.[29] Here the absence of ethnic war owes largely to astute leadership and the existence of political institutions capable of giving voice to opposing demands, thus providing a context in which working compromises can tentatively be reached.[30] Yet the result has been a continued absence of an overarching national identity, aside from that which is officially proclaimed. Early efforts to impose a unifying 'national idea' from the top down by western Ukrainian decision-making and intellectual elites had clearly failed by 1994. It proved impossible to generate broad support for a national self-image as culturally and historically unique, based on an inclusivist civic conception, while at the same time mollifying pan-Slavic, Russophile and neo-Soviet identity holders.[31]

Kazakhstan also offers an essentially comparable picture. While numerous smaller groups are scattered throughout the country, by far the largest nationalities are Kazakhs and Russians, the latter of which totals nearly 30 per cent of the population and is concentrated in the north. While the Russian diaspora remains highly problematic, it has not resulted in overt conflict or led to a stark polarisation of identities between Kazakhs and Russians in general.[32] This outcome can be traced to a prevailing official discourse that seeks to reconcile parallel identity projects. On the one hand, Nazarbaev's regime has worked hard to construct a national identity for the titular group through the familiar pattern of promoting the indigenous language and creating or reinventing national histories, cultural narratives and symbols in order to counter alternative identities of clan, tribe and region. While the delegation of this process to substate actors and their subsequent struggle for resources has actually led to some renewal of tribal identifications, Nazarbaev has succeeded in promoting a self-image of Kazakhstan as a Eurasian bridge.[33] On the other hand, Nazarbaev has been able to balance ethnic and civic variants of nation building, simultaneously championing the ideals of cultural traditionalism and republican multinationalism. He also allotted Russian an important role as the language of 'interethnic communication'. His success in these efforts is attributable in part to strategy and in part to his own leadership skill.[34]

Others in national identity

The construction of Others in Eurasia has taken place through intertwined processes which Graham Smith has called essentialisation, historicisation, and 'totalisation' or the use of absolute categories.[35] Here the use of dispositionally hostile and extreme imagery reproduces a situation of irreconcilable differences, which have proven extremely resistant to outside mediation. Essentialisation and totalisation have also tended to occur along ethnic lines. Such exaggerated and virulent myths of the Other are evident in Armenian and Azerbaijanian constructions of each other related to Nagorno-Karabakh[36] or in Georgia between ethnic Georgians and South Ossetians.[37]

Historicisation can be seen, for example, in the tendency of cultural elites in Russia and western Ukraine to construct myths of national inception and development which are consistent with their preferred mutual relations. For western Ukrainians this means asserting the existence of an 'original' Ukrainian state as well as the depiction of later Russian domination, while Russians have tended to stress traditional cultural commonalities between the two communities.[38] Consequently, although western Ukrainian elites often strategically employ the rhetoric of Slavic brotherhood for Moscow's consumption and to include Russophiles in the east, the everyday discourse in this part of the country delineates Russian imperialists (and alien Asians) as incompatible Others.[39] In Russia, the discourse of national identity reproduction overwhelmingly includes the explicit identification of hostile Others abroad, such as Islamic fundamentalists and organised criminal gangs.[40] This increasingly includes anti-Americanism as well, since frustration over Russia's inability to achieve claims to geopolitical influence in Eurasia and to resurgent great power status are connected with an image of America as arrogant and imperialist.[41] Elsewhere, deep historical expressions of enmity towards Turkey figure prominently in Armenian identity narratives, which as already mentioned centre on a self-image of suffering and grief inflicted at the hands of the Turks.[42] Without belabouring the point further, such constructions of the Other are fundamental aspects of the overall identity formations prevailing in all of the Eurasian states.

Not surprisingly, Russia itself is the most important Other for all the remaining Eurasian states, with an unenviable image ranging from imperialist aggressor (as core of the Soviet Union) to cunning wielder of influence. For Armenia, Russia embodies a melange of identity traits including Christian Orthodox, enemy of Islam, and regional hegemon. Such identification provides the basis for military cooperation, especially vis-à-vis Nagorno-Karabakh. In Kazakhstan, Russia is widely viewed in starkly different terms among the Russian ethnic and non-Russian ethnic populations, as Slavic defender and potentially (but not dispositionally) threatening hegemon. The latter image figures prominently in official discourse and is used to rationalise a policy of close institutional networking and sensitivity to Russian security concerns. The ethnicised variant of nationalist discourse in Moldova treats Russia in far more nefarious terms as historical antagonist to Moldovan self-assertion. Whether constructed as benign or hostile, however, the Russian Other invariably looms over Eurasian elites as a vast presence, central to the reproduction of national identity.[43]

An important additional set of Others is transnational Islam and its regional state representatives, especially Afghanistan and Iran as well as the breakaway Russian region of Chechnya. For Azerbaijan, Turkmenistan and Kazakhstan, Islam is an important constitutive feature of national identity as well as an external force. For each also, Islam is constructed primarily in ethnic and secular terms, and is therefore made compatible with the parallel civic national discourse. Azerbaijan under Aliev, like Turkmenistan and Kazakhstan, has turned to Islam mainly for appropriation as an instrument of state building.[44] Thus, like the remaining Central Asian states, they joined the Economic Cooperation Organisation and Islamic Confederation Organisation soon after the fall of the Soviet Union.[45] And yet Islam has also been tempered somewhat variously by Turkmenistan and Kazakhstan. Martha Brill Olcott observes that Turkmenistan has a larger devout population and has therefore pursued closer political and economic ties with the Islamic states of the Middle East than has Kazakhstan, which, given its image of Russia as potentially hostile, is committed to maintaining balanced relations with Moscow.[46] This has naturally influenced the nature of the imagery as well as the extent to which Islamic themes are included in national identity formation. Still, all three states share a deep concern over the prospect of fundamentalist unrest, which could undermine the dominant identity discourse and the state's social foundation.

In contrast Armenia and Russia, both of which border predominantly Islamic countries, share an image of an Islamic radicalism. This hostile Islamic Other has been linked closely to the process of identity formation in each state, producing constructs of the nation as Christian and 'Defender of Europe'. In Armenia one important identity narrative concerns historical conflicts with Ottoman foes; indeed the Nagorno-Karabakh conflict is frequently depicted as the latest in a long series of historical battles with 'the Turks'. A similar observation applies to a lesser extent in Russia as well. Nevertheless, especially within Russian political discourse, this demonic imagery is rivalled by competing narratives of Islam. Many Russian commentaries distinguish between aggressive and peaceful variants of Islam, reflecting the fact that roughly twenty million citizens profess Islam as their religion.[47]

In addition to negatively constructed Others, many Eurasian identity narratives include an array of potentially benignant Others in international society. Thus, for example, Turkey has played a key role in influencing Azerbaijan's post-Soviet identity formation and in providing more concrete forms of cooperation as well.[48] By far the most salient Other, however, is the

West and in particular the United States (although there is a salient strain of ambivalence towards America as well). Elites in all of the states of western Eurasia have sought to cultivate a 'European' identity in a broad cultural sense. This cultivation of a European identity serves domestic legitimating goals, in part by helping regimes distance themselves from the Soviet past. It has also been useful for gaining acceptance as members of the fraternity of 'advanced' states.[49] For some elites, normative gravitation towards the West is a way of demonstrating the political affinity needed to obtain military and economic assistance. This orientation is true in Ukraine, Georgia and Azerbaijan, where Russian imperial images are rife and where leadership elites have at times sought American security guarantees and even lobbied for admission to NATO. Yet identification with the West is more than merely instrumental. Western economic and political practices are often described as inherently positive and are typically equated with 'civilised' ways. Thus, across Eurasia national identity formation clearly includes not only nativist but also cosmopolitan features.

State capacity

In addition to analysing the way in which national identity determines the direction of foreign policy, it is necessary to consider state strength (or weakness). State capacity directly bears on the viability of state-brokered international institutions. It is useful to follow Michael Mann's conceptualisation of 'infrastructural power' as 'the capacity of the state to actually penetrate civil society, and to implement logistically political decisions'.[50] State weakness, then, in addition to meaning simply the absence of infrastructural power, involves a condition in which non-state elites retain their own cross-cutting segments of social control and may even operate through nominal state institutions.[51] The term also implies an absence of coordinated monitoring and policing mechanisms for managing diffuse security threats.[52] While institutional coherence and control over resources are thus important determinants of state capacity, so too is the existence of a prevailing and well-institutionalised national identity. The state's ability to promote – and link itself with – a consolidated national identity is vital to its exercise of authority.

The clear outlier with respect to state capacity in Eurasia is Turkmenistan, with its highly authoritarian and frequently coercive regime. While similar charges are sometimes levelled against the Aliev and Nazarbaev regimes in Azerbaijan and Kazakhstan, respectively, the latter do allow considerable room for dissenting opinion and independent civil society organisation. Indeed, on this score even Belarus appears relatively liberal in comparison with Turkmenistan. In any case the exercise of coercion and manipulation of fear in Turkmenistan makes it difficult to evaluate apparent state strength in some areas, such as the depth of consensus on core political matters. Yet the Niyazov regime does not seem to have a great deal of overall infrastructural strength regarding implementation or the ability to realise stated goals, owing largely to the fact that it remains so woefully poor that its physical and institutional capacity is limited.

The other states provide easier objects for interpretation. In Armenia the corollary of a unified national identity is indeed a strong state, one able to achieve popular mobilisation and implementation of central directives. This outcome is especially striking given the fact that state-building elites in Armenia faced the same problems of internal fragmentation that elites in Georgia and Azerbaijan did. While the resulting embattled identity has impeded development, most dramatically in blocking consideration of a 'peace pipeline' carrying Caspian oil from Azerbaijan, the state has succeeded in stabilising itself through close association with ethnic nationalist goals in Nagorno-Karabakh.[53]

Elsewhere, states experiencing at least substantial identity contestation do appear to have compromised state strength as a result. In Russia, for example, Putin's preferred means of accomplishing his state-building goals involves the introduction of fairly authoritarian practices, including centralisation of political authority, establishing direct ties with the regions, and putting pressure on the independent press.[54] These measures are intended to repair a condition of marked state weakness which has existed since 1991, in which central institutions have been repeatedly challenged by local organs and 'oligarchs', and have generally lacked extractive and enforcement capacity.[55] This picture appears to be changing, however, as Putin's emergence signals an effort to rebuild and strengthen the nation-state by invigorating a pragmatic statist discourse. Yet state weakness clearly remains a problem in autonomous ethnic republics, particularly in the Caucasus, where a jumbled assortment of unstable regions is either in the midst or on the verge of civil war.[56]

Similarly in Azerbaijan the state, highly personalised in the figure of Heydar Aliev, is extensively associated with official representations of national identity, such as showy parades and folk festivals. This strategy is part of an evident bid to enhance state legitimacy and authority. Nevertheless, the centre remains limited in its ability to coordinate and respond quickly to developments in the periphery.[57] Much the same might be said of Kazakhstan, where Nazarbaev has gone to great lengths to present the state as the very embodiment of national identity. Yet here too, in Almaty and especially in the Russian ethnic regions of the north, the centre struggles to achieve its developmental and organisational goals.

Georgia, finally, appears to be fast approaching the extreme of failed statehood. At the time of writing, the Shevardnadze regime had lost control over Abkhazia, Ajaria and much of South Ossetia, faced potentially major opposition in Javakhetia and Mingrelia, and was under siege in Tbilisi itself. Moreover, a massive Russian troop presence along the Abkhazian frontier and in several military bases underlined the ineffectual nature of the regime's domestic and foreign policies. In this context even to speak of a prevailing 'Georgian' identity is something of a misnomer. Instead, such references pertain to ideas held by those within the central heartlands around the capital. Certainly, the holders of such an identity are limited in their ability to contribute to any hypothetical Eurasian security institutions.

Conclusion: implications for institution building in Eurasia

Of course, the process of nation building is relevant not only for state building but also for establishing international institutions. The viability of such institutions is determined not only by their design or abstract functional capacity, but also by the degree to which the purposes they serve conform to the identities of their members.[58]

For example, exploring identity formation helps explain the operational tendency in Russia to conceptualise the 'near abroad' as its exclusive sphere of influence. The prevailing tendencies in discourse have expressed the self-image of an embattled great power surrounded by hostile or opportunistic Others. Accordingly, Russian approaches to the CIS generally incorporated assumptions of Russocentric control as well as a blurring of economic and security spheres.

In return, shared images of the Russian imperialist Other were instrumental in leading most states to reject this Russian approach and to resist joining, or fully participating in, the CIS structure.[59] Instead, informed by their Eurasian or European self-understandings and Other-images, they moved to join the EU-backed Transport Corridor Europe Caucasus Asia (TRACECA) plan for energy integration in order to by-pass Russia, despite the fact that on strictly pragmatic grounds such a notion was largely illusory.[60] Similarly, the combination of imperial understandings of Russia and self-understandings as European countries on the part of Georgia, Ukraine, Azerbaijan and Moldova facilitated the creation of GUAM, an economic and political association which has made overtures to the West. Even prior to GUAM, the reproduction of a European identity has played an important role in Ukraine's dealings with the West.[61] In the security sphere, this has included early entry into NATO's PfP Programme and obtaining western guarantees in return for joining the Non-Proliferation Treaty and eliminating its nuclear weapons; in the economic sphere, it has meant a Partnership and Cooperation Agreement with the EU as well as the provision of American development aid.[62] At the other extreme is Turkmenistan, which has steadfastly refused to join post-Soviet institutions, citing principled neutrality.

An exception is Kazakhstan, which under Nazarbaev has pursued an institutional membership policy that mirrors its complex identity discourse. As discussed above, Nazarbaev has pursued a skilful balancing act of promoting national identity on Kazakh ethnic lines while also embracing civic identity themes designed to assuage the fears of Russian ethnics and their protectors in Moscow. This wish to propitiate Russia and China, while still cultivating western investment, has resulted in an extremely flexible, if not protean, foreign policy. As one element of this overall balancing strategy, Nazarbaev has consistently pushed for a formal institutionalisation of Kazakhstan's interdependence with Russia. Not only did he support Mikhail Gorbachev's All Union Treaty concept, but after the fall of the Soviet Union he championed the formation of a 'Eurasian Union', which would resurrect some degree of trade integration and which prefigured the formation in 2000 of a Eurasian Economic Union (EEU) (along with Belarus, Kyrgyzstan and Tajikistan).[63] This notion of Eurasianism, however, has always had broader implications as well, including bringing together East and West through traditional trade routes and perhaps offering a vehicle for bridging and even reconciling their different sociopolitical systems.[64]

How much analytical purchase do we get, ultimately, through such an understanding of national identity formation? One valid response would be that it provides a partial corrective to approaches that would attribute the foreign policy conduct of Eurasian states to organisational and/or material conditions alone. Assuming that current constructs are not displaced by globalisation, a crucial factor will be national identity. Thus, the prevailing discourse in (heartland) Georgia under Shevardnadze has revealed a markedly European identity, consistent with its foreign policy orientation. In contrast, Kazakhstan – with an essentially similar geopolitical position – has been characterised by a Eurasianist discourse, and has taken a far more balanced approach than Georgia, including a willingness to commit to regional economic and security institutions.

It bears repeating that the above observations are not equivalent to an assertion that identity formation *caused* such policy outcomes. Making such a case formally would require ruling out liberal structural explanations at the domestic level as well as demonstrating causal directionality (identity shapes policy rather than the reverse) through careful content analysis and process tracing. Nevertheless, the consolidation of national identities, and their institutionalisation as part of state building, is consequential for understanding the current and prospective dynamic of interstate relations in post-Soviet space.

Where does this leave us with regard to the outlook for security institutions? Of course, the obvious first answer is that it depends on the type of institutional arrangement envisioned. After all, the range of multilateral institutions extends from issue-specific and pragmatic regimes all the way to general and highly principled security communities. At the low end of the gradient, relatively limited forms of functional cooperation do not require the existence of common or collective identities (except perhaps at the most basic level, such as the shared identity of sovereign statehood).[65] At the other end of the cooperative spectrum, however, shared identities are indispensable, especially in the security sphere. Even short of full-blown community formation, a significant degree of trust or perceived commonality would seem to be essential in order for shared security arrangements to emerge.[66]

The foregoing analysis of the Eurasian identity terrain suggests that there is currently no common, overarching identity among the post-Soviet successor states in Eurasia that might provide a sound basis for stable collective security institutionalisation. On the contrary, a general absence of shared identities bodes poorly for third-party-induced organisation, except perhaps among smaller groups of states which hold imperial or enemy images of Russia. Even in this case, however, a common identity foundation for cooperation may not suffice in the absence of state capacity. In Georgia and Moldova, for example, problems of state weakness have not only contributed to ethnic conflict but also impaired international peacekeeping efforts.[67]

The outlook for stable economic cooperation is probably not much brighter. An exception is the states of the EEU, which are either partly co-identified with Russia (Belarus) or dependent economically and militarily (Armenia and to a lesser extent Kazakhstan). Yet even here the disjunction between identity formation and institutional purpose suggests that the degree and duration of cooperative organisation may not be great. For that matter, the prospects for Eurasian involvement in international trade and investment flows remains poor, and few are strong candidates for future WTO membership besides Russia and Kazakhstan. Conditions for liberal development and interdependence are generally absent, while mercantilism is made more likely by prevailing threat perceptions and security anxieties.[68] Judging from prevailing identity narratives, then, the most likely prospect is for a continuation of weakly institutionalised economic and security space throughout post-Soviet Eurasia, at least for the foreseeable future.

Notes

1 See Irina Zviagelskaia and Vitali Naumkin, 'Non-Traditional Threats, Challenges, and Risks in the Former Soviet South', in Graham Smith, Edward Allworth and Vivien Law (eds), *Nation-Building in the Post-Soviet Borderlands: The Politics of National Identities* (Cambridge: Cambridge University Press, 1998), pp. 226–47.

2 Fredrik Barth, 'Introduction', in Fredrik Barth (ed.), *Ethnic Groups and Boundaries: The Social Organization of Cultural Difference* (Boston: Little, Brown, 1969), pp. 9–38.

3 I follow the distinction drawn by Kowert and Legro, who define norms as the 'regulative cultural content of international politics' and identities as 'regulative accounts of actors themselves'. Paul Kowert and Jeffrey Legro, 'Norms, Identity, and their Limits: A Theoretical Reprise', in Peter Katzenstein (ed.), *The Culture of National Security: Norms and Identity in World Politics* (New York: Columbia University Press, 1996), p. 453.

4 A second caveat is that this chapter represents only an illustrative, and rather tentative, overview of key themes in the public discourse of post-Soviet Eurasia, based almost entirely on secondary source materials. The point here is not to characterise or delimit definitively the prevailing identity constructs in this region, but rather to provide an indicative guide to the most salient patterns of identity formation and the influences upon this process.

5 Benedict Anderson, *Imagined Communities: Reflections on the Origin and Spread of Nationalism*, rev. edn (New York: Verso, 1991).

6 As Brubaker argues, '[W]e should focus on nation as a category of practice, nationhood as an institutionalized cultural and political form, and nationness as a contingent event or happening, and refrain from using the analytically dubious notion of "nations" as substantial, enduring collectivities.' Rogers Brubaker, *Nationalism Reframed: Nationhood and the National Question in the New Europe* (Cambridge: Cambridge University Press, 1996), p. 21.

7 On identity formation and the construction of Others, see Alexander Wendt, *Social Theory of International Politics* (Cambridge: Cambridge University Press, 1999), pp. 326–35. For Wendt, borrowing from symbolic interactionism, identity formation in international politics is relational and evolves through contact with Others. In contrast, other scholars emphasise the importance of pre-existing understandings or ontologically distinct developments concerning self–Other identification at home. See Naeem Inayatullah and David Blaney, 'Knowing Encounters: Beyond Parochialism in International Relations History', in Yosef Lapid and Friedrich Kratochwil (eds), *The Return of Culture and Identity in IR Theory* (Boulder, CO: Lynne Rienner, 1996), pp. 65–84; also Ted Hopf, *Social Construction of International Politics: Identities and Foreign Policies, Moscow, 1955 and 1999* (Ithaca, NY: Cornell University Press, 2002).

8 As David Campbell observes, 'the state more often than not precedes the nation: … nationalism is a construct of the state in pursuit of its legitimacy'. David Campbell, *Writing Security: United States Foreign Policy and the Politics of Identity*, rev. edn (Minneapolis: University of Minnesota Press, 1998), p. 11.

9 For example, leaders of states whose identity was constructed around the norm of pan-Arab solidarity were constrained to promote policies at odds with their insular preferences. See Michael Barnett, 'Sovereignty, Nationalism, and Regional Order in the Arab State System', *International Organization*, 49:3 (1995), pp. 479–510. See also Martha Finnemore and Kathyrn Sikkink, 'International Norm Dynamics and Political Change', *International Organization*, 52:4 (1998), pp. 887–917.

10 Phillip Roeder, 'Soviet Federalism and Ethnic Mobilization', *World Politics*, 43:2 (1991), pp. 196–232; Ronald Suny, *The Revenge of the Past: Nationalism, Revolution, and the Collapse of the Soviet Union* (Stanford, CA: Stanford University Press, 1993).

11 For example, see the following chapters in Smith *et al.*, *Nation-Building:* Andrew Wilson, 'National History and National Identity in Ukraine and Belarus', pp. 23–47; Viktor Shnirelman, 'National Identity and Myths of Ethnogenesis in Transcaucasia', pp. 48–66, and Edward Allworth, 'History and Group Identity in Central Asia', pp. 67–90.

12 Svante Cornell, *Small Nations and Great Powers: A Study of Ethnopolitical Conflict in the Caucasus* (Richmond: Curzon Press, 2001); Alexander Agadjanian, 'Revising

Pandora's Gifts: Religious and National Indentity in the Post-Soviet Societal Fabric', *Europe–Asia Studies*, 53:3 (2001), pp. 473–89.

13 Olivier Roy notes a 'growing contradiction between the juridical framework of the new constitutions, which privilege the concept of citizenship, and the real practices of the countries concerned, which emphasize ethnicity'. Olivier Roy, *The New Central Asia: The Creation of Nations* (New York: New York University Press, 2000), p. 175. See also Graham Smith, 'Post Colonialism and Borderland Identities', in Smith, *et al.*, *Nation-Building*, pp. 1–20. Although Russian discourse often demonises Chechens and swarthy Caucasians in general, even here the overall thrust of the dominant discourse embraces civic nationalism. See Valery Tishkov, *Ethnicity, Nationalism and Conflict in and after the Soviet Union: The Mind Aflame* (London: Sage, 1997), esp. pp. 259–71.

14 Ronald Suny, 'Provisional Stabilities: The Politics of Identities in Post-Soviet Eurasia', *International Security*, 24:3 (1999/2000), pp. 139–79; and Brubaker, *Nationalism Reframed*.

15 Shahram Akbarzededeh, 'National Identity and Political Legitimacy in Turkmenistan', *National Papers*, 27:2 (1999), pp. 271–90.

16 Leading examples are Hopf, *Social Construction*; Vera Tolz, 'Forging the Nation: National Identity and Nation Building in Post-Communist Russia', *Europe–Asia Studies*, 50:6 (1998), pp. 993–1022; and Astrid Tuminez, *Russian Nationalism since 1856: Ideology and the Making of Foreign Policy* (Lanham, MD: Rowman and Littlefield, 2000).

17 A contemporary example is Aleksandr Neklessa, who asserts that Russia is inherently opposed to the spread of 'Western European civilisation' and carries within itself an alternative, Orthodox basis for re-establishing global community. Aleksandr Neklessa, 'Konets tsivilizatsii, ili zigzag istorii', *Znamia*, 1:3 (1998), pp. 165–79. See also Timo Piirainen, 'The Fall of an Empire, the Birth of a Nation: Perceptions of the New Russian National Identity', in Chris Chulos and Timo Piirainen (eds), *The Fall of an Empire, the Birth of a Nation: National Identities in Russia* (Burlington, VT: Ashgate, 2000), pp. 161–96. On the increasing role of Orthodoxy see Agadjanian, 'Revising Pandora's Gifts'. For an historical perspective see Tim McDaniel, *The Agony of the Russian Idea* (Princeton, NJ: Princeton University Press, 1996), pp. 22–55; and Nikolas Gvosdev, 'The New Party Card? Orthodoxy and the Search for Post-Soviet Russian Identity', *Problems of Post-Communism*, 47:6 (2000), pp. 29–38.

18 For example, Aleksei Arbatov, *Rossiiskaia natsionalnaia ideia i vneshniaia politika* (Moscow: Moscow Social Science Foundation, 1998), pp. 6–18; see also Hopf, *Social Construction*.

19 Aleksandr Dugin, despite his hardline expansionist predilections, remains influential as an 'expert' on geopolitical matters. For a discussion, see Ilan Berman, 'Slouching Toward Eurasia?', *Perspective*, 12:1 (2001), on-line at www.bu.edu/iscip/. Zevelev suggests that this developed as part of the narrative of the New Soviet Man, which mobilised Russian nationalism by instituting a *de facto* russification of language and culture. Igor Zevelev, 'The Russian Quest for a National Identity: Implications for Security in Eurasia', in Sharyl Cross *et al.* (eds), *Global Security Beyond the Millennium: American and Russian Perspectives* (New York: St Martin's Press, 1999), pp. 110–30.

20 Algimantas Prazauskas, 'The Influence of Ethnicity on the Foreign Policies of the

Western Littoral States', in Roman Szporluk (ed.), *National Identity and Ethnicity in Russia and the New States of Eurasia* (New York: M. E. Sharpe, 1994), pp. 150–84; Jeff Chinn, 'Moldovans: Searching for Identity', *Problems of Post-Communism*, 44:3 (1997), pp. 43–52; William Crowther, 'Moldova: Caught Between Nation and Empire', in Ian Bremmer and Ray Taras (eds), *New States, New Politics: Building the Post-Soviet Nations* (Cambridge: Cambridge University Press, 1997), pp. 316–49.

21 Sherman W. Garnett and Rachel Lebenson, 'Ukraine Joins the Fray', *Problems of Post-Communism*, 45:6 (1998), pp. 22–33; and Ted Gurr and Michael Haxton, 'The Gagauz of Moldova: Settling an Ethnonational Rebellion', in Ted Gurr (ed.), *Peoples Versus States: Minorities at Risk in the New Century* (Washington, DC: United States Institute of Peace, 2000), pp. 140–63.

22 Nevertheless, even in Transdniestria the pattern of political opportunism and conflict has crystallised into embedded institutions which have so far stymied all efforts at resolution. Stuart Kaufman, 'Spiraling to Ethnic War: Elites, Masses and Moscow in Moldova's Civil War', *International Security*, 21:2 (1996), pp. 108–38.

23 Elin Suleymanov, 'Azerbaijan, Azerbaijanis and the Search for Identity', *Analysis of Current Events*, 13:1 (2001), pp. 3–6.

24 Mehran Kamrava, 'State-Building in Azerbaijan: The Search for Consolidation', *Middle East Journal*, 55:2 (2001), pp. 216–37; Audrey Altstadt, 'Azerbaijan's Struggle Toward Democracy', in Karen Dawisha and Bruce Parrott (eds), *Conflict, Cleavage, and Change in Central Asia and the Caucasus* (Cambridge: Cambridge University Press, 1997), pp. 110–55; and Tadeusz Swietochowski, 'Azerbaijan: Perspectives from the Crossroads', *Central Asian Survey*, 18:4 (1999), pp. 419–35.

25 Suny, 'Provisional Stabilities'; and Swietochowski, 'Azerbaijan'.

26 Cornell, *Small Nations and Great Powers*, pp. 78–125.

27 George Hewitt, 'Abkhazia, Georgia and the Circassians (NW Caucasus)', *Central Asian Survey*, 18:4 (1999), pp. 463–500.

28 Andrew Wilson, 'Redefining Ethnic and Linguistic Boundaries in Ukraine: Indigenes, Settlers, and Russophone Ukrainians', in Smith *et al. Nation-Building*, pp. 119–38.

29 Wilson, 'National History', pp. 23–47.

30 Alexander Motyl and Bohdan Krawchenko, 'Ukraine: From Empire to Statehood', in Bremmer and Taras, *New States, New Politics*, pp. 235–75.

31 Victor Stepanenko and Sergei Sorokopud, 'The Construction of National Identity: A Case Study of the Ukraine', in Christopher Williams and Thanasis Sfikas (eds), *Ethnicity and Nationalism in Russia, the CIS and the Baltic States* (Brookfield, VT: Ashgate, 1999), pp. 184–210; see also Taras Kuzio (ed.), *Contemporary Ukraine: Dynamics of Post-Soviet Transformation* (Armonk, NY, and London: M. E. Sharpe, 1998).

32 Emil Pain, 'Contagious Ethnic Conflicts and Border Disputes along Russia's Southern Flank', in Smith *et al.*, *Nation-Building*, pp. 177–202. Martha Olcott notes the existence of domestic policy constraints upon Nazarbaev owing to the combination of divergent ethnic identities and resource distributions, and therefore possible social tensions. See Olcott, 'Nation Building and Ethnicity', in Szporluk, *National Identity*, p. 225.

33 On the salience of Kazakh ethnicity over competing identities and the basic cleav-

age between Kazakh and Russian ethnicities in national identity, see Pal Kolsto, 'Bipolar Societies?', in Pal Kolsto (ed.), *Nation-Building and Ethnic Integration in Post-Soviet Societies* (Boulder, CO: Westview Press, 1999), pp. 15–43. On multiple identities in Kazakhstan, see also Martha Olcott, 'National Consolidation', *Harvard International Review*, 22:1 (2000), pp. 50–5; on unintended tribal identity effects, see Edward Schatz, 'The Politics of Multiple Identities: Lineage and Ethnicity in Kazakhstan', *Europe–Asia Studies*, 52:3 (2000), pp. 489–506.

34 Jorn Holm-Hansen, 'Political Integration in Kazakhstan', in Kolsto, *Nation-Building and Ethnic Integration*, pp. 153–226; and Azamat Sarsembayev, 'Imagined Communities: Kazak Nationalism and Kazakification in the 1990s', *Central Asian Survey*, 18:3 (1999), pp. 319–47. Martha Olcott points out that Kazakhstan is the only Central Asian state that neither officially celebrates any Muslim holiday nor refers to Islam in its constitution. Olcott, 'Nation Building and Ethnicity', pp. 218–19. As Suny suggests, 'Kazakhstan's relative success in the last decade in avoiding serious violence can in large part be attributed to a leadership adept at deploying discourses and policies that blur differences and lessen tensions'. Suny, 'Provisional Stabilities', p. 154. See also Martha Olcott, 'Nursultan Nazarbaev and the Balancing Act of State Building in Kazakhstan', in Timothy Colton and Robert Tucker (eds), *Patterns in Post-Soviet Leadership* (Boulder, CO: Westview Press, 1995), pp. 169–90.

35 Smith, 'Post Colonialism and Borderland Identities'.

36 Nora Dudwick, 'The Cultural Construction of Political Violence in Armenia and Azerbaijan', *Problems of Post-Communism*, 42:4 (1995), pp. 18–20.

37 Shnirelman, 'National Identity and Myths of Ethnogenesis'.

38 Serhii Plokhy, 'The Ghosts of Pereyaslav: Russo-Ukrainian Historical Debates in the Post-Soviet Era', *Europe–Asia Studies*, 53:3 (2001), pp. 489–506.

39 Mikhail Molchanov, 'Post-Communist Nationalism as a Power Resource: A Russia–Ukraine Comparison', *Nationalities Papers*, 28:2 (2000), pp. 263–89; Wilson, 'National History'.

40 Suny, 'Provisional Stabilities'; on the prevalence of anti-American imagery in Russia, see Stephen Blank, 'Partners in Discord Only', *Orbis*, 44:4 (2000), pp. 557–71. Hopf notes that the dominant Russian self-image as a 'European' country is meant partly to express rejection of America as well as embrace of Europeanism. Hopf, *Social Construction*.

41 *Ibid.*

42 For example, see Nora Dudwick, 'Armenia: The Nation Awakes', in Ian Bremmer and Ray Taras (eds), *Nations and Politics in the Soviet Successor States* (Cambridge: Cambridge University Press, 1993), pp. 261–87.

43 Prazauskas, 'Influence of Ethnicity', p. 169.

44 Graham Smith, *The Post-Soviet States: Mapping the Politics of Transition* (New York: Oxford University Press, 1999), Ch. 4. Despite official use of Islamic symbols, the Azeri elite has been from the outset overwhelmingly secular in orientation. See Tadeusz Swietochowski, *Russia and Azerbaijan: A Borderland in Transition* (New York: Columbia University Press, 1995), pp. 193–220.

45 Olcott suggests that this was done in part to balance the overall policy orientation and partly for purely opportunistic reasons. Olcott, 'Nation Building and Ethnicity', p. 215.

46 *Ibid.*

47 Aleksei Malashenko, 'Russian Nationalism and Islam', in Michael Waller, Bruno Coppieters and Alexei Malashenko (eds), *Conflicting Loyalties and the State in Post-Soviet Eurasia* (Moscow: Institute of Oriental Studies, Russian Academy of Sciences, 1998), pp. 187–202.

48 On early and deep attractions to Turkic cultural and religious forms, see Shireen Hunter, 'Azerbaijan: Search for Identity', in Bremmer and Taras, *Nations and Politics*, pp. 225–60.

49 On legitimation see Andrew Cortell and James Davis, 'How Do International Institutions Matter? The Domestic Impact of International Rules and Norms', *International Studies Quarterly*, 40:4 (1996), pp. 451–78. All the Eurasian successor states immediately turned for help and guidance to the West and to the major western-dominated international organisations. All joined the World Bank and International Monetary Fund (IMF), while Georgia and Moldova have joined the World Trade Organisation (WTO) and all others except Turkmenistan have observer status. Furthermore all joined the OSCE, and all but Kazakhstan and Turkmenistan, which are geographically ineligible, joined the Council of Europe.

50 Michael Mann, 'The Autonomous Power of the State', in Marvin Olsen and Martin Marger (eds), *Power in Modern Societies* (Boulder, CO: Westview Press, 1993), p. 315. Despotic power refers to the distributive power of state elites over civil society, without requiring any institutionalised negotiation. Thus the advanced capitalist democracies are 'despotically weak but infrastructurally strong'.

51 Joel Migdal, *Strong Societies and Weak States: State–Society Relations and State Capabilities in the Third World* (Princeton, NJ: Princeton University Press, 1988).

52 On Russian state weakness as leading to the emergence of 'mafia' groups which exert partial control over organised violence and taxation, see Vadim Volkov, 'Violent Entrepreneurship in Post-Communist Russia', *Europe–Asia Studies*, 51:5 (1999), pp. 741–54.

53 Suny, 'Provisional Stabilities'.

54 Sarah Mendelson, 'The Putin Path', *Problems of Post-Communism*, 47:5 (2000), pp. 3–12.

55 For example, see Michael McFaul, 'State Power, Constitutional Change, and the Politics of Privatization in Russia', *World Politics*, 47:2 (1995), pp. 210-43; and Vladimir Shlapentokh, Roman Levita, and Mikhail Loiberg, *From Submission to Rebellion: The Provinces Versus the Center in Russia* (Boulder, CO: Westview Press: 1997). Empirically, on the basis of extensive regional survey data, Stoner-Weiss attributes the central state's lack of authority and inability to attain policy implementation to the emergence of powerful group and regional interests which oppose the realisation of central state power. See Kathryn Stoner-Weiss, 'Wither the State? The Regional Sources of Russia's Post-Soviet Governance Crisis', paper prepared for the 2000 Annual Meeting of the American Political Science Association, Washington, DC, 31 August–3 September, 2000.

56 On Chechnya, see John Dunlop, *Russia Confronts Chechnya: Roots of a Separatist Conflict* (New York: Cambridge University Press, 1998); and Anatol Lieven, *Chechnya: Tombstone of Russian Power* (New Haven,CT: Yale University Press, 1998). On other conflicts in the Caucasus, see Cornell, *Small Nations and Great Powers*, pp. 197–284; Fiona Hill, *Russia's Tinderbox: Conflict in the North Caucasus and its Implications for the Future of the Russian Federation* (Cambridge, MA:

Harvard University, JFK School of Government, Strengthening Democratic Institutions Project, September 1995); and Jane Omrod, 'The North Caucasus: Confederation in Conflict', in Bremmer and Taras, *New States, New Politics*, pp. 96–139.

57 Kamrava, 'State-Building in Azerbaijan'.

58 As Cronin observes, neo-liberal accounts of the availability of international regimes can explain the emergence of cooperation, but cannot adequately explain the range of possible institutional outcomes. Bruce Cronin, *Community Under Anarchy: Transnational Identity and the Evolution of Cooperation* (New York: Columbia University Press, 1999).

59 Jan Adams, 'The CIS States: Going Global', *Post Soviet Prospects*, 5:1 (1997), on-line at www.csis.org/ruseura/psp/pspv1.html. Also William Crowther, 'Moldova: Caught Between Nation and Empire', in Bremmer and Taras, *New States, New Politics*, pp. 316–49.

60 David Mark, 'Eurasia Letter: Russia and the New Transcaucasus', *Foreign Policy*, 105 (1996/97), pp. 141–59.

61 Henry Hale, 'Integration and Independence in the Caspian Basin', *SAIS Review*, 19:1 (1999), pp. 163–89.

62 Jennifer Moroney, 'Frontier Dynamics and Ukraine's Ties to the West', *Problems of Post-Communism*, 48:2 (2001), pp. 15–25; also Molchanov, 'Post-Communist Nationalism'.

63 Olcott, 'Nursultan Nazarbaev and the Balancing Act'.

64 This point is made by Schatz, 'Politics of Multiple Identities'.

65 Indeed, under certain conditions narrowly functional regimes may be successful despite the lack of any substantial affinity among their members. See Oran Young, *International Governance: Protecting the Environment in a Stateless Society* (Ithaca, NY: Cornell University Press, 1994).

66 Charles Kupchan and Clifford Kupchan, 'The Promise of Collective Security', *International Security*, 20:1 (1995), pp. 52–61.

67 Dov Lynch, 'Euro-Asian Conflicts and Peacekeeping Dilemmas', in Yelena Kalyuzhnova and Dov Lynch (eds), *The Euro-Asian World: A Period of Transition* (New York: St Martin's Press, 2000), pp. 3–27.

68 Hendrik Spruyt and Laurent Ruseckas, 'Economics and Energy in the South: Liberal Expectations Versus Likely Realities', in Rajan Menon, Yuri Fyodorov and Ghia Nodia (eds), *Russia, the Caucasus, and Central Asia: The 21st Century Security Environment* (Armonk, NY: M. E. Sharpe, 1999), pp. 87–118.

3

Ethnic conflict and Eurasian security

Stuart Kaufman

What role does ethnic conflict play in Eurasian security affairs? Just breaking this question down into its component parts uncovers a vast array of apparent influences. Ethnic conflict is, first of all, clearly a cause of internal conflict and insecurity, as demonstrated by the problems in Bosnia, Kosovo, Macedonia, Cyprus, Georgia, Chechnya and Mountainous Karabagh. Furthermore, it is a key cause of international security problems, as the above list of ethnic civil wars illustrates: most of these conflicts have attracted involvement by neighbouring countries, and some have all along been as much interstate as intra-state disputes. But ethnic conflicts do not only *cause* international insecurity; they may also be in part a *result* of security competition. Bosnia's conflict, for example, was driven in large part by rivalry between Serbia and Croatia; Macedonia's violence is largely a spillover from the Kosovo conflict; and separatist conflicts continue in Azerbaijan and Georgia due in large part to Russian support for the separatists.

All of these dynamics combine with other sorts of security competition in the region to create significant security dilemma problems. Russian statesmen feel, for example, that a more or less exclusive Russian sphere of influence in the Caspian region, and especially in the Caucasus, is essential for Russian security. Indeed, they blame their Chechnya problems in large part on the absence of such predominance. Obviously, however, these hegemonic ambitions clash with the basic goals of security, sovereignty and territorial integrity of the states in the region, especially Georgia and Azerbaijan. The existence of those clashes, in turn, threatens the American and Turkish security interests of stabilising the Caucasus so they can obtain access to the energy resources of the region.

The key to sorting out these complex influences lies in rethinking the source and nature of the security dilemma both internally and internationally. In international relations theory, the debate has been primarily between neo-realists, who argue that international anarchy *ipso facto* causes security dilemmas, and neo-liberal institutionalists, who argue that institutions can help head off security dilemmas. Both sides have also tried to apply their ideas to internal ethnic conflicts. Self-identified constructivists cover this whole range of possible arguments, and much more territory besides.

Many of these arguments can be reconciled using a particular constructivist approach. As Randall Schweller has argued, the existence of an international security dilemma requires the existence of revisionist states – requires, that is, that states construct their security interests to require expansion.[1] When states construct their security needs in mutually accommodating ways, as within the western security community, there is no security dilemma.[2] The same insight applies to ethnic conflict: the critical cause of ethnic conflict is the construction of ethnic groups' vital interests in conflicting ways, typically in terms of mutually exclusive claims to the same territory. Where states or groups construct their interests in ways that are mutually reconcilable, neo-liberal institutionalist prescriptions for conflict management and conflict resolution can work. Where security interests are constructed in mutually exclusive ways, neo-realist objections to neo-liberal arguments apply.

In the hot spots of Eurasia, security dilemmas continue to exist within and between states because states and groups define their security in mutually exclusive ways. In ethnic conflicts such as those in the Balkans, institutional arrangements to manage conflict will remain fragile as long as and to the degree that ethnic attitudes and goals remain mutually hostile. Furthermore, even the fragile effectiveness of existing institutions will continue only as long as the distribution of power discourages the dissatisfied from trying again – which means, in large measure, only as long as the US remains engaged. In the Caucasus, the parties have constructed their interests to rule out compromise: those elites who might be inclined to seek a compromise settlement are prohibited by public opinion from reaching any agreements. There, renewed war is prevented only by the continuing military superiority of the victors of the last rounds of fighting. Effective institutional arrangements for conflict management do not exist and cannot be built in current circumstances. In both places, 'peace-building' efforts aimed at shifting public attitudes are necessary, and are the only available policy tools that can contribute to stability in the long run. However, peace-building efforts would face tough sledding in any case, and the Bush administration's 'realist' foreign policy has not contributed to the mitigation of the regional security dilemmas, especially in the Caucasus and the Balkan states.

Understanding Eurasia's ethnic wars

Scholars, practitioners and journalists have developed a number of different ideas about how to explain the ethnic violence in Eurasia. The most prominent of these include the 'ancient hatreds' argument most popular among journalists,[3] the 'elite manipulation' story favoured by most rational choice theorists,[4] the security dilemma argument focused on internal insta-bility,[5] and arguments focused on foreign influences – 'bad neighbours' and 'bad neighbourhoods'.[6] These diagnoses can lead to starkly different policy prescriptions. Misha Glenny, whose work tilts toward the ancient hatreds school, argues that the violence can stop only if outside powers intervene by force,[7] while Robert Kaplan, who represents the same school of thought, argues that such intervention can stop the violence only temporarily. Rational choice theorists focused on elite behavior and institutional struc-ture tend to argue that the solutions are found in appropriate institutional arrangements supplemented by international action as guarantors.[8] Security dilemma theorists argue that power-sharing institutions are hope-lessly ineffective, so only partition can resolve or at least reduce violent conflicts.[9] And those who study international factors focus on the impor-tance of deterring 'bad neighbours' from destructive interventions.[10]

All of these arguments, however, miss the central source of the problem: where do ethnic hatreds – which are not, in fact, 'ancient' – come from? Why do mass publics follow manipulative elites into war? Why do intermingled ethnic groups sometimes fight with each other when government is weak, but more typically avoid such fighting?[11]

The answers are found, in large part, in ethnic or nationalist mythologies and the manipulation of emotional symbols identified in those myths.[12] Ethnic groups are, as Benedict Anderson has said of nations, 'imagined communities'; they exist only because of a body of ethnic myths that define them. These myths, as Anthony Smith argues, typically identify who is in the group, how members are distinguished from non-members, a common set of cultural beliefs, a common name and history, what it means to be a group member, and, often, who the group's enemies are.[13] These divisions and identifications are always to some extent arbitrary. Serbs and Croats, for example, share a language but count each other as enemies on religious and historical grounds. Abkhazians, in contrast, though divided religiously, make common cause against the linguistically different Georgians, and ally with Russia to do so even though Russia was the perpetrator of Abkhazia's great historical tragedy, an ethnic cleansing campaign in the late nineteenth century.

What matters is the degree to which ethnic or nationalist myths justify hostility against other groups. Nationalist Serbs, for example, identify Croats with the World War II-era Ustashe fascists, and they identify Muslim Bosnians and Albanians with the hated Ottoman Turks – so they fought these groups in Bosnia and Kosovo. On the other hand, Serbs and Macedonians, though not particularly friendly towards each other, have tried to cooperate against the Muslim Albanians, who are seen by both groups as the national enemy.

These myths, and the hostility or hatred they generate, are not, however, ancient; they are modern. While Serbian mythology dates Serbs' hostility to Muslims to the 1389 Battle of Kosovo Field, for example, there was little popular ethnic tension before the myths of Kosovo were resurrected in the nineteenth century by Serbian propagandists, many working for the newly independent Serbian state.[14] And Serbs' hostility to Croats is based primarily on the symbolism of Croats as Ustashe fascists, which dates only to World War II and to postwar mythologising. Similarly, while Armenian mythology traces the roots of the nation to ancient times, and singles out Turks as historical enemies, Armenian national consciousness – and their national conflict with the Turks – dates only to the 1890–1915 period, when the Armenian national 'awakening' led to several rounds of ethnic violence between Armenians and Turks (including Azerbaijani Turks), culminating in the 1915 genocide.[15]

Such hostile myths are, however, more common than ethnic violence. If severe violence is to occur, hostile ethnic myths must be activated by some threat that leads members of at least one group to fear ethnic extinction. Thus the problem that set Yugoslavia ablaze was that Milosevic's grab for Serb domination provoked a countervailing Croatian nationalism, which in turn led the Serbs of Croatia to fear ethnic cleansing or genocide by a neo-fascist Croatian regime. The Armenians of Mountainous Karabagh in Azerbaijan, similarly, feared a creeping ethnic cleansing or 'white genocide' as a result of continuing, long-term Azerbaijani discrimination, while their response – a secessionist movement – threatened the dismemberment of Azerbaijan.

It is only in the context of such myths and fears that ethnic elites can mobilise popular opinion behind ethnic extremism, once they have the opportunity to do so. In some cases, most famously Milosevic's, incumbent leaders can manipulate myths like the Battle of Kosovo and symbols like Prince Lazar, doomed hero of that battle, by using their control over the media to dominate public debate and thereby promote an extreme national-ist program. The extremist program is key: ethnic war occurs only if the sides define their groups' security in mutually exclusive ways. Croats, for example, felt unsafe in a Yugoslavia dominated by Milosevic, so they decided to secede, while the Serbs of Croatia felt unsafe under an independent nationalist Croatian government, so they tried to split from Croatia. These conflicting security demands impelled both sides to fight.

Ethnic mobilisation does not, however, have to come as the result of elite manipulation. In some cases, popular myths and fears are strong enough for a street-corner agitator who harps on nationalist themes to become a nationalist hero, at least briefly. In Georgia, for example, the Communist Party leadership under First Secretary Jumber Patiashvili tried hard to suppress rising nationalist sentiment in the late 1980s, but was unable to arrest the rise of dissident journalist Zviad Gamsakhurdia to power, or to prevent the eruption of ethnic violence between Georgians and the minority South Ossetians. Georgian mythology painted the South Ossetians as 'recent' (seventeenth-century) migrants to Georgia with no right to their autonomous region; the South Ossetians, feeling threatened, counter-mobilised and the result, eventually, was war.[16]

Finally, foreign actors may play a critical role in turning ethnic conflict into war regardless of whether mobilisation is mass-led or elite-led. In the absence of external help, rebels or secessionists typically have little hope against the armed might of the state. With it, however, they are more likely to try to fight and more likely to win. Victims of 'bad neighbours' include Moldova and Georgia, whose secessionist groups would have lacked the ability to fight without Russian help, and Mountainous Karabagh, where the Armenians' victory over Azerbaijan was equally the result of Russian assistance. And the fights in Croatia and Bosnia occurred mostly because of the influence of Belgrade on their Serbian minorities. Macedonia's current troubles are more a case of a 'bad neighbourhood': no government in the region is trying to destabilise Macedonia, but the conflict there is none the less the result of spillover from Kosovo next door.

In sum, all four of the rival theories of ethnic violence offer insights, but none of them accounts for the whole picture. Journalists are right that violent ethnic conflicts are driven by popular hostility and hatred, but those attitudes are modern, not 'ancient'. Rational choice theorists are right that mass publics are often manipulated by ethnic elites, but they overlook the degree to which pre-existing myths and attitudes are needed to make such manipulation possible, and they ignore the importance of emotional symbolism in enabling leaders to manipulate their followers. Security dilemma theorists are right that ethnic violence escalates because of a security dilemma, but most underestimate the degree to which the insecurity is driven by simple hostile intent – the predatory goal of domination over the other group – rather than uncertainty.[17] Finally, international relations theorists are right that bad neighbours and bad neighbourhoods can have a critical influence, but they do not claim that such influences matter in the absence of the right (or wrong) internal conditions.

Furthermore, in evaluating the effects of foreign intervention in ethnic conflicts, it is important to take into account the various and powerful motives outsiders may have for such action. Ethnic chauvinism was Milosevic's ruling strategy, so he would have been pushed to intervene in Croatia and Bosnia even if he had not wanted to do so. The intervention of Russia's Fourteenth Army in Moldova's ethnic conflict in 1991–92, in contrast, was driven not so much by Moscow as by its officers who wanted to protect their own families resident in the region.[18] Russia continues to support the Abkhazian separatists against Georgia largely because they consider increased influence in Georgia essential for Russian security – including in Russia's fight against Chechnya, which borders on Georgia. The

NATO interventions in Bosnia in 1995 and Kosovo in 1999 expressed the Euro-American security policy of rebuilding NATO as the premier security organisation in Europe. Continued Russian intervention in the Caucasus can, in this light, be understood as a Russian effort, driven by the security dilemma, to prevent such NATO hegemony on its southern border. Encouraging constructive international intervention and heading off the destructive kind is, in this light, harder than it looks.

The dilemmas of policy intervention

Because all of these theorists are in part right, their prescriptions for conflict resolution all have merit. Rational choice theorists are right that designing workable institutions is critical if ethnically divided states are to be rebuilt, and that external intervention can play a critical role in setting up those institutions. But ancient hatreds theorists, and security dilemma theorists such as Chaim Kaufmann, are also right that neither intervention nor new institutions can change ethnic hatreds, especially after they have been renewed and entrenched by a recent round of violence. Furthermore, there are many different sorts of foreign intervention: helping one side win the fight, for example, may lead to a quick ceasefire but also cause a long-lasting political stalemate. Sometimes military intervention seems necessary to establish a secure environment; in other cases, mediation and other peaceful interventions suffice. In some cases, the key is to deter destructive external intervention. What mix of approaches is right, and how can the sides get past the hurdle of lasting hostility?

Thinking about ethnic conflicts in terms of a symbolic politics trap helps to fill in one of the key missing pieces. Interethnic stalemates stay in place not only because of the dynamics between the two groups, but because of the dynamics within them. Once extremist leaders have used extremist ethnic symbols to gain and hold power, they often become captive to those symbols. Thus even if leaders recognise that continued ethnic confrontation may no longer be in their group's interest, they may be unable to agree to a peace settlement because of the danger of being outflanked by even more extreme opposition figures who can use those same symbols against them.

Escape from the symbolic politics trap requires yet another set of tools for outside intervention. If the problem is hostile attitudes and social dynamics that make it hard to change them, the solution has to be policies aimed at changing those attitudes and social dynamics. This is the realm of 'peace-building' and 'conflict transformation' – efforts at encouraging non-hostile interethnic attitudes and cooperative relationships across communal lines.[19] Most typically, peace building programmes focus on dialogue between members of different ethnic groups aimed at undercutting their 'enemy image' of each other, helping participants find enough mutual empathy so that they find compromise not only thinkable but preferable to continued conflict. While such efforts work at the individual level, however,

their effects are usually limited owing to the re-entry problem: when participants return home, they find their friends and associates unsympathetic to
their new moderation, so they feel obliged to keep their views quiet.[20] This
points towards the need for more ambitious targets – changes in government
rhetoric, media coverage and school curricula aimed at creating an atmosphere that encourages moderate attitudes, plus well-crafted efforts at
promoting economic reintegration to create tangible incentives for a
compromise peace.

Eurasia's ethnic conflicts

To consider further all of these problems, I turn now to several of the more
prominent ethnic conflicts in Eurasia. I start with the internal dynamics of
the conflicts themselves, exploring the ethnic myths and symbols at the root
of the groups' conflicting identities. I then show how in each case the participants are caught in a symbolic politics trap, and are therefore locked into
intractable security dilemmas resulting from the sides' – or at least their
leaders' – irreconcilable, indeed predatory, goals. I then discuss the international dimensions of each conflict – the spurs and reins on international
intervention, and the resulting dynamics of those interventions.

Bosnia

The war in Bosnia-Herzegovina was the largest and most destructive of
Europe's ethnic wars in the 1990s, leaving over two hundred thousand dead
and over two million refugees and displaced persons after a four-year war of
a viciousness unseen in Europe since World War II. Since the outbreak of the
conflict is typically blamed on Serbian leader Slobodan Milosevic and his
allies in Bosnia, Radovan Karadzic and Ratko Mladic, it is important to point
out that in Bosnia, too, hostile ethnic myths and emotive symbols provided
the tinder which the sparks of Milosevic's propaganda set alight. Milosevic,
Karadzic and company are indeed the main reasons for the war, but their
efforts could not have succeeded in the absence of a climate receptive to their
appeals.

Among the Serbs, the critical myths stemmed from the traditions about
the Kosovo battle against the Turks, and from the experience (and myths) of
World War II. Kosovo is the founding myth of the Serbian nation, the lost
1389 battle against the Turks that led to five centuries of Ottoman Turkish
domination but, in the mythology, led also to a religious sanctification of the
Serbian nation as Christian heroes of Europe and martyrs to the terrible
Turk.[21] The Serbian habit of referring to all Muslims as 'Turks' allows Serbs
to feel about the Bosnian Muslims as they do about real Turks, in spite of the
fact that Serbs and Bosnian Muslims had far more in common with each
other than either did with Turks. At the same time, the mythologised
memory of the horrendous fight against the Nazis and the Croatian Ustashe

fascists inclined Bosnian Serbs to see Bosnian Croats (not entirely inaccurately) as the direct inheritors of the Ustashe.[22] Serbian propaganda added to this noxious mix an additional element, labelling the Bosnian Muslims as 'Islamic fundamentalists', raising fears for the survival of the Serbian community in Bosnia.

Croatian mythology paints the Croats as a single tribe, distinguished by their Catholicism and location as the 'outer wall' of Christian Europe's defence against the early modern Ottomans. It also emphasises over a millennium of Croatian 'statehood', and as a result is ambivalent about the Ustashe interlude: as Franjo Tudjman put it, the Ustashe regime was simultaneously 'a Fascist crime' and an authentic expression of Croatian nationalist aspirations.[23] The Croats of western Herzegovina, long associated with Croat extremism, were among the most avid followers of Tudjman's efforts to revive Croatian nationalism in the early 1990s and strong supporters of the dream of extending the revived Croatian statehood to their territory (dismembering Bosnia in the process).

The identity of Bosnian Muslims is more problematic. While there was, in fact, a medieval Bosnian kingdom – Bosnian King Tvrtko was a key ally of Prince Lazar and the Serbs at the Battle of Kosovo Field – no specifically Bosnian identity emerged from medieval times. Only in Tito's time did the Muslims of Bosnia make clear that they wanted recognition of their distinct identity. Since Serbs and Croats objected to construction of a 'Bosnian' identity that would include Bosnian Serbs and Croats, the 'Muslim' category was created in the Yugoslav census, and thence in Yugoslav political life. To the extent that the Bosnian Muslim identity had a political meaning, it was the vision of Alija Izetbegovic, the first president of independent Bosnia, who argued for a peaceful melding of secular western civilisation with Islamic spiritual values.[24] Mostly, however, the Muslim identity was a refuge for those trapped between the unacceptable Serb and Croat visions for the republic's future.

The main cause of Bosnia's war was less these identities, however, than the policy of the Serbian leadership. Slobodan Milosevic, the president of Serbia, created the apparatus of Bosnia's Serbian Democratic Party (SDS), led by Radovan Karadzic, and the Bosnian Serb army, led by Ratko Mladic. Using the Serbian myths and manufactured fears as justification, these leaders, with assistance from Serbia, formulated a policy of remaking most of Bosnia into an ethnically 'clean' Serbian state, leaving over a small Croat-Muslim rump. To implement this policy, the Bosnian Serbs launched their campaign of mass murder and ethnic cleansing, highlighted by the concentration camps at Omarska and elsewhere and the brutal siege of Sarajevo. Hardline Croats in Franjo Tudjman's HDZ simultaneously tried to carve out an ethnically Croat entity in western Herzegovina. The fighting continued until the Croatian counter-offensive of 1995, in alliance with the Bosnian Muslims and backed by NATO air strikes, presented the Serbs with the threat of military defeat, leading Milosevic to coerce his erstwhile Serbian allies into signing the Dayton peace accords that ended the fighting.

Those agreements established a rickety network of institutions that tried simultaneously to establish an effective central government for Bosnia and disperse virtually all effective power to two, and in practice three, ethnically based units: the Republika Srpska, the Muslim-Croat Federation, and the *de facto* Croat entity within the federation. On the one hand, the plan for *peace* centred on establishing a *de facto* partition: creating the ethnic entities, allowing the continued existence of separate armies and ethnically domi-nated local police forces, and establishing an arms-control regime. These provisions were all concessions to the predatory goals of the Serbs and Croats. On the other hand, the plan for *reintegration* aimed at undermining that partition in the long run: establishing a central Bosnian govern-ment, allowing for repatriation of refugees, and empowering NATO's Implementation Force (IFOR) to enforce the agreement and arrest the war criminals who were continuing to block reconciliation efforts.[25] These requirements were, of course, at the demand of the Bosnian government – whose goals the Serbs and Croats see as predatory.

In practice, the Dayton provisions that promote disintegration have proved stronger than those that promote reintegration, primarily because of the disinclination of IFOR (and its successor, NATO's Stabilisation Force (SFOR)) to coerce the Bosnian Serbs and Croats – whose leaders were still intent on carving up Bosnia – into implementing the provisions for reinte-gration. Thus IFOR refused to arrest war criminals, leaving Radovan Karadzic in power until 1996, and then accepting as his successor the initially equally hardline Biljana Plavsic. These criminal leaders, in turn, fought every effort at reintegrating Bosnia, repeatedly blocking efforts to repatriate Muslim refugees to Republika Srpska, and refusing even to accept a common licence- plate design for cars. The high representative established under the Dayton accords finally imposed the licence-plate design, but war criminals remain in control of local police and governments in Republika Srpska, have blocked most refugee repatriation, have prevented the estab-lishment of a single Bosnian economic space, and have undermined economic reconstruction by maintaining a corrupt system of payoffs linked to organised crime networks.[26] The Bosnian state remains a polite fiction, in spite of the fall of its most important external enemy, President Slobodan Milosevic of Yugoslavia.

Bosnia remains so in part because of hostile nationalist myths and atti-tudes, which were magnified by the horrors of the war. Serbs, Croats and Muslims all tend to deny or downplay the atrocities and murders committed by their own side, while exaggerating those committed by the others. But these attitudes are reinforced by incumbent local and entity leaders (and the media they control), all too often war leaders and war criminals with every incentive to obscure their own culpability. The November 2000 elections placed moderates in power in the central Bosnian government, but put the hardline SDS back in power in Republika Srpska. Not only was the SDS dominated by indicted or indictable war criminals – from wartime leader Radovan Karadzic behind the scenes to a legion of thugs in positions of local power[27] – but it also ran a thoroughly corrupt economic system in which bribery, smuggling and other sorts of organised crime flourished while reconstruction and other normal economic activity was choked off. These hardliners returned to power by exploiting the symbolic politics trap, blaming other ethnic groups and the international community for the economic misery their gangsterism causes. In this context, peace-building cannot by itself promote reconciliation: while some peace building efforts have made progress in neighbouring Croatia and even in Bosnia itself,[28] the general assessment of most foreign organisations in Bosnia is that the Serbs are simply not prepared to cooperate, due to hostile attitudes reinforced by hardline government officials. The symbolic politics trap in Bosnia thus remains elite-led.

Macedonia

Macedonia has, so far, managed to avoid the outbreak of all-out war between the Slavic Macedonian majority and the Albanian minority, which comprises at least a quarter of the population. The flare-up of fighting in the spring and summer of 2001 did, however, threaten to escalate into such a war, and full implementation of the fragile peace deal reached between the conflicting factions at Lake Ohrid in August of that year remains uncertain. Speaking mutually unintelligible languages, adhering to different religious faiths, and leading radically different styles of life (at least in rural areas), Macedonians and Albanians are distinctly hostile to each other, so their ability to head off full-scale war is all the more notable.

Macedonian nationalism is a new phenomenon. In the early twentieth century, there was no separate Slavic Macedonian identity; Macedonian villagers defined their identity as either 'Bulgarian', 'Serbian' or even 'Greek' depending on the affiliation of the village priest.[29] The separate Macedonian nationalist mythology and national identity are essentially a post-World War II phenomenon, a product of Tito's postwar nationality policy. According to the Macedonian mythology, modern Macedonians are the descendants of the subjects of Alexander the Great. Macedonian cultural identity stems from the ninth-century Saints Cyril and Methodius, who converted the Slavs to Christianity and invented the first alphabet for a Slavic language. Macedonians trace the roots of their nationalist movement to the turn-of-the-century Internal Macedonian Revolutionary Organisation (IMRO) – actually a pro-Bulgarian group – and celebrate the anniversary of the Ilinden uprising against the Ottoman Turks in 1903 as a national holiday. Unlike the Serbs, however, the Macedonians do not typically associate Albanians with the Ottoman Turks of history. There are

Macedonian fears of group extinction, but these fears have focused historically on the irredentist threat from Macedonia's neighbours – the 'four
wolves' of Serbia, Bulgaria, Greece and Albania – as much as on the internal
threat from Macedonia's Albanians.[30]

Albanians, for their part, claim (with more plausibility than the
Macedonians) descent from another ancient group in the region, the
Illyrians, and on this basis claim western Macedonia as historically theirs.
According to their mythology, they have never accepted foreign rule: their
national hero, Skanderbeg, led the Albanians' fight against the Ottomans in
the fifteenth century; their nineteenth-century national 'awakening' was
directed as much against the Turks as against their Slavic neighbours. These
ideas incline them to reject Macedonian authority as well. Furthermore, the
savagery of the Balkan Wars beginning in 1912 occurred largely in
Macedonia, so a twentieth-century precedent of extreme mutual violence is
also present.

When Macedonia achieved independence in 1991, therefore, hostile
myths, group fears and political opportunity were all present, and expressions of mass hostility were common. How, then, did it avoid large-scale
violence for a decade; and how did it manage to reach a compromise agreement on its ethnic conflict when fighting did break out in 2001? First,
Macedonians' fear of group extinction was assuaged because they had
predominant political power, while Albanian fears focused on prosaic
mistreatment rather than existential concerns. Second, and most importantly, politicians on both sides – presumably deterred by the example of
their northern neighbours – wanted to avoid violence, and were willing to
make efforts to prevent it. Macedonian leaders always included Albanian
ministers in their governments, and Albanian politicians refrained from
pushing their brinkmanship tactics to the point of violence. Given this
modicum of goodwill, the two sides managed to crawl slowly towards resolution of substantive issues, such as Macedonian government tolerance of
the Albanian-language university in Tetovo. The United Nations provided a
small peacekeeping force that helped reassure both sides of international
concern.

When violence did finally erupt in 2001, it was the result of spillover from
Kosovo, an uprising created by a few Albanian Macedonian extremists who
had experience fighting in Kosovo. These cadres created their 'National
Liberation Army' (NLA) based on the infrastructure and resources of the
Kosovo Liberation Army, and with some uncertain degree of connection to
the entrenched smuggling rings operating across borders in the region. The
Macedonian government's reaction to the outbreak of violence was schizo-
phrenic. On the one hand, hardliners led by Prime Minister Ljubcho
Georgievski spoke of a military solution to the problem, and even the moderate President Boris Trajkovski branded the NLA as 'terrorists' (which they
were not, in the sense that their usual targets of attack were Macedonian

military and police rather than civilians). On the other hand, Trajkovski also launched talks with Albanian political parties to address many of the Albanians' longstanding concerns: increasing jobs in government administration, expanding local self-government, and extending the use of the Albanian language in government and education. The NLA, for its part, staked out a strikingly moderate political platform largely corresponding to the demands made by the Albanian political parties, but complemented by the demand for changes in discriminatory language in the Macedonian constitution.

Prodded by US and EU mediators, representatives of Macedonia's main political parties (with the legal Albanian parties acting on behalf of the NLA) signed a peace agreement in August 2001, despite rising violence promoted by extremists on both sides. The agreement was a fair-minded compromise: for example, Macedonian was to remain the official language for the government's foreign relations, but any other language spoken by 20 per cent of the population of a locality was to be a 'service language' for that locality; higher education in Albanian was also to be provided. On the political level, the two sides agreed on a power-sharing deal, effectively requiring majority Albanian support in Parliament for legislation affecting the interests of Albanians. NATO peacekeepers were introduced to collect the NLA's armaments, and implementation of the deal was to be roughly synchronised with the arms-collection process, though in practice the constitutional amendments' ratification was delayed for two months by hardline Macedonian leaders. In implementing the deal, the most controversial issue turned out to be a provision for an amnesty for NLA fighters who had not committed war crimes: Macedonian hardliners did not want to let these 'terrorists' off the hook.

Neither Macedonia's approach to war nor its subsequent move towards peaceful conflict management was surprising. The preconditions for war were present, but Macedonia is blessed in that even its extremists are relatively moderate. War erupts when both sides pursue predatory goals, sticking to mutually irreconcilable positions; the NLA instead chose a moderate political programme, and agreed to disband when its demands were largely met. On the Macedonian side, some leaders did apparently want war in pursuit of ethnic domination, but President Trajkovski, the leader of the ruling nationalist VMRO-DPME party, was not among them. Thus while a security dilemma exists – Macedonians fear Albanian separatism and lawlessness, while Albanians fear repression by violent Macedonian police and paramilitaries – it remains manageable because the sides are not pursuing predatory goals. At the same time, none of the regional or great powers had an interest in fostering violence.[31] In these circumstances, the sorts of leverage available to the international community – diplomatic pressure, offers of a donor conference to implement a peace deal, pressure on foreign arms suppliers – were enough to tip the balance towards peace.

None of this means the conflict is over; implementation of the Lake Ohrid agreement will remain problematic as Macedonian hardliners try to manipulate emotional symbolism to block Albanian gains. In the medium term, continuing strong ethnic Macedonian hostility towards Albanians, a strong chauvinist presence in the Macedonian-language media, and the persistence of the nationalist VMRO government mean that Macedonia will remain for some time on the brink of war. If war comes, however, it will be elite-led: Albanians supported the (now defunct) NLA's goals but not its violent methods, while the VMRO government came to power by downplaying its nationalist programme and forming a coalition with an Albanian faction. On both sides, mass opinion is volatile but does not want ethnic confrontation.

Mountainous Karabagh

The first ethnic conflict to explode into war in this region was the conflict between Armenians and Azerbaijanis over Mountainous Karabagh. At the time the conflict started in late 1987, there were some 475,000 Armenians in Azerbaijan, a quarter of them in the Mountainous Karabagh Autonomous Region, as well as over 100,000 Azerbaijanis in Armenia. Ethnic tensions were longstanding, in large part reflecting deeply hostile ethnic mythologies.

Armenian mythology painted the Armenian people as ancient inhabitants of the region stretching from Karabagh to eastern Turkey, inheritors of a political tradition dating back over 2,000 years, and the first nation to convert to Christianity (in AD 301). The mythology also characterised Armenia as a martyr nation, repeatedly victimised over the centuries by Persian and Turkish adversaries. The defining experience for the nation is, in this narrative, the 1915 Genocide, in which virtually the entire Armenian population of eastern Anatolia, over a million people, was forcibly expelled in circumstances designed to ensure the deaths of most of them. The memory of this experience defined all Turks, including Azerbaijani Turks, as the national enemy, and rendered Armenians acutely sensitive to the perceived threat of a new expulsion from other lands of Armenian settlement, especially Mountainous Karabagh.[32]

Azerbaijanis, for their part, had a much more recent national tradition – their very name achieved wide currency only in the 1930s – but their mythology placed the roots of the nation in ancient times, even before the migrations that brought their Turkic language to Azerbaijan. The myths located this national tradition not, therefore, in Azerbaijan's Turkic language or Shi'ite Muslim culture, but in the tradition of politically autonomous entities in the region dating back to ancient times. The awakening of a self-conscious Azerbaijani nation occurred in the aftermath of the 1905–6 'Armeno-Tatar War' (Azerbaijanis at that time being called Tatars) and of the fighting between Armenia and Azerbaijan in 1918–20. Armenians thus came to be identified as the enemy of the Azerbaijani nation, and Karabagh's secessionist ambitions came to be seen as a mortal threat to the 'statehood' that was at the core of Azerbaijani identity.

Thus from the beginning of the conflict, both sides feared group extinction: the Armenian bugbear was 'genocide', and for Azerbaijanis it was dismemberment of their state. These hostile myths and group fears promoted predatory goals on both sides, with the Armenians calling from the outset for Armenian domination of Karabagh and its transfer to Armenia, while Azerbaijanis soon began calling for revocation of Karabagh's autonomy and its subordination to direct Azerbaijani administration. As a result, a security dilemma quickly emerged in spite of efforts by Communist Party leaders on both sides to dampen down violence: by the end of 1988, some 180,000 Armenians had been 'ethnically cleansed' from Azerbaijan, and 160,000 Azerbaijanis fled from Armenian-inhabited areas. In huge upswellings of mass nationalist sentiments, first Armenia and then Azerbaijan replaced its Communist leadership with nationalists focused on independence from Moscow and on the fight for Karabagh. Karabagh itself mobilised to fight the Turkic enemy, and once the Soviet Union collapsed – allowing the Karabagh Armenians to inherit part of the old Soviet army – the Armenians went over to the offensive, capturing and expelling the inhabitants of Azerbaijani areas in Karabagh, most notably the ancient town of Shusha.

By the time the shooting stopped in May 1994, the Karabagh Armenians, with overt support from Armenia and slightly less overt support from Moscow, had captured nearly 20 per cent of the territory of Azerbaijan, including virtually all of Mountainous Karabagh itself, and expelled the Azerbaijani inhabitants. Azerbaijan was left to cope with the loss of territory and a million refugees on the territory it did control, while it hoped for an oil and gas bonanza that would solve its economic problems and generate the military power to gain revenge on the Armenians. Armenia, for its part, had gained *de facto* military victory, but it faced a dismal economic picture, with trade shut off on two of its borders (with Azerbaijan and with Turkey), and a population haemorrhaging into the diaspora.

In spite of both sides' desperate need for a peace agreement, however, efforts to reach a deal were repeatedly blocked by the dynamics of the symbolic politics trap. Until 1998, Armenia was led by Levon Ter-Petrosian, hero of the independence struggle and leader of the Armenian National Movement. Ter-Petrosian might have been considered the one man capable of reaching a peace deal, but it became increasingly difficult as corruption, economic stagnation and a badly tainted re-election process sapped his legitimacy.

The most hopeful moment for peace came in September 1997, when Ter-Petrosian and Azerbaijani president Heydar Aliev accepted an OSCE proposal for a phased approach to peace, involving an Armenian withdrawal from Azerbaijani lands outside Karabagh, in exchange for an opening of economic ties in the region. The Karabagh authorities, however, adamantly rejected the idea of withdrawal from any territory before the status of Karabagh was settled, while the powerful Armenian émigré community also weighed in against the plan. In the ensuing backlash, Ter-Petrosian was forced to resign and was replaced by premier and former Karabagh president Robert Kocharian in 1998. This outcome vividly illustrates the symbolic politics trap: even the nationalist hero was unable to 'deliver' his constituents for a desperately needed peace agreement in the face of emotionally charged cries of betrayal.

After Kocharian's elevation, the pivotal place in Armenian politics was taken by the Yerkrapah movement of war veterans, and its political vehicle, the Republican Party led by the ex-defence minister and then prime minister, Vazgen Sarkisian. The road to peace would seem to have been blocked, but even hardliner Sarkisian, once confronted with the reality of Armenia's situation, seems to have swung over to a willingness to contemplate peace. A series of bilateral meetings between Kocharian and Azerbaijani leader Heydar Aliev in 1999 seemed to have been showing promise, but the process was undermined by the assassination of Sarkisian and several other Armenian politicians in a bizarre terrorist attack on a parliamentary session in October. Lacking support on his right flank, Kocharian backed away from a willingness to agree to any realistic compromise.

Aliev was similarly constrained. In spite of his authoritarian control of his country, partly charismatic and partly institutionalised, he, too, had to be sensitive to the virtually unanimous view of the political opposition that any compromise peace was tantamount to betrayal. He responded by conducting all of the Karabagh negotiations himself, fully trusting none of his advisors. But in the atmosphere of extreme nationalism in which Azerbaijani politics takes place, it was not at all certain that even Aliev could ensure the implementation of a peace agreement, should one be reached. Aliev's uncertain health, furthermore, meant that the implementation of any such agreement would be left up to his successor. It also meant that Aliev's attention was increasingly focused on trying to secure the succession for his son Ilham – a succession that might be jeopardised if Ilham were burdened with an unpopular peace agreement with Armenia.

Within Karabagh, a problem exists similar to that in Republika Srpska: the leaders of the rebel enclave have more of an interest in perpetuating the conflict than in solving it. Evidence is murky, but the region seems to be run by a corrupt coterie of politicians and warlords who enrich themselves by facilitating smuggling across the borders with Iran and Armenia. They are disinclined to agree to a settlement, because any deal – even one that leaves them in power and with continuing autonomy – would require that they give up control over Azerbaijani territory outside Karabagh, including the area on the border with Iran. Disinclined to give up any land, they are probably even less inclined to give up their chief source of income.

At the international level, the most important foreign influence on this conflict has been Russian military intervention. While Russian support was tilted towards Azerbaijan in 1990–93, that support ended once it became clear in the spring of 1993 that Azerbaijan would insist on the withdrawal of all remaining Russian troops, while Armenia would not. A Kremlin-supported military coup in Azerbaijan, and decisive Armenian military victory, followed. Continued Armenian military superiority was ensured by a continued flow of Russian weapons into Armenia's arsenal, while Russia used its leverage to maintain its military presence in Armenia. Meanwhile, owing to pressure from the Armenian-American community, the United States opened a generous flow of economic aid to Armenia and even to the unrecognised Mountainous Karabagh, while the controversial Section 907 of the Freedom Support Act blocked most American aid to Azerbaijan.

A critical background factor in the management of the Karabagh conflict was the growing push to exploit and market oil and gas from the Caspian basin, especially from Azerbaijan. The most contentious issue was the proposal for an oil pipeline from Baku through Georgia to the Turkish port of Ceyhan, in addition to a parallel pipeline from Baku to the Russian port of Novorossiisk, and a smaller one to the Georgian port of Supsa. US policy promoted the notion of 'multiple pipelines' – meaning, crucially, Baku-Ceyhan in addition to the others – on the principle that such competition would prevent one actor from gaining either an economic monopoly or a political stranglehold on the transportation of Azerbaijani oil. Azerbaijan hoped that a future oil bonanza shipped through multiple pipelines would shift the political and military balance in its favour, and it tilted towards the US in pursuit of influence that would balance Russia's. Russia, especially given its goal of an exclusive sphere of influence, therefore found itself in the position of wanting to block Baku-Ceyhan precisely in pursuit of a political-economic trump card in the region. To the considerable extent that unresolved ethnic conflicts in Karabagh and in Georgia were considered obstacles to the viability of Baku-Ceyhan, and to the extent that a resolution of the Karabagh conflict would open the door to increased US influence in Azerbaijan, Russia found that a resolution of the Karabagh conflict would not be in its best interests. It therefore refrained from using its considerable leverage to encourage Armenian flexibility in talks with Aliev.

The key diplomatic intervention was the establishment of the OSCE Minsk Group in 1992, and of its system of three (Russian, American and French) co-chairs in late 1994. The temporary breakthrough of September 1997 came in response to a proposal of the co-chairs, but after that period the group was largely sidelined by the process of bilateral Kocharian – Aliev meetings. The two tracks were brought together in a Minsk Group-sponsored negotiating session between the two presidents in Key West in April 2001, but the talks yielded nothing but atmospherics – and the observation by the US co-chair that domestic political constraints on both presidents remain a key obstacle. These official processes have at times been supplemented by an array of unofficial proposals and internationally sponsored peace-building programmes such as a parliamentary exchange programme.

The key failure of the international community has been its inability to bring the diplomatic, political and peace-building tracks together. The negotiating process turned into a way for both governments to pretend interest in a compromise peace while indulging in extremist rhetoric at home (in response to the even more extreme rhetoric of some opposition figures), while Armenia's foreign support was strong enough for it to feel itself able to resist compromise. The peace-building efforts were therefore marginalised. This is the result of a mass-led symbolic politics trap: any moves towards peace threaten the position of incumbent leaders, while leaders' efforts to stay in power block the road to peace. That problem is exacerbated by the most highly motivated outside force, the Armenian diaspora, which promotes the hardline position without suffering the ill effects of continued conflict. Until public opinion on both sides shifts to recognise those ill effects, and the corresponding benefits of a settlement of the conflict, the current deadlock will continue.

Conclusions and future prospects

There are two main themes in the argument of this chapter. The first is that ethnic civil conflicts such as the ones in Bosnia, Macedonia and Mountainous Karabagh are at the same time regional security issues whose trajectory is critically affected as much by external actors as by internal ones. The second theme is that the behaviour of all parties involved – ethnic groups within states, governments of other states, and others – depends on their construction of their interests. The construction of ethnic group interests, in turn, is heavily influenced by the ethnic mythology of the groups in question, and by the degree of mutual hostility and fear. Many of the groups are caught in a symbolic politics trap from which it is difficult to escape.

This applies also to other conflicts in the region. In Kosovo, for example, the Albanian majority insists so strongly on the goal of complete independence from Serbia that no major Albanian politician dares challenge it – or its implication of continued discrimination against the Serbian minority. The Serbian and Yugoslav governments, for their part, cannot concede the symbolism of Belgrade's sovereignty over the region even though the reality of political authority is irretrievably gone. A similar situation obtains in Chechnya, where legitimate political and guerrilla leaders are locked into the pursuit of independence, while the Russian president Vladimir Putin has built his presidency around a tough 'anti-terrorism' policy that allows him little room even to cede local autonomy to the puppet Chechen administration.

Two conclusions about conflict resolution follow from these thoughts, one commonplace, the other more controversial. The commonplace insight is that regional conflict resolution often depends in large part on whether external powers find it in their interest to push for it. Years of sanctions convinced Milosevic's Serbia, for example, to want an end to the war in Bosnia, but as long as Milosevic remained in power, the prospects of reconciliation in Bosnia were blocked by Bosnian Serb hardliners backed by Belgrade. In the Caucasus, Russia's hegemonic goals and the scramble for control of oil and gas routes interacted to give Russia little incentive to push for conflict resolution. Thus conflict resolution was blocked, in the one case at the implementation stage, and in the other case in pre-negotiations. In the Macedonia case, by contrast, all regional and great power actors had incentives to prevent escalation of the conflict, so none encouraged Macedonian hardliners.

The second insight is that ordinary diplomatic, political and even military interventions are not alone enough to achieve effective conflict resolution. Since groups' definition of their interests depends heavily on ethnic myths and group fears, reconciliation and conflict resolution require addressing the mythic roots of group interests, and assuaging the symbolic sources of group fears. This is the way out of the symbolic politics trap, and the tool for doing it is not diplomacy but peace building. To be sure, diplomacy and military coercion have their uses – peace-building efforts need to be backed by diplomatic muscle, and in the case of Bosnia, reconciliation requires coercion by peacekeepers to arrest the war criminals blocking implementation of the Dayton accords. Indeed, in the Bosnian case, destroying the crime nexus organised by war criminals, especially in Serb but also in Croat areas, is the only workable exit strategy for SFOR, and a necessary precondition for peace.

But ultimately, the problems are often attitudinal first, and political or criminal only second. For governments, the key access point to public opinion is the media. That means that foreign governments need to work much harder to push the local media towards more responsible and moderate reporting in all of these conflict areas. Efforts to do so might include the creation and funding of alternative media outlets, and pressure on governments to tolerate and facilitate their reporting. Other opportunities may be less intuitive. If Armenian myths and fears are the key driver of the Karabagh conflict, for example, then the key requirement for conflict resolution may be that Turkey help heal the Armenians' deepest wound by acknowledging and expressing regret for the 1915 Genocide. As with the Bosnia conflict, the key is to get the separatists' outside patron to push for conflict resolution (Serbia in the Bosnia case, Armenia for Karabagh); dealing with the business interests of the separatists must come later.

Supplying the need for peace building requires ever-closer cooperation between diplomats and international institutions such as the OSCE, on the one hand, and conflict-resolution non-governmental organisations (NGOs) on the other. The cultural and ideological clash between these communities is by no means the least of the obstacles to effective conflict resolution. Russian and US leaders, in particular, see themselves as hard-nosed realists with little patience for what they see as the soft-headed and impractical peace activists in the NGO community. NGO activists, on the other hand, are fiercely independent and inclined to resist the sort of top-down coordination by officials of any kind that could help them turn their disparate efforts into broadly effective peace-building programmes. While each side needs to adjust and accommodate to the other, the onus is on US and European officials to take the lead in encouraging, funding, coordinating and smoothing the way for the NGOs to do their work in places like Bosnia, Macedonia and Karabagh. Such a transformation does not presently seem to be in the offing. And that means that peace in all three regions will remain tenuous at best.

Notes

1 Randall L. Schweller, 'Neorealism's Status Quo Bias: What Security Dilemma?', *Security Studies*, 5:3 (1996), pp. 90–121.
2 A recent prominent convert to this view is Robert Jervis. APSA Presidential Address, APSA Annual Meeting, San Francisco, CA, September 2001.
3 Robert D. Kaplan, *Balkan Ghosts: A Journey Through History* (New York: Random House, 1993).
4 V. P. Gagnon, 'Ethnic Nationalism and International Conflict: The Case of Serbia', *International Security*, 19:3 (1994/95), pp. 130–66.
5 Barry R. Posen, 'The Security Dilemma and Ethnic Conflict', *Survival*, 35:1 (1993), pp. 27–47.
6 Michael E. Brown, 'The Causes and Regional Dimensions of Internal Conflict', in Michael E. Brown (ed.), *The International Dimensions of Internal Conflict* (Cambridge, MA: Center for Science and International Affairs, 1996), pp. 571–602.
7 Misha Glenny, *The Fall of Yugoslavia: The Third Balkan War*, 3rd rev. edn (London: Penguin, 1996).
8 Examples of works on institutional arrangement for managing ethnic conflict include Donald Horowitz, *A Democratic South Africa?: Constitutional Engineering in a Divided Society* (Berkeley, CA: University of California Press, 1991); David Lake and Donald Rothchild, 'Containing Fear: The Origins and Management of Ethnic Conflict', *International Security*, 21:2 (1996), pp. 41–75; Arendt Lijphart, *Democracy in Plural Societies: A Comparative Exploration* (New Haven, CT: Yale University Press, 1977); and Donald Rothchild, *Managing Ethnic Conflict in Africa: Pressures and Incentives for Cooperation* (Washington, DC: Brookings Institution, 1997). A prominent recent argument for foreign focus on institutional incentives is Barbara F. Walter, 'The Critical Barrier to Civil War Settlement', *International Organization*, 51:3 (1997), pp. 335–64.
9 Chaim Kaufmann, 'Possible and Impossible Solutions to Ethnic Wars', *International Security*, 20: 4 (1996), pp. 136–75; Chaim Kaufmann, 'When All Else Fails', *International Security*, 23:2 (1998), pp. 120–56.
10 Michael E. Brown, 'Internal Conflict and International Action', in Brown, *International Dimensions*, pp. 603–28.

11 James D. Fearon and David D. Laitin, 'Explaining Interethnic Cooperation', *American Political Science Review*, 90:4 (1996), pp. 715–35.

12 Stuart J. Kaufman, *Modern Hatreds: The Symbolic Politics of Ethnic War* (Ithaca, NY: Cornell University Press, 2001).

13 Benedict Anderson, *Imagined Communities: Reflections on the Origin and Spread of Nationalism* (Norfolk: Thetford, 1983); Anthony D. Smith, *The Ethnic Origins of Nations* (Oxford: Blackwell, 1986).

14 Jack Snyder, *From Voting to Violence: Democratization and Nationalist Conflict* (New York: W. W. Norton, 2000).

15 Ronald Suny, *Looking Toward Ararat: Armenia in Modern History* (Bloomington: Indiana University Press, 1993).

16 Kaufman, *Modern Hatreds*, Ch. 4.

17 For an exception, see Jack Snyder and Robert Jervis, 'Civil War and the Security Dilemma', in Barbara Walter and Jack Snyder (eds), *Civil Wars, Insecurity, and Intervention* (New York: Columbia University Press, 1999), pp. 15–37.

18 Brian D. Taylor, 'Commentary on Moldova', in Alexei Arbatov (ed.), *Managing Conflict in the Former Soviet Union* (Cambridge, MA.: MIT Press, 1997), p. 214.

19 John Paul Lederach, *Building Peace: Sustainable Reconciliation in Divided Societies* (Washington, DC: US Institute of Peace, 1997).

20 Stephen Ryan, *Ethnic Conflict and International Relations* (Aldershot: Dartmouth, 1990), p. 83.

21 See Kaufman, *Modern Hatreds*, Ch. 6.

22 Serbs, for example, have been quoted as saying 'Only three things grow [in western Herzegovina], snakes, stones, and Ustashes'. Cited in Glenny, *Fall of Yugoslavia*, p. 157.

23 Quoted in Kaufman, *Modern Hatreds*, p. 176.

24 Laura Silber and Allen Little, *Yugoslavia: Death of a Nation*, rev. edn (New York: Penguin, 1997), p. 209.

25 Jane M. O. Sharp, 'Dayton Report Card', *International Security*, 22:3 (1997/98), pp. 101–37, esp. 115.

26 International Crisis Group, *After Milosevic: A Practical Agenda for Lasting Balkans Peace*, International Crisis Group Report, 2 April 2001, p. 201. Available at website, www.intl-crisis-group.org.

27 International Crisis Group, *War Criminals in Bosnia's Republika Srpska: Who are the People in Your Neighborhood?*, International Crisis Group Report, 2 November 2000. Available at website, www.intl-crisis-group.org.

28 Nenad Dimitrijevic (ed.), *Managing Multiethnic Local Communities in the Countries of the Former Yugoslavia* (Budapest: Open Society Institute, 2000).

29 H. N. Brailsford, *Macedonia: Its Races and their Future* (London: Methuen, 1906), pp. 101–3.

30 Kaufman, *Modern Hatreds*, pp. 193–5.

31 Serbia's interest after its Kosovo defeat was in gaining international agreement for its forces to return to the Presevo Valley, an Albanian-inhabited region inside Serbia bordering on Kosovo and on Macedonia, which also happened to be a base for the Macedonian-Albanian NLA. In the wake of its defeat in the Kosovo conflict, Serbia's best bet was to avert a Macedonian war against Albanians, rather than promote one and provoke another backlash by NATO. The US and the EU wanted stability in the region, and Albania, dependent on the West, was

not inclined to make waves. Russia may have leaned towards supporting Macedonia's nationalists more than did the Western powers, but newly installed president Vladimir Putin had more pressing problems and did not want to promote trouble. While Ukraine did provide some heavy weapons to Macedonia, its motivations were purely mercenary and the aid did not continue for long.

32 Kaufman, *Modern Hatreds*, Ch. 3.

4

Eurasia and the transnational terrorist threats to Atlantic security

Phil Williams

The terrorist attacks of September 11 on the World Trade Center and the Pentagon were not only the most audacious and successful terrorist attacks the world has yet seen, but also marked the maturation of what had been described as the 'new terrorism'. It was a maturation in several senses. In the first place it revealed that trends identified by astute specialists such as Walter Laqueur, Bruce Hoffman and Ian Lesser were, in fact, well advanced.[1] These analysts had suggested that terrorists were increasingly pursuing grander and less specific political objectives than in the past, were moving towards greater ruthlessness and lethality, and were less likely to claim credit for their actions.[2] These characteristics were evident in the attacks of September 11. Traditionally terrorism was primarily about theatre – about lots of people watching rather than lots of people killed.[3] The terrorism of September 11 was about millions of people watching several thousand people being killed. Similarly, terrorism traditionally had been about the attainment of a well-defined political objective. The attacks on the World Trade Center and the Pentagon, in contrast, appeared to be an attack on American cultural and political hegemony, and an effort to galvanise a new pan-Islamic anti-western identity rather than a serious effort to make the United States withdraw its forces from Saudi Arabia or reduce its support for Israel. Moreover, Bin Laden and al-Qaeda denied responsibility in the hope that anonymity would enable them to avoid retribution. All that was lacking from the worst-case scenarios discussed by the terrorism analysts was the presence of weapons of mass destruction. Even without these, however, the attacks exacted a far higher death toll than any previous terrorist action.

If the attacks marked the maturation of the new terrorism they also compelled a rapid – if incomplete – maturation in the United States conception of security. Since the end of the Cold War, and the disappearance of the Soviet threat, the United States had enjoyed what appeared to be immunity to the business cycle and an absence of serious threats to its national security. Consequently, serious political debate over national security had been stultified. National attention had been fixated on scandals ranging from presidential indiscretions and pardons to the O. J. Simpson trial and the disappearance of a Washington intern. There had been voices in the national security community, including on the National Security Council itself, warning about transnational threats such as terrorism and organised crime.[4] Yet, the military focus had remained on threats from nation-states, whether an emerging China, a resurgent Russia, or rogue states suspected of acquiring weapons of mass destruction.

In launching an audacious, well-coordinated and conceptually sophisticated attack on the United States homeland, the al-Qaeda terrorist cells responsible for the hijackings transformed a narrow debate among specialists about threats to United States security into a national preoccupation. They also succeeded in galvanising the United States into mobilising national efforts and resources in ways reminiscent of the Cold War. The Bush administration, which in its first eight months in office had been unilateralist in its approach to international issues, embraced a multilateral approach to security that also harkened back to the Cold War. With NATO invoking Article 5 for the first time in its history, the European allies provided enormous diplomatic and law enforcement support to the United States – especially in the immediate aftermath of September 11. Subsequently, the United States military response in Afghanistan created some unease in western Europe, which was exacerbated by the 'axis of evil' reference in the president's 2002 State of the Union address. The European allies also became very concerned about possible United States plans to attack Iraq in a bid to oust Saddam Hussein. If the potential for Atlantic divisions remained very considerable, however, the common interests of the United States and its European allies in combating the challenge from radical Islamic terrorism are difficult to overestimate.

This is perhaps best illustrated by the series of arrests of terrorists and disruption of cells that took place in Germany in December 2000 and elsewhere in Europe throughout 2001, both before and after September 11. Close scrutiny of these events suggests that what well-informed observers described as a series of terrorist spectaculars was very narrowly averted.[5] The European cells exhibited the same lethality of intent, if not of execution, as the September 11 hijackers. The story is intriguing, with many details still obscure. In December 2000, German authorities in Frankfurt broke up a terrorist cell planning an attack in Strasbourg. Initial reports suggested that the target was a square in Strasbourg, while subsequent disclosures indicated that the target was Strasbourg cathedral. One report contended that a British cell had targeted the European Parliament and that poison gas, probably sarin, might have been the weapon of choice.[6]

The arrests also revealed an extensive network of terrorist cells in

Germany, Italy, Britain, Spain, Belgium and France. The cell structure operated under two large umbrella movements, the Egyptian movement, Anathema and Exile, and an Algerian counterpart, the Salafist Group for Preaching and Combat.[7] In effect, these loose multinational structures coalesced through three key individuals linked to al-Qaeda: Abu Doha (whom Italian police believe to be Rachid Kefflous), an Algerian who moved to London in 1999, was involved in the plot to bomb Los Angeles airport on the eve of the millennium, and was arrested in Britain in February 2001; Mohamed Bensakhria, leader of the Frankfurt cell; and Tarek Maaroufi, a Tunisian with Belgian citizenship, who is wanted in Italy. The Milan cell was led by a Tunisian, Essid Sami Ben Khemais, who had completed two years of training in al-Qaeda camps before moving to Milan in March 1998. Khemais helped to organise the sending of recruits to Afghanistan and was clearly linked to cells elsewhere in Europe. According to Italian authorities, the recruits met in Geneva, and used false Italian documents to fly to Pakistan, from where they were taken into Afghanistan. The Italians also inferred from the evidence that Khemais financed these activities by 'means of drug-trafficking, counterfeiting money and documents, recycling dirty money'.[8] The Milan cell also circumvented immigration and employment laws by creating a bogus cooperative to bring non-EU nationals into Italy, which enabled them to qualify for work permits.[9] In addition, this cell provided logistic support for its counterpart in Frankfurt as the latter planned the Strasbourg attack: stolen and false credit cards from Italy were used by members of the Frankfurt group to buy explosive materials.

When the Frankfurt cell under Bensakhria was disrupted, German authorities found a cache of automatic pistols, rifles with telescopic sights, handguns with silencers, directions for bomb building, and nails and pressure cookers.[10] Communication intercepts with the Milan cell also suggested that some kind of poison gas was being prepared.[11] The action by German authorities provided information that led to Operation Odin in Britain and the arrest of ten suspected terrorists in February 2001.[12] Although most of them were freed, Abu Doha – one of the three key members of the al-Qaeda network in Europe – and Mustapha Labsi, who was alleged to be a co-conspirator in the Los Angeles bomb plot, remained under arrest.[13] Members of the Milan cell were subsequently arrested in April 2001.[14] Bensakhria, who had avoided arrest in Frankfurt in December 2000, was arrested in June 2001 in Spain.[15] Further arrests occurred in Spain after September 11. In September, a cell that had provided logistic support was broken up, while in November another round of arrests was made.[16]

Although European law enforcement and intelligence agencies had considerable success in disrupting some of the al-Qaeda-related cells in several countries, the extensiveness of the structure and the links among the groups were surprising. Through a mixture of good luck, effective law enforcement and extensive intelligence cooperation among EU members, a number of potentially devastating terrorist acts were foiled. The arrests, however, revealed very clearly that Europe is as much of a target for radical Islamic terrorism as is the United States. Yet, this is only one part of a larger picture in which transnational threats to European and Atlantic security continue to loom very large. Accordingly, the next section of this chapter provides a conceptual analysis and assessment of these threats. The final section then considers the nature of the responses that are required as both the United States and European governments adapt to what is a very different kind of security challenge from that for which they prepared during the Cold War.

The new security paradigm

In the long term, traditional geopolitical competition could re-emerge in Europe. The more immediate threats, however, are transnational rather than national; the geographical sources of these threats are found along Europe's periphery and beyond. Indeed, there is a new threat paradigm that needs to be understood more widely if it is to be combated with maximum effectiveness. There are nine major characteristics of this paradigm that need to be taken into account.[17]

First, security threats are no longer stark, dramatic, and confined largely to direct external military aggression or threats of military attack; instead they are often insidious and indirect, with both external and internal dimensions. They include overt threats such as terrorism, in which the intent is to inflict significant harm, and more subtle threats such as organised crime, which uses corruption and co-option rather than confrontation. Indeed, organised crime is the HIV of the modern state, breaking down the defences of the body politic, eroding the rule of law, and undermining the integrity of institutions of social control. Although public institutions and the rule of law in the United States and most EU member-states are sufficiently robust to withstand such an assault, the ways in which corruption and organised crime can entrench themselves should not be underestimated. Organised crime from the former Soviet Union has made considerable inroads into western countries, often allying, at least temporarily, with local organisations to expand criminal markets and activities. Moreover, criminal organisations operating in Europe and the United States are more diverse (Russian, Ukrainian, Georgian, Albanian, Nigerian, Chinese, Colombian, Italian, Kurdish and Turkish) than ever before, have a wide portfolio of criminal activities from which they derive considerable profit, and deploy a sophisticated repertoire of risk-management techniques that help to protect them from law enforcement.

The second characteristic of the transnational threat paradigm is its enduring nature: transnational threats are neither simply the flavour of the moment nor 'boutique security issues' that pale in significance compared with traditional military threats. On the contrary, they pose continuing and serious challenges to national and international security and stability. Transnational threats have developed as a result of long-term secular trends that are likely to intensify rather than abate in the early decades of the twenty-first century. Even if al-Qaeda is defeated any time soon – which seems unlikely – terrorism will continue to be a major threat during the twenty-first century. Religious fundamentalism, political fanaticism and economic inequities and asymmetries will continue to feed a desire for revenge that is expressed in violent attacks against the citizens of countries that are viewed as the 'enemy' or the 'infidel'. If terrorist networks seek to get even with their enemies, then transnational criminal networks are motivated by the desire to get rich. And the targets are many of the advanced postindustrial countries that are also the major targets of terrorism. Not only do these countries wield political, economic and military power in ways that terrorist groups find unacceptable, they also provide lucrative markets for criminals. In short, the target countries are the same; the difference is that criminals seek to exploit them and terrorists to hurt them.

Third, there are few if any islands of security or safe havens in this new world. The United States prior to September 11 still considered itself as such, but this notion was dispelled as the towers of the World Trade Center collapsed. Part of the reason for this transformation is that in an age of unprecedented cross-border flows – whether of people, money, commodities or digital signals – the capacity of even strong governments to monitor who and what enters and leaves the country is limited. Smuggling can succeed either by circumventing monitoring systems and control points or by going through them with false documentation. Borders have always had a permeability about them that Westphalian conceptions of the state found convenient to ignore. With globalisation, however, permeability has increased enormously: borders are simply not what they were. In the era of military and territorial competition among great powers, lines on maps meant a great deal; for terrorists, however, borders are minor barriers that are easily circumvented and little more than boundaries for target sets. And for criminals, borders demarcate market opportunities, as many illegal goods such as drugs increase in value as soon as they cross certain borders. Yet, at the same time as criminals and terrorist networks transcend and violate borders, they also use them for defensive purposes, finding weak or sympathetic states that provide some kind of safe haven.

The weakness of border controls is particularly pronounced when the state itself is weak. In Africa and Central Asia, for example, long borders are often not patrolled and there are many points of entry that simply cannot be monitored by states with limited resources. As a result, illegal immigration has become commonplace. Furthermore, criminals and smugglers traffic in a variety of products including art and antiquities, stolen cattle, fauna and flora, guns, drugs, diamonds and gold. Customs and immigration services are generally poorly developed, poorly trained, badly equipped and inadequately paid. As such, they are easily circumvented by relatively sophisticated methods of concealment or bought off by fairly modest exercises in bribery and corruption. They facilitate what Bayart, referring to large parts of Africa, has termed 'the economy of plunder, fraud and smuggling'.[18]

Fourth, the helpful distinction that was made shortly after the end of the Cold War between zones of peace and zones of turmoil has to be refined to incorporate the notion of spillover.[19] In a globalised world, there is inevitable spillover from areas of turbulence and instability to zones of peace and tranquility. There are several vectors along which the connections are made. One of these is psychological: states in the zone of peace are held responsible for injustice or instability in the zone of turmoil. A second is immigration, which does not end old affiliations or moderate old enmities, but merely transfers them to new venues. Those in the diaspora retain links with the homeland and often send back financial remittances. The vast majority of these financial transfers take the form of legitimate economic assistance to families and are often eked out of relatively modest incomes. In some cases, however, financial proceeds generated through crimes such as drug trafficking and credit card fraud provide support for insurgency or ethnic conflict.[20] Another vector operates through the dynamics of illicit markets. Although there are some flows such as stolen cars (and, in some cases, arms) from zones of tranquility to zones of turmoil, most illegal commodities flow from areas of turmoil into zones of peace and prosperity where there is significant demand for 'products' such as drugs, foreign women for prostitution, rare antiquities and the like. Closely linked to these flows is the diffusion of networked actors from the more troubled areas. The way in which drug traffickers and organised crime groups from the Balkans have spread into western Europe and taken control of heroin markets in several countries, for example, illustrates the kinds of dynamics that are generated by the demand for narcotics in zones of peace and stability.

Fifth, the transnational actors challenging security operate largely through networked organisational structures. As such, they are difficult to destroy with traditional military means. They prefer to hide and strike with surprise and devastating effect rather than engage in direct head-to-head combat. The United States in Afghanistan succeeded in part in creating a head-to-head military contest. Yet it also encountered the problem of an amorphous networked enemy, as al-Qaeda forces dispersed and fled into a variety of other countries. The United States, by toppling the Taliban, removed Afghanistan as a safe haven for al-Qaeda; yet there is a very real possibility that the members of the network have found other safe havens – at least temporarily – in countries such as Somalia, Iran and Indonesia. One inadvertent – and disquieting – consequence of the United States success in Afghanistan is that al-Qaeda has been forced into becoming even a more diffused network actor. In the short term, this might inhibit its capacity to carry out further terrorist attacks; in the longer term, however, this might simply make it even harder to locate and combat.

There is also a danger of overestimating the impact of successful attacks on the core of the network: networks are not easily destroyed by decapitation strikes. Indeed, for decapitation to have a significant impact in degrading terrorist and criminal networks, it cannot be a single temporary measure. Decapitation has to be both successive and pre-emptive if it is to do more than temporarily destabilise the organisation. Yet another difficulty is that as networks become deeply embedded in societies and institutions, they are increasingly difficult to eradicate. Criminal networks, for example, are very successful in infiltrating legitimate industries and firms, and once embedded are difficult both to detect and to dislodge. Similarly, terrorist cells can operate in target countries, finding support and cover within ethnic and religious communities, and avoiding actions that arouse suspicions. Identifying them requires law enforcement strategies that are proactive rather than responsive, and that place an unprecedented premium on good intelligence. Unfortunately law enforcement agencies are not geared up to pursue such strategies. Instead, they are concerned with making cases that generate successful prosecutions and convictions and that serve to justify their budgets. The other difficulty is that both criminal and terrorist network connections are often transnational, whereas law enforcement remains stubbornly national. If this poses one kind of constraint, continued limits on the capacity of intelligence agencies to operate domestically create another. Even if cooperation between law enforcement and intelligence agencies is good, the result is still collection and analytical processes characterised by seams, gaps and disconnections. This absence of integrated processes is all the more debilitating because criminal activities, criminal transactions and the planning and implementation of terrorist strikes are seamless activities.

Even if law enforcement succeeds in disrupting networks, it will find them to be remarkably adaptable and resilient organisations with a capacity to regenerate themselves. Networks can learn and morph themselves: they can transform their shape, operations, modalities and size. They can contract and expand according to opportunities and constraints in their environment, and even when critical nodes are destroyed and critical connections severed, they are able to continue operating because of a high degree of redundancy. Although the United States and allied governments, since September 11, have begun the process of adapting to the particular requirements of combating networked adversaries, the learning curve is likely to be both long and steep.

The sixth dimension of the new security paradigm is that some states are part of the problem rather than part of the solution: the world has entered the era of the qualified state. If part of the new security paradigm revolves around a competition between traditional bureaucratic and hierarchical states on the one side and agile, networked actors on the other, the problem is compounded by the fact that many states lack effective, efficient, bureau-cratic structures characterised by integrity rather than susceptibility to corruption. Although the United States, after September 11, was very successful in mobilising not only its traditional allies but also other states in the effort to combat terrorism, two problems are inescapable.

The first is that some states ostensibly comply with the demands to join the war on terrorism, but tacitly defect from this effort. Saudi Arabia, for example, at one level has appeared to provide strong support for the United States in its efforts to attack the financial basis of al-Qaeda. Yet it is not clear that it has introduced vigorous measures to inhibit terrorist funding under the guise of charitable giving.

The second problem is that some states simply lack the capacity to combat transnational networks of criminals or terrorists. Many states along Europe's eastern and southern periphery suffer from lack of authority and legitimacy, low state capacity, and the existence of no-go zones that provide safe havens for a variety of illegal activities and those who engage in them. Endemic problems include capacity gaps and functional holes, which arise when the state fails to carry out responsibilities that are generally regarded as the norm for states. Many of these states are weak and have a very limited capacity to govern; they exhibit functional holes that are readily exploited by transnational criminals and terrorist networks. The most obvious manifestation of functional holes is the absence of effective social control and law-enforcement mechanisms, which allows organised crime and terrorist networks to operate in a low-risk environment. In effect, the networks exploit the space provided by the functional hole. Another such hole is the inability of many states to provide for the basic economic and social needs of their citizens. This failure can lead to migration from the legal economy to the illegal. It also provides opportunities for transnational actors to fill the hole. In many countries, for example, Islamic charities are increasingly providing the social safety nets that state authorities are unable to afford. In effect, a public function is fulfilled through private provision. Although such activities are obviously legitimate, they also provide opportunities for Islamic fundamentalists to spread militant forms of the religion that feed into terrorism. Terrorist networks that have embedded themselves in charitable organisations also use the opportunity to recruit new members. Moreover, as evidence from the trials relating to the United States embassy bombings in Kenya and Tanzania revealed, al-Qaeda has been particularly adept at using charities as cover for the movement of money and people. Another functional hole that has been particularly evident in Russia and other states of the former Soviet Union has concerned the regulation of business. Where the state has been unable to provide contract enforcement, arbitration of disputes or debt collection, organised crime has become a surrogate, in effect filling the functional hole and expanding its influence into the economy to a degree that is unprecedented.

In some cases, of course, the capacity gaps and functional holes are so large that the state simply collapses. This outcome occurs particularly where there are ethnic rivalries, secessionist aspirations, religious animosities or tribal divisions. Indeed, one of the most significant features of the late twentieth and early twenty-first centuries is the resurgence of warlordism. Although there are important regional variations, warlordism of one kind or another has helped to fuel conflicts in Afghanistan, Tajikistan and the Balkans. It is a complex phenomenon that both combines and blurs categories that in other parts of the world are regarded as separate and distinct. Warlords, who typically engage in criminal activities and in insurgent, military or terrorist activities, achieve what can be termed a symbiosis between politics and accumulation.[21] One manifestation of this is found in Africa, where the state is seen as the prize of politics, with the spoils to be distributed along tribal lines by the representative of the dominant tribe. This results in two phenomena: dictatorship where there is in effect a dominant warlord; and conflict among warlords where there is a struggle for dominance. Such conflicts revolve around control over resources, both in the legal economy and in the underground economy. Moreover, the resources that can be acquired through territorial control continue to fuel these conflicts, providing the wherewithal to continue fighting. Similarly, in Tajikistan's civil war from 1992 to 1997, conflict among rival warlords was intensified by the struggle for control over drug routes and markets, as heroin from Afghanistan was transshipped through Tajikistan. In Afghanistan itself, local warlords – prior to the consolidation of power by the Taliban and subsequent to the regime's overthrow – fought for control not only of drug cultivation areas, but also of trade routes, levying taxes on merchants passing through the territory under their control. One implication of all this is that political-military and sometimes terrorist activities on the one side and criminal activities on the other are combined as part of the warlord's day-to-day activities.

Nor are there easy solutions to these problems. In almost all cases of failed states, the lack of legitimacy and authority is reflected in the way in which many groups and individuals place their own narrow interests above the collective interest of the state and society.[22] It is hardly surprising, therefore, that state building is an extremely difficult enterprise. Nowhere has this been more evident than in Bosnia. The Dayton accords envisaged the emergence of a centralised state which would increase its resource base and pave the way for the gradual integration of different ethnic communities. What has happened instead is that the separatist national parties have worked in close cooperation with organised crime. These parties, in turn, have obtained control over criminal markets, corruption and rent-seeking opportunities, and have used their position to enrich themselves at the expense of the overarching state apparatus. The state, in effect, has been 'ripped off' and organised crime has become a spoiler not only in a peacekeeping contingency, but also in the state-building endeavour.[23] It seems likely that similar kinds of developments will bedevil Afghanistan as the United States tries to ensure that further neglect does not provide a continued safe haven, breeding ground and training camp for terrorists and drug traffickers.

The seventh feature of the new paradigm is the growing diffusion of technological capabilities. This is most obvious in the spread of weapons of mass destruction and the possible linkage between states that posses them and terrorist organisations that would be willing to use them against the United States and western Europe. Significant tensions between the Bush administration and western European governments over a possible attack on Iraq reflect divergent assessments of the salience and urgency of this issue. The Bush administration has regarded the terrorist use of weapons of mass destruction as a real threat that is inextricably linked to Saddam Hussein's programmes for developing or acquiring weapons of mass destruction (WMD). Whether or not Iraq is the supplier, the terrorist use of WMD is certainly not a contingency that can be excluded. As Bruce Hoffman pointed out several years ago, Aum Shinrikyo's use of sarin gas on the Japanese underground crossed a significant threshold.[24] Moreover, for terrorist networks whose goal is to create mayhem and inflict large-scale casualties, WMD are ideal. In spite of the lack of evidence found in Afghanistan, it would not be surprising if al-Qaeda had acquired enough radioactive material to make a 'dirty bomb'. In the latter half of the 1990s, nuclear and radioactive material stolen from Russian installations and stockpiles was increasingly smuggled through Central Asia, the Caucasus and the Balkans, all areas in which al-Qaeda had a significant presence. The critical point about the use of such weapons by terrorist networks is that they are more likely than not to be delivered in unconventional ways and not by missiles.

James Rosenau's identification of 'sovereignty-free actors' underscores the growing importance of technology and expertise diffusion from traditional great powers to other states with respect to computers and information technology.[25] Moreover, this is an area where entry costs for acquiring offensive capabilities are very modest.[26] This is linked, of course, to the notion of asymmetric warfare, in which enemies are able to exploit aspects of modern societies and economies that have traditionally been seen as strengths but increasingly create concomitant vulnerabilities. Indeed, the corollary of the diffusion of information technology is that the enormous reliance of postindustrial countries on computerised information and communication systems for the effective functioning of their economies and societies is a major vulnerability. United States infrastructure, for example, presents a tempting target set to terrorist organisations. If terrorist networks, using a mixture of physical and cyber attacks, succeeded in destroying Fedwire and CHIPS, the two systems that provide wire transfers and funds settlements domestically and internationally, the damage to the United States financial system as well as to global financial markets would be enormous. Although backup installations, based on a well-established risk management ethos, provide a high degree of redundancy within the system, there is little or no redundancy of the system. Consequently, a well-coordinated systemic attack could prove profoundly debilitating. The September 11 attack on the Word Trade Center was not designed primarily as an attack on infrastructure, but certainly caused short-term problems for the financial services sector. An attack that specifically targeted the electronic payments systems could overwhelm the existing safeguards. Getting even has never been so feasible or easy.

The eighth characteristic of the twenty-first-century security paradigm relates to the paradoxical and perverse consequences of globalisation. Although globalisation has been widely hailed as facilitating the spread of liberal democratic values and free market economics, it has both a downside and a dark side that liberal neo-institutionalists were slow to acknowledge. Legitimate businesses have benefited enormously from opportunities to exploit global markets, but the major beneficiaries of globalisation have been transnational criminal networks. These networks use the global trade system to embed illegal products in legal commodity flows, the global financial system to move and hide their money, the global telecommunications system to transmit directives and messages, and the global transportation system to move people and products. Terrorists have exploited globalisation in similar ways, using the global financial system to move and hide their money, and the Internet to transmit messages through either steganography (messages hidden in digital images) or more simply the use of encrypted emails. In addition, both criminals and terrorists have used global diasporas and transnational ethnic networks as cover and recruitment for their activities. As a result, combating criminal and terrorist activity has become very difficult without impeding the rapid flows of money, goods and services on which modern commerce and finance depend; and without violating the civil liberties which are the hallmark of western democracies and facilitate the efficiency of the market. Although the equation between security on the one side and freedom of movement on the other has swung in the direction of security after September 11, there is still a reluctance to interfere too much with a system of commerce based on just-in-time inventories and virtually unimpeded movements across borders. The adverse consequences of globalisation for national and international security must not be allowed to detract from the benefits of globalisation in economics and commerce. The subordination of security considerations, however, can have very serious consequences.

In addition to having a dark side, globalisation also creates discontents.[27] Regarded by its adherents as an unmitigated benefit, globalisation has disruptive effects on traditional societies, contributes to the marginalisation of groups within societies and in some cases of whole societies, and brings with it a form of cultural imperialism that is regarded with enormous hostility in certain regions and countries. There is also a gap between the speed with which ideas of the market economy have taken hold and the speed with which liberal democratic values and respect for human rights have become accepted as the norm. For many developing countries engulfed by globalisation, the result is growing prosperity for pro-western, non-democratic governments, and alienation of the large masses of the population who suffer from economic deprivation at the same time as their cultural norms are being eroded. In these circumstances, Benjamin Barber's notion of the clash between Jihad and McWorld proved to be prophetic.[28] Al-Qaeda's attacks on the United States and the foiled attacks on western European targets were simply the opening salvos in a struggle that is partly a clash of civilisations and partly a struggle over the pervasiveness of globalisation.[29] These attacks also reflected an anti-hegemonic impulse that, significantly, is manifested through transnational actors rather than emerging great powers. For those opposed to it, globalisation is not a neutral process so much as a project directed and dominated by the United States and its allies.

The ninth and final characteristic of the new security paradigm is the prevalence of disorder. Indeed, the management of great power rivalry has been superseded as a central theme of global politics by the issue of disorder versus governance. The security challenges of the twenty-first century are not the same as those of the twentieth: mass industrialised nations fighting one another to the finish have become passé. The obvious costs of such conflicts are compounded by the possibility that they will escalate to nuclear war either as a result of deliberate decision or through inadvertence and loss of control. Moreover, the source of most of these conflicts – struggle for geopolitical dominance in Europe – has been transcended by the evolution of the EU, a union that has tied together France and Germany, traditional enemies, in inextricable forms of political and economic interdependence. Western Europe – along with North America – has not only become the kind of 'security community' envisaged by Karl Deutsch but is extending this to selective states in central Europe. At the same time, the forces of disorder outside this security community, particularly emanating from Eurasia, have become increasingly formidable. Charles Tilly, in an oft-quoted comment, once noted that the state was simply the most efficient and effective form of organised crime.[30] In effect, the state legitimised organised crime by transforming extortion into taxation, brute force into authority, and rule by fear into rule by consent of the governed. Yet, in the last decade or so organised crime has been fighting back with a new vigour and some success – in many cases penetrating state institutions and dominating important economic sectors. Similarly, the fact that the main challenge to United States hegemony comes from a transnational terrorist network rather than other states suggests that the world has entered the twilight of the Westphalian system. It is likely to be a long twilight, however, as powerful states continue to function effectively, to deploy vast economic and military resources, and to combat the forces of disorder that embody the new security challenges. Yet for states to have any chance of maintaining their pre-eminence in the international system and defeating new security threats from organised crime and terrorist networks, they have to fight smart as well as hard. Consequently, the final section of this chapter looks at the kinds of strategies the United States and western Europe need to adopt to meet not simply the immediate challenge posed by al-Qaeda, but also the long-term challenge presented by the forces of disorder.

Conclusion: responding to the new security paradigm

The difficulty for the United States and western European states in responding to the new security paradigm is that they have well-established diplomatic and military systems and institutions based almost exclusively on the traditional state-centric security paradigm. Governments are prepared and equipped to deal with threats from other governments. They are familiar with a struggle of like versus like in which the actor with most resources generally comes out ahead. They are far less comfortable with asymmetric warfare, where there are no rules and no front lines, strengths and vulnerabilities are sometimes indistinguishable from one another, and fighting smart can sometimes compensate for limited resources. Against this background, this section does not seek to elaborate detailed strategies for countering terrorism or organised crime. Instead, it establishes some precepts that could be helpful not only in guiding these strategies, but also in developing a long-term approach to managing the new disorder.

The first injunction is to think and act strategically. While this appears so obvious as to be superfluous, there are, in fact, several ways in which governments typically fail to meet this requirement. Thinking strategically requires a long view going beyond a concern with immediate failures and successes; some analysis of root causes of security problems; an assessment of the consequences of success as well as failure in existing responses; and systematic efforts to turn assessments into actions.

The second imperative is to know the enemy. This requires far better intelligence than ever before. Much of the necessary intelligence can be collected only through multilateral efforts – and United States and European intelligence agencies need to collaborate and share intelligence with each other even more fully than in the past. They also need to cooperate with foreign agencies that can infiltrate al-Qaeda and similar terrorist or criminal networks with greater ease and lower risk of detection than can intelligence personnel from NATO countries. Similarly, it is necessary to develop and maintain intelligence assets in zones of turbulence, so that vectors creating spillover to zones of peace can be anticipated. Knowing the new enemies also requires extremely effective techniques for fusion of highly classified and open source material, traditional intelligence and law-enforcement intelligence, foreign intelligence and domestic intelligence, and strategic warning and tactical indicators. To have any chance of meeting the new security challenges with any degree of real effectiveness, intelligence superiority is essential. Indeed, it is far more important than weapons superiority. The United States obviously enjoys military superiority over any challenger, whether state or transnational network, but in many contingencies such superiority is meaningless.

The third imperative is to think out of the box and avoid the temptation of locating new challenges in old conceptual frameworks. It is essential to adopt new ways of thinking, beyond the conventional wisdom, and to deviate considerably from traditional ways of doing things. Old conceptualisations, categorisations and distinctions are no longer adequate and, in some cases, no longer relevant. The familiar distinction between domestic and foreign, for example, is of little utility when considering transnational threats that typically cross multiple borders. The way in which the threat from weapons of mass destruction is assessed is similar: it is conceivable, for example, that the delivery system of choice for a nuclear strike against United States citizens will be an intermodal container that is brought into a busy United States port as part of a legitimate shipment of goods. In the new security environment, container defence might be more important than ballistic missile defence – especially in relation to homeland security. While the Bush administration is fully committed to defence against ballistic missile attack, therefore, some of the effort and resources devoted to this could usefully be diverted to detection and prevention of other, less orthodox delivery systems. Another area where far more needs to be done is in identifying the requirements of network warfare and how it can be fought most effectively. Analyses by John Arquilla and David Ronfeldt have provided an excellent basis for this.[31] Indeed, in the aftermath of September 11, the US secretary of defence, Donald Rumsfeld, adopted the rhetoric of network warfare. Yet, in Afghanistan it is not clear the United States military undertook serious network damage assessment, or began to anticipate the ways in which the al-Qaeda network could adapt to the new security environment it now faces. For the most part, the United States relied on conventional military tactics supplemented by special forces. For United States military planners, therefore, the challenge is to think in very different ways about warfare. The United States is no longer involved in conflicts in which industrial or technological superiority is the simple key to victory. On the contrary, it has to confront enemies for whom traditional notions of victory and defeat mean very little so long as they can continue to inflict pain on the United States and its citizens.

Finally, the United States needs to reassess the institutions and procedures through which national security policy is made and implemented. Along with its NATO allies, the United States faces what is, in effect, a crisis of institutions: many of those institutions that still govern societies were organised primarily for the industrial age, not the digital age. They are essentially hierarchical, slow, bureaucratic organisations in which the chain of authority runs top-down, in which creativity is stifled, and in which standard operating procedures rule out innovative responses and solutions. Remedying the deficiencies will not happen overnight. As a matter of urgency, however, it is essential to break down the institutional stove-piping that characterises not only intelligence collection and analysis but also strategic and policy planning and task implementation. Institutional innovation needs to be encouraged at all levels, so that traditional bureaucratic distinctions and demarcations can be overcome. A premium must be placed on the creation of smart institutions to combat smart enemies. Anything less is unlikely to succeed.

In other words, as the United States and its NATO allies face a new strategic environment, particularly along Europe's eastern periphery, they need to develop new methods and procedures for responding to it. The enemies are flexible, nimble and innovative; governments are laboriously slow, wedded to established methods, and restricted by standard operational procedures. Unless the NATO member-states are able to transcend these limitations and respond to disorder in systematic and innovative ways, the forces of disorder will emerge triumphant and the Westphalian system will be doomed.

Notes

1 See Walter Laqueur, *The New Terrorism* (New York: Oxford University Press, 1999); Bruce Hoffman, *Inside Terrorism* (London: Indigo, 1999); and Ian Lesser *et al.*, *Countering the New Terrorism* (Santa Monica: Rand Corporation, 1999).

2 For a very succinct and useful analysis of these changing characteristics see Bruce Hoffman, 'Terrorism Trends and Prospects', in Lesser *et al.*, *Countering the New Terrorism*, pp. 8–38.

3 Brian Jenkins's comment 'terrorism is theater' is quoted in Hoffman, *Inside Terrorism*, p. 38.

4 See Anthony Lake, *Six Nightmares* (Boston: Little, Brown, 2000), esp. pp. 56–7 where he discusses the role of Richard Clarke in sounding the warnings and developing responses.

5 Martin Bright, Antony Barnett, Burhan Wazir, Tony Thompson and Peter Beaumont in London; Stuart Jeffries in Paris; Ed Vulliamy in Washington; Kate Connolly in Berlin; Giles Tremlett in Madrid; Rory Carroll in Rome, 'The Secret War: Part 1', *Observer*, 30 September 2001.

6 David Bamber, Chris Hastings and Rajeev Syal, 'Bin Laden British Cell Planned Gas Attack on European Parliament', *Daily Telegraph*, 16 September 2001.

7 Peter Finn and Sarah Delaney, 'Al Qaeda's Tracks Deepen in Europe: Surveillance Reveals More Plots, Links', *Washington Post*, 22 October 2001.

8 *Ibid.*

9 Bruce Johnston, 'Nerve Centre for Bin Laden Terrorists is Smashed in Italy', *Daily Telegraph*, 6 April 2001.

10 Wolfgang Krach and Georg Mascolo, 'Highly Alarmed', *Der Spiegel*, 9 April 2001, pp. 22–4.
11 Finn and Delaney, 'Al Qaeda's Tracks'.
12 Judith Miller and Sarah Lyall, 'Hunting Bin Laden's Allies, U.S. Extends Net to Europe', *New York Times*, 21 February 2001.
13 *Ibid.*
14 Johnston, 'Nerve Centre'.
15 Bright *et al.*, 'The Secret War: Part 1'.
16 Peter Finn and Pamela Rolfe, 'Spain Holds 8 Linked to Sept. 11 Plot: Direct Role, Ties to Cell in Germany are Alleged', *Washington Post*, 19 November 2001.
17 A tenth characteristic of the new security paradigm, although not yet relevant in this particular geopolitical context, is the rise of mega-cities, that is, cities with a population of over 10 million people. Mega-cities are often highly dysfunctional and incubators for all sorts of violence – both criminal and terrorist. They bring together the extremes of wealth and poverty and are increasingly characterised by growing levels of violence, facilitated, in part, by the global trade in light arms. It is not surprising, therefore, that these urban concentrations are also charac- terised by no-go zones where state authorities are conspicuously absent. These mega-cities, like Shanghai and San Paulo, are breeding grounds for disease, polit- ical violence and organised crime, as those who are downtrodden, deprived and alienated increasingly seek to get rich (through crime) or get even (through terrorism).
18 Jean-François Bayart, Stephen Ellis and Béatrice Hibon, *The Criminalization of the State in Africa* (Bloomington: Indiana University Press, 1999), p. 23.
19 Max Singer and Aaron Wildavsky, *The Real World Order: Zones of Peace, Zones of Turmoil* (Chatham, NJ: Chatham House, 1996).
20 Tamil communities in western Europe and Canada, for example, often include strong supporters of the Liberation Tigers of Tamil Elam (LTTE), who use crimes such as extortion, drug trafficking and various forms of fraud to generate proceeds to support the LTTE. See Peter Chalk, 'Liberation Tigers Of Tamil Eelam's (LTTE) International Organization and Operations: A Preliminary Analysis', *Commentary No. 77*, Canadian Security Intelligence Service (Winter 1999). This document can be viewed at www.csis-scrs.gc.ca/eng/comment/ com77_e.html.
21 Bayart *et al.*, *Criminalization of the State*, p. 8.
22 William Reno, *Warlord Politics and African States* (Boulder, CO: Lynne Rienner, 1998), pp. 2–3.
23 For the notion of a 'spoiler', the author is grateful to Stephen Stedman, 'Reflections on Implementing Peace Agreements in Civil Wars', www.glencree- cfr.ie/StedmanPaper.htm.
24 Hoffman, *Inside Terrorism*, p. 202.
25 On sovereignty-free actors see James N. Rosenau, *Turbulence in World Politics* (Princeton, NJ: Princeton University Press, 1990).
26 This is one of the themes in Roger Molander *et al.*, *Strategic Information Warfare* (Santa Monica: Rand Corporation, 1996).
27 See James H. Mittelman, *The Globalization Syndrome: Transformation and Resistance* (Princeton, NJ: Princeton University Press, 2000), p. 234.
28 Benjamin R. Barber, *Jihad Versus McWorld* (New York: Ballantine, 1996).

29 For the clash-of-civilisation thesis, see Samuel P. Huntington, *The Clash of Civilizations and the Remaking of World Order* (New York: Simon and Schuster, 1996).
30 Charles Tilly, 'War Making and State Making as Organized Crime', in Peter B. Evans, Dietrich Rueschemeyer and Theda Skocpol (eds), *Bringing the State Back In* (Cambridge: Cambridge University Press, 1985), pp. 169–91.
31 John Arquilla and David Ronfeldt, *Networks and Netwars* (Santa Monica: Rand Corporation, 2001).

5

Transboundary water management and security in Central Asia[1]

Stuart Horsman

Central Asia is subject to a number of major environmental concerns, including the desiccation of the Aral Sea, the depletion and degradation of river and irrigation waters, and the consequences of Soviet and Chinese nuclear weapons testing at Semipalatinsk and Lop Nor, respectively. Riverine water, particularly when linked with irrigated land, is perhaps the only one of these environmental issues that demonstrates a 'probable linkage between environmental degradation and the outbreak of violent civil or interstate conflict'.[2] This proposition reflects current research suggesting that globally fresh water is the renewable resource most likely to be a source of conflict in the near future.[3]

Historically water provided a cultural, economic and geographical focus for Central Asia. The khanates' political culture, including deferential collectivism, was associated with water scarcity and the organisational requirements of the construction and maintenance of irrigation systems.[4] Irrigation was 'one of the principle functions of state power'.[5] Conflict in the region was often linked to or affected water resources.[6] Tsarist and Soviet expansion of irrigation networks in the region heightened water's strategic importance, illustrated by the Bolsheviks' attempt to pacify the Ferghana Valley in the 1920s and by the national delimitation process of 1924–36.[7] During the late Soviet period, the Aral Sea and related irrigation crises provoked friction between Moscow and environmental and nationalist critics in Central Asia, and Uzbekistan in particular.[8] Competition for land and water was also cited as a contributory, if not the primary, cause of interethnic violence in the Batken-Isfara, Osh and Samarkand regions.[9] Since the Soviet Union's collapse, a number of academics and politicians have cited a relationship between Central Asia's water crisis and regional stability.[10] The recent extended drought in the region has renewed concerns about this dynamic. As well as the Aral Sea basin issue, another transboundary river dispute is emerging between China and Kazakhstan.

While riverine water is the environmental issue most liable to lead to war in the region, such an outcome remains improbable for a number of reasons, some related to water and others not. Water's security implications principally fall within the wider conceptualisation of security – as an indirect or contributory cause to instability. Poor water management affects diplomatic relations, economic development, public health and access to land. Thus, while interstate war directly associated with water disputes is not likely to take place in the near future, it is expedient to address Central Asia's water problem. There is a broad consensus that interstate cooperation is required if the problem is to be managed properly. Consequently, a number of international institutions, which range from the regional to the global, have been involved in addressing the issue. These represent a breadth of interests and bailiwicks, ranging from traditional and non-traditional security to economic development and integration to environmental sustainability.

Transboundary water resources in Central Asia

The 1.8 million km^2 Aral Sea basin encompasses all of Kyrgyzstan, Tajikistan, Turkmenistan and Uzbekistan, the two Kazakhstani provinces of Qyzylorda and Southern Kazakhstan, 40 per cent of Afghanistan and a small area of Iran. The basin supports 75 per cent of Central Asia's total population and contains 90 per cent of the region's surface water. Two rivers, the Amu Darya and Syr Darya, both of which drain into the Aral Sea, dominate the region. The former rises in the Pamir mountains and flows through Tajikistan, Uzbekistan and Turkmenistan before entering the sea. The Syr Darya's source is the Naryn River in Kyrgyzstan, and its subsequent route to the Aral Sea travels through Tajikistan, Uzbekistan and Kazakhstan.

Since the 1950s, the rapid expansion in irrigated agriculture has reduced the rivers' combined flow into the Aral Sea by 90 per cent and has resulted in an adverse environmental impact on the region. Between 1960 and 1998, the sea's volume and area declined by approximately 80 per cent and 50 per cent respectively. It has now divided into a small northern and larger southern section.[11] Riverine water in Central Asia is economically significant, politically sensitive and overutilised. The present water crisis can be attributed to a large extent to two Soviet-era polices: the establishment and demarcation of the five Soviet Socialist Republics (SSRs); and the rapid expansion of irrigation agriculture since the 1950s. Dams constructed upstream, in the Kyrgyz and Tajik SSRs in particular, stored water for irrigation and also hydroelectric production (HEP), which accounted for 35% of Central Asia's energy by the early 1990s.[12] These policies and processes created a regional economic complex, but also led to intra-regional problems and tensions.

The misallocation and overallocation of water, its economic significance and competing demands are expected to increase in the near future. Over 50 per cent of water supplies for Kyrgyzstan, Turkmenistan, Uzbekistan and the two southern Kazakhstani provinces are extra-republican in source.[13] While this in itself does not indicate an intractable source of tension, these supplies are overutilised and matters are further complicated by charges of inequitable water allocations. Under the existing water agreements the three downstream states (Kazakhstan, Turkmenistan and Uzbekistan) receive 73 per cent of total withdrawals from the Aral Sea Basin.[14] This contrasts with upstream Kyrgyzstan and Tajikistan. These two countries, the source of 90 per cent of all available waters, are allocated only 5 per cent and 11 per cent, respectively.[15]

These allocation problems are significant because of the importance of riverine water to agriculture, an important sector of these nations' economy. Irrigated land produces 90 per cent of the region's crops. Cotton, the single most important irrigation crop, underpins Uzbekistan and Turkmenistan's economies. It provides 30 per cent of Uzbekistan's gross domestic product (GDP), 35 per cent of its employment and 27.4 per cent of exports. Similarly, over 50 per cent of both Kyrgyzstan's and Tajikistan's electricity production is generated using HEP.[16]

Demographic pressures further increase the contested nature of the region's water. Between 1959 and 1989, the population of the basin states increased by 140 per cent.[17] It is expected that it will increase by a third again by 2020.[18] Fifty per cent of the region's population lives in 20 per cent of its area – the Ferghana Valley, Lower Zeravshan and Tashkent–Khujand Corridor.[19] These are the prime irrigated areas, emphasising the relationship between population pressures and competition for limited access to water and fertile land, as was evident in the Kyrgyz–Tajik violence, over land and water, during the 1980s.[20]

These problems existed in the Soviet period, but were manageable while the Soviet Union remained intact. The region's water resources were controlled by a unified system, the Ministry of Land Reclamation and Water Resources, based in Moscow.[21] While disagreements existed, there was a single and final arbiter – Moscow.[22] Downstream Kazakh, Turkmen and Uzbek SSRs were allocated the majority of the waters for irrigation, while the upstream Kyrgyz and Tajik SSRs were compensated by energy supplies from their neighbours. With the break up of the USSR, '[a]ll of a sudden, a very complex water management problem became a very complex *transboundary* water management problem'.[23] In other water-scarce areas the water problem and its management have gradually evolved in tandem with the development of relations between the riparians. This has not been the case in Central Asia, where the states have been rapidly forced to assume responsibility and develop management strategies.

Another distinct transboundary water management issue of regional significance is emerging between China and Kazakhstan. The two states share 24 rivers, the key ones being the Ili and Irtysh, both of which rise in

China.[24] Eighty per cent of Kazakhstan's Ili Valley water originates in China, while the Irtysh supplies the industrial regions of central and eastern Kazakhstan.[25] China plans to extract water from the Ili and Irtysh rivers for Urumchi and oilfield developments in the Xinjiang Uighur Autonomous Region.[26] The proposal has both economic and political objectives – to stimulate the economy of Xinjiang, to raise living standards, and to erode support for Uighur irredentism. As well as the constraints on Kazakhstan's economic growth and living standards, China's proposals have broader environmental implications. These include the increased salinisation and shallowing of these rivers as well as the Balkhash and Zaisan lakes, and adverse microclimate changes, problems already evident around the Aral Sea.

The regional response: institutional innovation

The most fundamental and important function that an international institution can undertake is actually managing and allocating the region's water resources. The Central Asian leaderships quickly acknowledged the need for indigenous responsibility with the signing of the 1992 Almaty Agreement. The agreement stated that 'only [through] unification and joint coordination of action' could the region's water crisis be managed effectively.[27] Under the agreement, the states agreed to retain their Soviet-period water allocations and refrain from projects infringing on other states, and promised an open exchange of information.[28] From this auspicious beginning the republics initiated a plethora of agreements and institutional structures. These included the Interstate Commission on Water Coordination (ICWC), the Amu Darya and Syr Darya Basin Management Authorities (BVOs) subordinated to the ICWC, the Interstate Council on Problems of the Aral Sea Basin (ICAS), and the International Fund for the Aral Sea (IFAS).

Institutional reforms in 1997 merged the ICWC and the ICAS, with the former subsumed by the later. It was hoped that the merger would simplify administrative procedures and resolve duplication of effort and bureaucratic inertia.[29] This step was a positive indication of the states' awareness of the seriousness of the crisis and the need to coordinate their response more effectively. IFAS's responsibilities after 1997 included deciding water allocations among the republics and the Aral Sea, overseeing the 'regulation, use and the protection of water courses', acting as a conduit for the states to give notification of intentions to act, and the avoidance of 'disputes before they arise'.[30] The IFAS increased its role further when it was provided with the managerial responsibility of Phase Two of the Aral Sea Basin Program (ASBP). The World Bank had played a more prominent managerial role in Phase One of the ASBP, a project discussed in more detail later in this chapter.[31]

The Central Asian presidents continue to reiterate their commitment to cooperative water management via the IFAS, other regional organisations and regional summits. Between March 1998 and January 2000, six framework agreements and nine annual operational agreements, including water-energy sharing agreements, were signed between different Syr Dayra states.[32] Similarly, a joint presidential proposal for further intergovernmental agreements on water use was proposed at the Central Asian Economic Union's (CAEU) June 2000 meeting.[33] Likewise the December 2001 Declaration of the Central Asian Cooperation Organisation (CAC), the CAEU's successor, stated that the 'heads of state are convinced that coordinated and agreed actions in the sphere of rational and mutually advantageous use of water facilities and hydro-energy resources based on the principles and norms of international law will serve as a basis for effective use of the existing agricultural and energy potential of the states'.[34] The CAC has one key attribute, which encourages such an optimistic assessment – its membership. It includes the four Syr Darya riparians and avoids the more difficult Amu Darya basin issue and the region's most difficult interlocutor, Turkmenistan.

Regional bodies, however, have been found wanting. None, and in particular not the IFAS, has established an effective institutional framework for regulating regional water disputes. As one commentator recently stated, there are 'too many intergovernmental agreements [which] remain just words on a piece of paper'.[35] The principle cause of this ineffectiveness has been the organisation's key stakeholders. Political differences, lack of political and financial commitment, and failure to implement agreements have weakened these bodies. Initially, it was proposed that the IFAS would rely on contributions from the member states of 1 per cent of their individual gross national products (GNPs), with additional international donations.[36] The IFAS then reduced the level of contributions to 0.3 per cent for Kazakhstan, Turkmenistan and Uzbekistan, and 0.1 per cent for Kyrgyzstan and Tajikistan. Despite this revision, the majority of its member-states have been unable or unwilling to pay their agreed contributions.[37] More generally, the Central Asian government's political and financial commitment to the IFAS and other regional initiatives has been poor, Kazakhstan being the exception. Although the IFAS has been underfunded, Kazakhstan, Turkmenistan and Uzbekistan have spent in excess of $650 million on projects within their own territory related to the Aral Sea.[38] The IFAS has been unable to develop an institutional identity or authority distinct from its members.

In an effort to provide some sense of permanency and consistency, the IFAS's Scientific Commission of the ICWC, which prepares the data for the annual irrigation plans, is now permanently based in Tashkent. This basing decision, however, caused difficulties when the ICWC refused to provide Turkmenistan, when it was the IFAS chair, with relevant hydrological data. As a result of such difficulties the IFAS's effectiveness has been limited. Similarly, the CAC's ambitious objectives are not matched by reality. Its goal of a single economic space by 2002, for example, did not materialise and its members have failed to implement the institution's decisions. In the long term the CAC may be the basis for an effective and indigenous organisation, but the present prognosis is not encouraging.

The republics and international donor community have increasingly acknowledged the nexus between energy supplies and water supplies formed by the Soviet management of regional waters. Kazakhstan, Kyrgyzstan, Tajikistan and Uzbekistan have initiated a number of relevant agreements, with encouragement from the EU-TACIS and the United States Agency for International Development.[39] The most promising of these initiatives is the Council of the Central Asian Energy System, established in August 2001. However, it remains a fragile structure and the issue is still as intractable as ever. The states have frequently failed to honour agreements – suspending supplies of water or energy, or not paying debts on time. Kyrgyzstan, for example, was still awaiting the delivery of 30,000 tonnes of coal from the 2000 agreement in April 2001. Similarly, Uzbekistan has sporadically cut gas deliveries to Kyrgyzstan because of Bishkek's energy debts and possibly as a means of political leverage.[40] A Kyrgyzstan–Uzbekistan energy–water agreement collapsed soon after it was signed in December 2000. Kyrgyzstan was forced to release waters for HEP, which were allocated for Uzbekistan's summer irrigation requirements, because the latter had cut gas supplies. A new agreement was signed in March 2001. Consequently, Uzbekistan may have received only a third of the water it should have been allocated. Tashkent estimated that this cost it $400 million in lost agricultural revenue.[41] Similar difficulties were reported in early 2002.[42]

The potential disputes over the Ili and Irtysh have attracted less international involvement. The most relevant organisation in this context is the SCO. Kazakhstan has attempted to draw the SCO into the problematic, with mixed results. At the 2001 SCO Shanghai Summit, President Nazarbaev stated that there is a need for cooperation in 'environmental-related interaction, first of all, in the border zones ... There are such issues as transboundary rivers [that] both sides are trying to resolve. In some cases, it would be preferable to conduct multilateral negotiations in the context of the Shanghai Cooperation Oganisation.'[43] China subsequently allowed Kazakhstan to survey the upper reaches of the Irtysh.[44] In fact, Amanbek Ramazanov, the chair of Kazakhstan's Water Resources Committee, suggested the preceding summit had provided a suitable opportunity for progress on the negotiations.[45]

In reality, the SCO has so far provided a limited forum to deal with transboundary water negotiations. The negotiations on the rivers remain bilateral in nature.[46] The Declaration of the SCO does state that the organisation aims to encourage 'further effective cooperation in politics, economy, science and technology, culture, education, energy, transportation, environmental protection and other fields'.[47] However, the fundamental interests of the SCO and in particular its most powerful members, China, Russia and Uzbekistan, are firmly linked to traditional security interests. This confluence of interests within the SCO reflects a common preoccupation with irredentism, terrorism and extremism. These three states also view and respond to new security challenges in a traditional manner. As a result, only modest expectations can be placed on the SCO's role in and effective management of regional water management issues.

The extra-regional response

Given the fact that Central Asian states have had only ten years to assume managerial responsibility and develop the institutional structures, it is understandable that indigenous institutions have not been entirely successful. In this milieu a number of extra-regional organisations have become involved in regional water issues. The principal role that these institutions can play is in technical assistance and institution building/capacity development.

The awareness in the donor community of the need for creating and strengthening an institutional framework for regional cooperation, based on a clear set of structures and institutional framework, has led to some successes. Both the ICAS and the IFAS were established under international donor pressure to improve regional cooperation on water management policies.[48] The World Bank, United Nations Development Program (UNDP) and United Nations Environmental Program have been involved with the Central Asian states in the ASBP. The three-phase, 20-year ASBP aims to stabilise and rehabilitate the environmental situation and develop the region's institutional capacity in order to implement the remedial work.[49] In Phase One, the World Bank temporarily moved out of its traditional financial and technical roles to become an active participant in related negotiations.[50] By Phase Two, however, the World Bank had returned to its more traditional role, focusing upon financial assistance and support of regional management and capacity building. Both the UNDP and EU-TACIS's Water Resources Management and Agricultural Production (WARMAP) have assisted in capacity building. [51] WARMAP has also sought to enhance water management strategies and information sharing.[52]

Another area in which extra-regional institutions have offered assistance is the application and implementation of international water law. This effort has had limited success to date. While water management agreements continue to be signed, none of the IFAS ones have been accorded the status of international law, as is the norm for other treaty-based river basin commissions. Neither of the BVOs is recognised by national legislatures and therefore they lack authority.[53] Similarly Eric Sievers reports that China has contravened both international law and bilateral agreements: in particular it has failed to notify and consult Kazakhstan on its intentions or provide environmental impact assessments.[54] Kazakhstan is the only Central Asian state to have acceded to the Helsinki Convention on the Protection and Use of Transboundary Watercourses and International Lakes.[55] However indirectly, international water law has penetrated the debate. The World Bank, for example, has supported only projects that do not contravene international water law principles.[56] WARMAP has likwise been involved in this sphere: 'Unlike the other aid projects with a technical focus, WARMAP had a specific legal and institutional agenda to create a framework for water sharing based on legal principles in accordance with the Helsinki Rules and International Law Commission recommendations'.[57]

Extra-regional organisations have played an important role in providing financial assistance to the region. The World Bank's Vice President for Europe and Central Asia, Johannes Linn, argues that the World Bank has two instruments, financial assistance and the appropriating of water resources, that can solve the Kazakhstan–Kyrgyzstan 'water problem'.[58] As Philip Micklin notes, although it is difficult to record the actual levels of foreign financial assistance, the World Bank had loans and credits of $605 million to the Central Asian states in 2000.[59] However, the relationship between the regional governments and extra-regional donors has been problematic. The regional governments' expectations that the international donor community would provide large-scale and unconditional financial assistance because the Aral Sea crisis is a 'global concern' is unrealistic. Conditionality and transparency have posed difficulties between the two parties, as have different expectations about the pace of related economic, environmental and management reforms. During 2001, these differences emerged when Uzbekistan sought financial assistance from the World Bank and United Nations (UN) as well as other donors to address the consequences of the ongoing drought.[60] The donor community was initially reluctant to offer further money – Tashkent had failed to implement any remedial policies, had in fact further exacerbated the drought by its water management and agricultural policies, and failed to account properly for previous loans.

While the potential for water-related conflict in Central Asia exists, water is unlikely to provoke interstate conflict by itself. Water-related issues remain none the less highly disputed and are discussed in a tense if not antagonistic manner. Water has also at times been incorporated, at least rhetorically, into the traditional security sphere. The rebel Tajik commander Mahmud Khudaberdiyev threatened to destroy a dam during his November 1998 insurrection.[61] There were also reports that groups in Tajikistan once discussed the idea of using the Syr Darya as 'an offensive weapon in any territorial dispute with Uzbekistan', and that Uzbekistan would threaten to use military force to seize the Toktogul Dam if Kyrgyzstan attempted to alter the existing distribution policy.[62] It is unclear whether any of these threats had any substance. They do indicate a regional political atmosphere from which confidence and cooperation are absent. In such a milieu, international institutions can provide essential assistance in conflict prevention and

confidence building. There are a number of security-orientated organisations which should be able to provide this function in this region, most
notably the UN, the OSCE and the SCO.

The OSCE's inclusive Eurasian membership, comprehensive security
concept (which includes an environmental dimension) and cooperative
approach to resolving security problems make it one of the most relevant
organisations in this context.[63] It is not surprising, therefore, that the
'Central Asian republics have called upon the OSCE to assist in addressing
the environmental issues of security in the region, particularly the question
of water resources'.[64] As a result, the OSCE has focused on the promotion of
consensus building and the support for negotiated and institutional
approaches to water management, which the OSCE regards as 'important
instruments for preventing potential conflict'.[65] Wilhelm Hoynck, special
representative of the chairman-in-office for Central Asia, recently highlighted this conflict-prevention role of the OSCE: 'Central Asia is a region
with a high potential for problems and also conflicts. But at this point ... is
not a crisis region. And here we have a challenge for the international
community to deal with a situation which is really a task of *crisis prevention*'
(italics added).[66] The Central Asian states and the OSCE have had a difficult
relationship, in particular in relation to the differing priorities over which of
the OSCE's three dimensions of security should take priority in the region.
The OSCE's Water Initiative, an attempt to encourage dialogue and cooperation, failed because of competing attitudes towards external intervention
and the value of bilateral or multilateral diplomacy. Similar problems have
affected the other water management scenario under discussion, the
Sino–Kazakh waterways. The SCO's original *raison d'être* was confidence
building and it successfully produced a multilateral agreement on military
reductions along the joint Sino–former Soviet Union borders.[67] However, as
noted previously, the SCO has not been able to provide more than an informal forum and indirect confidence-building measures on water issues.

Institutional involvement can also help define the norms of debate and
behaviour, and indicate what is environmentally, financially or technically
feasible. In 2001 there were reports that President Karimov had proposed
the revival of the Sibaral water diversion scheme. This plan was met with
broad international disapproval. The World Bank refused to fund even
preliminary analysis of the scheme.[68] Despite significant financial resources
and global credibility, the leverage that international institutions have on
encouraging cooperative and sustainable management structures should
not be overestimated.

Understanding the limitations of institutions

Regional and international organisations have had mixed success in managing Central Asia's water. Cooperation on water issues is attainable as long as

other, more deep-seated political differences can be managed. To a great extent the failings in regional water management are indicative of the broader political context. While interstate conflict or major diplomatic disputes have been avoided, it is not certain whether institutional bodies, within and outside of the region, have played a significant role in deterring them. Nor have there been significant improvements in water management or environmental protection – key objectives of the many institutions involved. As Daniel Bedford and Philip Micklin independently argue, regional institutional arrangements, such as the IFAS, could play a significant role in water management, but weak political commitment and cooperation, and financial and legal constraints, have hamstrung them.[69] Newly found and jealously guarded state sovereignty, lack of trust, of confidence and of compromise, unequal economic and political relationships, poor economic development, and the legacy of Soviet attitudes, infrastructure and norms have all hindered the development of regional cooperation. Political and personal rivalries between the Central Asian leaderships also weaken the potential for regional cooperation. For example, Niyazov's antipathy to Karimov's appointment as head of the IFAS marred the organisation's February 1997 summit meeting.[70] Problems and misunderstanding with and within the international donor community have also complicated the situation.

It is understandable that the region's governments have been keen to protect and promote their state sovereignty. However, this protection of sovereignty is also indicative of regional political thinking, in which policy-makers have at times applied nationalist, protectionist and 'zero-sum' calculi to the problem. For Turkmenistan and Uzbekistan, this feeds into their opposition to revisions of water allocations and the preference for bilateral diplomacy over multilateral engagement. Turkmenistan is the most obvious proponent of this approach. Despite the evident need for interstate cooperation, President Niyazov has stated that multilateral organisations 'shall not infringe upon [Turkmenistan's] sovereignty'.[71] When invited by the OSCE to participate in collective water discussions, both Asgabat and Tashkent declared that they favoured bilateral approaches.[72] Uzbekistan's refusal to participate in the multilateral discussions was accompanied by the statement that Uzbekistan had a thousand years of resolving its own water problems.[73] Similarly Henning places China's behaviour in the Irtysh scenario within Asia's broader and bleak environmental security dynamic. Beijing's assertive water policy is indicative of a trend in Asia, where states are keen to ensure their national water supplies, often to the detriment of the stability of other states and the region.[74] This attitude was also evident in Asgabat's redefining of the Kara Kum Canal as a river and entirely on its own territory. In Asgabat's view, this meant that the related allocation and management issues would not require interstate consultation.[75]

Unequal power relationships pervade the ongoing water disputes. There are in essence conflict of interests between 'status quo' and 'revisionist' states. The former have the most to lose if allocations are renegotiated, while multilateral negotiations provide the best option for the latter to reverse what they perceive as inequitable quotas.[76] This dynamic is evident in the Kazakhstan/Uzbekistan/Turkmenistan–Kyrgyzstan/Tajikistan, Turkmenistan–Uzbekistan and China–Kazakhstan cases.

Most of the Central Asian leaders lack a genuine commitment to finding a viable solution to the regional water crisis. The lack of commitment is evident in the republics' limited support of the relevant organisations. It is also noticeable in a pervasive attitude within the region that because the problem is of Soviet origin and of considerable magnitude, the present governments should not be expected to shoulder the burden on their own.[77] Unless regional ownership and initiative are enhanced it is difficult to see how the problem will be resolved or why external actors should be seriously involved. Economic policies and priorities have hampered cooperative water management. The continuation of Soviet-style and unsustainable environmental and economic practices has been a major impediment for Turkmenistan and Uzbekistan. Admittedly, there has been a modest decline in acreage under cotton since 1991, and a corresponding expansion in less 'water-thirsty' grain production. This change in the composition of crops under cultivation has been undertaken principally to promote national food self-sufficiency, rather than to reduce water consumption and forestall an ecological disaster.

During 2001, the fourth year of a regional drought, both Turkmenistan and Uzbekistan sought to find new water sources, drilling new boreholes, for example, rather than reduce state-planned targets for cotton and grain production. Similarly both Turkmenistan's planned Lake of the Golden Age and the reported revival in the Sibaral scheme suggest outdated and unsustainable developmental and environmental thinking.[78] After a decade of independence, an Uzbekistani water expert could state: 'the re-routing of Ob-Irtish [*sic*] appears to be the only tangible solution to the ecological and other problems caused by the drying of the Aral Sea. ... [T]he international community could conceivably provide funding to support a project ... re-routing the Ob-Irtish to [the] Aral Sea'.[79] This statement suggests that international institutions and norms on water management may not have penetrated the regional understanding on the water crisis as deeply as many advocates have hoped or suggested.

The divisions between the republics' individual economic priorities, between HEP and irrigation requirements, and between HEP-reliant states and hydrocarbon producers have also weakened institutional agreements and management. The fragile nature of the recent energy–water transfer agreements demonstrates that while the republics are aware of the potentially symbiotic relationship between water and energy, they have not found a robust or mutually beneficial mechanism to regulate this dynamic. As a result water remains a scarce, strategic resource which the states find diffi-cult to compromise on. Without a shift in economic thinking and priorities, a viable compromise over the distribution of water among the riparian states will remain elusive.

Management prospects and implications for Eurasian security

Water remains a contested and strategic asset for the four countries of the Aral Sea Basin and may become so between China and Kazakhstan in the near future. How far water-related conflict is likely in the future is difficult to gauge. International evidence, particularly from the Middle East, suggests that interstate water-related conflict is the exception rather than the rule.[80] It is fortunate that water rarely results in interstate violence. Demand for water is, however, intense and predicted to increase in the near future. Moreover, rising demand is accompanied by a number of negative political factors: poor collective management, proposals for further water extraction, tension in interstate relations, bellicose diplomatic rhetoric, and sporadic but low-level violence at the communal level.

The countries of the Aral Sea Basin do not appear to have acknowledged either individually or collectively the seriousness of the situation, the expedi-ency of cooperative political action, or the need for an integrated manage-ment system to resolve this issue. As Micklin notes:

> Looking at the future, the only rational avenue for the Aral Sea Basin states to follow is cooperation and compromise in managing and sharing their trans-national water resources. This is not only necessary to avoid interstate conflict, perhaps even military confrontation, but to develop an integrated basin-wide strategy to optimize water use efficiency and maximize efforts to restore and protect key water related eco-systems.[81]

The republics have taken tentative steps towards collective water manage-ment, although 'progress is slow and uneven, and the most critical problems remain formidable and largely unresolved'.[82] Further pressures – the deteri-oration of the existing irrigation infrastructure, the continued economic reliance on irrigation agriculture, demographic growth, and Afghanistan's and China's demands for water, as well as non-water-related disputes – suggest a heightened sense of water insecurity and an inability to cooper-ate.[83] As a result the region's water security milieu is and will continue to be tense, although not openly hostile.

The role of external actors in this strained and confused security environ-ment is on the whole positive but limited. Extra-regional organisations can play a useful but essentially supportive role. Encouragement and incentives for more efficient water provision, cooperative water management and conflict prevention have not necessarily found a receptive audience in Central Asia. Although the Central Asian republics have been resistant to some initiatives, the international community is also to blame for this failure. International organisations and individual states have failed to maintain clear and consistent objectives, with economic and strategic objectives often running counter to policies encouraging collective regional behaviour. Confusion and competition between the initiatives of different organisations have also hindered the goal of cooperative water management.[84]

The focus of future international attention with respect to Central Asia's water resources should include increased and simplified cooperation within the donor community and with regional bodies in order to produce a more coherent, efficient and less adversarial management structure. It should also include the provision of 'a know-how transfer concerning the legal basis of international river basins [and] the organization of water management', and induce a shift from the alleviation of the symptom (the drying up of the Aral Sea) to reform of the fundamental cause, the cultivation of cotton. Two other categories of policy response are also essential: increased support for civil society activities in general and those related to agricultural and environmental sectors in particular; and, depending upon the Central Asian states' response to the World Bank's 1996 *ASBP Review*, financial support.[85]

Interstate relations in Central Asia are far less tense than those in the Middle East, and the existing institutional framework and shared political norms at the elite level in Central Asia suggest that, while there have been disputes and tensions over water, violent conflict is unlikely. The sub-state situation has greater potential for environmentally related conflict. Here violent incidents associated with access to water have been evident, although limited in scale. The most significant of these conflicts was the 1992 'kolkhoz war' in Kurgan Teppa.[86] Low-level tensions over water poaching and rerouting of irrigation canals have been reported elsewhere.[87] However, these are unlikely to escalate into interstate conflict.

Although interstate conflict may be avoided, water does have wider security implications.[88] The interaction between economic and environmental issues is particularly acute and problematic in the rural sector. Given the fact that the majority of the region's population is employed in the agricultural sector, this has serious implications for social stability, and possibly for security. It was reported that ecological deterioration led to the internal migration of 70,000 Kazakhstanis in 1996.[89] Similarly, it is estimated that 20 per cent of agricultural jobs in Uzbekistan are superfluous.[90] Degradation of agricultural land, demographic pressures, unemployment and underemployment may translate into major population movement, group competition for economic, political and social resources, social instability, the rise of political Islamist movements and the erosion of regime legitimacy.[91]

Given the limited scale of recent examples of water-related population and economic dislocation and instability, the security implications for the wider region and Europe in particular are limited and indirect. Also, the geographical distance between the main water flashpoints and European energy investments in the region and western Europe itself means that unless any potential water war escalated considerably, it would not adversely affect Western interests. However, these may be affected indirectly. Some of the interests at risk are national self-interests and material. These include risks to current and potential investments in the region, a worsening security environment in Central Asia, which could draw in significant near neighbours including Russia and China, and the possibility of massive refugee flows. Other interests are more universalist and benign in character, including the promotion and defence of human rights and conflict prevention, good governance, international and social stability, security and (sustainable) development, equitable resource allocation and environmental protection, for example. It is more likely, however, that interest in the region will be a function of narrow national interests.[92]

Prior to September 11 2001, western interests in the region were relatively modest. The exceptions to this rule were perhaps the concern about the Aral Sea and the investment into the energy sector. International assistance to and interest in the immediate Aral Sea region was relatively forthcoming. However, much of this was misplaced, diverting attention, energy and funding away from the fundamental causes – water mismanagement and irrigation-based cotton agriculture – to what is essentially a symptom of the basic factors.[93] Since September 2001, there has been a substantive increase in western interest in the region and the resources available for implementing recent and long-term objectives there. Western European involvement in the region is more than a strategic reaction to the American-led campaign against the Taliban regime in Afghanistan and to the American presence in Central Asia more generally. It reflects, for example, an effort to promote good governance and economic reform in the region. As a result of both self-interested and universalist objectives, it is expedient that the West retains and increases its engagement in Central Asia. Despite the difficulties faced by international institutions' activities in Central Asia, they remain probably the most effective vehicle for promoting effective regional management and European engagement on this issue. Ultimately, however, both the international donor community and the Central Asian leadership should recognise the limitations of extra-regional parties in this dynamic. The key role for 'the international donor community [is] to remind the Aral Basin governments that whereas the international community is committed to assisting the region in resolving the Aral Crises, fundamental responsibility for this rests with the Aral Sea Basin countries'.[94]

Notes

1 The views expressed are the author's own and should not be regarded as a statement of government or Foreign and Commonwealth Office policy. I would like to thank Sarah O'Hara and Madalene Lock for their comments on this chapter.

2 Leigh Sarty, 'Environmental Security After Communism: The Debate', in J. DeBardeleben and J. Hannigan (eds), *Environmental Security and Quality after Communism: Eastern Europe and the Soviet Successor States* (Boulder, CO: Westview Press, 1995), p. 19. Environmental security, a highly contested concept, is usually applied to at least one of five spheres: (1) the environment as a cause and/or objective of conflict; (2) the environment used as an instrument of war; (3) environmental degradation resulting from military action; (4) the indirect influence of environmental degradation on security via development and welfare issues; and (5) environmental degradation and protection, distinct from its political and security implications. For a critical review of the environmental security debate, see Nils Gleditsch, 'Armed Conflict and the Environment: A Critique of the Literature', *Journal of Peace Research*, 35:3 (1998), pp. 381–400.

3 Thomas Homer-Dixon, 'Environmental Scarcities and Violent Conflict: Evidence from Cases', *International Security*, 19:1 (1994), pp. 5–40.

4 Gregory Gleason, 'The Struggle for Control over Water in Central Asia: Republican Sovereignty and Collective Action', *RFE/RL Report on the USSR* (21 June 1991), p. 11; and Karl Wittfogel, *Oriental Despotism: A Comparative Study of Total Power* (New Haven, CT: Yale University Press, 1957).

5 Hélène Carrere d'Encausse, *Islam and the Russian Empire: Reform and Revolution in Central Asia* (London: I. B. Tauris, 1988), p. 8.

6 See, for example, Gregory Wheeler, *The Modern History of Central Asia* (London: Weidenfeld and Nicolson, 1964), p. 3; Philip Micklin, *Managing Water in Central Asia* (London: Royal Institute of International Affairs, 2000), pp. 26–7.

7 Michael Rywkin, *Moscow's Muslim Challenge: Soviet Central Asia* (New York: M. E. Sharpe, 1982), p. 42.

8 Z. Goldman, 'Environmentalism and Nationalism: An Unlikely Twist in an Unlikely Direction', in John Massey Stewart (ed.), *The Soviet Environment: Problems, Policies and Politics* (Cambridge: Cambridge University Press, 1992), p. 9.

9 S. Abashin and V. Bushkov, *Sotsial'naya napryazhennost i mezhnatsional'nye Konflikty v severnykh raionah Tadjikistana*, Document 24, (Moscow: IEA, 1991); *Pravda*, 19 July 1989; Yacoov Ro'i, 'Central Asia Riots and Disturbances, 1989–90: Causes and Context', *Central Asian Survey*, 10:3 (1991), pp. 21–54, esp. p. 24.

10 See Gleason, 'Struggle for Control'; D. J. Petersen, *Troubled Lands: The Legacy of Soviet Environmental Destruction* (Boulder, CO: Westview Press, 1993); David R. Smith, 'Environmental Security and Shared Water Resources in Post-Soviet Central Asia', *Post-Soviet Geography*, 36:6 (1995), pp. 351–70. For example, see President Nursultan Nazarbaev, 'Speech at the Meeting of the Leaders of the Shanghai Cooperation Organisation States', Shanghai, China, 15 June 2001, quoted in Center for Foreign Policy and Analysis, *Shanghai Cooperation Organization* (Almaty: Center for Foreign Policy and Analysis, 2001), p. 7.

11 For detailed information on the rivers and the sea, see Nazarbaev, 'Speech', pp. 13–20.

12 See Sarah O'Hara, 'Water and Conflict in Central Asia', in Andrew Dobson and Jeffery Stanyer (eds), *Contemporary Political Studies 1998* (Nottingham: University of Nottingham, 1998), pp. 171–9.

13 Smith, 'Environmental Security', pp. 361–2.

14 Uzbekistan receives 38 per cent and Turkmenistan 26 per cent of the basin's total withdrawals. Kazakhstan receives 30 per cent of Syr Darya withdrawals, Tajikistan 11 per cent and Kyrgyzstan only 0.4 per cent. The Aral Sea has been allocated 16 per cent of total withdrawals. Micklin, *Managing Water*, pp. 46–51 and Table 5.1.

15 *Ibid.*

16 N. F. Vasil'yev quoted in Philip Micklin, 'The Water Crisis in Soviet Central Asia', in P. Pryde (ed.), *Environmental Management in the Soviet Union* (Cambridge: Cambridge University Press, 1991), p. 217; Economist Intelligence Unit, *Uzbekistan Country Profile 2001* (London: EIU, 2001), p. 18; and Stefan Klötzli, *The Water and Soil Crisis in Central Asia: A Source for Future Conflicts?*, ENCOP Occasional Paper No. 11 (Zurich: Center for Security Policy and Conflict Research; Berne: Swiss Peace Foundation, May 1994), Table 3, on the importance of hydroelectric power in the Aral Sea basin (defined by number of power plants for differing categories of electricity production per year).

17 Gleason, 'Struggle for Control', p. 12.

18 Based on 1996 figure. Tashkent Institute of Engineers of Irrigation and Agricultural Mechanization and the Aral Sea International Committee, *The Mirzaev Report* (May 1998), Table 1, cited in Micklin, *Managing Water*, p. 68.

19 Philip Micklin, 'The Aral Sea Crisis: An Introduction to the Special Edition', *Post-Soviet Geography*, 33:5 (1992), pp. 269–82, esp. p. 89.

20 Valery Tishkov, *Ethnicity, Nationalism and Conflict: The Mind Aflame in and after the Soviet Union* (London: Sage, 1997), p. 74.

21 It was renamed the Ministry of Water Management Construction (MinVodKhoz) and then restructured as a scientific research institute, in 1990. Luis Viega da Cuhna, 'The Aral Sea Crisis: A Great Challenge in Transboundary Water Resources Management', NATO Advanced Research Workshop on Transboundary Water Resources Management: Technical and Institutional Issues, Skopelos, May 1994, p. 17.

22 *Inside Central Asia*, 25 (31 March 1996), p. 4.

23 Viega da Cuhna, 'Aral Sea Crisis', p. 6.

24 Bruce Pannier and Edige Magauin, 'Kazakhstan: China Discusses Future of Irtysh Rivers', *RFE/RL Weekly Magazine* (28 May 1999); and Kazakh Commercial Television, Almaty (1300 GMT, 26 June 2001).

25 Gleason, 'Struggle for Control', p. 146; and Temirbolat Bakhytjan, 'Water Dispute Threatens Central Asian Stability: Astana is Seriously Concerned over Plans by China to Divert Several Cross-Border Rivers', *Turkistan Newsletter*, 4:111 (29 May 2000) www.eurasianet.org/resource/cenasia/hypermail/200005/0109.html.

26 See Eric Sievers, 'China Set to Divert the World's Fifth Largest River', *Ecostan*, 7:7 (July 2000), www.econoline.ru/news/JUN00/00062904.TXT.

27 Sarah O'Hara, 'Managing Central Asia's Water Resources: Prospects for the 21st Century', ICREES Seminar on Environmental Issues in Central Asia, University of Nottingham, 9 December 1998, p. 13.

28 *Ibid.*, pp. 13–14.

29 Micklin, *Managing Water in Central Asia*, pp. 50–1.

30 See, for example, *Ibid.*, pp. 49–51; O'Hara, 'Managing Central Asia's Water Resources', pp. 13–14; and Smith, 'Environmental Security', p. 366.

31 Micklin, *Managing Water*, p. 29.
32 *Central Asia Regional Water, Environment and Energy Agreements*, www.ce.utexas. edu/prof/mckinney/ce/Topics/central_asia_regional_water.htm.
33 *RFE/RL Newsline*, 4:112, Pt 1 (9 June 2000).
34 CAC Declaration, Article 3; and Uzbek Television, *First Channel*, Tashkent (1630 GMT, 28 December 2001).
35 Kazakh Commercial Television, Almaty (1130 GMT, 20 February 2002).
36 Viega da Cuhna, 'The Aral Sea Crisis', p. 13.
37 Philip Micklin, 'Regional and International Responses to the Aral Crisis', *Post-Soviet Geography and Economics*, 39:1 (1998), pp. 399–416, esp. p. 15.
38 Micklin, *Managing Water*, p. 52.
39 See for example *ibid.*, p. 46; *RFE/RL Newsline*, 3:104, Pt 1 (28 May 1999); and Kabar, Bishkek (1231 GMT, 13 June 2001).
40 BBC World Service (1506 GMT, 13 December 1999); *RFE/RL Newsline*, 4:11, Pt 1 (17 January 2000); and *Inside Central Asia*, 364 (26 February–4 March 2001), p. 3.
41 *Inside Central Asia*, 363 (19–25 February 2001), p. 3.
42 Interfax news agency, Moscow (1627 GMT, 15 February 2002); and *Kazakh Commercial Television*, Almaty (1130 GMT, 20 February 2002).
43 Nazarbaev, 'Speech at the Meeting of the Leaders'.
44 *Kazakh Commercial Television*, Almaty (1300 GMT, 26 June 2001).
45 *Ibid.*
46 Kazakhstan–China negotiations began in 1999. They are now in the fourth round.
47 See *Declaration of Shanghai Cooperation Organization*, english.peopledaily.com.cn/ 200106/15/print20010615_72738.html; and the Center for Foreign Policy and Analysis, *Shanghai Cooperation Organization*, pp. 9–11.
48 Micklin, *Managing Water*, p. 48; and Erika Weinthal, 'Making Waves: Third Parties and International Mediation in the Aral Sea Basin', in Melanie Greenberg, John Barton and Margaret McGuiness (eds), *Words over War: Mediation and Arbitration to Prevent Deadly Conflict* (Lanham, MD: Rowman and Littlefield, 2000), pp. 280–1.
49 Weinthal, 'Making Waves', p. 278.
50 *Ibid.*
51 *Ibid.*, p. 280; and Micklin, *Managing Water*, p. 50.
52 Micklin, *Managing Water*.
53 O'Hara, 'Managing Central Asia's Water Resources', p. 15.
54 Sievers, 'China Set to Divert'.
55 Daniel Linotte, 'Water Resources Management in Central Asia: Addressing New Challenges and Risks', *Analyst* (15 August 2001); and *Vek* (6 July 2001).
56 Weinthal, 'Making Waves', p. 287.
57 Micklin, *Managing Water*, p. 13.
58 *Kazakhstan Today*, Almaty (0925 GMT, 22 October 2001).
59 Micklin, *Managing Water*, p. 53.
60 Owen Bowcott, 'Drought-Hit States Facing Famine', *Guardian* (30 October 2001).
61 BBC, 'Tajik Rebels: "We Will Blow Up Dam"' (6 November 1998).
62 Shirin Akiner, 'Conflict, Stability and Development in Central Asia', in C. J. Dick (ed.), *Instabilities in Post-Communist Europe* (Portsmouth: Carmichael and Sweet,

1996), p. 14; and B. Roberts, 'More on Water in Central Asia', *Cenasia. Email Discussion Group* (14 April 1996).

63 OSCE, *The OSCE Handbook* (Vienna: OSCE, 1999), pp. 1–133. See also 'Seventh Economic Forum Focuses on "Security Aspects in the Field of the Environment"', *OSCE Newsletter*, 6:5 (May 1999), pp. 2–3.

64 *OSCE Newsletter*, 6:11/12, (November–December 1999), p. 14.

65 *OSCE Newsletter*, 6:5 (May 1999), p. 3.

66 Hoynck quoted in 'Central Asia: New OSCE Chief. The OSCE's Role in the Region', *Times of Central Asia* (2 August 2001), p. 4.

67 Roy Allison, 'Central Asia: A Region in the Making', paper presented at the conference on Central Asia in a New Security Context, Swedish Institute of International Affairs, Stockholm, 2–3 September 1999, p. 9.

68 Galima Bukharbaeva, 'New Uzbek Water Crisis', *Institute for War and Peace Reporting*, 48 (19 April 2001).

69 Daniel Bedford, 'International Water Management in the Aral Sea', *Water International*, 21 (1996), pp. 63–9; and Micklin, *Managing Water*, p. 52.

70 The position rotates between the two presidents every two years. Karimov was eventually appointed head of the Fund in 1997. *OMRI Daily Digest*, 43, Pt 1 (3 March 1997).

71 S. Niyazov, *Komsomolskaia Pravda* (27 October 1994), quoted in Kirill Nourzhanov, 'Turkmenistan: Halfway Through to the Golden Age?', *Central Asian Monitor*, 1 (1995), p. 12.

72 Roland Eggleston, 'OSCE Seeks Agreement on Central Asian Water', *RFE/RL Newsline*, 4:110, Pt 1 (7 June 2000).

73 *Ibid*.

74 John Henning, 'Water: Potential Spark of Asian Regional Conflict', *Analyst* (24 May 2000), www.cacianalyst.org.

75 O'Hara, 'Water and Conflict in Central Asia', p. 21.

76 *Ibid*.

77 Thus, as one billboard in Karakalpakstan states, 'the catastrophy [*sic*] of the Aral Sea, which has shocked the entire world is an ecological disaster on a global scale which Uzbekistan and its neighbours cannot cope with alone'. See Stuart Horsman, 'Water, Security and Development in Central Asia', in EBRD (ed.), *The Next Ten Years: Mapping the Challenges* (London: EBRD, 2001), p. 67.

78 Linotte, 'Water Resources Management'; and *Uzbek National News Agency* (web site), Tashkent (9 April 2002).

79 Abdukhalil Razzakov, 'Water Shortage in Central Asia and the Re-Routing of Siberian Rivers to Central Asia', *Analyst* (6 June 2001), www.cacianalyst.org.

80 Thomas Naff and Ruth Matson (eds), *Water in the Middle East: Conflict or Cooperation?* (Boulder, CO: Westview Press, 1984), quoted in Smith, 'Environmental Security', p. 357.

81 Micklin, 'Aral Sea Crisis', p. 80.

82 *Ibid*.

83 Richard Dion, 'Decline of Central Asian Integration', *Analyst* (29 March 2000), www.cacianalyst.org.

84 See Micklin, 'The Aral Sea Crisis'; and Micklin, *Managing Water in Central Asia*, pp. 51–3.

85 Micklin, *Managing Water*, p. 49; and Weinthal, 'Making Waves'.

86 Olivier Roy, 'Islam in Tajikistan', *Project on Open Society in Central Eurasia, Occasional Paper No. 1* (New York: Open Society Institute, 1996), p. 7.

87 Personal communication with the author.

88 For a discussion of the environmental security concept and its application in Central Asia, see Stuart Horsman, 'Security Issues Facing the Newly Independent States of Central Asia: The Cases of Kazakhstan and Uzbekistan', PhD dissertation, University of Sheffield, 1999.

89 International Organization for Migration, *CIS Migration Report* (Geneva: IOM, 1997), pp. 56–60, cited in 'Migrations in Kazakhstan', *Eurasian File, 96* (April 1998), p. 7.

90 Government of the Republic of Uzbekistan/TACIS, *Uzbekistan Economic Trends 1997*, First Quarter (Tashkent, 1998), p. 49.

91 For the relationship between political Islam and economic and social crises, see R. Hrair Dekmejian, 'Islamic Revival: Catalysts, Categories, and Consequences', in Shireen Hunter (ed.), *The Politics of Islamic Revivalism: Diversity and Unity* (Bloomington: Indiana University Press, 1988), p. 7; and James P. Piscatori (ed.), *Islam in the Political Process*, (Cambridge: Royal Institute for International Affairs/Cambridge University Press, 1983).

92 As Gregory Gleason states, 'The provision of assistance to Central Asia is closely related to the value that the outside world attaches [to the region and] the degree to which assistance can be expected to build long-term relationships that are valuable to the donor'. Gregory Gleason, *The Central Asian States: Discovering Independence* (Boulder, CO: Westview Press, 1997), p. 154.

93 Weinthal, 'Making Waves'.

94 Micklin, 'Regional and International Responses', p. 17.

6

The geopolitics of
Central Asian energy

Jaewoo Choo

This chapter assesses the rising geostrategic and geoeconomic importance of Central Asian oil and natural gas for China and the United States – the most transparent source of Sino-American conflict in this region. The initial rationale for Chinese engagement in Central Asia, despite the emergence of China as a net oil-importing nation in 1993, was not driven by the search for an alternative and secure source of oil and natural gas.[1] Rather, Chinese policy reflected a set of domestic and foreign policy concerns, particularly the desire to address unresolved border disputes with its many neighbours, to dampen ethnic unrest in the Xinjiang autonomous province, to foster regional economic cooperation, to open new markets for Chinese arms, and to reduce the incidence of drug trafficking and illegal migration.[2] American interest in the region was closely linked to the Clinton strategy of engagement and enlargement, particularly the desire to facilitate the transition to democracy and the market economy in the states spawned by the dissolution of the Soviet Union. But as the gap between the demand and domestic supply of oil widened in both countries, the oil-producing states of Central Asia took on a new significance. Both the Chinese and American governments have sought privileged access to this region for their national oil firms.[3]

Sino-American competition in this region began in earnest in 1994.[4] China seemed to be better positioned initially, owing to successive annual summit meetings with the regional oil-producing states – Russia, Kazakhstan, Kyrgyzstan and Tajikistan. These meetings resulted in the creation of the 'Shanghai Five' in 1996, a grouping that was subsequently enlarged with the addition of Uzbekistan in 1999 and formalised in 2001 with the creation of the SCO.[5] The Shanghai process generated cooperation agreements in various issue areas, ranging from border disputes to economic cooperation to anti-terrorism measures. In this way, China established a firm diplomatic presence in the region.

The September 11 terrorist attacks on New York and Washington, DC, however, have had a lasting effect on the trajectory of Sino-American competition in Central Asia. The subsequent American retaliation on the Taliban and al-Qaeda in Afghanistan generated the not unwelcomed externality of expanding the American sphere of influence in the region. American military operations required the acquisition of military basing rights, and the United States was able to deploy and base its troops along Afghanistan's perimeter in Uzbekistan, Turkmenistan and Kyrgyzstan in exchange for considerable sums of humanitarian aid and economic assistance. The basing of American forces in these Central Asian states initially raised concerns in Russia, China, Iran and even Turkey. Despite the American claim that the US military presence in the region was temporary and contingent on the war on terrorism, the world in general, and Russia and China in particular, were very much concerned that this temporary deployment of American troops would become permanent and formalised in a set of bilateral treaties. At this juncture, it appears certain that the duration and nature of the US military presence in Central Asia will extend into the medium term, an assessment in keeping with the immediate challenge of counter-insurgency warfare in Afghanistan and the longer-term challenge of waging the war on terrorism.

The longer the duration of the American military presence in Central Asia, the more anxious will China be. Just as the United States was discomfited by the rising influence of China and Russia in the region prior to September 2001, China and Russia are now discomfited by the rising American role and influence there, despite their (self-interested) support of the US campaign against terrorism.[6] China, in particular, faces an acute geostrategic dilemma. Whether it be NATO's PfP programme, the OSCE, or the signing of bilateral military agreements with states in the region, China views these American initiatives, even if they have been directed at the disinterested goal of regional stability, as a putative threat to Chinese regional interests (just as many in Washington have viewed the SCO as a threat to American interests). These divergent geostrategic assessments raise a few interesting questions: are American and Chinese interests in fact opposed in the region? Is the nascent security regime embodied in the SCO inherently incompatible with the Atlantic security system? Will the development and exploitation of Central Asian energy be hindered or precluded by the clash of Chinese and American geostrategic interests in the Pacific? Answers to these questions will inevitably be conditioned by the negative perceptions that Chinese and American foreign policy elites have of one another and the power vacuum in Central Asia that has invited the major powers to stake an exclusive leadership claim there. While Chinese diplomatic options are increasingly constrained by the rapprochement between Russia and NATO and the dependence of Pakistan and India on American patronage to broker the Kashmir dispute, the 'Great Game' for influence and control of this region could none the less be replayed by the United States and China.

Increasingly, such an outcome could be fuelled as much by a competition for future rights to Central Asian oil reserves as by concerns over geostrategic advantage.

The rising geostrategic and geoeconomic importance of Central Asia

Prior to the September 11 terrorist attacks, Central Asia was already an important region in the world for two reasons, one positive and the other negative. Central Asia is potentially an alternative to the Persian Gulf as a major source of oil and natural gas.[7] American, European and Chinese interest in Central Asia embodies similar diversification strategies designed to lessen dependence on unstable Middle Eastern governments and an unpredictable Organisation of Petroleum Exporting Countries. Central Asia offers two prominent advantages for oil consumers. First, its reserves are much larger than previously assumed and continue to be revised upwards as recovery technologies improve and prices rise. Second, the oil-production capacity of the Middle East and Saudi Arabia, which account, respectively, for 63% and 25% of the world's proven oil reserves, has stagnated over the past 20 years.[8]

American, Chinese and Russian interest in Central Asia is driven by the fragility of Central Asian regimes and the potential threat they pose to regional stability. The difficult transition process has stalled in many cases and outstanding conflicts, territorial and other, continue to plague inter-state relations and complicate the process of exploiting, extracting and delivering oil and natural gas from the region.[9] The ability of the great powers, particularly China and the United States, to mitigate the causes of regional instability, to mediate interstate conflict, and to avoid the outbreak of war will largely determine whether Central Asia can become a stable and reliable source of supply. The states of the region have already proven themselves incapable of managing their own affairs and have relied heavily on outside help for solutions to the economic and political challenges attending statehood. The region remains potentially volatile owing to water-allocation conflicts, Islamic militancy and ethnic tensions. The prospects for regional peace and stability will depend, at least in the short term, on the sustained interest and intercession of the great powers, especially China, Russia and the United States.

These three powers have made sustained and competitive diplomatic overtures to the Central Asian states. The United States, for instance, has made an effort to integrate these states into the Atlantic security system via the PfP programme and the Euro-Atlantic Partnership Council. China and Russia, in turn, adopted a more traditional strategy of limited multilateralism with the creation of the 'Shanghai Five', which was later institutionalised as the SCO. Both China and the United States have sought preponderant influence, if not hegemony, in the region. Moreover, the

Sino-American competition means that China and the United States, almost by definition, view each other's ambitions in the region as virtually inimical to each state's own interests.

Illustrative of this trend is the American marriage of convenience with Uzbekistan, which reflects Washington's effort to manage the tension between ideals and self-interest in a critical area of the world. Washington designated Tashkent a strategic partner in 1995, despite the latter government's non-democratic and totalitarian nature.[10] Washington's embrace of Tashkent later served the short-term American interest in the war against terrorism and reinforced the American presence in the region. That policy, however, may make long-term solutions to regional problems more difficult to come by, particularly from the need to find a multilateral solution for the routing of oil lines to eastern Asia as well as to Europe.[11] The potential danger of the American intimacy with Uzbekistan is that 'the inertia and the logic of events may tempt the Bush administration to let a temporary expedient grow into an enduring policy shift'.[12] In other words, propping up Uzbekistan as a regional hegemon not only would fail to address, but would actually exacerbate, a key source of Central Asian instability: the domestic political repression that fosters the radicalisation of Islamist movements and galvanises popular support behind them. Moreover, viewing the Islamist threat primarily as a military problem will not mitigate the various transnational concerns plaguing the region, particularly water-allocation disputes and unwanted flows of drugs, refugees and weapons.[13] This danger is particularly acute since the Caucasus and Central Asian states could become zones of interstate competition similar to that in the Middle East or the Korean peninsula. The intensification of war in Chechnya and the evolution of post-Taliban Afghanistan already point to the region's potential for 'Balkanisation'. Were this process to accelerate and spread throughout the region, it could precipitate military intervention by any one of the regional or global major powers, including Turkey and Iran, both of which threatened to intervene in the Nagorno-Karabakh war in 1992–93.[14]

A second negative development in the region is the gradual shift in the goals and objectives of the SCO. Russia, and particularly China, are potential challengers to the American design for and role in the region. The SCO, for instance, shifted its focus from the resolution of border conflicts and enhanced economic cooperation to addressing the common problem of Islamic militancy when the members established an 'anti-terrorism centre' in Biskek (Kyrgyzstan) in 1999. Although the SCO claims that the sole purpose of the Biskek centre reflects a growing recognition of the threat posed by terrorism to the region, the United States has not fully accepted that explanation. Rather, the Bush administration suspected that it was a harbinger of a joint Sino-Russian strategy of eventually stationing Chinese and Russian troops in Central Asia, moving towards creating a military and political bloc. But this fear has been allayed by the evolution of the

Russian–American relationship, particularly the amicable personal relationship of the presidents, George Bush and Vladimir Putin, and Russia's virtual *de facto* membership of NATO. Russia's concern with the SCO has changed correspondingly. No longer interested in creating a balancing alliance against the United States, Russia now sees the SCO as an institutional basis enabling it to act as Asia's interlocutor with the United States. Sino-American relations have not experienced a similar evolution. Washington and Beijing remain suspicious of each other's intentions and strategic interests, particularly in Central Asia. In the Chinese strategic calculus, the SCO remains an institution designed to balance American power in the region. The United States, on the other hand, suspects that China's ultimate objective is Chinese hegemony and an American loss of presence in Eastern and Central Asia.[15]

American and Chinese energy policy and strategy

Both the United States and China were forced over the course of the 1990s to reassess their growing vulnerability to disruptions in the supply of oil from the Middle East. Each has had to reconsider the economic and political consequences of an unanticipated energy shortfall, as well as the need to fashion policies that would encourage the development of new sources of oil outside the Middle East. There is a growing consensus that there may eventually be an unsustainable gap between the supply and demand for oil.[16] The chief reasons for the anticipated gap between global supply and demand are attributed to the secular decline in the production of oil, limited reserves in the OPEC states, a rising demand for oil outside the wealthy countries of the Organisation for Economic Cooperation and Development, and an inadequate refining capacity. The rapid rise in oil consumption by the developing states of Asia, particularly China and India, underscores the concern over a future, major oil shortage and has accelerated the search for new sources of oil. As a Brookings Institution study warned, the 'growth in international oil demand will exert increasing pressure on global oil availability', and the growth rate of Asian economies and populations – particularly in China and India – will be 'major contributors' to this increased demand.[17] In a similar vein, the US Energy Information Administration projects that the demand for oil in developing Asian countries will increase by 129 percent over the next 20 years.[18] Another study forecasts that China will need to import some 60 percent of its oil and at least 30 percent of its natural gas by 2020.[19]

The anticipated gap between the domestic supply and demand for oil has forced the Chinese government to look abroad to meet China's future energy needs.[20] Similar concerns in the United States led the Department of Energy to recommend in May 2001, for example, that the Bush administration take aggressive measures to meet America's future energy needs.[21] The suggested policy initiatives, particularly drilling for oil in the Arctic National

Wildlife Preserve, pose a formidable domestic political challenge to the administration.[22] A confluence of domestic politics and foreign policy imperatives has turned Chinese and American attention to Central Asia as a solution to their respective future energy requirements. The oil-rich states of Central Asia have been accorded a privileged place in the American and Chinese foreign policy calculations. As a consequence, these states may become the fodder in any Sino-American competition for geopolitical and geoeconomic predominance in the region.

The United States will face fierce competition from China and other Asian states in the race to exploit and develop Central Asian energy resources. While it is true that Asian states have been important consumers of oil, they have been content to buy that oil on the open international market rather than to undertake the capital investment necessary to discover and exploit new oil fields or lay claim to existing reserves. That time has passed. The Asian states now possess the financial and technological wherewithal to compete on a near equal footing with the European and North American oil companies. Western dominance in this area of the international economy is coming to an end, a development which will no doubt enhance the energy security of the Asian states, but at the same time diminish the energy security of Europe and North America. The Asian advantage is particularly marked in the oil-rich states of the Caspian Sea area: geopolitics will allow China and other Asian states to pose a direct challenge to the West, especially the United States, when it comes to exploiting new sources of oil and natural gas and controlling the all-important energy supply networks. The potential for conflict, rather than cooperation, has been conditioned by Chinese and American foreign policy initiatives in the region after the breakup of the Soviet Union in 1992.

US policies in the region

The Bush administration's policy in Central Asia remains very much within the framework of the Clinton administration's policy of engagement and enlargement. When the Central Asian states became independent of Soviet rule in 1992, the United States focused on promoting political and economic stability among Kazakhstan, Kyrgyzstan, Tajikistan, Turkmenistan and Uzbekistan. The goals and objectives of American policy towards the region remained congruent with those of the grand strategy pursued by the Clinton administration: to institutionalise democracy and the free market economic system; to improve human rights and underwrite the rule of law; and to stop the proliferation of weapons of mass destruction, particularly nuclear weapons.[23] At the outset, the Clinton administration sought to foster regional cooperation, relying on multilateral initiatives such as NATO's PfP and the Central Asian Economic Community (CAEC).[24] The overall goal of the administration's policy was to create a favourable environment in which to achieve America's strategic goal of extending its influence in the region.

Arguably, an important secondary strategic goal of American policy was the facilitation of energy exploration in the region by American corporations. For the Bush administration, the search for new sources of energy was close to the top of the foreign policy agenda in the region, but that goal has been displaced by the war on terrorism, a war which poses a threat to national and regional security as well as any future effort to exploit a significant, alternative source of energy.[25] This fusion of America's geopolitical and geoeconomic objectives in the region has produced a constellation of policies that may persuade regional governments to favour American over European or Chinese corporations in the energy field.

The Uzbek–American relationship illustrates this fusion of the geopolitical and geoeconomic. At the outset, the United States was interested in fostering the emergence of Uzbekistan as a regional hegemon serving American interests. In the early 1990s, only Uzbekistan was viewed by the United States as a reliable partner, although some in the Clinton administration cautioned against choosing a 'preferred' customer in the region. Some analysts believed that the administration's policy was too ad hoc and insufficiently sensitive to Chinese and Russian interests in the region; others felt that the administration was too confused to promote and secure the nation's interests, not to mention the interests of corporate America.[26] Arguably, the United States did lack a concrete plan for achieving stability in the region. The administration was initially unable to engage the regional leadership by identifying or creating a common or coincidental set of interests that would facilitate cooperation. Instead, it provided generous amounts of financial support in exchange for their support of American policy preferences.[27] The Bush administration's war on terrorism has not provided the necessary policy coherence that would sustain cooperation over the long term, but instead has substituted a diffuse agenda with an agenda of one item – terrorism.

American diplomatic activity in Central Asia prior to September 2001 focused on creating an environment that would privilege American corporations in the exploitation of regional economic and financial opportunities. The main thrust of that policy was the building of firm political connections with the Central Asian regimes and governments.[28] Moreover, the United States relied on other regional actors to accomplish this end. As Edward Morse and James Richard observed, 'until September 11, the United States pursued two often conflicting goals: encouraging Russia to better protect US corporate investment in the Russian energy sector, and assisting the Caspian countries in developing and exporting their own hydrocarbons, thereby avoiding pipelines routes through Russia'.[29] Thus, the United States sought to engender political stability in the region – either by its own efforts or the efforts of others – to facilitate the exploration of Central Asian oil and natural gas fields. After September 11, however, energy interests were conjoined to the war against terrorism. This change in the definition of American security interests led the Bush administration to forge stronger bilateral political and military relationships with the regional states. The consequence of the administration's foreign policy shift was a significant change in the regional balance of power.

The Bush administration's response to the terrorist attack on the World Trade Center and the Pentagon has had the collateral effect of furthering its long-term objectives in Central Asia; viz., creating a political environment conducive to the exploration of the region by American energy firms and to a regional military and political order conducive to the furthering of American strategic interests *vis-à-vis* China. In the process, however, the United States could not escape the dilemma of protecting its strategic and political interests – responding to the terrorist threat and gaining privileged access to Caspian Sea oil – at the familiar cost of its rhetorical dedication to American values, democracy, freedom and liberty, the inescapable and persistent tension between ideals and self-interest identified by Robert Osgood over fifty years ago.[30] As in the past, the Bush administration opted to protect its interests at the expense of its professed ideals. As noted by Pauline Jones Luong and Erika Weinthal, the war against al-Qaeda and the Taliban required the United States to enlist Uzbekistan's authoritarian ruler, Islam Karimov, who has long been regarded as one of the region's most undemocratic and repressive leaders.[31] None the less, the United States succeeded in securing access to Uzbek air bases to station its troops, airplanes and helicopters and to make use of Uzbek territory to launch offensive strikes on Afghanistan. In exchange, Uzbekistan received $125 million in grants between September 2001 and January 2002.[32]

On the surface, the evolution of US policy in Central Asia could be seen as facilitating the exploration and development of new sources of oil and natural gas by American corporations. However, regional instability and volatility demands more than a diplomatic environment facilitating the signing of contracts. It requires, instead, a long-term American commitment to regional stability in order to reduce the financial risks attending the exploration and development of new energy sources. Thus, American policy has had to shift from the relatively painless task of facilitating contracts between American firms and regional governments to the more difficult and costly task of ensuring regional political stability.

Chinese policy in the region

Beijing's original goals and interests in Central Asia are still very much directed towards mitigating ethnic conflicts along its borders, the favourable resolution of outstanding border conflicts, and other non-military threats like drugs and ethnic unrest.[33] In recent times, however, the Chinese orientation has evolved along lines similar to those of the United States: China is increasingly concerned with the task of ensuring a secure supply of energy, and views Central Asian oil and natural gas reserves as central to that strategic necessity.[34] China is now actively involved in Central Asian energy exploration, which reflects China's long-standing fear of dependency on uncertain sources of foreign supply.[35]

As China's economy continues to grow, its demand for all sources of energy, notably oil and natural gas, will increase. Oil demand is projected to grow at an average annual rate of 3.8 percent during the period of 1996–2020, increasing consumption from 3.5 to 8.8 million barrels per day. In tandem with the rising demand for oil, China's domestic reserves and production have steadily declined. Conservative estimates of Chinese oil reserves indicate a reserves/production ratio of just 20 years. On the brighter side, the share of oil in China's primary energy consumption will remain at 20 percent, in part because of the Chinese government's effort to expand natural gas production and consumption.[36]

Natural gas demand is expected to grow at an average annual rate of 11.7 percent over the same period, increasing consumption from 0.7 to 9.5 trillion cubic feet. China's demand for natural gas is growing at a more rapid pace than that for other sources of energy, with the result that natural gas is expected to grow from 2 percent of China's energy consumption in 1996 to 11 percent in 2020. Rising natural gas consumption will be largely responsible for the projected decline in the use of coal from 73 percent to 65 percent of total energy consumption between 1996 and 2020, although demand for coal is still expected to grow at an average annual rate of 3.6 percent during this period.[37]

Besides the recent decline in China's domestic oil exploration and production, there are two other reasons why China has sought to develop both domestic and foreign natural gas reserves: to end chronic energy imbalances and shortages; and to stem rising petroleum imports.[38] China has been faced with sporadic, yet chronic, energy imbalances and shortages. The uncertain rate of future economic growth makes it very difficult to predict Chinese energy needs with any precision.[39] To reduce uncertainty, China made two strategic decisions in the 1990s regarding its future energy needs. First, as it became clear that the volume of crude oil imports was set to rise dramatically, China started to import ever-larger quantities of oil from the Middle East and to diversify its sources of supply.[40] Second, the government committed its state-owned enterprises in the oil business to undertaking substantial international investments related to the extraction of oil and gas resources, as well as to the improvement of transport networks.[41] In general, the overall purpose and intention behind these decisions were to ensure that China would have the energy supplies necessary to sustain its future economic growth.

China will play a more active role in Central Asian energy politics in the coming decade, which may well bring it into conflict with America's strategic goals in the region. China is already engaged in one energy exploration project in Iran and is refurbishing two refineries for oil swaps from the

Caspian region; China has committed substantial financial resources for oil exploration in Kazakhstan; Chinese service companies are active in Turkmenistan; and China hopes to increase oil and gas shipments from Turkmenistan via Iran. As important, China plans to commit capital to build long-distance pipelines running to and from the region. Moreover, the seriousness of the Chinese concern about its future energy security is underscored by China's long-term negotiations with the Iraqi government to secure rights to an oil field, despite the American animus towards Saddam Hussein's Iraq and the American-led and enforced embargo on that country.[42]

Perception and misperception in the Sino-American relationship

The United States and China would seem to share coincidental, if not common interests and goals in the region, particularly the need to create a favourable political and strategic environment facilitating the exploitation of Central Asian oil and natural gas reserves. However, the strategies and tactics employed to achieve this goal suggest that the two states are having a different dream in the same bed. While the United States has earnestly striven to improve its political profile as the means to secure its economic interests in the region, China is fearful that an American presence in the region will frustrate its own pursuit of not dissimilar objectives. Historically, China has been discomfited by the presence of a great power along its border and has sometimes responded militarily, the Chinese intervention in the Korean conflict providing the prime example. The heightened American profile in Central Asia and the indefinite basing of American troops in China's backyard suggests that the United States runs the risk of inflaming Chinese suspicions of American intentions and ambitions in the region.

There has been a progressive realignment of the American military presence in Asia during the past decade. The United States has very slowly, perhaps haphazardly, crept into the Chinese neighbourhood – from Singapore to Indonesia, from the United Arab Emirates to Oman, and now from Uzbekistan and Pakistan to Kazakhstan. This development reinforces the Chinese preoccupation with an American strategy of neo-containment in Asia.[43] How is China going to perceive and react to this untoward change in its external environment? Will the US military presence in the region have a negative or positive effect on China's effort to secure a new channel of supply from Central Asia? A similar question can also be raised with respect to the Indian Ocean and South China Sea lanes: how will American policy towards Southeast Asia affect Chinese strategic thinking and its future acquisition of foreign oil and natural gas? What are the consequences of a Sino-American dispute over issues of territorial sovereignty (i.e., the Taiwan question) or the direction of the pipelines from Central Asia?

China and the United States are wary of one another's interests and intentions in Central Asia, a legacy of their postwar relationship and different conceptions of international order. Real conflicts of interest, which are magnified by mutual misunderstandings and misperceptions, will inevitably complicate the task of developing, extracting and delivering oil and natural gas from the region. Two examples illustrate this mutual wariness. First, the United States perceived the 'Shanghai Five' and the subsequent SCO as a military alliance aimed against the United States and as a mechanism for isolating it in the region, if not excluding it from the region.[44] The Bush administration in particular regarded the SCO as a platform for joint Russo-Chinese denunciations of American policies and as the legal basis for enabling either Russia and/or China to project military force into the area. The administration also assumed, incorrectly, that the SCO would be manipulated to enhance Chinese leverage with Russia on the Taiwan question. The American preoccupation with a set of unfounded strategic assumptions about the purpose of the SCO and the *idée fixe* that China is a 'peer competitor' have distracted attention from the Chinese effort to defend its interests in Central Asia against separatism, terrorism and Islamic extremism – areas where the United States and China should be able to find common ground.[45] The fundamental logic informing the Bush administration's understanding of the SCO has reflected the deeply held assumption that China seeks regional hegemony and the diminution of the American presence in the western Pacific. The administration's pessimism about the destabilising role of the SCO – at least from the American perspective – has been reinforced by the inevitable competition for Central Asian oil and natural gas. Although the SCO cannot be viewed as an institution that is capable of excluding the United States from the region, it can be viewed as a regional effort to check American influence. None the less, the SCO is likely to have a limited impact on the American freedom of action for two reasons: first, the emerging framework of understanding in Europe between the United States and the Russian Federation is likely to spill over into Central Asia; and second, China cannot yet act alone against the United States without Russian support.[46]

Were one to persist in arguing that the SCO presents a serious challenge to the US role in Central Asia, it would be equally clear that the ongoing American military and political penetration of Central Asia presents a direct challenge to China. First, the American military action taken in Afghanistan has certainly shifted the regional balance of power in the American favour. The United States has concluded military cooperation agreements with Uzbekistan, Kyrgyzstan and Kazakhstan. Second, these agreements have laid a solid foundation for the United States to realise its long-sought objective of expanding its political influence in regional affairs. With a military presence legitimised by a set of bilateral agreements, the United States is now in a much better position to secure and promote its energy interests in the region. Third, the US military presence is indefinite and provides a source of considerable anxiety for China, which 'would prefer not to have the US next

door (again), as it did during the wars in Vietnam and Korea'.[47] The stationing of 1,000 American troops in Uzbekistan, a limited deployment by any
standard, has had important regional implications. Although those troops
were tasked to provide security for an airport central to the success of the
war against the Taliban and al-Qaeda in Afghanistan (as well as to the ancillary tasks of humanitarian aid and search-and-rescue missions), Uzbekistan
now provides the staging ground for military action against any regional
power threatening American objectives or allies. The United States is now
positioned to support the governments of Turkmenistan, Kazakhstan and
Uzbekistan as well as smaller Kyrgyzstan and even the Russian client-state
Tajikistan in exchange for the favourable treatment of American interests,
particularly the construction of energy pipelines and major infrastructure
projects in the region. This prerogative may enable the United States to
determine the direction, path and end point of the energy transport networks
in the region. Were the United States to wield this kind of influence, it would
seriously compromise the Chinese goal of securing its own channel of supply
from the region.[48]

Conclusion: different starting point, different end point?

The set of interests pushing China and the United States into Central Asia
were initially quite different. China's engagement reflected a desire to resolve
outstanding border disputes as well as ensure regional stability, which was
jeopardised by the disintegration of the Soviet Union. Beijing desired stability
and peace along the country's long border with the Central Asian states; it
also had an equally compelling interest in stopping the transfer of arms from
the radical Islamic states and terrorists in support of the Uigor minority independence movement in the Xinjiang autonomous region.[49] By contrast,
American policy objectives for the states of this region were not dissimilar
from those held for the Russian Federation during the early years of the
Yeltsin administration. The Clinton administration provided economic and
financial assistance in an attempt not only to resuscitate weak regimes in the
region, but to lay a strong foundation for the spread of democracy and the
free market economic system.

Starting from the mid-1990s, American and Chinese policy priorities
shifted towards devising foreign policies that would best develop and exploit
Central Asian energy reserves towards the goal of enhancing national
energy security. Neither state desires an increased dependence upon Middle
Eastern oil; neither wants future economic growth held hostage to supply
shortages – real or manufactured – or price rises. Despite a common interest
in regional stability and the exploitation of Central Asian oil reserves, China
and the United States have so far acted independently of one another.
Arguably, Sino-American cooperation would be one avenue for reducing the
high costs and risks attending the development of Central Asian oil and

natural gas fields. None the less, Sino-American cooperation remains limited by the two states' deep distrust of one another, which is aggravated by their ongoing strategic competition for Pacific and Asian dominance.

The United States has sought to maintain its dominant position in the Pacific. For Beijing, the cumulative impact of the Bush administration's policies in Asia has been an increased wariness of American intentions in the region. President Bush's state visits to India and Pakistan for the first time since the late 1970s were freighted with important military and strategic implications, at least for China. In the wake of September 11, the United States has succeeded in building military posts on the basis of official military cooperation agreements that have strengthened its strategic and military position in the South China Sea, the Malacca Strait and Central Asia.[50] American policy towards Russia in Europe has weakened the SCO as a bulwark against undue American influence in Asia; the stationing of a sizeable US military force in the region has also meant that there is now an opportunity for the weaker members of the SCO 'to escape from Russo-Chinese efforts to dominate them'.[51] China is specifically worried that the Central Asian states, in siding with the United States in the war against terrorism, have traded their penury relationship with Russia and China for a much more munificent dependence on the United States. Uzbekistan and Kazakhstan, in promising Washington access to military bases, over-flight rights and intelligence sharing, have purchased insurance against a Sino-Russian condominium. The Central Asian states are engaging in a balancing diplomacy in an effort to maximise their freedom of movement, not only from Russia and China – their proximate neighbours – but from the United States were it to become an overbearing protector. Unsurprisingly, Beijing views these trends and developments as inimical to its own long-term strategic interests in Asia.

Sino-American goodwill will probably remain shallow at best and Sino-American cooperation episodic and contingent on shared calculations of interest. In 2001 and the first half of 2002, for instance, China and the United States have seemed to be on good terms, with China winning the hosting rights to the 2008 summer Olympics and entering the WTO as a full member in the winter of 2001. These positive developments were disrupted by the US spy plane incident on the island of Hainan in April 2001. Moreover, despite Beijing's support of the American action against terrorism in Afghanistan, tensions re-emerged when the Bush administration invited Taiwan's minister of defence to visit Washington, DC, in March 2002. This chequered recent past, which is indicative of the deep mutual mistrust existing between these two important states, in combination with their not easily reconciled strategic ambitions, suggest that the exploitation and development of Central Asian energy is an unlikely basis for Sino-American cooperation. As important, the Central Asian states may face the unpalatable choice of choosing between Washington and Beijing.

Notes

1 Erica Strecker Downs, *China's Quest for Energy Security* (Santa Monica: Rand Corporation, 2000); Li Zhisheng, 'Zhongguo de Nengyuan Weiji' ('China's Energy Crisis'), in Li Ming (ed.), *Zhongguo de Weiji (Xia)* (*The Crisis of China II*) (Beijing: Gaige chubanshe, 1998), pp. 611–30; and Wang Qingyi, 'Zhongguo de Nengyuan Weiji' ('China's Energy Crisis'), in Li Ming *The Crisis of China II*, pp. 631–9.

2 Liu Hong Xuan (ed.), *Zhongguo Mulin Shi: Zhongguo yu Zhoubian Guanxi Shi* (*The History's of China Relations with its Neighbouring States*) (Beijing: Shijiezhishi chubanshe, 2002), p. 227; Zhongguo Xiandai Guoji Guanxi Yanjiusuo (China Contemporary International Relations Institute) (ed.), *Shanghai Hezuo Zuzhi: Xin Anquanguan yu Xin Jizhi* (*Shanghai Cooperation Organisation: New Security Perceptions and System*) (Beijing: Shishi chubanshe, 2002); Hsue Chuntu and Xing Guangcheng (eds), *Zhongguo yu Zhongya* (*China and Central Asia*) (Beijing: Shehuikexue chubanshe, 1999); Wang Zhiyi and Pan Zhiping, 'Lishi Huigu: Zhongya de Dongdang he Xinjiang de Wending' ('History Recollection: Turbulence in Central Asia and Stability of Xinjiang'), in Pan Zhiping (ed.), *Minzu Zijue, Haishi Minzu Fenlie: Minzu he Dangdai Minzu Fenlie Zhuyi* (*Ethnic Sovereignty or Ethnic Separatism*) (Urumuchi: Xinjiangrenmin chubanshe, 1999), pp. 228–80; and Xing Guancheng, 'China and Central Asia: Towards a New Relationship', in Zhang Yongjin and Rouben Azizian (eds), *Ethnic Challenges Beyond Borders: Chinese and Russian Perspectives on the Central Asian Conundrum* (New York: St Martin's Press, 1998), pp. 32–49.

3 Sherman W. Garnett, 'The United States and the Caspian Basin', in Sherman W. Garnett, Alexander Rahr and Koji Watanabe (eds), *The New Central Asia: In Search of Stability. A Report to the Trilateral Commission*, 54 (New York: Trilateral Commission, 2000), pp. 20–38.

4 The year 1994 is significant for two interrelated reasons. First, Chinese Premier Li Peng and government representatives made their first visits to the regional states. Second, the United States, by inviting the Central Asian states into NATO's PfP program, took a first step towards enhancing its political influence in the region. See Liu (ed.), *China's Neighbour History*, pp. 216, 222, 224.

5 In this context, Niklas Swanstro and Svante E. Cornell note that the inclusion of Uzbekistan in the SCO in 1999 was a success for Chinese and Russian foreign policy. See Niklas Swanstro and Svante E. Cornell, 'China's Trepidation in Afghanistan', *Central Asia Caucasus Analysts* (Washington, DC: Central Asian Caucasus Institute, Johns Hopkins University, 10 October 2001), p. 5.

6 David M. Lampton, 'Small Mercies: China and America after 9/11', *National Interest*, 66 (2001/02), pp. 106–13.

7 Estimates show that Central Asia, including Azerbaijan, has oil and natural gas reserves which could make the region the world's second most important source of energy exports by 2020. See Anthony H. Cordesman, *The US Government View of Energy Developments in the Caspian, Central Asia, and Iran* (Washington, DC: Center for Strategic and International Studies, 2000).

8 Edward L. Morse and James Richard, 'The Battle of Energy Dominance', *Foreign Affairs*, 81:2 (2002), pp. 16–31, esp. p. 23.

9 The high cost and low return of exploiting oil reserves in the near and mid-term is discussed in Downs, *China's Quest*, pp. 20–40; Zhang Wenmu, *Zhongguo Xin*

Shiji Anquan Zhanlue (*China's Security Strategy in the New Century*) (Jinan: Shandongremin chubanshe, 2000), p. 179; and Morse and Richard, 'Battle of Energy Dominance', p. 25.

10 Uzbekistan was an attractive diplomatic partner for the United States, because it was the nation with the strongest pro-American sentiment in the region, it possessed a significant military force and infrastructure, and it was not a member of the 'Shanghai Five'. The Uzbek–American relationship could be seen as an effort to thwart the development of a Sino-Russian coalition in central Asia. See Robert M. Cutler, 'Cozying up to Karimov?', *A Global Affairs Commentary*, Foreign Policy in Focus, 4 October 2001.

11 See Robert M. Cutler, 'U.S. Intervention in Afghanistan: Implications for Central Asia', *A Global Affairs Commentary* Foreign Policy in Focus, 21 November, 2001; 'China Schemes to Win Support Against the US', *Financial Times* (13 June 2001).

12 Mark Burles, *Chinese Policy Toward Russia and the Central Asian Republics* (Santa Monica: Rand Corporation, 1999).

13 Pauline Jones Luong and Erika Weinthal, 'New Friends, New Fears in Central Asia', *Foreign Affairs*, 81:2 (2002), pp. 61–70.

14 Robert M. Cutler, 'The Key West Conference on Nagorno-Karabakh: Preparing Peace in the South Caucasus?', *A Global Affairs Commentary*, Foreign Policy in Focus, 4 October 2001; and Fiona Hill, 'The Caucasus and Central Asia', *Policy Brief No. 80* (Washington, DC: Brookings Institution, May 2001), p. 1.

15 See Cutler, 'U.S. Intervention'; and Thomas J. Christensen, 'Posing Problems without Catching Up: China's Rise and Challenges for U.S. Security Policy', *International Security*, 25:4 (2001), pp. 5–40.

16 For the United States, see Department of Energy, *New Energy Policy Report* (Washington, DC: GPO, May 2001); National Energy Policy Development Group, *National Energy Policy: Reliable, Affordable, and Environmentally Sound Energy for America's Future* (Washington, DC: GPO, May 2001); and National Energy Policy Development Group, 'Strategic Energy Policy: Challenges for the 21st Century', *Baker Institute Study No. 15* (April 2001). For China, see Li Peng, 'Xin Nengyuan Zhengce' ('New Energy Policy'), *Renmin Ribao* (*People's Daily*), 28 May 2002; Zhou Fengqi, *Prospect of Petroleum and Natural Gas Supply and Demand in China and in the World by 2010 and by 2020* (Beijing: Energy Resources Institute, State Development Planning Commission, November 1998); and Ni Weidong, Li Zheng and Xue Yuan, 'National Energy Futures Analysis and Energy Security Perspective in China', and Shi Zulin and Xu Yugao, 'The Impact of China's Accession to the World Trade Organization on China's Energy Sector', papers presented at Strategic Thinking on the Energy Issue in the 10th Five-Year Plan (FYP) Workshop on East Asia Energy Futures, Beijing, June 2000.

17 See Fiona Hill and Regine Spector, 'The Caspian Basin and Asian Energy Markets', *Conference Report No. 8* (Washington, DC: Brookings Institution, September 2001), p. 1.

18 *Ibid.*

19 Downs, *China's Quest*, p. xi.

20 Hill and Spector, 'Caspian Basin'; Sergei Troush, 'China's Changing Oil Strategy and its Foreign Policy Implications', *CNAP Working Paper* (Washington, DC: Brookings Institution, 1999); Burles, *Chinese Policy*; Zhang,

China's Security Strategy, pp. 173–5; China Contemporary International Relations Institute, 'Nengyuan Anquan Shingshi' ('Energy Security Situation'), in *Strategic and Security Review 2001/2002* (Beijing: Shishi chubanshe, 2002), pp. 129–54.

21 Department of Energy, *New Energy Policy Report*.

22 See National Energy Policy Development Group, *National Energy Policy*.

23 See Garnett, 'United States and the Caspian Basin', pp. 23–31; and Stephen Blank, 'The United States and Central Asia', in Roy Allison and Lena Jonson (eds), *Central Asian Security: The New International Context* (Washington, DC: Brookings Institution, 2001), pp. 127, 146.

24 Luong and Weinthal, 'New Friends, New Fears', p. 61.

25 See National Energy Policy Development Group, *National Energy Policy*; Denise A. Bode, 'Energy Shortage in Energy-Rich America: Why?', *Heritage Lectures* (Washington, DC: Heritage Foundation, 16 November 2000); Charli Coon and James Phillips, 'Strengthening National Energy Security by Reducing Dependence on Imported Oil', *Backgrounder* (Washington, DC: Heritage Foundation, 24 April 2001).

26 See, Blank, 'United States and Central Asia', p. 143; Cutler, 'U.S. Intervention in Afghanistan'; and Luong and Weinthal, 'New Friends, New Fears', p. 61. According to critics of the Clinton administration's policies in the region, American policy interests amounted to a laundry list of likes and dislikes that shifted in response to crises and lacked a stable set of policy preferences. Instead, issues 'such as oil and gas pipelines, conflict resolution, and human rights were targeted at different junctures, but an overall strategy – which was essential given limited government resources for the regions – was never fully anticipated. As a result, American priorities were not communicated clearly to local leaders, resulting in frequent misinterpretations of intentions.' See Hill and Spector, 'Caspian Basin', p. 2.

27 The American government has provided transition and humanitarian aid and loans to Kazakhstan ($311 million in 1994); to Kyrgyzstan ($250 million in 1995); and to Uzbekistan ($500 million in 1995). From 1997 to 2000, aid increased by 61%, from $620 million to $1 billion. Furthermore, from 1997 to 2000, further financial assistance of approximately $1 million was made when joint military exercise or training was held. In April of 2000 when the then secretary of state, Madeline Albright, toured three Central Asian states – Kazakhstan, Kyrgyzstan and Uzbekistan – an additional pledge of $3 million was made to each state for anti-terrorism purposes. See Zheng Yu (ed.), *Dulianti Shinian: Xianzhuang, Wenti, Qianjing 1991–2001* (*The Ten Years of the CIS: Present Situation, Problems and Prospects 1991–2001*) (Beijing: Shijie chubanshe, 2002), pp. 282–6.

28 For detailed analysis on functional relations between the US military/political interests and business interests, see Anatol Lieven, 'The (Not So) Great Game', *National Interest*, 58 (1999–2000), pp. 69–81.

29 Morse and Richard, 'Battle of Energy Dominance', p. 26.

30 Robert Endicott Osgood, *Ideals and Self-Interest in American Foreign Policy* (Chicago: University of Chicago Press, 1952).

31 Luong and Weinthal, 'New Friends, New Fears', p. 62.

32 *Ibid.*

33 For an assessment of China's traditional national interests in the Central Asian region, see Hsue and Xing, *China and Central Asia*; Xing Guangcheng, 'China and Central Asia', in Allison and Johnson, *Central Asian Security*, pp. 152–70; Zhang and Azizian, *Ethnic Challenges Beyond Borders*; and Wang and Pan, 'History Recollection'.

34 Philip Andrews-Speed and Sergei Vinogradov, 'China's Involvement in Central Asian Petroleum: Convergent or Divergent Interests?', *Asian Survey*, 40:2 (2000), pp. 377–97, esp. pp. 390–3.

35 Downs, *China's Quest*, p. xi.

36 On the prospect of an energy shortfall in China, see Ni *et al.*, 'National Energy Futures'; International Energy Agency, *World Energy Outlook* (Vienna: IEA, 1999); and Department of Energy, *International Energy Outlook, 1999* (Washington, DC: GPO, 1999), pp. 141, 145.

37 Department of Energy, *International Energy Outlook, 1999*, pp. 141, 146–7.

38 Hill and Spector, 'Caspian Basin', p. 5.

39 Andrews-Speed and Vinogradov, 'China's Involvement', pp. 386–7.

40 Frank C. Tang and Fereidun Fesharaki, 'China: Evolving Oil Trade Patterns and Prospects to 2000', *Natural Resources Forum*, 19:1 (1995), pp. 47–58; Li, 'New Energy Policy'; and Zhang, *China's Security Strategy*, pp. 175–9.

41 In the late 1990s, for instance, the Chinese National Petroleum Corporation committed about $800 million on two field development projects in Kazakhstan, at Aktyubinsk and Uzen, that have total oil reserves of about 2.5 billion barrels. See Burles, *Chinese Policy*, pp. 23–5; and Andrews-Speed and Vinogradov, 'China's Involvement', p. 389.

42 Hill and Spector, 'Caspian Basin', p. 7; and Andrews-Speed and Vinogradov, 'China's Involvement', p. 377.

43 China Contemporary International Relations Institute, *Strategic and Security Review: 2001/2002*, pp. 61–79; and Zhang, *China's Security Strategy*, pp. 166–72.

44 Bates Gill, 'Shanghai Five: An Attempt to Counter US Influence in Asia?', *Newsweek Korea* (May 2001).

45 It is difficult to understand how anyone could view the SCO as potential legal cover for a joint Sino-Russian military action against Taiwan. See Stephen Blank, 'Towards Geostrategic Realignment in Central Asia', *Central Asia-Caucasus Analysts* (Washington, DC: Central Asia-Caucasus Institute, Johns Hopkins University, 10 October, 2001), p. 7.

46 Swanstro and Cornell, 'China's Trepidation'; and Lena Johnson and Roy Allison, 'Central Asian Security: Internal and External Dynamics', in Allison and Johnson *Central Asian Security*, p. 19.

47 Swanstro and Cornell, 'China's Trepidation'.

48 Robert M. Cutler, 'Central Asian Energy and Security in Light of the Afghanistan Crisis', *Central Asia-Caucasus Analysts* (Washington, DC: Central Asia-Caucasus Institute, Johns Hopkins University, 10 October 2001), p. 9; and Blank, 'Towards a Geostrategic Realignment', p. 7.

49 Andrews-Speed and Vinogradov, 'China's Involvement', p. 380.

50 The reintroduction of American forces into the Philippines to fight terrorist cells linked to al-Qaeda has led some to call for the restationing of American troops on a permanent basis. See Paolo Pasicolan, 'Strengthening the U.S.–Philippine

Alliance for Fighting Terrorism', *Executive Memorandum* (Washington, DC: Heritage Foundation, 13 May 2002).

51 Blank, 'Towards Geostrategic Realignment in Central Asia', p. 7.

III

Institutions of
security governance

7

Geopolitical constraints and institutional innovation: the dynamics of multilateralism in Eurasia[1]

Sean Kay

This chapter assesses the relationship between traditional state-based security concerns and the development of multilateral institutions in Eurasia from 1992 to 2002. Multilateral institutions matter in Eurasia, but multilateral cooperation is highly contingent upon power relationships. Large states have used multilateral institutions to exert power and small states have used them to constrain larger ones. States have also used these institutions to signal their intentions and to reinforce their domestic identity. None the less, international institutions in Eurasia have neither mitigated the security dilemma nor facilitated cooperative approaches to the new security challenges of transnational terrorism, ethnic strife, environmental degradation, food and energy scarcity, drug trafficking, unchecked population growth, rampant migration and organised crime.[2] Eurasia hosts several variations in institutional forms, including the CIS, GUUAM, and the SCO. Yet these three principal regional institutions have largely failed to cultivate cooperative multilateralism. Can they do so singularly or in combination in the future?

Multilateral form and the security dilemma

The basic conditions underlying western models of multilateral institutional cooperation do not exist in Eurasia.[3] In the transatlantic context, the major institutions reflected a benign American hegemony and acquiescent western European states. NATO, for example, survives because its combination of American power and institutional attributes enhanced cooperation between its members over time. NATO has promoted transparency and information sharing, facilitated issue linkages, fostered the norm of multilateralism, and helped lower the transaction costs of collective action among its member-states. This transatlantic institutional configuration of power and cooperation has not taken hold in Eurasia, where Russia retains a degree of postcolonial hegemonic influence through the CIS. Nevertheless, smaller former Soviet republics have sought to exert their independence through multilateral balancing of Russian influence and by signalling their national identity preferences through the GUUAM group. Meanwhile, the growth of American military engagement in Eurasia has the potential to transform another multilateral institution – the SCO – into a mechanism for a renewed Sino-Russian alliance.

Despite potential fissures arising from great power competition in the region, the states of Eurasia share some important interests in multilateral cooperation. Russia and China, as well as key medium-sized states such as Kazakhstan and Uzbekistan, are status-quo oriented and seek to ensure that no single power can dominate. Moreover, the states of Eurasia and interested external powers such as the United States all view radical political Islam and international terrorism as common threats and share interest in the quest for international order. Eurasia is not a region where interstate war is likely.[4] And yet, traditional security concerns dominate the dynamics of multilateralism. The inability of the Eurasian states to develop western-style institutions or to embrace cooperative multilateralism effectively is not the result of intrinsically opposed political cultures or a new political divide reflecting a 'clash of civilisations'.[5] The key variable affecting the dynamic and form of multilateralism in Eurasia is divergent state interests.

The security dilemma

Security dilemmas stem from the assumption that the international system is based on self-help and comprised of states with an egoist definition of interest. In the absence of a global leviathan, international relations are inevitably anarchic. States will eventually position themselves in an offensive or defensive posture depending on their perceived security needs. States operating under such threat perceptions confront a situation where a country's efforts to increase its own security (even if for defensive purposes) can be perceived by other states as an offensive threat.[6] Consequently, states will make adjustments in their defensive or offensive position – through self-help or via alliances – to ensure survival. Such a security dilemma can produce arms races or preventive war if a balance of power is not attained or breaks down. States therefore must worry about both the absolute and relative gains of their competitors.[7] That is, states must worry about their overall international position relative to the power of other states.[8]

States have a variety of multilateral options to pursue in response to a threat.[9] States might balance the existing threat by increasing their capabilities or forming alliances with like-minded countries sharing the same threat perception.[10] Alternatively, states might align with a dominant power by bandwagoning towards it to reap distributive gains.[11] Balancing or bandwagoning through multilateral alliances represent one variation in institutional form of multilateralism. Each approach can result in peace if a functional balance of power is achieved. Among a coalition of states, the dominant power can exert the greatest degree of influence and, in the process of exercising institutional hegemony, may also contribute to peaceful relations among alliance members. From hegemony, effective multilateral cooperation can emerge and be applied to issue areas separate from that for which the institution was originally intended.[12]

Confronted with a relative decline in power, large states often seek to maintain influence by making concessions to prevent defection and balancing by previous allies. Smaller powers may seek to sustain multilateral institutions, but also to adapt them to gain more influence. Moreover, great powers are positioned to lead coalitions with smaller states – which make residual institutions useful in lowering transaction costs. Institutional forms reflecting hegemonic influence can alleviate the security dilemma, because smaller states receive security reassurance against each other as the dominant power provides a public good of general security.[13] Nevertheless, as hegemonic influence declines, states will not necessarily bandwagon towards the declining power and rather might pursue balancing strategies. At this stage new forms of multilateralism can emerge with new institutions replacing old ones, or old ones being transformed. Alternatively, conflict and instability can emerge as institutions become unable to moderate the security dilemma given changed geopolitical realities.

International institutions and security

International institutions are persistent and connected sets of rules that prescribe behaviour roles, constrain activity, and shape expectations through informal regimes and formal organisations.[14] As a possible means of modifying the security dilemma, international institutions have become a dominant part of international politics. Though institutions remain dependent upon the will and interests of member states, they are increasingly seen as enhancing security and facilitating crisis management. Institutions are used by states to maximise their individual or mutual security interests because they are presumed to make cooperation easier to attain than in their absence. By encouraging reciprocity, international institutions help states manage the uncertainties of international anarchy better. Multilateral cooperation, conducted over time, might become an international norm if states were socialised into new patterns of cooperative behavior. Consequently, security could be enhanced because states would perceive gains from learning about each other. By enhancing transparency among states, the security dilemma might be reduced, as states can better signal their intentions and reduce the risk that misperception or miscalculation will lead to tension or conflict.[15]

Institutions are thought to impact on interstate relations positively because the shadow of the future and the uncertainty of anarchy in the international system allow for an environment in which international insti-tutions embody and affect state expectations.[16] Institutions play a variety of roles including aiding the exercise of influence, constraining bargaining strategies, balancing or replacing other institutions, signalling govern-ments' intentions, specifying obligations, and shaping or defining the inter-ests and preferences of states.[17] Institutions are seen as relevant to security because they increase the level of information available to states by enhanc-ing transparency, raising the costs of defection and defining what constitutes defection, increasing the likelihood of issue linkage, and advancing inter-state socialisation towards the concept of an international community.[18]

Unlike multilateral forms of hegemonic stability and alliance formation, some institutional approaches to security offer positive inducements to multilateral cooperation. For example, concert diplomacy is an institutional form emphasising state interest in maintaining great power equilibrium. A concert is a self-regulating means of systems management. If the principal regional powers have a common interest in maintaining a systemic status quo, they may avoid steps to revise it. Conversely, if concert powers see a state making efforts to overturn the status quo, then those states will form a common alliance to challenge the defector and ensure that it does not succeed. Concerts are generally organised around informal structures with powerful states cooperating to resolve crises. If each major regional power shares in the benefits of an existing international order, a concert system will function. However, if any one actor successfully dominates and balancing fails, then the system will be transformed. Historically, war is the most common byproduct of a failed consensus on international order by the great powers.[19] The historical track record of concert diplomacy is strong when the conditions are favourable. The Concert of Europe lasted, at various levels of strength, well into the nineteenth century.[20] This institutional form was replicated in the arrangements providing for the permanent members of the UN Security Council and is evident in the Contact Group/Group of Eight diplomacy used to settle the 1990s Balkan conflicts.

A contemporary institutional form, cooperative security, has emerged in the post-Cold War era, building on a more inclusive approach to systems management than concert diplomacy, while also being more realistic than the legalistic, hierarchical arrangements of the failed League of Nations. Cooperative security provides for less automatic but prospectively more successful approaches to organising states to act on mutual security concerns. Cooperative security implies that no state acting alone can solve all regional security problems and thus respectful multilateral solutions are necessary. Cooperative security is intended to be inclusive and to promote consultation over confrontation, reassurance over balancing, and informa-tion sharing, transparency and burden sharing among security partners.[21] Cooperative security promotes both dialogue and socialisation into shared norms as a crisis-prevention mechanism via confidence- and security-building measures. Cooperative security is also a model for forming ad hoc military coalitions for crisis management by lowering the transaction costs of multilateral cooperation. Thus intervention in a crisis is thought to be easier to attain under coalitions of the willing facilitated through the institutional mechanisms of cooperative security.[22]

In Eurasia, the security dilemma drives the nature of state choices for international cooperation. Eurasia is also, however, a region where the status quo has not been changed by deep military alignments or security cooperation. The variations in institutional form illustrate that states are primarily signalling their security concerns via institutional membership choices. While such security cooperation is not deeply ingrained, it could become so in the future. Thus the dynamics of multilateralism in Eurasia do provide a framework for understanding the general geopolitical trends in the region. Consequently, as the following discussion shows, the institutional forms that reflect hegemonic stability, regional balancing and global balancing are key to understanding the geopolitical trend-lines of Eurasia. As this chapter illustrates, many of the core components are in place for a general regional concert system in Eurasia. Whether that concert system can successfully be translated into a new cooperative security arrangement is a critical policy and theoretical question confronting Eurasian security.

Geopolitics and the institutions of Eurasia

Much strategic analysis of Eurasian geopolitics focuses on access to oil and related transportation routes. Many strategists thus predict increased competition over natural resources in a new 'great game', as historically practised between Great Britain and Russia in the nineteenth century.[23] This historical analogy gained currency with the 2001 war in Afghanistan and the resulting extension of American access to military bases in Uzbekistan, Tajikistan, Kazakstan and Kyrgyzstan. Nevertheless, the 'great game' assessment of Eurasian power competition is oversimplified. In the words of one regional expert: 'The misplaced belief among US, Russian and other analysts in the central importance of geopolitical rivalry represents a cumulative failure of imagination'.[24] In reality the priority concern of the Eurasian states is status-quo maintenance. This quest has led to a combination of divergent threat perception and shared interests on specific issues such as counter-terrorism.

The Eurasian geopolitical spectrum reflects three major trends: Russian efforts to sustain hegemonic influence, met by the actions taken by some former states to balance Russian influence and assert their sovereignty; American efforts to project power and promote regional stability, generating nascent cooperation between Russia and China to balance American engagement; and a shared interest among all regional actors in diffusing the encroachment of radical political Islam and associated terrorism. The confluence of these geopolitical trends reflects the persistence of the security dilemma, which forms an intractable barrier to the duration and effectiveness of multilateralism. These geopolitical trends make Eurasia not especially receptive to multilateral institutions addressing the 'new security agenda', which raises the prospects that instability will grow and in turn impact on the existing strategic concerns of states. These trends are illustrated by the three most prominent multilateral security institutions of early twenty-first-century Eurasia: the CIS, GUUAM, and the SCO.

The CIS and hegemonic stability

The CIS is a manifestation of some structural aspects of the Soviet Union. Established through the Minsk Treaty of 1991, the CIS emerged as a loose confederation of 12 countries seeking to harmonise various economic and, to a much lesser extent, security policies after the collapse of the Soviet state. In 1993, Russia completed a military doctrine that defined the frontiers of the former Soviet Union as the strategic frontiers of Russia. In 1995, a presidential statement identified Moscow's goals in the CIS as making the region an exclusive area of Russian influence, minimising the expansion of external presence and influence in CIS territory, facilitating regional crisis management, and protecting Russians living outside Russia within the CIS.[25] For non-Russian members, support for the CIS has varied from the enthusiastic responses of Belarus to the antagonistic compliance of Ukraine. In the absence of significant western assistance, states like Ukraine, with their continued economic dependence on Russia, have little choice but to bandwagon reluctantly towards Moscow.

Russia's residual hegemony in the CIS is primarily economic and is exercised through pre-existing, Soviet-era personnel networks and bilateral linkage strategies. Power is increasingly exerted through fuel and energy, which Moscow can turn on and shut off to those states still depending on the Soviet-era pipeline system. For example, to pressure Georgia into allowing a continued presence of Russian military bases on its territory, Moscow has shut off the flow of natural gas. When Georgia refused to allow Russia to enter the Pankisi Gorge area on the border with Chechnya, Moscow retaliated by introducing visas for Georgian citizens and by halting gas supplies until past debts were repaid. Russia has also used the flow of energy supplies as a means of pressuring Ukraine and Moldova to make payments on debts owed to Moscow.[26]

Russia has sought to develop within the CIS a customs union, economic integration, converging standards of international economic legislation, a payments union, integration of production in science and technology (and the defence industry), common legal conditions and a common capital market.[27] Moscow has also sought to destabilise CIS countries not cooperating with Russia through intelligence activities, blackmail, coercion, subversion of problematic political leadership, and support to violent groups amenable to Russian influence.[28] Russia's overall military influence is receding. Russia maintains 8,000 forces in Tajikistan (in high combat readiness status), 2,900 troops in Armenia, 4,000 in Georgia and 1,500 in Moldova.[29] With a base in Tajikistan, Moscow has organised joint exercises with Central Asian armies and seeks to supply arms and equipment to Kazakhstan, Kyrgyzstan and Tajikistan, which Russia sees as important allies.[30] However, Russia has declining capacity to project military power within the CIS. Russia hopes to develop a 50,000-member rapid deployment corps at the Russia–Kazakhstan border, but whether it can fund and sustain full readiness is doubtful. Airlift capabilities are severely limited and what remains of Russia's air capacity is largely medium-range bombers and operational-tactical missiles – most of which are of little value in a fight against terrorism, the major security threat.[31] In a worst case, Russia might, given its conventional military weakness, have to rely on tactical nuclear weapons to deter attacks on forward-deployed forces.

Other aspects of Russian influence within the CIS area are in steady decline. Between 2025 and 2035 the last generation socialised during the Soviet era will retire and leave leadership positions. Russian is no longer a priority language in non-Russian Eurasian countries, though it remains a primary language of business and government.[32] Moreover, the Russian public had little appetite for shedding blood and treasure to keep Russia intact in Chechnya – let alone to sustain the CIS. Russia has thus used economic leverage to exercise its residual hegemonic influence. While Russia's economic pressure has some effect, CIS states increasingly define their relationship with Moscow on their own in the absence of the credible threat of military force. This trend is especially true as trade and other forms of international contact have diversified among the non-Russian CIS states, to include alternative transport corridors for oil and natural gas. Russia's ability to exert its regional influence is complicated by the hegemonic design of the CIS, which does not foster trust among its member-states, in combination with a variety of competing national agendas among the smaller members. The more Russia leverages its residual hegemony in the region, the lower the prospects for cooperative multilateral relationships through the CIS. Indeed, Azerbaijan, Georgia and Uzbekistan opted in 1999 to withdraw from formal CIS security cooperation, while Azerbaijan, Uzbekistan and Turkmenistan have refused to participate in CIS political and economic structures.

While Russian influence is declining, a number of post-Soviet states have bandwagoned towards Russia, and thus the CIS persists. The trade-off for Russian influence is the provision of some degree of stability – especially for states like Tajikistan, which have post-Communist leaders drawing from their Soviet background to facilitate distributive gains and enhance their domestic authority (in the absence of democratic legitimacy). Even non-CIS state (and NATO member) Turkey has made some important moves towards Russia to enhance its own relative economic-security needs. In June 2001, Turkey completed a deal to build the Blue Stream natural gas pipeline with Russia, which would increase its dependence on Russian natural gas from 66 to 80 per cent (Turkey imports some 98 per cent of its energy needs). This deal was completed over strong American opposition.[33] For Russia, the result has been sustained regional involvement which satisfies Moscow's basic interests in maintaining influence on its periphery. However, Russians may increasingly question these gains as they see core CIS partners as resource burdens diminishing Moscow's international prestige. Of particular concern has been the degree to which Russia has discounted energy prices to CIS members in order to promote the objectives of integration.[34] Since becoming president, Vladimir Putin has increasingly prioritised Russia's bilateral relations with CIS members over multilateral action.

To make Russia's regional hegemonic goals more palatable within the CIS, Moscow presents its efforts to foster hegemonic stability as a cooperative effort. In 1992, Russia negotiated a 'Collective Security Treaty' with most of the CIS members. As security developments under this framework largely reflected all institution and no cooperation, little effective action was taken to develop the CIS at the multilateral level of security cooperation. By 1999 some multilateral programmes did emerge, with the development of a CIS Joint Air Defence System headquartered in Moscow and headed by the Russian Air Defence Forces command. Participants in the air defence system include Russia, Belarus, Azerbaijan, Armenia, Kazakhstan, Kyrgyzstan, Tajikistan and Uzbekistan (which has kept its participation limited to what it describes as 'coordinated' rather than 'joint' operations). CIS security functions received additional competencies in October 2000 when an agreement was signed in Biskek to create a joint rapid reaction force, consisting of troops from Russia, Kazakhstan, Kyrgyzstan and Tajikistan, to respond to regional crises and to fortify porous border areas against terrorist attacks and incursions.

In March 2001, the CIS Collective Security Council secretary, Valery Nikolaenki, visited Kazakhstan, Kyrgyzstan and Tajikistan to discuss military integration of rapid reaction forces, to include headquarters planning as 'the first step in setting up collective rapid deployment forces' under the Collective Security Treaty.[35] For Russia the purpose of such an organisation would be to facilitate the transfer of military equipment and technology within the CIS to limit the influence of other purveyors of military equipment, particularly the United States, and to organise responses to radical political Islam and associated terrorism. On 25 May 2001, the participating countries – now including Armenia and Belarus – completed plans for a CIS rapid deployment force. Each participant contributes at least one battalion to this force. The force includes a 3,000-strong contingent for Central Asia including battalions from Kazakhstan, Kyrgyzstan and Tajikistan, and includes elements of the remaining Russian 201st division deployed for peacekeeping purposes in Tajikistan. A separate arrangement includes Russian and Armenian forces totalling 1,500 for crisis management in the Caucasus.

The mandate of the CIS rapid deployment force was put in geostrategic terms, declaring that: 'We, the leaders of the states participating in the Collective Security Treaty, state our strong resolution to promote the formation of a multipolar, fair, and democratic world order based on respect for the United Nations Charter and the norms of international law'.[36] For Russia, the CIS was also a means of signalling its security interests to the United States and its worries over the projection of American power. The culminating effect of CIS security developments has been to allow Moscow to extend a defence perimeter away from its borders via air defence, border guards, and the possible development of small-scale rapid deployment forces. This outcome runs contrary to many assumptions of the mid-1990s that the CIS would be strengthened, perhaps as a counter-weight to balance NATO enlargement. Rather, the CIS has become a progressively weaker security institution.

GUUAM: regional balancing

Efforts by some Eurasian states to minimise the effects of lingering Russian hegemony have produced mixed results. Most former Soviet states are torn between their desire to enhance their sovereignty *vis-à-vis* Russian influence and the reality that Moscow dominates their economies. The most significant attempt at regional balancing against Russia's residual hegemony is the GUUAM grouping of Georgia, Ukraine, Uzbekistan, Azerbaijan and Moldova.[37] The GUUAM states officially describe this institution as a 'strategic alliance designed to strengthen the independence and sovereignty of these former Soviet republics'.[38] At the same time, the members of GUUAM assert that their institution is organised against no particular state. Rather, GUUAM members stress it is a cooperative means to address a range of issues via: political cooperation; joint efforts on energy production (including a Transcaucasian energy supply route); mutual support for sovereignty and territorial integrity; opposition to ethnic and religious intolerance; combating illegal drugs; and working closely with NATO, the OSCE and the UN. Conceptually, the GUUAM members identify economic security, energy security, environmental security and territorial security as their main concerns. None the less, it is highly significant that GUUAM is the only security institution in the former Soviet space not including Russia.

Western officials generally view GUUAM as an anti-Russian balancing effort. This perspective was shared in Moscow, which watched cooperation in GUUAM accelerate during the Kosovo war in side-meetings held during NATO's fiftieth anniversary summit in Washington, DC. Russian foreign minister Igor Ivanov noted:

> How should we understand the fact that the new regional organisation GUUAM has been created in Washington during a NATO summit? What aims are pursued by demonstratively creating this organisation at the time of the latest events in the Balkans? This is a reflection of the policy of the leaders of the states who make such steps rather than a mere coincidence.[39]

GUUAM began informal consultations and produced joint declarations beginning at the Conventional Forces in Europe review conference held in 1996, and formalised their status as a cooperative structure at the 1997 Summit of the Council of Europe meeting in Strasbourg.[40] The principal organising elements of GUUAM include promotion of: political interaction, combating separatism, peaceful resolution of conflicts, peacekeeping activities, and development of a Eurasian-Transcaucasian transport corridor. Strategically, GUUAM members signalled their intent to hedge against Russian power through their integration into Euro-Atlantic and European structures of security and cooperation, including 'the development of a special relationship and dialogue with NATO'.[41] By combining elements of cooperative security and balancing simultaneously, these countries have signalled a general desire to pursue a political and economic path divergent from Russia's vision while seeking to constrain Russia's influence. As the Georgian ambassador to the United States, Tedo Japaridze, declared in November 2000, 'GUUAM's birth mother is the CFE [Conventional Forces in Europe] negotiations, and our foster mother is NATO'.[42]

The level of members' interest in GUUAM varies. Both Moldova and Uzbekistan engage inconsistently. Uzbekistan, Ukraine and Moldova moved closer (to varying degrees) in their alignments towards Russia in 2001–02, although those alignments face the countervailing pulls of a heightened economic reliance on Moscow and the general desire to signal a non-Russian security policy orientation. By June 2002, Uzbekistan effectively suspended its membership in GUUAM and Ukraine announced its desire to be considered a formal candidate for NATO membership, even while at the same time its economic fortunes grew more deeply embedded with those of Russia. Moreover, the GUUAM architecture remains informal, with high-level ministerial meetings occurring, but with little effort to create institutional mechanisms to coordinate multilateral action on declared objectives. Nevertheless, GUUAM made modest steps towards institutionalisation by creating a secretariat in 2001 and exploring the establishment of a parliamentary assembly. At a June 2001 summit, the GUUAM members signed the Charter of GUUAM, which codified it as an international organisation. Yet GUUAM's significance is symbolic in that these states pursue, to the extent feasible, a policy separate from that of Russia, or seek a balance between a western and a Russian orientation.

Concerns over residual Russian hegemony are a driving force behind

GUUAM. However, the organisation is a reflection of only nascent multilateral balancing efforts. GUUAM members have avoided deep security cooperation within this framework, as they generally prioritise their individual relationships with NATO's PfP.[43] The leaders of GUUAM stress that the success or failure of their institution lies in the degree to which it gains assistance from the United States. The United States has trodden carefully so as not to over promote GUUAM as the sole western alternative for Southeast and Central Eurasian states, while simultaneously encouraging the development of cooperative security programmes. US assistance included (for the fiscal year 2001): $5 million in foreign military financing grants, $2 million in non-proliferation and export control assistance, $500,000 in international military equipment and training funding, and $1 million in anti-terrorism assistance.[44] Some members of GUUAM are ambivalent about giving the institution true balancing power. Ukraine, for example, still exists under significant Russian economic influence.[45] President Leonid Kuchma insisted that GUUAM members not turn the organisation into a military-political structure.[46] Ukraine and Uzbekistan are increasingly deviating politically from some of the declared normative goals of the institution, while at the same time moving closer to Moscow out of economic necessity and a shared fear of the spread of international terrorism.

GUUAM does force Russia to account for balancing forces affecting its foreign policy. This trend could moderate Russian hegemonic ambitions if Moscow worries that its exercise of power might contribute to a deepening of balancing institutions. Consequently, the prospect of significant countervailing pressures within Eurasia might force Russia to consider more cooperative or issue-linked bargaining strategies that eventually are reflected in new institutional forms. However, in the short term, Russia would be more likely to favour working bilaterally with each GUUAM member (as it has with Ukraine and Moldova) to undermine institutional cohesion. It is possible that with the growing US–Russian accommodation, reflecting a common interest in combating terrorism, the historical fears of Russian hegemony in the region will be allayed – particularly for states such as Uzbekistan, which hosted US troop deployments in the 2001–2 campaign against the Taliban in Afghanistan.

The SCO: great power balancing

In June 2001, the leaders of China, Russia, Kazakhstan, Kyrgyzstan and Tajikistan transformed an informal grouping established in 1996 and known as the 'Shanghai Five' into a formal international institution, the SCO, which was expanded to include Uzbekistan. The official objectives of the institution are to promote trust, stability and mutual understanding between members, including confidence building in the military sphere and mutual reductions of armed forces in border areas.[47]

The SCO is viewed in western circles as a potential balancing mechanism designed by China and Russia to frustrate American global dominance. Indeed, the founding SCO document specifies that promoting multipolarity is a core institutional objective. Both China and Russia use the advancement of multipolar international relations to balance American power. At the political level, this objective is reinforced by the specific requirement that states accept the primacy of the UN, respect for sovereignty, and non-interference in the domestic affairs of states. While specifying that the organisation is not an alliance directed against any other states, there are important elements of balancing behaviour in the SCO. For example, to bolster Russian and Chinese efforts to frustrate US plans for national missile defence, SCO members agreed to preserve the global strategic balance. The members stated that they all saw the 1972 Anti-Ballistic Missile Treaty as crucial to that objective. According to Chinese vice-foreign minister Zhang Deguang, the SCO is in agreement that missile defence 'would have a negative impact on the safeguarding of world strategic balance and security'.[48] None the less, the application of the SCO to this global balancing dynamic demonstrated the relative weakness of even a combined Russian–Chinese position as the United States announced its intent to withdraw from the Anti-Ballistic Missile Treaty in late 2001.

The balancing prospects of the SCO can be overstated. Russia had serious misgivings about including Uzbekistan in the institution, largely because Tashkent has pursued a strident independence. Meanwhile, the smaller SCO members – Kazakhstan, Kyrgyzstan and Tajikistan – have have been reluctant to place too much emphasis on purely Russian-led institutions. As Uzbek president Islam Karimov asserts: 'This organization must never turn into a military political bloc . . . It should not be against any country, should not join certain trends, should not organise subversive activities against third countries'.[49] Russia's interest in the SCO may be as much guided by a desire to constrain the growth of China's influence in the region as to hedge against American power. Russia might also bandwagon towards the United States if Chinese power continues to grow. Russian–Chinese accommodation must also be viewed in the light of their history of deep tensions and rivalry for influence in northeast Asia.

The issue generating the highest convergence of interests among the SCO members is the spread of radical political Islam and associated international terrorism. The SCO has agreed to create an anti-terrorist centre in Biskek, Kyrgyzstan, and a 2,000-soldier unit of Russian, Kazakh, Kyrgyz and Tajik troops was organised. Although there are American concerns that this institution was designed to counterbalance the United States, the SCO could alternatively move more closely towards American interests in combating international terrorism. This trend-line is true even for China, which has a significant ethnic separatist movement in its northwest Xinjiang province. China asserts that Islamic groups in Xinjiang were supplied with money, arms and leadership by the al-Qaeda terrorist organisation.[50]

Given the proximity of these states to Afghanistan and other areas of terrorist basing, the SCO could even complement American strategic interests as the SCO pursues its open-ended campaign against terrorism. Conversely, the SCO could be used by Russia and China to ensure that the United States does not gain a strategic foothold in Eurasia justified by counter-terrorism. By further institutionalising the SCO in the area of counter-terrorism, Russia and China would advance their goals of limiting American influence in Eurasia and justify efforts to secure their own state authority in Chechnya and Xinjiang. In early 2002, the SCO issued a joint statement declaring that regional and sub-regional structures were best suited to fighting terrorism, and implied that the post-September 11 environment had provided a rationale to institutionalise further the SCO's anti-terrorism capabilities. Yet, for medium and smaller regional powers, the increased American presence in Central Eurasia might make the SCO less attractive – particularly for Kyrgyzstan and Uzbekistan.

Conclusion: geopolitics, multilateralism and twenty-first-century Eurasia

The prospects for building cooperative multilateral institutions for addressing the complex new security agenda of Eurasia are not promising. The security dilemma remains strong in the region as Russia continues to seek hegemony via the CIS; former Soviet republics seek to balance against or bandwagon towards Russian power; America has significantly increased its Eurasian regional interests during the war against terrorism; and Russia and China remain poised to balance continuing assertions of American power. All the regional actors remain united in a shared fear of radical political Islam and international terrorism. While these geopolitical constraints are a major inhibitor of the development of western-style cooperative security institutions, it does not mean that multilateralism is irrelevant. Rather, as an institutional form, multilateralism remains at best an intervening, and more likely dependent, variable determining regional security outcomes. Nevertheless, Eurasia is poised to function as a regional concert system that might eventually foster cooperative multilateral efforts towards addressing the new security agenda.[51]

Prior to the September 11 2001 attacks on the United States, conditions favouring a regional concert system were largely in place in the Eurasian area. The United States, Russia and China appeared prepared to sustain an informal triangular framework for relations among major regional actors. Of these countries, currently none can exercise complete hegemony over the Eurasian area. While American influence ascended in 2001–2, Washington's interests in the region are transitory and limited to counter-terrorism and transit routes for oil rather than issue-based multilateralism. The key pivot point is Russia, which has the opportunity to shift between the

United States and China. Meanwhile, the medium-sized states of Kazakhstan and Uzbekistan serve as keystone powers between Russia and China. Both large and medium powers want to sustain domestic regime stability, especially in the light of the challenge of a rising tide of radical Islam. Ultimately, Eurasian states hope to sustain international stability so they can address pressing domestic challenges.

Formal institutions that can constrain state behaviour through the extension of hegemony or specific rules and norms, such as the CIS, GUUAM and the SCO, are not likely to provide cooperative means of addressing Eurasia's new security agenda. These institutions remain highly conditioned by the regional balance of power. Indeed, they are best understood as important reflections of an informal concert framework. Should China or the United States become too powerful, Russia can use the CIS as a peripheral defensive measure. However, the weaknesses of the CIS may force Russia to bandwagon and make a truly historic decision as to whether its interests lie with the West or with Asia. Should the United States become too powerful in a way that undermines the Eurasian balance of power, Russia and China can use the SCO to balance American power. Conversely, while Russia may bandwagon towards the West, Moscow might undermine American primacy by elevating its relationship with Europe over Washington. Alternatively, should Russian power increase or a functional Russian–Chinese accommodation emerge, then GUUAM might serve to project American security interests.

The defeat of the Taliban in Afghanistan in late 2001, however, raises important questions as to the longevity of the concert model. While political Islam remains a serious challenge to regional stability, the absence of the Taliban regime makes it more difficult for radical Islamic groups to organise and wield international influence. Consequently, this shared threat perception could recede if stability reigns in Afghanistan. The utility of the concert model lies in its flexible capacity to ebb and flow depending on the interests of the major powers. Should, for example, the Islamic Movement of Uzbekistan ever succeed in taking over Uzbekistan and further threaten its neighbours, the existing concert framework would be strengthened among the major powers in a manner similar to that exercised by the 2001–02 anti-Taliban coalition. Even without the collapse of a key state, smaller areas such as Chechnya, the Ferghana Valley and the Xinjiang province provide sufficient reason for the major powers to share ongoing fears of radical political Islam.

American military engagement could also upset the Eurasian status quo. The nascent concert framework places heavy emphasis on states' preference for the existing status quo and particularistic quest for domestic regime stability. Conservative Eurasian regimes fear radical Islam and increasingly use that threat to avoid addressing human rights concerns or opening to democratic reforms. The global pressures towards democracy, free markets and respect for human rights that accompany the expansion of American power may run directly counter to the status-quo state interests in Eurasia. Even more problematic, as conservative and repressive regimes work to sustain the status quo they are able in the short term to combat international terrorism. However, in the long term, it is this very state repression of freedoms that often fuels the radicalisation of Islam. Thus the United States faces an uncomfortable policy choice between promoting stability and values.

The prospects for a lasting regional concert system for Eurasia will depend on whether the United States asserts its regional role with restraint and whether it pursues multilateral or unilateral security engagement. During the war in Afghanistan, Russia acquiesced to the United States and allowed American military deployments in former Soviet bases in Kyrgyzstan, Tajikistan and Uzbekistan. Indications that American troops would not be likely to leave this area in a timely manner might eventually heighten the security dilemmas of Russia and China. Russia, in particular, will be put under increasing pressure to overturn the status quo or seek balancing arrangements if the United States does not act with restraint. Russia's historic sensitivities to traditional encirclement are well known – and now Russia faces an expanding NATO to the west, American military forces on its southern borders, and the rising power of China to the east. The core question of the future of Eurasian security may be which side Russia will choose: West or East. This long-standing question for Russia's identity will in large part be determined by how the United States adapts its policies in the region, and by whether Washington builds cooperative security institutions that include Russia and account for Moscow's interests.

To sustain its regional presence, the United States might pursue trade-offs with Russia on economic assistance or on future NATO enlargement. Or America might withdraw and thus instigate a return to regional bandwagoning and balancing behaviour. Such a move would seriously damage expectations raised among the smaller states of Eurasia and contribute to a persistence of unresolved traditional and new security challenges. Alternatively, the United States presence could be the precursor of the development of a cooperative security dynamic for the region. This outcome would require Washington to pursue a multilateral and inclusive framework for its engagement, involving Russia and China as co-equal regional partners, and to create institutional mechanisms to engage the smaller regional powers in multilateral dialogue. Western models of cooperative security might subsequently evolve in Eurasia, but only as an evolutionary process that fosters trust. Such an effort might use conference-style diplomacy to create a network of multilateral issue-based regimes. For example, by making the existing Cooperative Threat Reduction programme (for reducing the risks of nuclear proliferation out of Russia) into a multilateral regional framework, new patterns of security cooperation might emerge and be transferred into other issue areas.

The United States has important gains to make by achieving a regional foothold in Eurasia. A US military presence in Central Asia could facilitate containment of either Russia or China should the need arise in the future. An American presence could also facilitate access to proven and unproven oil reserves that could supply the world with significant energy resources well into the twenty-first century. Moreover, a military presence could assist American power projection should it lose access to bases in the Persian Gulf. If the extension of American power into Eurasia were accompanied by a gradual extension of cooperative multilateral forms, rather than a quest for extending unilateral gains, Russia might overcome its historical security dilemma and join the West while constructive engagement with China was fostered. However, if poorly handled by Washington, there is significant risk that its policies in Eurasia will drive Russia and China towards a balancing architecture. As with the cooperative multilateral institutions that have evolved in Europe, the prospects for international institutions in Eurasia will depend on the nature and exercise of American leadership – and restraint.

Notes

1 For this chapter, I conducted research as a Visiting Fellow at the International Institute for Strategic Studies in London during summer 2001. I am grateful to many individuals for their support and observations, including: Klaus Becher, Mats Berdal, Douglas Blum, Archie Brown, Richard Caplan, Jonathan Chipman, Chris Coker, Chris Donnelly, Richard Fusch, Robert Grant, Stuart Horsman, Stuart Kaufman, Margot Light, Neil MacFarlane, Dov Lynch, Andrew Michta, William Park, M.J. Peterson, Jean-Mark Ricci, Karl Ryavec, James Sperling, Joshua Spero, Kristina Spor and Paul Taylor.
2 International Institute for Strategic Studies, *Strategic Survey: 2000–2001* (London, International Institute for Strategic Studies, 2001), pp. 269–70.
3 See Patrick M. Morgan, 'Multilateralism and Security: Prospects in Europe', in John Gerard Ruggie (ed.), *Multilateralism Matters: The Theory and Praxis of an Institutional Form* (New York: Columbia University Press, 1993), pp. 327–64.
4 Richard Sokolsky and Tanya Charlick-Paley, *NATO and Caspian Security: A Mission Too Far?* (Santa Monica: Rand Corporation, 1999), pp. 13–21.
5 Samuel Huntington, *The Clash of Civilizations and the Remaking of World Order* (New York: Simon and Schuster, 1996).
6 See Robert Jervis, *Perception and Misperception in International Politics* (Princeton, NJ: Princeton University Press, 1976); and Alexander Wendt, 'Anarchy is What States Make of It: The Social Construction of Power Politics', *International Organization*, 46:2 (1992), pp. 391–425.
7 See Joseph Grieco, 'Anarchy and the Limits of Cooperation: A Realist Critique of the Newest Liberal Institutionalism', *International Organization*, 42:3 (1988), pp. 485–507.
8 See John J. Mearsheimer, 'The False Promise of International Institutions', *International Security*, 19:3 (1994–95), pp. 10–12.
9 See Robert Jervis, 'Cooperation under the Security Dilemma', *World Politics*, 30:2 (1978), pp. 167–214.

10 See Glenn H. Snyder, 'The Security Dilemma in Alliance Politics', *World Politics*, 36:4 (1985), pp. 461–96; and Stephen M. Walt, *The Origins of Alliances* (Ithaca, NY: Cornell University Press, 1987).

11 See Randall L. Schweller, 'Bandwagoning for Profit: Bringing the Revisionist State Back In', *International Security*, 19:1 (1994), pp. 72–107. Neil MacFarlane demonstrates that the distribution of power in Eurasia favours a Russian strategy of assertion and consolidation in its periphery but, at the global level, Russia has bandwagoned towards the United States. Neil MacFarlane, 'Realism and Russian Strategy after the Collapse of the USSR', in Ethan B. Kapstein and Michael Mastanduno (eds), *Unipolar Politics: Realism and State Strategies after the Cold War* (New York: Columbia University Press, 1999), pp. 218–60.

12 See Robert O. Keohane, *After Hegemony: Cooperation and Discord in the World Political Economy* (Princeton, NJ: Princeton University Press, 1984).

13 See Lisa Martin, 'The Rational State Choice', in Ruggie, *Multilateralism Matters*, pp. 91–117.

14 See Robert O. Keohane, *International Institutions and State Power* (Boulder, CO: Westview Press, 1989).

15 See Oran R. Young, 'The Effectiveness of International Institutions: Hard Cases and Critical Variables', in James N. Rosenau and Ernst-Otto Czempiel (eds), *Governance without Government: Order and Change in World Politics* (Cambridge: Cambridge University Press, 1992), pp. 160–94.

16 Robert Axelrod and Robert O. Keohane, 'Achieving Cooperation under Anarchy: Strategies and Institutions', in Baldwin, *Neorealism and Neoliberalism*, pp. 85–115.

17 Robert O. Keohane, Joseph S. Nye and Stanley Hoffmann (eds), *After the Cold War: International Institutions and State Strategies in Europe, 1989–1991* (Cambridge, MA: Harvard University Press, 1994), pp. 2–3.

18 Charles Kupchan, 'The Case for Collective Security', in George Downs (ed.), *Collective Security After the Cold War* (Ann Arbor: University of Michigan Press, 1994), pp. 50–1.

19 Robert Gilpin, *War and Change in World Politics* (Cambridge: Cambridge University Press, 1981).

20 See Paul W. Schroeder, 'The Transformation of Political Thinking: 1787–1848', and William H. Daugherty, 'System Management and the Endurance of the Concert of Europe', in Jack Snyder and Robert Jervis (eds), *Coping with Complexity in the International System* (Boulder, CO: Westview Press, 1993), pp. 47–70, 71–106.

21 Craig A. Snyder, 'Regional Security Structures', in Craig A. Snyder (ed.), *Contemporary Security and Strategy* (London: Macmillan, 1999), pp. 114–15.

22 See Janne E. Nolan (ed.), *Global Engagement: Cooperation and Security in the 21st Century* (Washington, DC: Brookings Institution, 1994).

23 See Ariel Cohen, 'The New "Great Game": Pipeline Politics in Eurasia', *Eurasian Studies*, 3:1 (1996), pp. 2–15; and Zbigniew Brzezinski, *The Grand Chessboard: American Primacy and its Geostrategic Imperatives* (New York: Basic Books, 1997).

24 Kenneth Weisbrode, *Central Eurasia: Prize or Quicksand? Contending Views of Instability in Karabakh, Ferghana and Afghanistan* (London: International Institute for Strategic Studies, 2001), p. 9.

25 'Strategic Policy Toward CIS Published', *Foreign Broadcast Information Service*

Daily Report: Central Asia SOV-95 (28 September 1995), pp. 19–20.

26 International Institute for Strategic Studies, *Strategic Survey*, p. 122.
27 'Strategic Policy Toward CIS Published', pp. 19–20.
28 See Stephen J. Blank, *Energy, Economics, and Security in Central Asia: Russia and its Rivals* (Carlisle Barracks, PA: US Army War College, 1995).
29 International Institute for Strategic Studies, *The Military Balance: 2001–2002* (London: International Institute for Strategic Studies, 2001), pp. 117–18.
30 In April 2000, Russia organised, and Tajikistan hosted, CIS Southern Shield 2000 exercises, which involved the additional participation of Kazakhstan, Kyrgyzstan and Uzbekistan and were designed to prevent rebel forces from infiltrating Uzbekistan via Tajikistan. *ITAR-TASS* (2 April 2000) (FBIS-NES-2000–0402).
31 Dmitri Trenin, 'Central Asia's Stability and Russia's Security', *PONARS*, 168 (November 2000).
32 Sokolsky and Charlick-Paley, *NATO and Caspian Security*, p. 28.
33 Douglas Frantz, 'Russia's New Reach: Gas Pipeline to Turkey', *New York Times* (6 June 2001).
34 International Institute for Strategic Studies, *Strategic Survey*, p. 121.
35 *Interfax* (31 March 2001).
36 Haroutiun Khachatrian, 'Creation of Rapid Deployment Force Marks Potential Watershed in Collective Security Development', *Eurasia Insight* (2 July 2001).
37 The June 2002 Uzbek announcement that it would suspend membership in GUUAM means that the institution's acronym will revert to GUAM.
38 'The GUUAM Group: History and Principles: Briefing Paper', at www.guuam.org/.
39 Quoted in Charles Fairbanks, C. Richard Nelson, S. Frederick Starr and Kenneth Weisbrode, *Strategic Assessment of Central Eurasia* (Washington, DC: Atlantic Council of the United States, 2001), p. 59.
40 Uzbekistan joined GUAAM in 1999.
41 Anatol Lieven, 'GUUAM: What Is It, and What Is It For?' *Eurasia Insight* (18 December 2000).
42 *Ibid.*
43 See Taras Kuzio, 'Promoting Geopolitical Pluralism in the CIS: GUUAM and Western Foreign Policy', *Problems of Post-Communism*, 47:3 (2000), pp. 25–35. Some military cooperation goals include creating a joint peacekeeping unit, and information exchange on regional security issues. GUUAM has also adopted a calendar of forthcoming events to facilitate cooperation among ministries of defence. Some external cooperative military programmes have developed, including the signing of a defence protocol between Azerbaijan, Georgia and Ukraine in March 1999, which was followed by joint military exercises designed to protect oil pipelines. Meanwhile, Azerbaijan, Georgia and Turkey established a nascent multinational approach to regional security, focusing on combating terrorism and organised crime as well as protecting oil pipelines.
44 For further discussion, see Chapter 10 by Willerton and Cockerham in this volume.
45 Ukraine's interdependence with other GUUAM states is limited. In 2002, Ukrainian exports to GUUAM countries were 2.5 per cent of its exports. The corresponding share for imports was 1.8 per cent. Total turnover in trade with Ukraine's four GUUAM partners was 70 per cent of that with Belarus and slightly

over 50 per cent of that with Turkmenistan. Igor Torbakov, 'GUUAM's Potential to Play Role in Anti-Terrorism Alliance Appears Limited', *Eurasia Insight* (11 January 2002).

46 Iryna Solonenko, 'Quo Vadis, GUUAM?', *Central Europe Review* at www.ce-review.org. Limited public awareness of GUUAM is another constraint on its potential: 62.6 per cent of Ukrainians have not heard of GUUAM and only 3.6 per cent were well informed about the activities of the institution.

47 'Joint Statement by the Heads of State of the Republic of Kazakhstan, the People's Republic of China, the Kyrgyz Republic, the Russian Federation, the Republic of Tajikistan, and the Republic of Uzbekistan'.

48 'Central Asia Bloc United Against Missile Shield', *CNN World* at cnn.com.

49 'Russia Has Misgivings about Shanghai Cooperation Organization', *Eurasia Insight* (20 June 2001).

50 In early 2002, China blamed separatist forces in Xinjiang for 200 explosions, assassinations and other attacks over an 11-year period, resulting in 111 deaths and 440 injuries. As many as 1,000 Chinese Muslims may have trained in al-Qaeda terrorist camps in Afghanistan. Philip P. Pan, 'China Links Bin Laden to Separatists', *Washington Post* (22 January 2002).

51 The emergence of a contemporary regional concert for Eurasia was first identified by Kenneth Weisbrode. See Weisbrode, *Central Eurasia*.

8

The OSCE role
in Eurasian security

P. Terrence Hopmann

A wide range of institutions have appeared in the Eurasian region since the end of the Cold War that have a role to play in Eurasian security. Indeed, it has often been observed that Europe after 1989 is 'institutionally thick', that is, it is crisscrossed by an extensive web of multilateral institutions designed to prevent, deter, manage and resolve conflicts that might appear in the region once occupied by the former Communist states of the Soviet Union and its Central and East European allies. Among these institutions the OSCE is unique, mainly because it is the one institution that has a clear-cut mandate in the field of security that also includes all of the parties involved in Eurasian security, including 55 participating states extending from 'Vancouver to Vladivostok' the long way around.

The Conference on Security and Cooperation in Europe (CSCE),[1] the forerunner of the OSCE, opened in Helsinki in 1973 and produced the Helsinki Final Act signed at a summit conference in the Finnish capital on 31 July–1 August 1975. During the Cold War years, the CSCE focused primarily on ten principles for security (the 'Decalogue'), a series of confidence-building measures to reduce fears of surprise attack between NATO and the Warsaw Treaty Organisation, and on human rights and expanded human contacts across the East–West divide through the centre of Europe.

Since the end of the Cold War, conflict prevention and resolution have moved to the forefront of the OSCE's agenda. Yet these roles performed routinely by the OSCE and its missions and field activities have gone largely unnoticed in governments and especially in the general public, not only in the United States but in much of Europe as well. We are all painfully aware of the failures of conflict prevention in the former Communist regions of central and eastern Europe and Eurasia. Names like Bosnia-Herzegovina, Kosovo and Chechnya – previously known only to regional specialists – have become household words and appear in our media almost daily. Yet successful conflict prevention receives virtually no attention since, by definition, 'nothing happens' – and we all know that 'nothing' never makes the news or excites the attention of policy-makers and public officials.

Therefore, when the 'dogs don't bark' – when a potential conflict does not erupt into violence or when an old conflict remains dormant for many years – we may easily overlook the fact that this may be due to skilful and fore-sighted diplomatic initiatives taken outside the glare of public attention. In fact, patient but often overlooked preventive diplomacy by OSCE missions and field operations has frequently made a significant contribution to the avoidance of violence in a number of potentially dangerous situations in the OSCE region, and that other conflicts have been moderated or prevented from escalating is further due to the rapid, but often unseen, work of these OSCE officials.

Within the Eurasian region only the OSCE – in particular the Conflict Prevention Centre (CPC), with its missions and field activities, as well as the High Commissioner on National Minorities (HCNM) – has a clear mandate, organisational structure, and significant acquired experience in the field of conflict management. When combined with the 'human dimension' that infuses all of the OSCE's work, this conflict-prevention capacity constitutes the special contribution that only the OSCE brings to the European security 'architecture'. This is an especially important function that needs to be nurtured and strengthened with the active support of the OSCE's largest, wealthiest and most powerful participating states, especially the United States.

The special role of the OSCE

In the field of medicine, the principle that 'an ounce of prevention is worth a pound of cure' has long been accepted. The US government and private sources devote billions of dollars every year to research on preventive medicine, because the best way to deal with the most deadly killers such as cancer and heart disease is by preventing their occurrence in the first place. Unfortunately, this simple principle has not yet been widely accepted in the field of foreign policy. For whatever reason, it seems to be easier to achieve a political consensus behind the deployment of large and expensive military peacemaking and peacekeeping operations than to provide the much smaller resources generally needed to carry on the activity of multilateral preventive diplomacy. Thus, for example, the entire annual US assessment for all OSCE activities, including its missions, amounted to only about $20 million in fiscal year 2002. At the same time the United States spent over $4 billion annually to pay for the cost of US forces stationed with SFOR in Bosnia-Herzegovina and with KFOR (Kosovo Implementation Force) in Kosovo. Thus the US contribution to conflict prevention in the OSCE region was approximately equivalent to what it spent in just two days to maintain its military presence in those two regions where violence occurred. As budgetary pressures become more stringent, and political opposition grows against the large-scale deployment of US troops overseas, perhaps US political leaders will learn that the need for such interventions might be averted if they invested even a small fraction of those resources into the less visible, but often more important, work of conflict prevention. But this too requires a shift in institutional focus: while it is NATO that implements peacekeeping operations, the North Atlantic alliance has little or no capacity to engage in conflict prevention. That vital role in conflict prevention, management and resolution represents the comparative advantage of the OSCE, and it is to the OSCE that the United States should give its support to perform this role more effectively.

It is interesting to speculate about how much might have been saved if the United States had only devoted more resources, attention and effort to conflict prevention *before* either of the conflicts in Bosnia-Herzegovina and Kosovo exploded into violence. But this is not just a matter of saving budgetary resources, however important that is. Nor is it first and foremost a question of avoiding politically difficult choices about deploying US troops in yet one more overseas operation, although that too is an important consideration. It is mostly about preventing the tragic consequences of war for the innocent people who are its inevitable victims. Before the NATO-led deployments took place in Bosnia and Kosovo, thousands of residents of these regions lost their lives; physical infrastructure, homes, farms, schools and factories were destroyed; the bare rudiments of social connections across different ethnic groups were severed; and the human spirit of the peoples surviving in all of these regions was crushed by the violence that swept across their societies.

Rebuilding from the physical damage is the easy part; re-establishing mutual trust among peoples who have lived alongside one another for centuries and who must inevitably continue to do so for the foreseeable future will be far more difficult. Yet this is essential if the foundations of a functioning civil society are to be constructed, if individual human rights and the rights of persons belonging to minorities are to be respected, and if democratic governance is to be established. For all of these reasons, one clear lesson that emerges from the recent experience in Bosnia-Herzegovina and Kosovo (and for that matter from the Russian experience in Chechnya) is that it is a lot harder to 'put Humpty Dumpty back together again' than it would have been to prevent him from falling off the wall in the first place.

Preventing the outbreak of war throughout the entire OSCE region is the principal challenge that faces the OSCE today. Furthermore, there is no other multilateral institution or individual country at present that can perform this role. Even before the end of the Cold War, Europe was crisscrossed with a wide variety of multilateral security institutions. Since 1990, most of these have expanded their functions, and the web of institutions has become even thicker: NATO has been enlarged and transformed, the EU has expanded and adopted a 'common foreign and security policy', and the OSCE has created institutions such as the CPC, the Office of Democratic Institutions and Human Rights (ODIHR) and the HCNM. The UN continues to have an important role to play in European security, as does the Council of Europe. Yet within this region only the OSCE has a clear mandate, an organisational structure, and significant acquired experience in the field of conflict prevention and resolution.

NATO has long been an important institution for deterring aggression against its members by promising a collective response in defence of its member-states if they are attacked from outside. Since the early 1990s, it has developed a significant peacekeeping capability as well. By its very nature, NATO is a military organisation that can support but not supplant diplomatic institutions in preventing the outbreak of violence and promoting the resolution of existing conflicts. Almost by definition, the introduction of NATO troops into a country experiencing conflict means that the point of no return is about to be, or already has been, crossed. At this point, efforts to achieve political solutions have usually been abandoned in favour of providing some form of 'temporary' military security. The role of the OSCE missions and of the HCNM, by contrast, is ideally to enter into a situation long before it reaches the violent stage. By trying to assure full rights for all citizens in multinational states and by providing facilities for mediation and conflict resolution at the grassroots level, these institutions seek to head off incidents before they reach the boiling point.

A further limitation of NATO is that it is still viewed with considerable scepticism in many of the regions of Eurasia most threatened with conflict, a legacy of the Cold War and of the fact that some countries, especially Russia, are not members and are not likely to become so within the foreseeable future. To be effective in conflict resolution at the local level, it is necessary that outsiders not be perceived to be injecting global political issues into the already complex set of local issues. Once again the OSCE has a comparative advantage over other institutions owing to the universal participation of all states in the region where it operates.

The EU has also sought to play a major role in some conflicts in the OSCE region, and the adoption at Maastricht in 1991 of a 'common foreign and security policy' was supposed to signal a more active collective diplomatic effort on the part of the EU. However, so far EU efforts have been plagued with considerable inconsistency and policy differences among its member-states, and the outlines and priorities of the common foreign and security policy have emerged slowly, if at all. Furthermore, there has been a tendency for the EU to try to demonstrate its bona fides in the field of conflict prevention and resolution by intervening in situations where other institutions and NGOs were already at work, often causing confusion and 'institution shopping' on the part of disputants, and at times even undermining other efforts that might have promoted a successful resolution of disputes. The EU also suffers from the fact that two states – namely the United States and the Russian Federation – that play a fundamental role in European security are not among its members. In short, the EU has an essential role to play in contributing to the economic recovery and development of its neighbours to the east; the prospect of eventual membership provides a compelling reason for those states to undertake the difficult tasks required by democratisation and economic reform. But its role in conflict prevention, resolution and peacekeeping has yet to be established or validated on the basis of its record to date.

Many of the same limitations apply as well to the Council of Europe, whose membership automatically excludes the United States and Canada and is likely to restrict the participation of Russia and other post-Soviet states. Furthermore, the focus of the Council of Europe has been primarily on issues of human rights and democracy building. Although the Council sets up strict standards for admission, once admitted a country largely escapes long-term monitoring and enforcement. This contrasts with the OSCE long-term monitoring that observes over time and on-site how well participating states actually live up to the obligations they have taken on. Thus, the Council of Europe has not been engaged in long-term security building on the ground in zones of potential or actual conflict.

This leaves the OSCE as the only multilateral institution with a mandate and capacity to carry out the functions of conflict prevention and resolution in areas of tension within the broad European region it covers. Furthermore, this capacity has grown considerably throughout the past decade and, as I will argue below, its potential for further growth is great. When the CPC was first created by the Charter of Paris in 1990, it had a very limited mandate and a minute budget and staff. After the sad experience of the former Yugoslavia in 1991, the CPC's capacity gradually grew to the point where in 2002 there were OSCE missions and other field activities in eighteen countries and regions of Eurasia: six in Southeastern Europe, three in post-Soviet Eastern Europe, four in the Caucasus, and five in Central Asia. In the cases of Bosnia-Herzegovina, Croatia and Kosovo those missions have also grown quite large, as the OSCE has been charged with significant political roles in rebuilding these war-torn regions, operating in two of those venues alongside the NATO-led forces of SFOR and KFOR. The missions have also been supported by two OSCE organs based outside of the country, namely the ODIHR, which supports missions activities in areas such as democratisation, elections, the rule of law and human rights, and the HCNM, who works with missions in conflict-prevention and conflict-resolution activities in disputes involving ethno-national groups or between central governments and persons belonging to minority groups. The chairperson-in-office and other member governments serving in the OSCE troika (the chair, past-chair and chair-elect), as well as officials of the OSCE Secretariat and CPC in Vienna, frequently provide assistance at the highest levels to the field missions and activities.

The OSCE institutional capacity for conflict management
in the Eurasian region

In the aftermath of the collapse of the Berlin Wall, the OSCE began to increase its capacity to manage conflicts despite the very modest mandate of the CPC. After the outbreak of violence that occurred in both the former Soviet Union and the former Yugoslavia in the first two years of the decade, the OSCE substantially strengthened its institutional capacity in this area at the Helsinki Summit of 1992. The mandate for the CPC was reinforced, and the first mission of long-duration to be stationed in a region of conflict was created for the regions of Kosovo, Vojvodina and Sandjak within the Federal Republic of Yugoslavia. Of equal importance, the office of the HCNM was created. Together, these two institutions have functioned as the core of the OSCE's conflict management work throughout the Eurasian region.

The CPC is located within the secretariat in Vienna and is primarily responsible for coordinating the work of the OSCE missions and other field activities. It is largely responsible for staffing and training missions, for coordinating their work in the field, and for liaison between the missions and other OSCE institutions and participating governments. It is thus the CPC that provides the primary point of contact between each of the field missions and activities and OSCE officials in Vienna. Prior to the 2000 reorganisation, all arrangements to staff and supply the missions with necessary materials were provided by the CPC. Presently, the CPC still serves as the communications link through which instructions are normally relayed to mission heads, and mission heads normally convey all reports, both routine and special, through the CPC office in Vienna. Although the staff of the CPC in Vienna was recently enlarged, it is still quite small in proportion to the number of missions that must be supported, a reflection of the limited budgetary resources available to it. The staff in 2001 consisted of three professional officers, including a director and deputy director, supported by 14 contracted staff members. Therefore, it is often necessary for the staff to prioritise their responses to the requests of each of the field missions.

At the time of its founding, the CPC focused mostly on the implementation of various military confidence- and security-building measures (CSBMs), especially those included in the agreement known as Vienna Document 1990. These included the following:

- providing an information and database regarding military forces and activities in the OSCE region, including force size and deployment, military budgets, and a calendar of annual manoeuvres and other military movements that were required to be reported under the terms of Vienna Document 1990;
- providing a locus and infrastructure for consultation and coordination regarding any unusual military activities not reported through the

Vienna mechanism that might give rise to concern of impending military activity of a threatening nature;
• coordinating the responses of countries with regard to hazards resulting from military activities or incidents involving military forces before they could set off a chain reaction of potentially violent responses;
• organising annual meetings to assess the performance of participating states with regard to the implementation of all CSBMs agreed to under CSCE provisions.

The Charter of Paris thus anticipated the possibility that the CPC's initial functions might be expanded as the need arose. Following the outbreak of fighting in the former Yugoslavia, the CSCE ministerial meeting in Prague in January 1992 created the framework for expanding the functions of the CPC, opening the door to the creation of its present structure. Based on the concept of responding to unusual military activities, the possibility of long-term monitoring to provide 'early warning' of impending threats to the security of states and persons in the region became a central function of the CPC during and immediately after the 1992 Helsinki follow-up meeting. Therefore, the concept of the 'mission of long duration' emerged, and the CPC was given the task of organising and overseeing the operation of these missions.

In the event that missions provide 'early warning' to the CPC of incipient conflict, it is the CPC's primary responsibility to see that OSCE institutions and participating states are alerted to the potential danger, as well as to prepare to implement any decisions taken by the Permanent Council or other high-level institutions. This often requires the director to deliver 'early warning' messages to the appropriate OSCE institutions and to prepare to implement decisions taken by those institutions. The director also frequently travels to the site of potential conflicts to meet with local officials or with parties involved in local conflicts to provide assistance and backing for the work of the mission.

A further reorganisation of the CPC took place in 2000 as a result of the Istanbul Summit conference and the decision to create the Rapid Expert Assistance and Cooperation Teams (REACT) system for recruiting and training mission staff. As a consequence an Operations Centre was created within the CPC to provide for advanced planning of all aspects of future OSCE missions, including the deployment of civilian police. The Operations Centre also created the position of liaison officer to become a point of contact between the OSCE and other international organisations, both military and civilian, that might be involved alongside the OSCE in regions experiencing conflict. The new Operations Centre includes a 'situation room' which can maintain contact at all times (24 hours a day, seven days a week) with all field operations and can relay information from the field to secretariat officials and to the chairman-in-office on very short notice. The mandate for the Operations Centre includes three major tasks:

- helping to identify crisis areas by maintaining close liaison with other international organisations and NGOs involved in conflict-management activities, including but not limited to the role played by OSCE missions and field activities, but also extended to regions where no OSCE mission is currently on the ground so that information must be obtained from other international actors operating in these regions;
- serving as the planning unit for all future OSCE missions and field operations;
- acting as a point of coordination during the initial mobilisation and subsequent deployment of any future field operations mandated by the OSCE Permanent Council. This new function first operated to set up a reinstated OSCE mission to the Federal Republic of Yugoslavia in early 2001.

The CPC, directed in 2002 by Ambassador Marton Krasznai, coordinates implementation and verification of OSCE agreements on CSBMs (i.e., the 1986 Stockholm agreement, the Vienna Document 1990 and the Vienna Document 1992), although separate consultative groups promote the implementation of the Conventional Forces in Europe and Open Skies Treaties. The CPC also coordinates the work of the Forum for Security Cooperation, which meets regularly in Vienna to discuss long-term policy issues and to negotiate on arms control and CSBMs.

The HCNM in The Hague is a senior official, initially the former Dutch foreign minister Max van der Stoel, who has considerable independent authority to investigate and assist in responding to potential or actual incidents of violence where national minorities play a significant role. Many specialists on international organisations view the creation of this position at the Helsinki Summit in 1992 as one of the most creative decisions taken by the OSCE in its 25-year history, as the office has provided a function not found in most other global or regional international institutions.

Supported by a small staff, the HCNM provides early warning of brewing conflicts and intervenes in such situations where he deems it appropriate in order to assist the parties to find non-violent solutions to their disputes. Under the mandate given to the HCNM by the Helsinki Summit, he is only supposed to deal with issues involving persons belonging to *national* minorities, he is not permitted to deal with groups practising terrorism, and he is only supposed to deal with conflicts that have the potential to affect inter-state relations or regional security. Although the HCNM reports regularly to the Permanent Council, he does not receive instructions from it (unlike the CPC and the missions and field activities which it coordinates), and he is free to respond according to his own judgement whenever he believes it to be appropriate. Under van der Stoel's leadership, this became a very active office in the OSCE that has operated with considerable political independence. Van der Stoel retired in 2001 and was replaced by Rolf Ekeus of

Sweden, who is likely to continue van der Stoel's broad interpretation of the mandate for his office and be actively engaged in monitoring relations between governments and persons belonging to minorities throughout the Eurasian region.

Typically the HCNM responds to any incidents that fall within his mandate by travelling to the scene of the event and meeting immediately with the parties involved, including government officials and aggrieved parties. On the basis of his observations he may offer immediate advice to the parties, engage in third party mediation, prepare recommendations for the parties, or organise seminars or round tables at which parties may discuss their grievances. As a representative of the OSCE – an international organisation composed of national governments – the HCNM must always be aware of his obligations to the governments to whom he is responsible. Thus his role is not necessarily to act as an advocate on behalf of minorities; rather it is to promote dialogue between persons belonging to minority groups and governments or other institutions and organisations representing the national majority. His goal is to promote the successful integration and acceptance of persons belonging to minority groups within the structures of a multinational state and, in so far as it is possible, to seek to head off pressures for secession by regions heavily populated by persons belonging to minority groups.[2]

Frequently the HCNM has travelled to countries and regions where there is not an established OSCE mission or field activity. In this way, he has been able to intervene in situations where short-term assistance is needed, but where a longer-term presence is not necessary. However, whenever the HCNM has concluded that a more continuous presence by OSCE representatives is desirable in a region, he has recommended to the Permanent Council that a mission or field activity be set up. Indeed, a substantial number of the missions now fielded by the OSCE have come into existence in part as a consequence of recommendations by the Commissioner. Once a mission is on location, however, that does not necessarily mean that the role of the HCNM disappears from the region. Although most OSCE missions and field activities have at least one human rights specialist on their staff, their work can often be supplemented by the involvement of the Commissioner, especially when the issue concerns the rights of persons belonging to minorities as opposed to violations of individual human rights.

Therefore, the HCNM has often appeared in countries where OSCE missions are established and functioning. In these cases, the on-site mission has been in part responsible for arranging the logistics of the visit by the Commissioner, for briefing him about the situation on the ground, and for assisting him with the follow-up to his visit. On rare occasions there have been tensions between mission members, who often feel that their continuous presence gives them a more in-depth knowledge of the situation in a particular country, and the Commissioner, who enters into many regions of conflict where he necessarily must operate on the basis of a concern for general principles of minority rights rather than according to the details of the local situation. On the other hand, in most cases the OSCE missions and the office of the HCNM have collaborated closely in their effort to resolve underlying tensions involving the rights of persons belonging to minorities. Ideally, their relationship should be complementary rather than competitive. The local mission members typically do have more intimate knowledge of the local situation, whereas the prestige and international standing of the HCNM generally give him the clout necessary to persuade governments and leaders of minority groups to pay serious attention to his recommendations, which is not always the case with regard to recommendations made by OSCE mission staffs. Therefore, the HCNM and the mission human rights specialists each have their own special role to play, and through close collaboration they can best advance the OSCE's role in resolving tensions surrounding national minority issues in many of the OSCE participating states.

One of the most innovative roles performed by van der Stoel during eight and a half years in office was to create what has come to be known as 'seminar diplomacy'. Typically, this approach involves inviting leaders of national minorities and leaders of majority groups as well as government officials to small seminars, often in isolated locations where they can deliberate outside of public attention. In general, the HCNM also invites to these seminars a small set of international 'experts' from OSCE countries on issues such as human rights, minority rights, constitutional law, shared power and autonomy, and federalism/confederalism. Through intense interactions over several days, the Commissioner seeks to acquaint all parties with international norms and practices for dealing with minority groups and their integration into multinational states. These seminars also provide an opportunity for the parties to express their own grievances in the presence of an audience of international experts, who may then make recommendations to the parties about how to overcome their differences. In most cases, the HCNM follows up these seminars with a set of written recommendations to the parties based on what he learned from the seminar, as well as a series of follow-up visits to promote direct negotiations between the parties in an effort to resolve their differences. Through a continuing series of back-and-forth exchanges of information and ideas, therefore, the High Commissioner may hope both to educate the parties about international standards and norms and to bring them together around solutions based on those broadly acknowledged principles. The HCNM has thus been one of the OSCE's most effective instruments for promoting conflict resolution throughout central and eastern Europe and the former Soviet Union (FSU).

Specific OSCE conflict prevention and resolution activities since 1991[3]

OSCE field activities may be categorised into five different functions that they perform in countries experiencing potential or actual violent conflict. Most missions and field activities perform multiple functions, but for purposes of this chapter I focus on prominent examples that illustrate each of these different functions. I will thus highlight each of these five functions and present a brief evaluation of the major accomplishments and shortcomings of the OSCE in performing each of them:[4]

- Virtually all OSCE missions promote long-term conflict prevention through encouraging the development of democratic institutions and procedures and respect for human rights and the rights of persons belonging to minorities, and for many missions this serves as the principal task assigned by their mandates.
- Many OSCE missions seek to prevent the escalation of conflicts to the level of violence through various forms of diplomatic intervention, including efforts at conciliation and mediation of disputes.
- Occasionally, but rarely, OSCE missions may actively mediate ongoing violent conflicts, seeking a ceasefire as a precursor to introducing non-violent methods for the eventual resolution of the conflict.
- Once violence has ceased, OSCE missions often seek to promote through negotiations a long-term resolution to the underlying issues of the conflict.
- Many OSCE missions have focused on rebuilding societies and re-establishing security in the aftermath of violent conflict.

Long-term conflict prevention through democratisation

It has become a generally established finding of social science research that democracies generally do not go to war with other democracies; furthermore, intra-state or civil conflicts are less likely to occur in societies that have well-established procedures for the non-violent resolution of conflicts of interest among their citizens.[5] Therefore, the establishment of democratic processes, the creation of governments of laws and not of individuals, and processes to integrate persons belonging to minorities fully into the institutions of the state are together the best long-run guarantors of peace. Examples include Estonia and Latvia, where the OSCE played a significant role on behalf of large minorities of ethnic Russian denied citizenship rights in these Baltic states; indeed, these missions achieved sufficient results so that they were closed down at the end of 2001. Furthermore, the OSCE has embarked since 1998 upon an effort to defend democracy in Belarus against an authoritarian government that has reversed that country's early post-Soviet progress in the field of democratisation. As one of a very few international institutions operating in Belarus, the OSCE Advisory and Monitoring Group has played a vital role in providing international protection for NGOs and a severely restricted political opposition within that country.

Difficulties in the process of democratisation have also arisen in the five Central Asian states that emerged from the collapse of the Soviet Union with strong leaders in charge, and the democratisation process has been slow to take hold. Therefore, in 1995 an OSCE Liaison Office in Central Asia was established in Tashkent, the capital of Uzbekistan. This effort was enlarged in 1998 with the establishment of OSCE centres in the capitals of three other Central Asian republics: Kazakhstan, Kyrgyzstan and Turkmenistan. (The fifth Central Asian state, Tajikistan, has a full-scale OSCE mission operating on its territory with a more specific mandate in the field of conflict management that will be discussed below.) The focus of OSCE efforts in Central Asia has been on stimulating education about democratisation and human dimension issues. In each case, numerous seminars have been organised with local political elites and NGOs in which outside specialists on topics such as criminality and drug trafficking, legislative changes that would promote greater foreign investment, regional environmental problems, sustainable development, and CSBMs among ethnic communities and with neighbouring states. In addition, the OSCE has worked closely with local universities and other educational institutions to try to institutionalise these topics in their curriculum.

In all of these efforts, it is important to realise that democratisation is an extremely difficult and long-term task even in the best of circumstances. Centuries of authoritarian rule throughout the region have created a climate in which few persons if any were alive in 1990 who had ever lived in a democratic state. As a result, the transition to a fully democratic society, in which more than the outward appearance of democracy is established and in which democratic values are truly internalised throughout the population, is unlikely to take place rapidly. Democracy is inherently fragile in all transitional societies, and more immediate measures of conflict prevention and resolution will frequently be required in order to avoid an outbreak of violence that might set back the democratisation process by a decade or more. The linkage of security to political and humanitarian concerns epitomises the special role that the OSCE missions have come to play in societies undergoing political transformation since the collapse of communism.

Prevention of violent outcomes in potential conflict situations
As noted above, a major function of the OSCE has been to prevent 'Humpty Dumpty' from falling off of his wall. The organisation's record in this case is mixed. However, the OSCE has often been blamed unfairly for failing to prevent conflicts. Too often OSCE inaction was the result of the refusal by one or more of its participating states to take action recommended by OSCE mission heads or other officials such as the HCNM; that is, by the failure to obtain the consensus that is required to take decisive action. Furthermore, in the early post-Cold War years the OSCE did not have a sufficient structural capacity to respond to brewing conflicts.

Thus the conflicts in Croatia and Bosnia-Herzegovina were well under way by the time the first CSCE mission of long duration was sent into the field in late 1992, following the Helsinki follow-on meeting that summer. In the case of Kosovo, the OSCE was hamstrung by the fact that it had suspended the Federal Republic of Yugoslavia from participation in May 1992. Although there were many good reasons for this action, it also had the perverse effect of preventing the OSCE from having any access on the ground in the Kosovo region until tensions had passed the point of no return. By the time the United States, led by Ambassador Richard Holbrooke, persuaded the parties to accept an OSCE Kosovo Verification Mission on the ground in October 1998, it was too late to realise a peaceful resolution of the conflict. A similar decision a year or more earlier, however, might have prevented the bloody war and subsequent international occupation of Kosovo, although of course it is always impossible to prove 'what might have happened if . . .'. But it is very clear that the OSCE and especially the special representative of the chairman-in-office, Ambassador Max van der Stoel, provided substantial 'early warning' of impending disaster in Kosovo. It was the failure of key participating states – including the United States – to take 'early action' in the form of active diplomacy prior to late 1998 that permitted the outcome in Kosovo to be so violent and the subsequent task of reconstruction so enormous.

Looking at the other side of the coin, the OSCE has contributed to the successful resolution of potentially violent conflicts in several regions of Eurasia. Perhaps most notable is the role played by the OSCE in mediating between nationalistic ethnic Russian politicians in Crimea and the central government of Ukraine, which was critical in reaching a solution to that volatile conflict that could have easily exploded into violence. Russian nationalists wanted to separate Crimea from Ukraine and perhaps return it to its pre-1954 status as a part of the Russian Federation, and the Ukrainian government was prepared to do anything necessary to prevent this from happening. Special credit here goes to the OSCE's HCNM, van der Stoel, whose continuing intercession, often using the problem-solving workshops referred to above as 'seminar diplomacy', played a major role in promoting a non-violent outcome in this potentially grave situation. Van der Stoel's work was also backed up by continuous efforts of the OSCE mission members in both Kyiv and Simferopol to broker a solution guaranteeing substantial Crimean autonomy while preserving the territorial integrity of Ukraine. Furthermore, this effort was especially important due to the strategic significance of the region. Needless to say, a war in the mid-1990s between Russia and Ukraine would have created a severe international crisis that would have affected the vital interests of the entire West, including the United States. Even if this were the only accomplishment of the OSCE in the decade of the 1990s, I would argue that this alone was worth all of the effort and resources that have been put into the entire organisation by the United States and its European allies.

But this is, of course, not the only significant accomplishment of the OSCE during the 1990s. At least until 2001, the OSCE mission to Skopje (the former Yugoslav Republic of Macedonia) played an instrumental role in preventing that former Yugoslav republic from falling into the kind of violence that has swept across Croatia, Bosnia-Herzegovina and Kosovo. Of course, the results of those efforts were placed in doubt as violence expanded in regions of Macedonia inhabited by large ethnic Albanian populations throughout 2001. Several factors largely beyond the control of the OSCE conspired to push the situation in Macedonia towards the brink of violence, including the collapse of the government of Albania in 1997 and the looting from its storehouses of large supplies of light weapons and munitions, which made their way into Kosovo and subsequently into Macedonia; the removal of the United Nations Preventive Deployment Force (UNPREDEP) from the northern border regions due to Chinese opposition in the UN; and the growing ambitions of some ethnic Albanian politicians to follow up their 'success' in Kosovo with a similar effort to split heavily Albanian-populated regions of Macedonia off from the rest of the country, perhaps eventually creating a 'greater Albania'.

Fear that violence was imminent, however, in turn led to a rise in nationalism among the Macedonia majority and greater restrictions on minorities, especially Albanians. At the same time, some parts of the Albanian minority, in the aftermath of the defeat of Serbian forces in neighbouring Kosovo, began to advocate separation from Macedonia and joining with Kosovo and Albania. Their separatist ambitions were fuelled by a ready availability of weapons that crossed the border from neighbouring Kosovo. As a result violence flared up in the spring of 2001 between Albanians near the border areas and the Macedonian armed forces. After a ceasefire was negotiated in the Ohrid Framework Agreement of 13 August 2001, several units of NATO troops entered Macedonia to disarm the parties, following which the armed forces were withdrawn. At the same time, the OSCE enlarged its mission in Macedonia to a total of about 210 unarmed monitors, protected by some 1,000 soldiers from France, Germany and Italy. While the OSCE's mandate remained basically unchanged, the necessity for intensive conflict prevention at the local level had been clearly indicated by the outbreak of violence and the increased radicalisation of the two communities that lay behind the violence. In the autumn, deteriorating conditions in Macedonia seriously challenged what was previously regarded as one of the more successful preventive diplomacy missions. None the less, the OSCE Spillover Monitoring Mission in Macedonia, with some timely help from NATO and the continued engagement of the OSCE HCNM, managed by the end of 2001 to head off the escalation of violence and to prevent Macedonia from proceeding down the violent path that Bosnia-Herzegovina and Kosovo had taken in the recent past.

Ceasefire mediation

Once violence breaks out in a country, the OSCE role has generally been limited. One exception, however, was the first war in Chechnya, which started with the Russian military assault in December 1994. Shortly afterwards the OSCE Permanent Council created the OSCE Assistance Group to Chechnya, which set up operation in Grozny in 1995. Russia, as a country that still clings to its self-image as a great power, was of course reluctant to permit any presence by a multilateral organisation on its soil. Therefore, it was somewhat surprising when the Russian government permitted a small OSCE 'assistance group' to be established in the very vortex of the fighting. Under the able leadership of the second head of mission, Ambassador Tim Guldimann of Switzerland, the OSCE expanded its activity beyond monitoring human rights violations and war crimes and assumed a role as an active mediator between the Chechen leaders and officials in Moscow. Guldimann's shuttle diplomacy, involving numerous trips between Grozny and Moscow, was largely responsible for setting up the meeting at Khasavyurt between Alexander Lebed and Zelimkhan Yanderbiev that brought an end to fighting and a withdrawal of Russian troops from Chechnya in August 1996.

Subsequently, the OSCE assumed the major role in preparing, conducting and monitoring the presidential elections in Chechnya in January 1997, in which Aslan Maskhadov was elected. Sadly, the internal situation in Chechnya degenerated into anarchy, with frequent violence directed at outsiders, even those representing international humanitarian organisations. This was followed by a renewal of Russian military action against Chechnya in 1999, after the OSCE Assistance Group had moved its offices to Moscow because of fear about the safety of mission members if they remained in Chechnya. Tragically, this also resulted in a decline of OSCE influence over the parties, and extensive efforts to re-establish a mediating role for the OSCE, undertaken at the Istanbul Summit in November 1999 by the United States and several other countries, failed to bring results; indeed, only in June 2000 did the OSCE Assistance Group finally return to Chechnya. This tragic outcome, however, should not cause us to overlook completely the potential for the OSCE to play an important mediating role, even in the midst of violent conflict, as it did in Chechnya in 1995–96.

Conflict resolution after a ceasefire is in place

Since the major OSCE conflict prevention functions were created after the spate of post-Cold War violence in the early 1990s, a major focus for OSCE missions has been the effort to broker longer-term resolution of the conflicts that had produced the previous chain of violence. In addition, the OSCE has sought to prevent the renewal of violence in situations where serious tensions remain. This has been the major focus of the OSCE missions in Moldova (regarding Transdniestria), Georgia (especially regarding South Ossetia and to a lesser degree Abkhazia, where the UN has taken the lead role), Tajikistan, and the so-called Minsk Group dealing with the conflict in Nagorno-Karabakh.

In this area, the OSCE record is clearly mixed, and there is probably no single aspect of the work of the OSCE where performance has fallen so short of aspirations. On the positive side of the ledger, in none of these regions has large-scale violence reappeared since the OSCE missions entered. In most cases, the OSCE has played a useful role in monitoring the performance of peacekeeping forces, mostly from Russia, operating under a CIS umbrella. In addition, OSCE activities in democratisation, human rights, the rule of law, refugee resettlement, and support for the rights of persons belonging to minorities has assisted local authorities in keeping tensions below boiling point. Perhaps of greatest importance, in each case the OSCE has played a third party role in keeping lines of communications open and negotiations under way between former belligerent factions to try to resolve some of the important issues underlying these conflicts. Most of these conflicts have become frozen in place: there is no settlement, but also no return to mass violence. These outcomes are no small accomplishment, but they also leave open the potential for the OSCE to improve its effectiveness at managing negotiations to enhance its ability to bring about long-term settlement of frozen conflicts, so that life in these divided states may return to some semblance of normality.

Post-conflict reconstruction and security building

After episodes of significant violence, social relations within society are usually badly broken. Hatred, anger and the desire for revenge become dominant emotions that often reinforce the differences that produced conflict in the first place. Rebuilding war-torn societies is often a long and difficult task. It would not be appropriate to expect Serbs, Croats and Bosnians to forget about their long and bitter struggle in a few short years. Thus one of the major challenges facing the OSCE has been to try to assist societies torn by conflict in their efforts to rebuild. NATO and other multinational forces can help by providing security, both for international personnel and to prevent opposing sides from resuming violence. The EU and other international financial institutions can assist by contributing desperately needed economic aid to rebuild infrastructure and jump start economies so that they can begin to grow on their own, and thus reduce the poverty that so often becomes a breeding ground for violence. But in virtually all cases of violence in the Eurasian region, the primary responsibility for reconstructing political institutions and developing a democratic political framework for resolving differences peacefully – the most difficult task these regions face – has fallen overwhelmingly to the OSCE.

This activity has been the major focus of some of the largest of the OSCE missions, including those in Croatia, Bosnia-Herzegovina and Kosovo. It has also been the primary task of the OSCE presence in Albania, as well as an important function of the missions in Georgia and Moldova. In many ways, the OSCE's activities in this category are those of long-term democracy building, where the OSCE faces the especially difficult challenge of operating in a post-conflict situation. The OSCE's close cooperation with other security institutions, especially the UN, NATO and the EU, is particularly necessary in these regions. In the effort to revive these war-torn societies, the OSCE cannot succeed alone, but its contribution is none the less essential to the successful accomplishment of this task.

Evaluation and recommendations

In summary, when one surveys all of the myriad activities that the OSCE has undertaken since the early 1990s in the field of conflict prevention and resolution, one cannot escape the conclusion that, in spite of all its shortcomings and failures, it plays a much more significant role than it is generally credited with. The OSCE deserves a place of at least equal status with NATO when evaluating the role that multilateral institutions play in contributing to security in the North Atlantic and pan-Eurasian region. The OSCE's role often goes unrecognised, in part because it works in so many relatively obscure locations, and because most of its successes are the consequence of thousands of small accomplishments achieved day by day, village by village, rather than any single, dramatic result that can readily be pointed to.

Furthermore, as noted previously, when it is most successful, very few people notice and thus very little credit is given where credit is due. The failures – Bosnia-Herzegovina, Chechnya and Kosovo – make headlines. The successes can be uncovered by outsiders only with painstaking and difficult research about potential crises that never materialised. The many accomplishments on a daily basis, often small achievements individually, but of great importance collectively, are easily overlooked. The men and women who serve in OSCE missions, in the staff in Vienna, The Hague and Warsaw, and in national delegations to the OSCE institutions, are often making significant accomplishments in heading off crises for which they seldom, if ever, receive the credit they deserve. The OSCE is certainly not a panacea and cannot bring peace to Eurasia alone, but without its steadfast work throughout the region, it is extremely likely that violence, violation of human rights and degradation of the human spirit would be far more widespread than they are today.

That having been said, the next question naturally arises: can the OSCE do better at its conflict-prevention and conflict-resolution functions? And if so, what needs to be done to strengthen it? The answer to the first question is definitely 'yes'. The question of how to strengthen the OSCE is somewhat more complex.[6] One of the strengths of the OSCE is that it is a relatively small, non-bureaucratic and flexible body, in notable contrast to many other multilateral organisations. Any effort to strengthen the organisation must be careful not to undermine its flexibility and resilience, which are essential to its ability to respond in a timely fashion to brewing conflicts.

None the less, there are several modest steps that might strengthen the OSCE's capacity to work effectively in conflict prevention and resolution without entailing great costs or the creation of a large, cumbersome bureaucracy. First, the OSCE needs a more professionally competent, well-trained staff, especially in its missions. At present, it depends too much on short-term volunteers and personnel seconded to the OSCE by the participating states. Many of these people go into the field with little or no knowledge about the region where they are being sent, and little or no training about the process, skills and techniques of conflict resolution. Many are selected to serve on missions because they are available for short-term assignments, or they are seconded by governments that do not need their services elsewhere. Most are on short-term contracts that too often expire just as the people are beginning to get a grasp of the issues with which they are supposed to be dealing. In spite of these limitations, many OSCE personnel have done an excellent job. Yet they could do much better with proper training and enough time in the field really to learn their job and how to perform it effectively.

The REACT program was initiated at the Istanbul Summit in 1999 to recruit and train staff for OSCE missions, especially for emergency missions that must be established with a short lead-time. Each participating state is expected to maintain a roster of qualified and trained individuals who can be called up at short notice to be deployed in areas of developing conflict. REACT has produced some enhancements in training OSCE personnel, but this programme still depends on each participating state to train its own volunteers, and the results are inconsistent at best. Heads of missions are generally very qualified senior diplomats, but they too often have to work with very limited resources and inexperienced, inadequately trained personnel. And the challenge of finding the right people quickly, when they are most needed to head off developing emergencies, remains a serious one that the OSCE must figure out how to surmount.

Similarly, the OSCE could benefit from a strengthened analytical office and information resources in the CPC in Vienna. A small group of highly trained specialists in each of the major mission functions – elections, human rights, rights of persons belonging to minorities, democratisation, freedom of the media, conflict prevention, mediation and conflict resolution – could provide enhanced support to each of the missions when needed. A better library and access to Internet resources could provide enhanced information for missions in the field, which often work in isolated locations. Although the recently created Operations Centre in Vienna has substantially improved the OSCE's capacity to receive and process 'early warning' messages about incipient conflicts and get that information rapidly into the hands of those capable of developing an early response, it depends heavily on the quality of information received from the field and has only a limited capacity to analyse and evaluate that information when it reaches Vienna. Therefore, the OSCE is still often challenged by the difficult task of authorising action *prior* to the point of no return; when the cycle of violence has escalated out of control, OSCE preventive action is no longer sufficient to head off an escalatory spiral.

Second, the OSCE also needs to develop a greater capacity to engage proactively in order to mediate serious conflicts that appear to be on the brink of violence or that have become frozen in the aftermath of violence. The HCNM represents a model of an OSCE official who can enter into disputes rapidly and without any special mandate, enabling him or her to respond on the spur of the moment. Many other OSCE institutions, however, remain mired in potential paralysis created by the need to find consensus (or approximate consensus) within the Permanent Council, where all 55 partic-ipating states are represented. Moving from the recognition that a problem is brewing to a political decision to initiate a timely response remains the Achilles heel of almost all international organisations.

In order to begin to overcome these obstacles to timely response, the OSCE should create a greater institutional capacity to bring 'eminent persons' to intervene on their own initiative in extremely sensitive or urgent situations. This can be done in part by upgrading the status of the OSCE's secretary general, who now plays primarily an administrative role; as a consequence, the secretary general is not generally available to play the kind of role played by the UN secretary general in many severe crises where his or her personal intervention may produce positive results when all other efforts have failed. Political leadership for the OSCE is provided by the chairperson-in-office, but this position rotates every year, so that there is not sufficient continuity or consistency from one individual to the next to enable this person to play a long-term role as ombudsman or mediator. Sometimes, of course, the OSCE can rely on eminent persons coming from among its participating states, as was the case when Richard Holbrooke assumed an important mediating role on behalf of the United States in the conflicts in both Bosnia-Herzegovina and Kosovo. However, it is far better in principle for such individuals to operate within the OSCE framework, except in extraordinary circumstances, since the representative of a multilateral institution will generally be accorded greater legitimacy by disputing parties than will the representative of any single participating state.

In addition, the OSCE often lacks the instruments to influence states to change behaviours that undermine the commitments undertaken under the Helsinki Final Act and the other subsequent documents that have been adopted by the OSCE. In many cases, the more influential states will have to support the OSCE by exerting pressure on intransigent states that resist OSCE efforts to promote democratisation and other improvements in the 'human dimension'. For example, the United States and the Russian Federation need to cooperate to encourage highly authoritarian states such as those in Central Asia and the Caucasus, as well as Belarus, to live up to their commitments undertaken within the OSCE framework. They also should work together more effectively to reinforce OSCE efforts to broker solutions to the most important 'frozen conflicts', such as those in Moldova, Georgia and Nagorno-Karabakh.

Therefore, the US government needs to encourage the Russians to take their own rhetoric about the potential for the OSCE seriously. In the early post-Cold War years, Russian rhetoric emphasised the primacy of the OSCE among European security institutions. The Russians seem to have largely abandoned that effort following their failure to block the enlargement of NATO. But that does not mean that the United States should give up encouraging them to make more effective use of the OSCE to deal with the many and serious security threats that surround them on all sides. Furthermore, the United States can best convince the Russians to take the OSCE seriously by taking it seriously itself. The United States should give the OSCE the same priority it gives to NATO in dealing with broad European security issues, while recognising the different strengths of both institutions. Unless the United States can help enhance the OSCE's capacity to prevent new violent conflicts and to resolve conflicts that recently produced violence, we are likely to be faced with a continuing series of hard choices: either the United States will have to send more troops abroad in politically unpopular missions, an especially difficult task since the US military priority shifted to combating terrorism; or the United States will be forced to stand by while violence and instability spread across regions of Europe and Eurasia, creating, among other negative consequences, fertile ground for terrorist groups to form and flourish.

Similarly, European institutions like the EU or the Council of Europe cannot be counted on to deal with all crises that arise on their own continent. The Europeans also need to give the OSCE significant priority alongside their efforts to enlarge and strengthen the EU. They need to be realistic about the ability of an expanding EU to reach a consensus about foreign and security policy. Even if they are successful in that endeavour, their capacity to implement effective action is likely to be limited without the close cooperation of the United States and/or Russia. And such cooperation can best be achieved when they work within the framework of the one European security institution in which those two countries are represented, that is, the OSCE.

In the process, US officials and the attentive public might come to realise that the OSCE also serves long-term US interests by helping to create a more stable, peaceful and democratic regime in those regions of Eurasia formerly ruled by Communist governments. Indeed, this is a vital interest that all OSCE participating states share, even though they do not always fully recognise this convergence of interest. Promoting collective action to support these goals of cooperative security throughout the OSCE region thus ought to be a high-priority goal for US foreign policy.

Finally, the United States should encourage other regions of the world experiencing insecurity and violence to consider borrowing, when appropriate, concepts and approaches to regional security that have been successful in the Eurasian context. Of course, security in each region is influenced by different cultural, political and strategic environments. But the OSCE has shown that intervention by a regional security institution may be undertaken with greater sensitivity to the local conditions, greater awareness of the underlying issues, and deeper understanding of specific regional concerns than is generally possible for global international organisations like the UN or global hegemonic powers like the United States. In several instances the Organisation of African Unity and the Asian Regional Forum have begun to experiment cautiously with some of the confidence-building measures and techniques of preventive diplomacy developed by the OSCE. Thus, with due sensitivity to regional variations, the OSCE also offers a model of how a regional security organisation can strengthen security and promote democratic development in volatile regions of the world, and its value as a model ought to be taken seriously in all regions of the globe threatened with instability and violent conflict.

Notes

1 The CSCE was renamed the OSCE in 1995 to reflect the fact that it had evolved from a series of itinerant conferences to a fully institutionalised organisation.
2 Ambassador van der Stoel has summarised his philosophy for responding to conflicts involving the rights of persons belonging to minorities as follows: '...the protection of persons belonging to minorities has to be seen as essentially in the interest of the state and of the majority. Stability and security are as a rule best served by ensuring that persons belonging to national minorities can effectively enjoy their rights. If the state shows loyalty to persons belonging to minorities, it can expect loyalty in return from those persons who will have a stake in the stability and well-being of that state ... solutions should be sought as much as possible within the framework of the state itself'. Quoted in Connie Peck, *Sustainable Peace: The Role of the UN and Regional Organizations in Preventing Conflict* (Lanham, MD: Rowman and Littlefield, 1998), p. 45.
3 Throughout the decade from 1992 through to 2001, I was engaged in research to evaluate the effectiveness of OSCE missions and field activities. I was assisted in this endeavour by support from the Center for Foreign Policy Development at Brown University in 1992, a Fulbright Fellowship to the OSCE based in Vienna in 1997, and a Jennings Randolph Senior Fellowship at the US Institute for Peace in Washington in 1998. As part of this research, I conducted extensive interviews with heads of mission; attended numerous OSCE meetings, including regular meetings of the Permanent Council; read the activity reports of missions from throughout this period; and made on-site visits to several OSCE missions in the field. The evaluations and conclusions presented below draw primarily from my own observations and analysis in conducting this research rather than from secondary sources.

4 For a further exploration of these roles and some primary examples of their successful performance by the OSCE, see my chapter in a book released by the Committee on International Conflict Resolution of the US National Academy of Sciences: P. Terrence Hopmann, 'The Organization for Security and Cooperation in Europe: Its Contribution to Conflict Prevention and Resolution', in Paul C. Stern and Daniel Druckman (eds), *International Conflict Resolution After the Cold War* (Washington, DC: National Academy Press, 2000), pp. 569–615.

5 See Bruce M. Russett and John Oneal, *Triangulating Peace: Democracy, Interdependence and International Organizations* (New York: Norton, 2001), Ch. 1. For a more sceptical assessment of the democratic peace hypothesis, see Joanne Gowa, *Ballots and Bullets: The Elusive Democratic Peace* (Princeton, NJ: Princeton University Press, 1999).

6 A more detailed set of suggestions about how to strengthen the OSCE may be found in P. Terrence Hopmann, *Building Security in Post-Cold War Eurasia: The OSCE and U.S. Foreign Policy* (Washington, DC: United States Institute of Peace, Peaceworks No. 39, 1999).

9

Paths to peace for NATO's partnerships in Eurasia

Joshua B. Spero

This chapter examines the role of multilateral cooperative efforts and institutionalised security cooperation in the Eurasian area through a study of NATO's PfP programme. In terms of measuring the capacity to increase Eurasian security, the general track record of the post-Cold War security institutions in non-traditional areas of societal democratisation, economic modernisation, civil and cross-border war prevention, and Eurasian integration presents a mixed picture.[1] By focusing on the Eurasian politico-military partnerships created with NATO, it is possible to gain an understanding of how targeted policies supported by multilateral institutions can increase security in the Eurasian area. NATO's PfP provides a myriad of programmes between NATO and non-NATO states utilising multilateral military cooperation to educate, train, exercise, and allow military staff and civilian officials to operate effectively together.[2] Since its January 1994 inception, the PfP has created substantial security enhancements in Eurasia and contributed directly to the capacity of allied nations to deploy troops to the region in the post-September 11 anti-terrorist coalition.

The PfP has evolved into an exemplary model of institutionalised civil-military cooperation among over forty European and Eurasian states. The success of the PfP has had an important impact feeding back into NATO, thus facilitating NATO's own post-Cold War survival. None the less, the future of PfP will depend heavily on whether NATO can adapt adequately to the kinds of post-September 11 threats confronting both allies and partners. By incorporating the experiences of the PfP into NATO planning, the alliance may be in a stronger position to adapt to current and future challenges.[3] Almost six years of PfP cooperative planning and operations in Eurasia have laid part of the foundation to counter such non-traditional threats as terrorism, the proliferation of WMD, ethnic conflict, resource depletion and narcotics trafficking in Eurasia. The PfP provides the principal mechanism through which NATO cooperates with individual and regional groupings of non-NATO nations. These cooperative mechanisms focus on long-term training regimens and have integrated the Eurasian participants into NATO planning facilities at NATO headquarters in Belgium and at all NATO military commands. This chapter concentrates on several aspects of the PfP's contribution to Eurasian security.

The origins of the PfP

During the early to mid-1990s a handful of key American officials, in the Departments of Defense and State, developed the PfP concept. PfP was born in 1993, largely from concepts developed by Joseph Kruzel, deputy assistant secretary of defence for Europe and NATO, and General John Shalikashvili, chairman of the joint chiefs of staff, who had served previously as NATO supreme allied commander of Europe. Though the initial demand for PfP reflected a desire to provide a short-term alternative to expanding NATO's membership, the concept eventually evolved so that it truly changed early post-Cold War thinking about multilateral European security cooperation. At its core, the PfP is premised on a belief that the more civilian strategists and military operators plan together within an integrated civil-military command structure like NATO, the greater the likelihood of peaceful international relations. Moreover, by introducing states to western models of civil-military relations, NATO might help to stabilise weak post-Soviet states throughout eastern Europe and Eurasia – even those states that would not eventually seek NATO membership. Such a design required significant building-block initiatives to proceed in earnest and develop institutionally. NATO represented the ideal institution through which to promote this goal because of its multilateral and cooperative focus on shared politico-military approaches, norms, standards and operating procedures developed over decades of multilateral cooperation.

American strategic planners, mainly in the Pentagon, however, needed to ensure that PfP first survived its early tests. Such challenges included American initiatives to pursue long-term linkages and then enhanced relationships through NATO institutionally with the unstable states in the Caucasus and Central Asia – frequently seen by NATO's European allies, except Turkey, as outside the area of European security. Senior US officials, reinforced with crucial staff initiatives (mostly emanating from the joint chiefs of staff), made this happen during the administration of President William J. Clinton.[4] Each participant in the interagency debate had different reasons for backing the PfP, with some seeing it as a means of deferring debate over expanding NATO membership and others seeing it as facilitating NATO's expansion over time. Either way, had this coalition of key senior US policy-makers not thrown its support and leadership behind the Kruzel–Shalikashvili initiative, the PfP process, without American leadership, would probably have floundered within NATO.[5]

US and NATO allies projected PfP as a non-threatening security strategy across Europe and Eurasia during the 1990s. Indeed, the PfP process evolved to become a force multiplier strategy eventually serving the interests of stability throughout the region. Through PfP, NATO and PfP nations could project their forces collectively to confront traditional and non-traditional security threats, as was demonstrated by their crucial role in providing a baseline for successful engagements in the Balkans and Afghanistan.[6] The PfP initiative became one of the most important tools for the US national security strategy of engagement and enlargement to promote multilateral dialogue, planning and operating mechanisms for cooperative security. Significantly, as the PfP process progressed during the latter part of the 1990s, particularly in Georgia, Azerbaijan, Kazakhstan, Kyrgyzstan, Uzbekistan and Tajikistan, joint efforts to reduce consistent problems posed by non-state actors arose from PfP multilateral regional cooperative security that promoted, for example, counter-terrorist education, training and planning among Eurasian PfP members.[7]

Establishing durable procedures and processes for PfP initially presented a major challenge to NATO planners. By working with key allies such as Great Britain, Germany, Norway, Denmark, the Netherlands, Italy, Greece and Turkey, and critical PfP partners such as Poland, Ukraine, Finland, Sweden, Albania, Georgia, Kazakhstan, Kyrgyzstan and Uzbekistan, America led the shaping of PfP. Washington gave early impetus to galvanise PfP with congressionally appropriated funding, titled the Warsaw Initiative. By working closely on multilateral policy recommendations at NATO head-quarters and throughout the NATO military command structure, the US-allied strategy stemmed from the belief that through multilateral leadership Eurasian security could be enhanced. Even with this political dynamism, American civil-military planners knew instinctively that the military held the quickest, most pragmatic capabilities to reinforce the early, nascent and fragile PfP process in every region involved, including the Caucasus and Central Eurasia. Crucial US congressional staff members on the Senate Armed Services Committee and the Senate Foreign Relations Committee convinced members of Congress to allocate Warsaw Initiative funding to the joint chiefs of staff in late 1994 to initiate the PfP process.

The first Warsaw Initiative instalment of $30 million allowed US joint chiefs of staff planners to formulate and recommend a broad multilateral vision of PfP to General Shalikashvili, coordinating closely with Kruzel and his European, Eurasian and NATO staffs in the Office of the Secretary of Defense. To achieve such a vision, General John Shalikashvili, in turn, forged a dynamic political and military strategy with his strategic plans and policy staff who covered NATO and Eurasia. As chairman of the joint chiefs of staff, Shalikashvili gained support from US and NATO European and Atlantic commanders and built a strong consensus in support of PfP with the secretary of defence, William Perry, and the secretary of state, Warren

Christopher. That consensus was then taken by the national security advisor, Anthony Lake, to President Clinton with the necessary game plan to implement PfP. President Clinton, in turn, was able to persuade NATO allies and PfP participants alike of the intrinsic value of this programme.

Long-term civil-military exercise programmes across Europe and Eurasia were soon developed through the PfP. These often involved thousands of civilian planners and troops conducting training events and deployments several months long. In addition to formal PfP activity, US and other NATO members conducted hundreds of bilateral and multilateral 'in-the-spirit-of - PfP' programmes. As initially conceived by the US joint chiefs of staff and the Office of the Secretary of Defense, many 'in-the-spirit-of-PfP' programmes evolved into formal NATO activities. These institutional mechanisms for NATO's PfP process drew, along with important allied and partner contributions, considerably on American resources, financial support, and equipment leases or purchases to the majority of PfP nations. Consequently, US Warsaw Initiative funding, increased in subsequent years, gave PfP states important financial breathing space. Within the constraints of limited PfP nation budgets, often consumed by personnel and pension costs, American and NATO strategists pushed PfP states to modernise their militaries as best they could, while also maintaining or increasing their training and readiness. These were crucial steps for any serious effort to meet the multiple post-Cold War security challenges in Eurasia. As a result of this vision being taken from theory into practice, the PfP process accelerated and solidified throughout NATO's political and military committees and command structures while also taking root in many allied and PfP nations' national planning structures. As a result, PfP emerged as perhaps the most significant operational bridge between Europe and Eurasia.[8]

Bandwagoning towards PfP

While it is clear why PfP was so appealing to the NATO members, a key question remains: why was this particular form of multilateral cooperation so successful among the participating countries of Eurasia? International relations theory, especially that which assesses the dynamics of bandwagoning and balancing behaviour among states, helps to a considerable degree in answering this question – and also in explaining the sources of regional stability in post-Cold War Eurasia. As Randall Schweller explains, bandwagoning portrays actions that states conduct to gain reward and profit from aligning with the stronger side, while balancing characterises efforts that states take to align with the weaker in order to achieve the security of the state.[9] The results from balancing, however, frequently entail more costs to states because such alignment involves balancing with a state or coalition vigorously against a strong predatory state or coalition. This balancing, whether offensively or defensively, by a state or coalition against an external threat perceived as serious aims to preserve and protect the state.[10] As Glenn Snyder also maintains, 'the choice between conciliation and balancing involves optimising among security, autonomy, and intrinsic values: conciliation buys security at some cost to intrinsic values; balancing buys it at the cost of autonomy'.[11] Moreover, antagonistic or aggressive alignment often comes at a higher cost than cooperative or conciliatory alignment. Security-seeking states can reduce the potential for conflict by revealing benign motivations, demonstrating foreign policy transparency, and signalling reassurance to decrease the risks of misperception leading to conflict, therefore avoiding spiralling tensions that can lead to a regional security dilemma.[12] This defensive concept of cooperative alignment might describe state alignment more accurately, as states are choosing multilateral forms of enhancing their perceived security interests.[13] This approach generally provides the best conceptual framework for understanding why Eurasian states have chosen to align with NATO through the PfP.

By choosing a strategy with the least costly alignment policy, a state decides on its balance of interest. If, as Schweller states, the objective of bandwagoning centres on the opportunity for a state to gain by joining the security system it values, the state determines that its cost to achieve security defensively might be lower than to defend the existing order, which may be more unfavourable. The security system comprises a stronger state or coalition of stronger states and the bandwagoning state attempts to align, usually during a time of geopolitical change, and not in a manner threatening to other states – especially those states outside existing security institutions. Building on Schweller's bandwagoning definition, Mark Kramer offers what he characterises as non-predatory bandwagoning alignment. States ally with others not solely because of the external security and stability sought, but also because of the expectation of distributive gains for many of the states involved.[14] Kramer's concept of 'non-military' state alignment or non-predatory bandwagoning provides insights as to how the PfP led both NATO and its participants towards multilateral cooperative security strategies. Non-predatory bandwagoning states, as those joining the PfP, generally try to attain gains not through aggression, but from extending the bandwagoning state's value system. Encouraged by NATO, PfP states have sought to institutionalise the values of cooperative security even if they do not actually seek formal NATO membership.

By becoming more 'western' in their geopolitical orientation, PfP countries hope to achieve a variety of distributive gains resulting from the positive-sum experiences of non-predatory bandwagoning. PfP participants have chosen a particular form of cooperative security behaviour as an alternative to behaviour motivated by power and threat – which can lead to aggression and war. Within this conceptual framework, the motivations behind the general Eurasian trend towards PfP can best be understood. Seen as the most threatening entity by the majority of current PfP members during the Cold War, a post-Cold War NATO provided the non-predatory bandwagoning states with a practical path for adapting their predominantly non-threatening foreign policy and military postures, while also signalling to the international community the depth of their own state identity choices, as in the post-Soviet geopolitical space. Consequently, aggressive interstate behaviour in historically war-torn Eurasia has not emerged among PfP members.

Despite these historical achievements, there are some negative assessments of the NATO/PfP outreach process in Eurasia. A primary criticism views the PfP as a means of delaying NATO's promise to maintain an open door for absorbing new members – with the collective defence security guarantee accompanying membership. Additionally, some critics saw the PfP as not providing enough of a comprehensive strategy for ensuring the security of the signatory states. Another critique centres on the risks of overextending NATO member resources in outreach ventures to non-member PfP countries – thus diluting NATO's traditional core mission of collective defence. An additional concern reasons that overextending already resource-strapped militaries emerging from the former Warsaw Pact and post-Soviet states only undermines their prospects for democratisation. Finally, PfP advocates, both in NATO countries and in the participating non-NATO states, have generally seen the programme as receiving inadequate resource investment for it to succeed. Despite these criticisms, PfP has been the principal means for organising effective multilateral military coordination that both broadens and refines NATO's new missions and serves as the centre of geopolitical gravity for the interested post-Communist countries of Eurasia.[15]

Cooperation between NATO and non-NATO nations, even nations that contributed troops outside the PfP framework from Latin America, Africa, the Middle East and Asia, became important foundations of NATO's post-Cold War missions in operations such as Bosnia, Albania, Kosovo and the Former Yugoslav Republic of Macedonia. The PfP's consultative functions cannot solve the often ingrained domestic problems within any given PfP member-state. Rather, PfP ultimately provides a critical baseline for NATO and non-NATO nations to begin grappling effectively with twenty-first-century perils: WMD proliferation, international narcotics trafficking, resource depletion and environmental degradation. An important question arises in the context of these security threats: can the Eurasian countries achieve more concerted cooperation via the PfP process to overcome, or significantly reduce, such regional security challenges? Will the relatively short history of the PfP process lead Eurasian states towards the kind of successful historical reconciliation witnessed between former enemies such as France and Germany or Germany and Poland?[16] Given the critical American role in European security within NATO's intricate structures that established the basis for Franco-German and German–Polish reconciliation, arguments might favour similar possibilities for the Caucasus and Central

Asia, albeit taking into account Eurasia's uniqueness.

When regarded as inducing multilateral political and military cooperation, the PfP promotes an enhanced capacity for states to align with NATO as a means to avoid historic great power struggles. Such interstate behaviour may help generate western ideas and state identities based on the norms and standards defined by NATO as key criteria for PfP cooperation. Nevertheless, even in such ideal circumstances, anarchy still prevails in the international system, and state leaders must choose from political alignments that will first and foremost help them ensure the security of their states. None the less, as when the United States deployed forces in Eurasia during the autumn 2001 campaign in Afghanistan, its state strategies were indirectly aided by the years of multilateral cooperation gained through the PfP.

PfP pragmatism: multilateral and cooperative

How did PfP evolve to reach the stage where its mechanisms and procedures provide a supporting baseline for counter-terrorist coalition operations as in Afghanistan? The PfP processes represent a practical cooperative security framework between NATO and individual PfP states involving defence, operational and budgetary planning, military exercises and civil emergency operations. Its defensive principles and incentives for states to bandwagon politically and militarily with, but not necessarily to join, NATO make PfP both practical and realistic. Such cooperative security options presented Europe's neutral states (Austria, Finland, Ireland, Switzerland and Sweden) with creative post-Cold War policy options. These states, as well as most in the post-Soviet Caucasus region and Central Asia, continually reiterate that they do not need to join NATO. Rather, they want to strengthen PfP and not jeopardise relationships with other non-NATO states, particularly Russia. Therefore, a total of 46 PfP countries plan and operate for crisis management and directly enhance NATO-led operations. In turn, these states also contribute significantly to NATO's post-Cold War adaptation. However, the way the US-led and non-NATO coalition against international terrorism develops in Eurasia will amount to a test of the future viability of the PfP. The sustainability of the PfP will be especially tested after NATO's November 2002 enlargement. For example, as NATO enlargement supersedes PfP, there will be fewer incentives remaining to invest resources in this form of multilateralism.

Because it does not guarantee the security of its signatories, PfP challenges the traditional views of NATO as a solely collective defence institution designed to defend against a threat to its members.[17] Increasingly, the operational distinction between NATO and PfP members barely exists. The blurring of the distinction, however, strengthens rather than detracts from NATO's evolution and concomitant missions. As testified to by the hundreds of PfP events annually and the numerous ties with NATO's politico-military command headquarters and staffs, PfP mechanisms bring together, rather than separate, Eurasian states. Such a tool provides politico-military link-ages and critical consultative ties without requiring PfP members to join NATO. For example, few observers thought it would be possible in NATO's first PfP exercise, 'Cooperative Bridge', to behold German troops crossing the Polish border unobstructed for the first time since World War II. As the newly unified German military re-entered Poland in September 1994, post-Cold War troops peacefully exercised alongside Americans and half a dozen other NATO and new PfP nations to conduct a platoon-level peacekeeping mission.[18]

Within less than a decade the PfP process has developed considerably. For example, by 2001, the annual Black Sea-based NATO-led multinational exercise, 'Cooperative Partner 2001', involved 4,000 troops from 13 NATO and PfP countries, including ships, fighter aircraft and helicopters. Hosted for the first time by Georgia in June 2001, 'Cooperative Partner 2001' entailed a large-scale anti-terrorism operation to release hostages, peace-keeping operations, and disaster-relief and rescue missions.[19] Consequently, the September 2001 terrorist attacks on New York and Washington, DC, only underscored the vital importance of the PfP exercise in Georgia and the Black Sea the preceding June, which tested the skills and procedures required to deal with real world crisis scenarios. From Poland to Georgia, Europe and Eurasia have experienced the evolution of a cooperative security process that provides the framework for former enemy states to train and operate together. This framework allows post-Cold War European and Eurasian states to conduct twenty-first-century missions more effectively, whether via NATO-led operations or through coalitions of the willing. In effect, PfP has helped to increase security in Eurasia by lowering the transaction costs of multilateral joint military action should states decide to act within a multi-lateral framework for managing regional security threats.

Eventually, PfP's practical tools went well beyond NATO's initial outreach efforts to former enemies, which initially took the form of confer-ences, seminars and workshops. Indeed, nearly every major development in NATO's post-Cold War transformation can be linked in some respect to the PfP initiative and evolution. NATO enlargement now proceeds with a base-line of indicators and criteria developed from PfP. The NATO relationships with Russia and Ukraine build on and use PfP's mechanisms and underlying principles. NATO's important operations in the Balkans depended upon initial training and exercises via PfP and utilised PfP's civil-military interac-tion between NATO and non-NATO nations to make national force planning more effective and efficient. Such exercising and organisation, within a cycli-cal planning–execution–evaluation process, formed the embryonic head-quarters, staffs and command structures in Bosnia; enabled the procedures for dealing with the aftermath of the Albanian collapse; provided the foun-dation for the operations in Kosovo; and figured prominently in the NATO mission to the Former Yugoslav Republic of Macedonia. The PfP framework also indirectly facilitates NATO's Mediterranean Dialogue with North African (Morocco and Tunisia) and Middle Eastern states (Egypt, Israel, and Jordan). The concept underlying the PfP concept has even been raised in US policy-making circles for application to other parts of the world, even if without engaging the direct institutional structure of NATO.

Alone, the PfP cannot be adjudged as having prevented the emergence of Eurasia's multiple security dilemmas or resolved them. The PfP framework did not avert the carnage and destruction in the Balkans or stop the terrorist attacks emanating from the borders of Central Asia in Afghanistan. Moreover, PfP cannot give its members the absolute security guarantee many of them want. The crucial security contribution involves the evolution, operationalisation and institutionalisation of PfP mechanisms at NATO headquarters and within individual national planning and bureaucratic processes. By building upon the early PfP baseline of national defence and budgetary transparency that upholds the tenets of democratic control of national armed forces, NATO and PfP nations bolstered military effectiveness of multinational forces that can operate with NATO.[20] Such a broad, fundamental application by states working within NATO allows politicians, policy-planners and military commanders to grapple together with global trans-sovereign challenges.[21]

Deepening PfP partnerships in Eurasia

Eurasia is an area challenged by a variety of domestic political, economic and ethno-national security dilemmas that PfP alone cannot resolve. Moreover, PfP is unlikely to influence the direction of future challenges stemming from growing corruption, autocracy, oil and natural gas competition, great power competition between Russia, China and America, or competition between regional powers such as Iran, Turkey and Pakistan – all are quite beyond the capacity of a programme like PfP to influence directly. Only the states of Eurasia themselves, working in cooperation with other key states and international institutions such as the UN, World Bank and IMF, can deal with these problems directly.[22] However, NATO's ongoing PfP process can apply the successful experiences of nearly a decade of multilateral cooperative programmes within the region towards an ongoing stabilising role. NATO's planning for regional and international contingencies, such as counter-terrorist operations or WMD counter-proliferation, reflects the value of such planning, training and operational linkages developed over time. Without the PfP baseline established during the latter half of the 1990s, potential stabilisation, even future democratisation and modernisation, might not occur as effectively in Eurasia – extending as far east as Afghanistan.[23]

If it continues to receive significant support from the NATO countries, PfP can maintain the bridge of greater political and military understanding between Europe and Eurasia. PfP can remain as a directory for its Eurasian participants to follow for reducing the volatility and danger sparked by potential civil and international conflicts throughout the region. Without the consistent PfP cooperation and coordination that allow US and NATO members to survey potential military training centres and even future basing areas, regional tensions and attendant state instabilities might increase in the future.[24] Yet, in the aftermath of the terrorist attacks on America, the galvanisation of the world community's opinions on counter-terrorism may now generate a historic opportunity for reducing future regional security problems in Eurasia via a deepening PfP process.[25]

Some of PfP's prospects, however, may be constrained by the various mixed signals emitted by NATO towards Eurasia. These limitations include the criticism that no clear strategic thinking exists for NATO's efforts and that individual members such as America and Turkey often pursue goals diverging from NATO as a whole, while antagonising Russia, China and Iran. Such problems influence regional security while potentially involving some NATO members in missions that they would rather avoid.[26] Although some aspects of these contentions appear accurate, there is often a tendency among some analysts to misrepresent the intent of the PfP process. NATO never intended, for example, that the PfP define a policy to oppose states such as Russia, China or Iran. Moreover, although many PfP members may never seek to join NATO, these countries can continue to forge multilateral political and military cooperation aimed at reducing regional instability and preventing future conflict. This alignment reflects non-predatory bandwagoning that PfP signatory states in Eurasia seek *vis-à-vis* NATO. Some Eurasian states also need reassurances that they will not, in the future, be threatened by Russia. Consequently, some PfP members will continue to use their participation as a means of signalling their relative geopolitical independence from Moscow. However, the most important gains for these states stem from their broader linkage with the West as established through the PfP – and such trends include Russia, too. Alternative regional security groupings such as GUUAM (Georgia, Ukraine, Uzbekistan, Azerbaijan and Moldova) and the SCO (Russia, China, Kazakhstan, Kyrgyzstan and Tajikistan) have not yet emerged as functional alternatives to the PfP. Indeed, tensions in Eurasia have often risen as a result of these kinds of nascent balancing institutions that run counter to the sort of bandwagoning being pursued through PfP's cooperative security architectures. Potentially, the historical balance of power notions that have driven some of the Russian or Chinese alternatives to NATO programmes may decline even further as China and Russia engage in the mutual gains of counter-terrorist cooperation with western institutions in Eurasia. Given the rapid emergence of American influence in Eurasia via the US-led international coalition to combat global terrorism, entirely new links among nearly all the region's states appeared more possible in 2002 than ever before.[27]

Developments following the September 11 2001 terrorist attacks indicate support for the possibility of accelerated cooperation in Eurasia. China and Russia quickly endorsed UN resolutions in support of US efforts against terrorism, as did the NATO–Russia council in Brussels. Neither country raised significant concerns when US troops were deployed in Eurasian states surrounding Afghanistan. Within the region, the US-supported Central Asian Peacekeeping Battalion ('Centrasbat') is comprised of units from Kyrgyzstan, Uzbekistan and Kazakhstan. 'Centrasbat' trains Eurasian participants in the spirit of the PfP process. These alignments serve both as a key basis for multilateral cooperation and for American power projection in the region. By monitoring the Tajik–Afghan border, 'Centrasbat' prevents elements of Tajikistan's extremist Islamic opposition, which had fled to safe havens in Afghanistan, from returning.[28] The regional cooperative security arrangement among all eight Trans-Caucasus and Central Asian states against the proliferation of dangerous materials and goods is another important PfP activity that promotes multilateral cooperation in the region.[29] Finally, Central Asia and the Caucasus, because of their geostrategic location, now serve as key staging grounds for operations that the international coalition initiates against terrorist networks. These deployments included American, British, Turkish, French and other forces already familiar with the territory because of their years of experiences gained through the PfP.[30] Taken together, these crucial international cooperative steps, based on a new willingness to set aside seemingly intractable geopolitical differences in order to fight terrorism, delineate a larger framework expanding on PfP objectives and goals.

Such expansive PfP cooperation in Eurasia did not arise spontaneously. Since the mid-1990s, the NATO allies have methodically established and implemented numerous long-term training and education programmes, including exercise cycles and familiarisation with facilities across Eurasia. Without this preparation, the rapid insertion of NATO and PfP nation troops for operations into and out of areas in Afghanistan and the Pankisi Gorge on the border with Georgia would have been greatly slowed. The PfP process took firmer hold in Eurasia when the Americans launched a series of bilateral 'in-the-spirit-of-PfP' interoperability programmes, and when NATO coordinated the 'Combined Endeavor', 'Regional Cooperation', and 'Centrasbat' exercise series. These multiple phased programmes and exercises evolved from dozens of preparatory seminars, workshops, conferences and small-scale training projects that have annually culminated in field training, command post exercising, and command, control, communications and computer systems development.

Interoperability characterises one of the primary capabilities for PfP states to possess in order to link and operate with NATO for the range of PfP missions. The US Defense Department realised from the outset of the PfP process that some of its nascent bilateral programmes from the pre-PfP and post-Cold War era could be adapted to fulfil critical PfP country interoperability objectives. The American strategy of aiding PfP nations to achieve interoperability with NATO centred on three main programmes intended for all PfP nations. For the Eurasian participants in PfP, the US Warsaw Initiative still provides critical assistance towards participation in these multilateral 'in-the-spirit-of-PfP' interoperability efforts. The first key area, the Regional Airspace Initiative (RAI), focused on developing civil-military airspace regimes fully compatible and interoperable with west European civilian airspace organisations and NATO.[31] Second, the PfP Information Management System (PIMS) represents a system of communications connectivity and information management using off-the-shelf hardware and software designed to link PfP nation capitals with US and NATO facilities for planning exercises, sharing information and deepening daily cooperation. Establishment of close communications between PfP and NATO not only overcomes practical problems of communications with PfP capitals, but also ensures that PfP nations feel linked in a close, cooperative relationship to NATO. PIMS remains fundamental to distance learning and emergency planning. Finally, the Defense Resource Management Studies Program (DRMS) provides country-specific exchanges concerning defence planning and force structure methodology that both sides use to guide resource management and procurement decisions. DRMS facilitates establishment of a rationalised defence management system similar to those already in use by NATO allies. This crucial NATO-related budgeting and planning approach aids civil-military restructuring, especially infrastructure requirements. All of these US programmes reach well into the Eurasian area and provide an instrumental foundation for regional cooperation and integration.[32]

Since most of the Eurasian signatories started their PfP programmes during the mid-1990s, the NATO nations now operating in these regions for counter-terrorist contingencies can acquire an additional operational foothold via multilateral participation in PfP processes. In the case of exercise 'Combined Endeavor', conducted under the auspices of the US, European Command (EUCOM – Stuttgart, Germany), synchronised with NATO's Supreme Allied Commander Europe (SACEUR) at Supreme Headquarters Allied Powers Europe (SHAPE), and held mainly at key US training facilities in Germany, the participants identify and document command, control, communications and computer interoperability between NATO and PfP nations' equipment to attain compatibility. This exercise now includes most of the Caucasus and Central Asian states among nearly 25 NATO and PfP nations. By broadening this training, the US Central Command (CENTCOM – Tampa, Florida) worked with EUCOM and individual NATO states to start the 'Regional Cooperation' exercise series. This German-based command post and computer-assisted exercise, located at the US-run Warrior Preparation Center, concentrates on peace enforcement training for contingencies of the designated Central Asian peacekeeping battalion and Caucasus contingents. By 2000, the event involved all of the key PfP states, except Tajikistan, with observers from Mongolia, Turkey and Ukraine. Finally, CENTCOM shapes the 'Centrasbat' field training exercise to enhance the Central Asian battalion's capabilities to conduct peacekeeping operations to support either UN or NATO missions, while also advancing cooperation between and among Eurasian states and other non-NATO nations.[33]

Like 'Cooperative Partner', 'Cooperative Determination 2001', held in Azerbaijan in November 2001, broadened regional, multilateral cooperation. Through a sophisticated 600-person command post exercise that focused on a multinational brigade staff and mobile medical centres for helping civilians, this first-time PfP exercise in Azerbaijan involved significant crisis management contingencies. Comprised of many NATO and PfP nations, including Greece and Turkey, the US and the International Committee of the Red Cross, the exercise utilised a scenario for both peacekeeping and humanitarian operations.[34] Given the success of PfP exercises in the Caucasus, there is every possibility that such exercises can be expanded throughout Eurasia and possibly extend to include Afghanistan, Pakistan and even, over time, China and Iran.

Toward future NATO partnerships in Eurasia

This chapter has addressed several issues for the PfP process and its cooperative security framework within the larger security context of Eurasia. First, PfP reflected cooperative security policies and processes, best understood within the theoretical framework of realistic and pragmatic state alignments. These alignments symbolise non-predatory bandwagoning with PfP signatories seeking close relations with the once-threatening NATO institution they opposed as part of the Warsaw Pact and former USSR during the Cold War. This broad Euro-Atlantic, European and Eurasian post-Cold War structural transformation affects the way its members have defined NATO's new missions, specifically via PfP. NATO members and PfP signatories synchronised their threat perceptions over the last half of the 1990s and formed the practical cooperative security needed to change NATO as an institution.

Second, PfP has evolved into an important international cooperative security framework since the early 1990s. The PfP mechanisms underscored the progressive and advanced international security standards and procedures required for former enemies to operate together and to confront the complexities and often violent upheavals of the twenty-first century. The PfP process serves as one counter-measure against such crucial security threats as terrorism. From the practical civil-military cooperation and coordination arising from thousands of political and military events and real world operations during the 1990s, PfP stands alone as the principle NATO means of multilateral security cooperation in Eurasia. PfP provides a unique set of tools for NATO and non-NATO policy-makers, planners and operators to tackle together the challenges of the twenty-first century.

As the PfP process gains greater acceptance in Eurasia, NATO appears destined for unforeseen, although not surprising, further evolution.[35] Indeed, NATO's 1999 New Strategic Concept established the basic framework for a broader concept of NATO's twenty-first-century mission. The 1999 Strategic Concept provides PfP states with the ability to consult, cooperate and coordinate during crises, and to operate with NATO forces in a variety of contingencies. Although the NATO outreach to Eurasian nations cannot begin to solve all of the region's security challenges, PfP has served as a crucial baseline from which to forge the political and military ties needed for the United States and its allies to establish and maintain an effective international coalition against global terrorism.

More lessons can eventually be learned about how well policy-makers, planners and operators functioned in and around PfP countries surrounding Afghanistan as well as in the Caucasus and in Southeastern Europe. As a region long left out of Euro-Atlantic security calculations, the Eurasian area conceivably will represent a more important geostrategic space for the major world powers. Whether interests lie in access to natural resources, environmental challenges, or multilateral efforts to combat international terrorism, the Eurasian area is destined to become increasingly important to NATO's operational interests. PfP's pragmatic and realistic mechanisms provide the needed foundation from which a far different type of international coalition can confront non-traditional security challenges. Ultimately, the PfP's future success will depend on its resource requirements and NATO member resource investment. With an adequate degree of NATO attention, progress can be sustained towards enabling international coalitions of the present and future to launch operations – counter-terrorist and otherwise – based on lessons learned and training areas provided. As NATO's most important member, the United States must figure prominently, however, in this multilateral cooperative security process if PfP is to survive. Moreover, the United States, its NATO allies and PfP partners together must reshape NATO to deal more effectively with training, planning and operating to counter the twenty-first-century challenges of terrorism, WMD proliferation, ethnic conflict and narcotics trafficking.[36]

Countering the original criticism that NATO's PfP project signalled western hesitation and lack of resolve on NATO enlargement in the early 1990s, PfP now provides the key operational planning tools for multilateral security cooperation in Eurasia. PfP remains the only proactive multilateral, cooperative and political/military institutional procedure for NATO and Eurasia to test, modify and develop current and future plans for joint efforts at combating the non-traditional security challenges in the region. The initial American unilateralism in its war on terrorism and its policies towards 'rogue' states have no doubt increased transatlantic tensions more than the regional problems of Eurasia. As a result, the means for ensuring the preservation of the NATO and PfP regional Eurasian cooperation requires a consensus – particularly between Americans and Europeans – on their interests inside and outside of Europe. In the absence of such a consensus, it will become increasingly difficult to coordinate the effective planning of future operations out of area. If a consensus can be reached and sustained, then troop deployments will occur multilaterally, or US planners will synchronise their much more powerful and rapidly deployable US troop contingents for phased multilateral PfP operations after first-stage deployments. The question remains of whether NATO itself can adequately adapt to the dramatically changed twenty-first-century security environment by going sufficiently beyond its core Altantic orientation.

Notes

1 For example: S. Frederick Starr, 'Making Eurasia Stable', *Foreign Affairs*, 75:1 (1996), pp. 80–92; Strobe Talbott, 'A Farewell to Flashman: American Policy in the Caucasus and Central Asia', address at the Johns Hopkins School of Advanced International Studies, Washington, DC, *U.S. Department of State Dispatch*, 8:7 (1997), pp. 10–13; Glen E. Howard, 'NATO and the Caucasus: The Caspian Axis', in Stephen Blank (ed.), *NATO After Enlargement: New Challenges, New Missions, New Forces* (Carlisle Barracks, PA: Strategic Studies Institute, US Army War College, 1998), pp. 151–228; Rachel Bronson, 'NATO's Expanding Presence in the Caucasus and Central Asia', in Blank, *NATO After Enlargement* pp. 229–54; Robin Bhatty and Rachel Bronson, 'NATO's Mixed Signals in the Caucasus and Central Asia', *Survival*, 42:3 (2000), pp. 129–45; Anatol Lieven, 'The Caucasus and Central Asia Ten Years After the Soviet Collapse', eurasianet.org (21 August 2001); and Pauline Jones Luong and Erika Weinthal, 'New Friends, New Fears in Central Asia', *Foreign Affairs*, 81:2 (2002), pp. 61–70.
2 For early overviews of cooperative security and PfP, their conceptualisation and impact, see James M. Goldgeier and Michael McFaul, 'A Tale of Two Worlds: Core and Periphery in the Post-Cold War Era', *International Organization*, 46:2 (1992), pp. 467–91; Ashton B. Carter, William J. Perry and John D. Steinbruner, *A New Concept of Cooperative Security* (Washington, DC: Brookings Institution, 1992); Janne E. Nolan (ed.), *Global Engagement: Cooperation and Security in the 21st Century* (Washington, DC: Brookings Institution, 1994); and 'Partnership for Peace: Invitation', *NATO Ministerial Communiqué M-1(94)2*, issued by the heads of state and government participating in the meeting of the North Atlantic Council, 10 January 1994.
3 Sean Kay and Joshua Spero, 'Keep NATO Relevant for 21st Century', *Defense News* (17–23 December 2001), p. 27.
4 Officials giving the PfP process high priority included the secretary of defence, William Perry, and his key assistant secretaries, among them Joseph Nye, Ashton Carter and Franklin Kramer. Also supportive were the secretary of state, Warren Christopher, and his deputy, Strobe Talbott, along with the assistant secretary of

state for Europe and Canada, Richard Holbrooke. The national security advisor, Anthony Lake, the joint chiefs' strategic plans and policy director, Army Lieutenant-General Wesley Clark, Army Lieutenant-General Daniel Christman and Air Force Lieutenant-General Richard Myers also provided key support for the PfP.

5 As the senior civilian strategic planner, the author shaped the heart of the PfP evolution, developing, operationalising and implementing its many intricate and multilateral cooperative initiatives and enhancements in Europe and Eurasia from 1994 to 2000 in the Joint Chiefs of Staff's Directorate for Strategic Plans and Policy. For published accounts of the phases of the US and PfP processes, see Catherine M. Kelleher, *The Future of European Security: An Interim Assessment* (Washington, DC: Brookings Institution, 1995), pp. 67–105; Sean Kay, *NATO and the Future of European Security* (Lanham, MD: Rowman and Littlefield, 1998), pp. 61–87; James M. Goldgeier, *Not Whether But When: The U.S. Decision to Enlarge NATO* (Washington, DC: Brookings Institution, 1999), pp. 14–44; and David S. Yost, *NATO Transformed: The Alliance's New Roles in International Security* (Washington, DC: US Institute of Peace Press, 1998), pp. 97–187.

6 Stephen Blank, *U.S. Military Engagement with Transcaucasia and Central Asia* (Carlisle Barracks, PA: U.S. Army War College, Strategic Studies Institute, June 2000), pp. 14–16.

7 These two states also became members of the PfP and this relationship served as the foundation for their broader relationships with NATO via a NATO–Russia council and a NATO–Ukraine special relationship.

8 Impressions by the author and *U.S. Annual Report to Congress on the Partnership For Peace*, jointly prepared by the State Department and the Defense Department, pursuant to section 514 of the *Foreign Relations Authorization Acts, Fiscal Years 1994–2002*.

9 Randall L. Schweller, 'Bandwagoning for Profit: Bringing the Revisionist State Back In', *International Security*, 19:1 (1994), pp. 72–107, esp. pp. 74–5; Randall L. Schweller, *Deadly Imbalances: Tripolarity and Hitler's Strategy of World Conquest* (New York: Columbia University Press, 1998), pp. 76–7; and Kenneth N. Waltz, *Theory of International Politics* (New York: Random House, 1978), p. 126.

10 Schweller, 'Bandwagoning for Profit', pp. 104–7.

11 Glenn H. Snyder, 'Alliances, Balance and Stability', *International Organization*, 45:1 (1991), pp. 121–42, esp. p. 128.

12 Andrew Kydd, 'Sheep in Sheep's Clothing: Why Security Seekers Do Not Fight Each Other', *Security Studies*, 7:1 (1997), pp. 114–55, esp. p. 152; and Andrew Kydd, 'Trust, Reassurance, and Cooperation', *International Organization*, 54:2 (2000), pp. 325–57, esp. pp. 325–7.

13 For example, see Charles L. Glaser, 'Realists as Optimists: Cooperation as Self-Help', in Michael E. Brown *et al.* (eds), *Theories of War and Peace: An International Security Reader* (Cambridge, MA: MIT Press, 1998); Jeffrey W. Taliaferro, 'Security Seeking under Anarchy: Defensive Realism Revisited', *International Security*, 25:3 (2000/01), pp. 128–61, esp. p. 159; and Gideon Rose, 'Neoclassical Realism and Theories of Foreign Policy', *World Politics*, 51:1 (1998), pp. 144–72.

14 Mark Kramer, 'Neorealism, Nuclear Proliferation, and East-Central European Strategies', in Ethan B. Kapstein and Michael Mastanduno (eds), *Unipolar Politics: Realism and State Strategies After the Cold War* (New York: Columbia University

Press, 1999), pp. 428, 437–8, 462.

15 For a survey of assessments of the PfP, see Henry Kissinger, *Diplomacy* (New York: Simon and Schuster, 1994), pp. 824–6; Charles Kupchan, 'Strategic Visions', *World Policy Journal*, 11:1 (1994), pp. 112–22; Nick Williams, 'Partnership for Peace: Permanent Fixture or Declining Asset?', in Philip H. Gordon (ed.), *NATO's Transformation: The Changing Shape of the Atlantic Alliance* (Lanham, MD: Rowman and Littlefield, 1997), pp. 221–33; Daniel N. Nelson, 'Post-Communist Insecurity', *Problems of Post-Communism*, 47:5 (2000), pp. 31–7; Sean Kay, 'NATO's Open Door: Geostrategic Priorities and the Impact of the European Union', *Security Dialogue*, 32:2 (2001), pp. 201–16; and 'Peacekeeping and War: No, they're Not Incompatible', *The Economist* (16 August 2001).

16 See Michael Loriaux, 'Realism and Reconciliation: France, Germany, and the European Union', in Kapstein and Mastanduno, *Unipolar Politics*, pp. 378–9; and Joshua B. Spero, 'Enhancing Great Powers: Medium Size State Impact on Regional Security Cooperation', manuscript.

17 For general discussion of NATO's post-Cold War transition see Kelleher, *Future of European Security*; Robert McCalla, 'NATO's Persistence after the Cold War', *International Organization*, 50:3 (1996), pp. 445–75; Kay, *NATO and the Future of European Security*; Yost, *NATO Transformed*; and Celeste A. Wallander, 'Institutional Assets and Adaptability: NATO after the Cold War', *International Organization*, 54:4 (2000), pp. 705–36, esp. pp. 721–3, 728–31.

18 US Department of Defense, *United States Security Strategy for Europe and NATO* (Washington, DC: GPO, 1995); and US Department of Defense, *Partnership for Peace* (Washington, DC: GPO, 1996).

19 Vladimir Socor, 'Major NATO Exercise Successfully Held in Georgia', Jamestown Foundation, *Monitor* (26 June 2001), available from NEDB@Latvia-USA.org.

20 Transcript of interview by General John M. Shalikashvili, chairman, joint chiefs of staff, with reporters from the *International Herald Tribune, USA Today, Defense News*, and *Jane's Defense News* (16 June 1997); and 'Partnership for Peace: An Enhanced and More Operational Partnership', *NATO Fact Sheets* (6 September 2000), available from www.nato.int/docu/facts/2000/PfP-enh.htm.

21 For NATO's current strategy and rationale for twenty-first-century missions, see *The Alliance's Strategic Concept*, approved by the heads of state and government participating in the meeting of the North Atlantic Council in Washington DC, 23 and 24 April 1999, NATO Press Release NAC-S(99)65 (24 April 1999), available from www.nato.int/docu/pr/1999/p99–065e.htm.

22 For background, see S. Frederick Starr (ed.), *The Legacy of History in Russia and the New States of Eurasia* (Armonk, NY: M. E. Sharpe, 1994); Zbigniew Brzezinski, *The Grand Chessboard: American Primacy and its Geostrategic Imperatives* (New York: Basic Books, 1997), pp. 123–50; Rosemarie Forsythe, 'The Politics of Oil in the Caucasus and Central Asia', *Adelphi Paper 300* (Oxford: Oxford University Press for the International Institute for Strategic Studies, 1996); Pavel Baev, *Russia's Policies in the Caucasus* (London: The Royal Institute of International Affairs, 1997); and Jan H. Kalicki, 'Caspian Energy at the Crossroads', *Foreign Affairs*, 80:5 (2001), pp. 120–35.

23 Joel E. Williamson and Jennifer D. P. Moroney, 'Security Cooperation Pays Off: A Lesson from the Afghan War', *Current Defense Analyses*, (2002), pp. 1–3.

24 Vladimir Socor, 'War Draws Central Asia's "Stans" Closer to the U.S.', *Wall Street*

Journal Europe (18 January 2002), available from Johnson's Russia List No. 6029, davidjohnson@erols.com; Todd S. Purdum, 'The Allies: Uzbekistan's Leader Doubts Chances for Afghan Peace', *New York Times* (14 March 2002); and Armen Khanbabyan, 'Georgia is Only the Beginning: The American Presence in the Transcaucasus Will Quickly Expand', *Nezavisimaya Gazeta* (14 March 2002), available from Johnson's Russia List No. 6136, davidjohnson@erols.com.

25 Sunanda K. Datta-Ray, 'A Central Asian Initiative that Could Eliminate bin Laden', *International Herald Tribune* (20 September, 2001).

26 See Bhatty and Bronson, 'NATO's Mixed Signals', pp. 131–8.

27 'Turkey Might Get Two Azeri Military Airports', *BBC Monitoring/Azerbaijani TV station ANS* (9 January 2002), NEDB, available from NEDB@Latvia-USA.org; Eric S. Margolis, 'Russia Checkmated its New Best Friend', *Los Angeles Times* (28 November 2001); and Patrick E. Tyler, 'The Morning After Dawns on Moscow', *New York Times* (16 December 2001).

28 See, for example, *U.S. Annual Report to Congress on the Partnership For Peace* (2002); and Bruce Pannier, 'Central Asia: Ten Years After', *Radio Free Europe-Radio Liberty*, Johnson's Russia List, No. 5436 (11 September 2001), available from davidjohnson@erols.com.

29 See the draft text (October 2001) of the 'Multilateral Agreement on Transit of Goods Subject to Export Controls', arranged by the US Department of State. According to this, the governments of the Republic of Armenia, the Azerbaijan Republic, Georgia, the Republic of Kazakhstan, the Kyrgyz Republic, the Republic of Tajikistan, and the Republic of Uzbekistan will be guided by the Treaty on Non-Proliferation of Nuclear Weapons, the Convention on Banning Chemical Weapons and the Convention on Banning Bacteriological Weapons, aimed at facilitating the transit of goods subject to export controls and preventing unauthorised transit, thus enabling them to strengthen national, regional and international security, and expanding economic ties, transshipments and international trade.

30 Michael R. Gordon with C. J. Chivers, 'U.S. May Gain Use of More Air Bases to Strike Taliban', *New York Times* (5 November 2001); Ariel Cohen, 'Moscow, Washington and Tbilisi Wrestle with Instability in the Pankisi Gorge', *New York Times* (19 February 2002); 'NATO Backs Anti-Terror Operation in Pankisi Gorge', *Interfax* (8 March 2002), available from NEDB@Latvia-USA.org; and David Fillipov, 'US Troops Help Ex-Soviet State fight Militants', *Boston Globe* (19 March 2002), available from Johnson's Russia List No. 6143, davidjohnson@erols.com.

31 Phase I of RAI is a study of PfP nation requirements to build and operate an effective air sovereignty system. Phase II is implementation of the study results by the PfP nation. Equipment purchases between US and PfP nations depend partially on PfP funds to build Air Sovereignty Operations Centres (ASOCs), or command and control centres in each country as the PfP states integrate the ASOCs.

32 *Report to Congress on the Partnership for Peace: Developments through July 15, 2001*, pursuant to section 514 of the *Foreign Relations Authorization Act, Fiscal Years 1994–1995* (P.L. 103–236) and section 205 of the *NATO Participation Act of 1994* (Title II of P.L. 103–447), pp. 27–9.

33 *Report to Congress on the Partnership for Peace: Developments through July 15, 2001*, pp. 15–17. Another important bilateral 'in the spirit' of PfP exercise, namely Peaceful Star 2001, sponsored by Turkey, builds on the US bilateral

series in the Caucasus and Central Asia and involves nearly all the seven Eurasian states in conducting field training based on pooling PfP experiences from the NATO-led operations in Bosnia. 'Peaceful Star-2001 Exercises Begin in Istanbul', *Turkish News Agency*, Anatolia/BBC monitoring (19 September 2001), available from NEDB@Latvia-USA.org.

34 'NATO Command and Staff Exercises Begin In Baku', *Interfax* (5 November 2001), available from NEDB@Latvia-USA.org.

35 *Alliance's Strategic Concept*.

36 For overcoming the declining policy and resource commitment to PfP within the context of NATO–EU relations, see Kay, 'NATO's Open Door'; and Kay and Spero, 'Keep NATO Relevant'.

10

Russia, the CIS
and Eurasian interconnections

John P. Willerton and Geoffrey Cockerham

Central to post-Soviet Eurasian security calculations and economic stabilisation efforts are Russia's power interests and efforts to reclaim a leadership role in the region. Since the break-up of the USSR, states of the FSU have pursued foreign policies based upon their own mix of interests and preferences rather than those of a central set (Moscow) of policy-makers. It is hardly surprising that more than a decade after the Soviet collapse, all FSU states remain wary of the Russian Federation's intentions as it struggles to re-establish its lost regional leadership position. Yet the disintegration of the Soviet Russian empire did not obviate the numerous significant economic and security linkages among the FSU states and to Russia. Russia still possesses many resources with which to assert its Eurasian power interests. Russian authorities have used various means toward this end, promoting the CIS, participating in other Eurasian multilateral fora, and giving special attention to the country's own bilateral relations with FSU states. Moscow has used both military and trade arrangements to reassert its interests in Eurasia.[1]

Nationalism has continued to be widespread throughout the area of the FSU and it has further invigorated post-Soviet concerns over national autonomy.[2] States once dominated by Moscow have pursued various bilateral and multilateral means to consolidate their sovereignty, lessen their economic and security dependence on Russia, and integrate into the mainstream global system. All of these states face the reality of geographical location and a history of economic and security interconnections, while they still share considerable common infrastructure. As demonstrated by an eager Belarus's desire for stronger integration with Russia or by a reluctant Ukraine's need to maintain and even expand commercial and military connections with Moscow, reality dictates that the FSU states rely on one another – and to varying degrees on Russia – to safeguard their security and commercial vitality. The manoeuvrings of Belarus and Ukraine, however, also reflect the complexities of balancing entangling external linkages with the preservation of unique domestic economic and political programmes and prerogatives.

There has been an understandable post-Cold War tendency to discount Russia's continuing regional capabilities and commitment to its Eurasian leadership position. Indeed, the dramatic September 11 2001 terrorist attacks on the United States and consequent insertion of American military power in Central Asia further complicated Russia's FSU leadership aspirations and may launch a new era in the Eurasian 'Great Game'.[3] Western scholarship on post-Soviet Russian foreign policy and the FSU has predictably emphasised Russian power contraction and dilemmas in the conduct of Russian–FSU relations.[4] This development may be inspired by the sort of western triumphalism some have noted, but it does reflect the realities of significant Russian power contraction.[5] Yet, while Russia's power has been diminished, it continues to be the state of regional standing with an ambitious agenda of Eurasian infrastructural and policy arrangements which has been promoted by all Russian Foreign Ministry teams. Russian officials have used the FSU states' heavy reliance on Russian fuel, among other dependencies, to influence those states' actions. Meanwhile, international economic conditions have complicated the efforts of FSU states both to distance themselves fully from Russia and to build extensive commercial – and security – ties with the more advanced western economies. Destabilising conflicts or political instability in selected areas (e.g., Caucasus, Tajikistan and Transdniestria) have significantly complicated the policy choices of involved states while providing Moscow with enticing openings for involvement. For all of their highly publicised failures, FSU multilateral fora such as the CIS have permitted intergovernmental policy coordination in a number of areas, not only in the economic transformation of states but in collective security and anti-terrorism arrangements as well. These fora suggest an FSU 'economic and security space', and they have been manipulated by Russia to bolster both the legitimacy and viability of a Russia-led grouping of concerned states.

We argue that all FSU states, in spite of natural desires to distance themselves from the legacy of the Russian empire and Soviet Union, must countenance relatively high levels of regional economic interaction and cooperative security arrangements. Indeed, some of these states (e.g., Belarus and Kazakhstan) have promoted longer-term and intrusive economic and political intergovernmental arrangements.[6] Both multilateral and bilateral relations amply demonstrate the push–pull relationship between integrative and disintegrative tendencies in post-Soviet Eurasia, and they illuminate the challenges in ensuring some level of regional inter-state cooperation. A major function of the CIS has been to help identify and coordinate common security arrangements among members, and it has been the primary intergovernmental vessel used by the Russian Federation to consolidate its security relationships with FSU partners. Unfortunately for

Moscow, a decade of CIS multilateral arrangements has yielded little by way of common policy solutions.[7] Russia and other FSU states have relied primarily on bilateral arrangements with one another to advance their agendas. Yet, even a decade after the Soviet collapse, we wonder if a common FSU economic and security space continues to obtain, and – if so – what its implications would be for efforts at long-range Eurasian cooperation under Russian tutelage. We think this is an especially important question given President Vladimir Putin's energetic commitment to consolidating Russia's position in the FSU area; its importance only underscored by the region's changed power politics in the wake of the September 11 terrorist attacks and resultant enhanced western power presence.

In this chapter, we examine the fledgling organisational arrangements, under the aegis of the CIS, which have been used to channel the transformation of the FSU area and to re-establish a zone of linked FSU states. We adopt a two-pronged approach. First, we look at CIS security arrangements, with our examination revealing the problems in consolidating firm intergovernmental institutions and effective policy positions. We contend that the confused and evolving interests of FSU states must be considered against the background of ongoing entangling infrastructural, resource and security needs among these very states. While loaded with powerful connotations, the term 'interdependence' may be appropriate in describing numerous FSU bilateral relationships. Second, we turn to underlying resource and economic realities which structure states' actions, using the limited trade data available to explore systematically the potential for a 'common economic space' among FSU states. Our desire is to balance the predictable focus on dynamic, country-specific considerations by giving attention to those underlying interconnections which structure long-term behaviour; interconnections which could facilitate longer-term engagement among FSU states, especially under assertive Russian prodding.

Continuing Russian hegemonic interests and the FSU

Governing elites of collapsing multinational empires struggle to maintain their hegemonic position even as their relations with the regions of the periphery are fundamentally restructured.[8] This has proven true in the Soviet and Russian case, as all Moscow-based politicians endeavoured to maintain Russian influence in Eurasia. The desire of anti-Soviet Russian Republic officials to maintain Russia's sphere of influence and to limit full independence for the Soviet republics was communicated during 1990–91, well before the August coup and subsequent appearance of the CIS.[9] Boris Yeltsin's government may have championed the rights and policy prerogatives of the republics as it challenged the Gorbachev government's position, but it simultaneously manoeuvred to reinforce other republics' political and economic linkages with Russia. The Yeltsin government did not unduly support republics' independence drives. Rather, it used often broad-ranging political agreements and more focused economic treaties to tie the republics together – and to Russia. In November 1990, Russia, together with Belarus and Ukraine, agreed to coordinate price changes: the first multilateral agreement to enhance economic cooperation among the successor states.[10] Only a few months later, the presidents of these three republics, together with the Kazakh president, met to consider a new union arrangement as an alternative to Gorbachev's Union Treaty. Thus, the logic of common FSU economic and security needs and structures had already been laid out when the CIS emerged in December 1991.

Russian priorities in the immediate post-Soviet period

After the Soviet collapse, Russia's major strategic goal within the area of the FSU was the establishment of a relatively unified and reliable system of military control and mutually advantageous economic cooperation. The CIS was to be the major organisational mechanism for ensuring these goals. From Moscow's perspective, the CIS would help prevent and resolve conflict within the FSU, help defend the CIS's external borders, and serve as the primary forum for addressing common regional infrastructural and economic issues as all countries moved towards regulated market economies.

In this environment, multidimensional issue agendas drove multilateral bargaining efforts. President Yeltsin and other Russian officials stressed the common economic and security needs which bound the FSU states together, while the representatives of the other FSU states postured against potentially intrusive intergovernmental arrangements involving Russia.[11] It is not surprising that initial CIS meetings entailed unilateral chest beating, with politicians predictably opportunistic in advancing their own states' resource claims as multilateral jockeying intensified. But the exhilaration of national independence quickly gave way to the growing awareness that domestic economic and political problems transcended national borders and were interconnected. Worsening economic conditions within all of the FSU states compelled politicians to acknowledge their states' continuing economic reliance on Russia, its natural and energy resources, and its markets. During 1992, Russia had a 1.5 trillion rouble trade balance with other CIS states, with its early unilateral moves (e.g., the introduction of non-cash rouble accounting to settle bilateral trade transactions for rouble-zone countries) revealing a continuing proclivity to manipulate its resource and infrastructural advantages to influence other states' commercial and security calculations.[12]

The June 1992 Russian–Ukrainian summit and the Minsk CIS heads of government meeting brought momentum to reinforcing more collective ways of addressing policy problems. Whether in finalising a scheme for the division of Soviet property or in agreeing to establish joint peacekeeping forces for eastern Moldova, FSU states became more engaged in regional multilateral fora. Substantial agreements on economic and trade issues resulted, while some FSU states committed themselves to collective security and 'peacekeeping' activities.[13] As the momentum for regional intergovernmental cooperation grew, Russian officials pressed for an acknowledgement by both the FSU states and the West of Russia's unique regional leadership role.[14] It was Russia that would assume primary responsibility for the conduct of relations among the successor states.

Meanwhile, most FSU states, including those building firmer intergovernmental ties with Russia, concomitantly attempted to balance Russia's power position by creating smaller regional associations and arrangements which excluded the regional hegemon. Such efforts at interstate policy coordination were generally among states of a common region (e.g., the Baltic, Central Asia). The developmental pattern was, in the initial phase, to address broad policy concerns, with more specific agreements and resource commitments negotiated later.

Throughout the decade 1992–2001, multilateral protocols and agreements revealed a potential attitudinal and policy base for viable multilateral institutions, but dilemmas in policy implementation – combined with dynamic domestic situations within the FSU states – indicated the inherent fragility of all arrangements geared towards the reintegration of the FSU. Thus, while security and economic agreements were hammered out, states did not commit the necessary resources or engage in the development of intergovernmental institutional arrangements necessary to translate stated common interests into tangible policy results. Meanwhile, Russian unilateralism in its economic policies took precedence over its stated foreign policy multilateralism.[15] With the massive costs of regional economic and security reintegration becoming more immediate, Russia exhibited mounting caution in transforming its hegemonic power interests into concrete external resource commitments. Formal multilateral and bilateral negotiations did not yield large-scale Russian financial or resource commitments. There was a decided gap between Russian rhetoric and actions.

The push–pull of Russian unilateralism and FSU regional cooperation
The irony of FSU regional developments by the mid-1990s was the coming to power of FSU regimes more willing to engage Russia just as Moscow was becoming more cautious about potentially costly foreign entanglements. A fundamental reality of post-1991 Eurasia has been the near-impossibility of reconciling the contrasting domestic agendas of evolving states, especially in the context of government turnovers and consequent policy reformulation. We cannot survey all of the unique domestic settings within the FSU, but it is fair to observe that domestic economic imperatives and the desire to engage positively with Russia encouraged many states to re-evaluate the payoffs of CIS and other multilateral arrangements. Once strongly anti-Russian

governments in Azerbaijan and Lithuania were replaced by regimes headed by more moderate leaders (with significant past experience with Moscow), while hotly contested presidential elections in Belarus and Ukraine brought to power more pro-Russian and pro-CIS officials. These regimes, and their voting publics, confronted the structural realities of now-independent states' mounting unpaid bills for deliveries (e.g., of energy) from Russia and their continued need for Russian credits to finance such deliveries. Resource and market needs compelled even sceptical states such as Turkmenistan and Ukraine to engage with Russia.

These developments, however, were met by Russian policy caution, reflective of Russia's own unilateral concerns over the resource costs of external commitments. Developments within the Russian polity, including the autumn 1993 executive-legislative crisis and the December 1993 elections, led to a more cautious Yeltsin government stance towards external entanglements, even though those domestic developments also required the articulation of a more assertive public line towards the FSU.[16] Russian officials maintained a careful balancing act, with their often blunt and occasionally harsh rhetoric masking the absence of substantial and binding external commitments. In all policy areas – from the use of 'peacekeeping forces' to the setting of new banking and currency policies – the Yeltsin government's public positions reflected national calculations rather than Commonwealth interests.

In its public profiling, Russian efforts to consolidate regional cooperation efforts relied much more on high-level summits, formal protocols and regularised multilateral negotiations to convey the image of common community interests and obligations. These ongoing meetings centred on the construction of common CIS issue positions to reinforce the notion of a regionally defined community.[17] Meanwhile, Russian politicians used economic and even military pressure to advance their policy interests *vis-à-vis* the FSU.[18] But the divergent interests of individual CIS members, with their continuing worries over the re-emergence of a domineering regional hegemon, led Russia to rely more upon bilateral negotiations and smaller multilateral fora to consolidate its Eurasian position. An impressive diversity of formal economic and security arrangements was negotiated with most FSU states, ranging from the economic and troop withdrawal agreement with Lithuania in November 1993 to the 1997 formation of Turkmenrosgaz, a Russian–Turkmenian gas joint-stock company, to the 1999 (re-)establishment of Russian military bases in Tajikistan. Such arrangements signified that Russia would regularise its regional security and economic interests in a more focused and piecemeal way. Moreover, external pressures, in particular those stemming from western political and economic influence eastward, only further reinforced Russia's use of such bilateral and focused multilateral means.

Overall, Russian resource constraints, combined with unclear strategies of action, complicated Moscow's efforts to re-establish its former regional leadership position. Comparable dilemmas within the CIS, compounded by the lack of common perspectives and goals, denied the CIS the ability to be an effective instrument for advancing common (Russian-led) regional interests. Russian officials seemed to have lost confidence in the utility of the CIS, with one observer characterising Russian actions involving the FSU as 'complacent'.[19] Even the March 1996 'group of four' accords among Russia, Belarus, Kazakhstan and Kyrgyzstan – intended to forge such multilateral consensus on economic and security issues – could take on meaning only when Russia had sorted out and normalised its bilateral relations with each member. A lack of Russian strategic focus and listlessness would characterise the duration of the Yeltsin period, with a re-energised FSU policy emerging only with Vladimir Putin's ascension to power.

Two illustrative bilateral relationships

A dilemma in characterising Russian policy interests in the FSU involves the diversity of states involved, each with its own dynamic domestic environment and evolving political and security needs. Russian–Belarussian relations reflect one extreme of potentially intrusive intergovernmental arrangements between Russia and a former Soviet republic. Relatively compatible security concerns and interrelated economic needs, set against a background of shared historical and cultural interests, made this bilateral relationship a promising candidate for a more profound integration process. The April 1996 Russian–Belarussian Union and December 1999 Russian–Belarussian Treaty specified the institutional arrangements and common policy positions that would undergird the mounting cooperation – and anticipated future integration – of the two countries. These union agreements were said to entail the development of common political and economic organisational arrangements and policies to facilitate long-term integration.[20] Institution and policy-building efforts within this framework would help in developing arrangements that could be applied to a broader regional or CIS community (e.g., creation of a customs union, setting of common duties, tax standardisation, and the creation of common civil and economic laws). Irrespective of the political implications of Belarussian deference to Russian regional leadership, the Russian Federation would assume considerable resource costs for a bilateral economic union.[21] As an intermediary step, the Russian–Belarussian 'union' would be suggestive for the FSU 'group of four', which had committed itself to the lowering of economic barriers and the enhancement of multilateral security arrangements.

Russian observers complain that Belarus has made few real policy concessions while securing political and economic gains.[22] In reality, the peculiarities of the Lukashenko regime and its unpredictability, combined with the anticipated massive costs inherent in integration, contributed to uncertainties in the bilateral relationship. Such uncertainties continued to be evident in the post-1999 Putin–Lukashenko period, as both presidents publicly promoted an acceleration of the integrative process without committing serious resources to it.[23] Overall, Belarus has been as active a CIS member as any, and it has loyally supported Russian regional security preferences, but the domestic base upon which this posturing is constructed has not been fully reliable.[24]

As a suggestive contrast, Russian–Ukrainian relations have proceeded cautiously as both countries contend with the past legacy of bilateral cleavage and Russian imperial control. The reduction of economic barriers and the regularisation of bilateral political and security consultations became policy priorities of both the Kuchma and Yeltsin governments. A series of lengthy and tortuous high-level negotiations permitted the two regimes to realise piecemeal economic agreements, while domestic opposition in both countries undercut tentative security arrangements arrived at by the two countries' executive branches. Resolution of fundamental disagreements was not helped by Russian efforts to link Ukraine's energy dependence with concessions on political-security issues. Such issue linkage was highly risky – and could be counterproductive to longer-term cooperation – but negotiations between the Kuchma government and Yeltsin's second-term government did eventually result in concessions on both sides regarding the Black Sea Fleet and trade issues.[25] Indeed, the 1997 Russian–Ukrainian Treaty of Friendship, Cooperation and Partnership, in effect for ten years and with an automatic extension, yielded a trade-off between Russia's payments to use Black Sea facilities and Ukraine's state debt to Russia (each worth between $2.5 and $3 billion). Subsequent negotiations led to an agreement to end value-added taxes on one another's exports, thus ending a costly trade battle which complicated efforts to consolidate CIS trade structures.

Russian attempts to maintain Ukraine's more extensive bilateral relationships with both the CIS members and with Russia bore some fruit at least in terms of ongoing economic interactions. The two countries' chief executives publicly acknowledged Ukraine's continuing intention to 'make sparing use' of the CIS even while bilateral economic relations were consolidated.[26] Indeed, after eight years of debate, Ukraine finally joined the CIS Inter-Parliamentary Assembly and pushed to make the CIS area a free trade zone.[27] Ukraine's limited engagement with the CIS and the modest improvements in Russian–Ukrainian relations were realised fundamentally through direct bilateral arrangements – hammered out by high-level executive branch officials – rather than through multilateral negotiations under CIS auspices. The underlying mistrust and suspicions each country has of the other's intentions have made all negotiated political arrangements tenuous and vulnerable to domestic pressures.[28]

Belarus, caught by compelling security needs, and Ukraine, vulnerable to pressing economic and energy needs, confront continuing dependencies on

Russia a decade after the Soviet collapse. Each has developed a unique bilateral relationship with the Russian Federation which entails vulnerabilities that are simultaneously dynamic and unpredictable, and subject to exploitation by Moscow. Such a characterisation could be offered for nearly every FSU state, whether considering Armenia and its security and economic needs, Georgia and the Russian Federation's involvement in its secessionist problems, Moldova and the Russian Federation's role in the Transdniestria conflict, or Uzbekistan and continuing sales of Uzbek cotton to Russian consumers. Russian authorities have attempted to utilise such vulnerabilities and dependencies to recreate a common FSU space, with the Putin regime exhibiting an energy seemingly absent throughout most of the Yeltsin period.[29] Indeed, in the wake of the September 2001 terrorist attacks in the United States and the new Russian–American strategic relationship, Russian regional power consolidation efforts only grew – and along not only political and security but economic dimensions.

The CIS and an unrealised common security space

The CIS was to be the central intergovernmental institutional focus for the expression of FSU regional security maintenance, with Russian support critical to its long-term viability. A decade after its formation, the CIS has accomplished little, its mandate is minimal, and its resources are extremely limited. Its primary achievements have had less to do with foreign states and external threats and more to do with arranging capabilities and interests within the CIS/FSU region.[30]

Reviewing the wide array of issues addressed by CIS fora during the past decade, this international organisation proved most effective in helping structure the smooth dismantling of the USSR. Its early years yielded a semblance of intergovernmental cooperation, but with the emergence of internal decision-making norms such as the 'dissent norm' – whereby members are free to ignore any collective CIS decision – it has not proven possible to construct a consensus agenda of issues, let alone adopt binding policy responses. There is a predictable irony in the long-term negative impact of decision-making rules such as the 'dissent norm': these rules were essential to draw reluctant states into the CIS, but they then served to reinforce states' unilateral resolve to diverge from common CIS positions. Thus, wary states could countenance CIS participation, but they were provided with an effective institutional means to void CIS action.

In the security realm, the fundamental goals of CIS operation revolved around three basic concerns: the acknowledgement and creation of a 'common FSU security space'; the creation of formal integrated security structures; and the development of a coordinated system of member states' security forces. Russia's security calculations were intimately tied to all three of these broad concerns, with top Russian officials communicating this from the CIS's earliest days.[31]

The overriding goal of creating a common FSU security space emerged with the first CIS summit in Minsk in late December 1991. Nine FSU countries (excluding Turkmenistan and Ukraine) ultimately signed the May 1992 Tashkent Collective Security Treaty, with subsequent documents suggesting interconnected security interests and regional collective response. All states had concerns regarding Russian power and its potentially hegemonic role in the CIS and the region, making it difficult to construct a meaningful regional security regime with confidence-building arrangements. Russia's continuing disproportionate military assets meant there would be a central role for Russian forces: a reality that encouraged member-states to focus on external threats rather than security dilemmas within the FSU. Russia's efforts in promoting an extended border defence did yield some fruit, for instance, as Central Asian states confronted mounting terrorist threats. However, the CIS's inability to cope collectively with threats within the region was evident from the start, as Azerbaijan learned in 1994 when it sought CIS help over the Karabakh conflict. Security dilemmas within the CIS/FSU area were addressed through bilateral – or more regionally focused multilateral – means. All states, starting with Russia, resorted to bilateral arrangements, but a decade of such arrangements did not cumulate into a broader regional collective security network.

Regarding the goal of creating a formal integrated security structure, a fair amount was accomplished on paper, suggesting multilateral progress in basic CIS institutional preparation. The key issues of border cooperation, constructing an air defence system and peacekeeping operations necessitated immediate institutional construction, with many key bodies created during the CIS's first year. Especially notable were the Councils of Heads of State and Heads of Government, along with subordinate Councils of Defence Ministers and other top government officials, and dozens of other coordinating multilateral bodies. Beneath these broader guiding entities were specialised bodies such as the General Headquarters of the CIS Joint Armed Forces and the Council of Commanders of Border Guards. The utility of creating these bodies was immediately apparent, as numerous multilateral consultations addressed wide-ranging issue agendas. Difficulties in crafting common policy responses, however, quickly overwhelmed such formal institutions. The over three dozen high-profile meetings of the Heads of State and Heads of Government Councils proved more useful in at least permitting the articulation of members' concerns and grievances, with modest policy results. Lower-level bodies, useful for consultative purposes, were more effective when less formalised, leading to the replacement of 'standing' organisations (e.g., the General Headquarters of the CIS Joint Armed Forces) with looser coordinating staffs.

Looking beyond broad CIS goals and institutional preparation, were there identifiable policy results? As regards establishing a formal coordinated system of CIS members' forces, piecemeal agreements were hammered out that reflected individual states' unilateral security capabilities and needs rather than a genuinely collective multinational entity with a supranational identity and mission. In a fiscally constrained environment, regional security concerns were a low budget priority as states' scarce resources were devoted to unilateral security capabilities. Under the CIS aegis, both command and support capabilities were brought together for joint defence planning, military training and conducting of military exercises. Commencing as early as December 1991, integrated border guard units emerged with a continuing interest and commitment made by roughly half of the CIS members.[32] Arrangements varied by state, ranging from Russia providing technical assistance and training (e.g., Belarus and Kazakhstan) to Russia participating in joint forces with a host CIS member (e.g., Armenia, Georgia and Tajikistan).[33] Likewise, after a number of years of difficult negotiating and a severe push by Moscow, several CIS states committed to the 1995 CIS Unified Air Defence Agreement, though not all actively participated in joint operations.

More important in these cases were bilateral arrangements between Russia and individual CIS members which, like the border guard arrangements, varied by state. The CIS's putative air defence system included the active involvement of six members' forces,[34] though the regional gaps left in the FSU area raised questions about the system's overall strategic value.[35]

Under the rubric of CIS-sponsored 'peacekeeping missions', Russia used the cloak of supposed joint action to legitimate and bolster its military presence in a variety of settings throughout the FSU. Active CIS/Russian peacekeeping operations arose in Georgia (Abkhazia and South Ossetia), Moldova (Transdniestria) and Tajikistan. CIS meetings and agreements have been used to justify what is essentially Russian involvement (e.g., the October 1994 CIS conference addressing Abkhazia). The CIS took credit for contributing to the ceasefires reached in all four of these conflicts. These brokered ceasefires only legitimated Russian meddling and underscored the continued inability of local actors to resolve their fundamental differences.

Overall, the CIS facilitated consultations and piecemeal security arrangements that are member- or region-specific, but with no emergent common security space. Where the CIS has been relatively forceful, we find strong Russian interests and the commitment of Russian resources, including military forces. What have proven central in the security arena are the unilateral responses of member states, whether in Belarus seeking security *vis-à-vis* perceived western threats, Armenia addressing the Karabakh issue and Azerbaijan, or Kyrgyzstan coping with destabilisation from the Tajik civil war and threat of terrorism. In addressing these security concerns, CIS states have primarily relied on their bilateral relationships with Russia, whether in gaining access to Russian equipment and intelligence information or seeking a more intrusive Russian military presence.

By the end of the 1990s, the various forces driving individual states' security calculations had led to discernible regional alignments among selected CIS members. Surveying the constellation of FSU states, with their varying degrees of commitment and involvement in the CIS, we find that essentially two groupings of states emerged. The first, a seemingly 'pro-Moscow' grouping, and including Armenia, Belarus, Kazakhstan, Kyrgyzstan and Tajikistan, encompassed states which had remained in collective security arrangements, had sought more intense bilateral political, economic and military ties with the Russian Federation, and were members of – or considering inclusion in – a newly formed and Russian-sponsored EEU. Meanwhile, the second group was more active in developing ties with western countries and more circumspect in their political and economic proximity to Moscow. This grouping included Azerbaijan, Georgia, Moldova, Ukraine and Uzbekistan, and together they composed a new political-security-economic pact, GUUAM. Beginning in 1999, several of the GUUAM states had begun to explore a wide array of initiatives (e.g., lessened trade barriers, creation of common transportation projects, peacekeeping activities) outside of CIS and Russian Federation auspices. Their September 2000 decision to form their own free trade zone had serious implications for developments in the Caspian area and Central Asia, and it was no accident that the other CIS members, at a meeting in Moscow a month later, were spurred on to form the EEU. These divisions within the CIS ranks only further accentuated the importance – for Moscow – of creatively using more focused bilateral means to advance its interests *vis-à-vis* individual FSU partners. Russian regional leadership became a top priority of Vladimir Putin, as he tried to revive the notion of a common FSU space and give new life to moribund CIS arrangements.

A common FSU economic space?

We have seen piecemeal FSU military-security arrangements, but also a profound inability to create firm, institutionalised regional arrangements that tie CIS members together in politically meaningful ways. Yet after ten years of tedious negotiation and frequent public disagreements among member-states, the CIS survives. Surveying the entirety of the CIS's history, we wonder if other factors – besides security concerns – continue to bind together even reluctant member-states. Geographical realities interconnect the security needs of the FSU states, but underlying infrastructural and resource linkages constantly complicate any CIS member's unilateral calculations and behaviour. Such ongoing interconnections – or to use a more loaded term, interdependencies – compel some level of regional cooperation, and it would be naive to judge security arrangements without reference to underlying infrastructural and economic linkages. In the wake of a decade of powerful centrifugal forces, are such underlying linkages still present and strong? We think that they may be, and as a fundamental precondition for any common FSU space – economic or security – they merit our attention.

To suggest the existence of a common FSU economic zone, we must at least demonstrate systematic evidence of commercial interconnection among CIS members. We wonder if, holding economic and geographical factors constant, CIS states will exhibit relatively high levels of trade between themselves. This is not to deny the reality that the Soviet collapse loosened all the states of the FSU's ties with one another and permitted them to develop new or more extensive relationships with other states. Indeed, by definition, the removal of Moscow-based Russian central planners signified that the newly independent states would have a more diverse group of trading partners.[36] The proportional share of FSU states' trade with one another would automatically decline as a result of the collapse of the Soviet empire.[37] A cursory examination of available FSU trade patterns reveals that trade levels among FSU states dropped significantly, by one estimate from $139 billion in 1991 to $59 billion in 2000.[38] However, FSU historical, infrastructural and other logistical realities would severely constrain any state from fully escaping significant economic intercourse with other FSU states.

In the past decade there has been an explosion of political science litera-ture concerning trade flows and their political and security consequences. The initial interest was concern about the impact of interstate conflict and/or diplomatic cooperation upon trade flows. Several studies found that conflict generally has a negative impact on trade, while cooperation gener-ally has a positive, if smaller and less robust, impact.[39] Progressively more complex research has sought either to establish the direction of causality between conflict and trade or to investigate the impact of other types of polit-ical conflict or cooperation upon trade.[40] Most relevant here is work that deals with institutionalised or quasi-institutionalised political arrangements and their impact upon bilateral trade.[41]

It is undeniably in Russia's best security and economic interests to attempt to foster trade to develop the degree of dependence necessary to create a *de facto* if not *de jure* alliance structure.[42] Furthermore, we might expect to see FSU states, beyond Russia, trade among themselves, if for no other reason than to strengthen themselves *vis-à-vis* the regional hegemon.[43] And those FSU states which calculate that their security is dependent upon Russia (e.g., Belarus) may choose to trade with it to create positive trade externalities which would mollify any future Russian aggres-sion.[44]

A favourite political factor employed by both economists and political scientists in their models of trade flows is some measure of preferential trading arrangements (PTAs).[45] These range from the virtually inconse-quential Commonwealth Preferences to such extensive common markets as the EU and even the old Council of Mutual Economic Assistance. It stands to reason that trade flows between nations that have negotiated some sort of preferential arrangement should be greater than those between nations that have neither bilateral nor multilateral arrangements between them.

The CIS is neither a strong PTA nor a true alliance. However, the CIS leaders' own stated commitment to the 'economisation' of the CIS and the creation of a free trade system reveals their ongoing commitment to regionally defined preferential arrangements.[46] We borrow from the estimation strategies of those investigating alliances or PTAs and model the impact of CIS membership upon bilateral trade flows of member-states. We wonder if there exists a common economic space inhabited by these states and whether, as a result, even though they attempt to trade with other nations, they must still engage in considerable trade with each other.

We model the bilateral trade flows of FSU states using the IMF's data set for the most recent period for which complete data are available, 1992–97. Our examination includes all dyads involving a CIS member-state. Our strategy is dependent on being able to estimate a model of trade flows that controls for economic and geographic factors. Fortunately, such a model exists, commonly referred to as the 'gravity model' of bilateral trade flows; it is well known and often used in the econometrics literature.[47] The gravity model is based upon the premise that trade flows are a function of the size of participating economies. The theory is a simple one: bilateral trade between small economies will be exponentially smaller than trade between two large economies. Economic size is operationalised as both income and population. Thus, we hypothesise that both of these factors have positive effects on trade. Factors other than the size of the economies involved are taken into account as so-called resistance terms. Economists commonly include the physical distance, or proximity, between the two trading partners as the primary resistance term. By using the gravity model we are able to control for economic determinants of trade flows and turn our attention to the political ties between CIS states that we will factor into the resistance term in the simplest possible manner.[48]

What we find when we systematically examine the trade of CIS countries for the period 1992–97 is that the bilateral trade between pairs of member states is *consistently and significantly higher* than economic factors alone would suggest (see Table 1). The results reveal that the dummy variable for the CIS has a robust, consistent, statistically significant and positive impact upon trade flows for all years considered. Pairs of CIS members trade more between themselves than standard economic theory would suggest. This result points to a common FSU economic space which continued at least throughout most of the Yeltsin period. This is unmistakable evidence of the *continued* interdependence of the CIS area, though these economic data and findings do not permit us to assess the impact of CIS negotiations and fledgling arrangements. Moreover, when we look at trade flows involving three leading FSU states, Russia, Ukraine and Belarus (Table 2), we also find the dummy for CIS member state dyads to be consistently positive and consistently statistically significant for the 1992–97 period.[49] The estimated coef-

Table I *Ordinary least squares (OLS) estimates of the determinants of trade for all CIS states, 1992–97*

Parameters	1992–97		1992		1993		1994		1995		1996		1997	
ln GDP	0.43***	(0.032)	0.60***	(0.136)	0.36 ***	(0.086)	0.51***	(0.078)	0.47***	(0.069)	0.47***	(0.066)	0.42***	(0.067)
ln population	0.26***	(0.043)	0.44***	(0.149)	0.32 ***	(0.126)	0.263***	(0.103)	0.128	(0.094)	0.231***	(0.091)	0.239***	(0.094)
ln distance	–1.12***	(0.047)	–1.45***	(0.194)	–0.82 ***	(0.126)	–1.08 ***	(0.114)	–1.20***	(0.104)	–1.24***	(0.096)	–1.22***	(0.099)
Dummy for CIS	1.24***	(0.100)	2.09***	(0.439)	1.35 ***	(0.253)	1.41***	(0.232)	1.44***	(0.219)	0.929***	(0.211)	1.04***	(0.225)
Dummy for Ukraine	1.15***	(0.118)	0.78	(0.469)	1.15 ***	(0.314)	0.445	(0.280)	1.68***	(0.259)	1.20***	(0.249)	1.38***	(0.254)
Dummy for Belarus	0.64***	(0.115)	0.44	(0.454)	0.59 *	(0.313)	0.32	(0.286)	1.00***	(0.249)	0.55**	(0.238)	0.73***	(0.246)
Dummy for Russia	1.30***	(0.109)	0.66*	(0.341)	0.75 ***	(0.270)	1.45***	(0.263)	2.04***	(0.254)	1.39***	(0.242)	1.61***	(0.245)
Constant	–12.52***	(0.663)	–20.88***	(2.94)	–11.82***	(1.76)	–14.78***	(1.61)	–11.32***	(1.47)	–12.65***	(1.38)	–11.58***	(1.40)
N	3125		190		478		556		610		673		613	
Adjusted R^2	0.36		0.41		0.36		0.42		0.42		0.40		0.41	

Notes: Numbers in parentheses are standard errors. ***indicates statistical significance at the >0.01 level. **indicates statistical significance at the >0.05 level. *indicates statistical significance at the >0.10 level.

Table 2 *Ordinary least squares (OLS) estimates of the determinants of trade for selected CIS states, 1992–97*

Parameters	Russian trade 1992–97		Ukrainian trade 1992–97		Belarussian trade 1992–97	
Ln GDP	1.07***	(0.184)	0.85***	(0.107)	0.42***	(0.089)
Ln Population	1.19***	(0.305)	0.42**	(0.180)	0.19	(0.126)
Ln Distance	−1.08***	(0.118)	−1.56***	(0.107)	−1.30***	(0.123)
Dummy for CIS	1.44***	(0.333)	0.61**	(0.281)	0.71**	(0.284)
Dummy for Ukraine	1.84*	(1.05)		N/A	1.42*	(0.810)
Dummy for Belarus	0.23	(0.900)	1.00	(0.760)		N/A
Dummy for Russia		N/A	2.17**	(0.859)	1.23	(0.810)
Constant	−45.92	(5.56)	−25.62	(3.11)	−10.44***	(2.09)
N	515		322		308	
Adjusted R^2	0.31		0.51		0.43	

Numbers in parentheses are standard errors. ***indicates statistical significance at the >0.01 level. **indicates statistical significance at the >0.05 level, *indicates statistical significance at the >0.10 level.

ficients on the dummy variables for trade with each of the three countries, while consistently positive, are variable. Russian–Ukrainian relations look more consequential, especially for Ukraine, though the trade coefficients involving Belarus – while positive – are not always statistically significant.

These results reveal that CIS members trade more between themselves than they trade with other states, once economic and geographical factors have been controlled for. The results are especially impressive given the time period considered: all CIS states had experienced economic collapse and significant domestic political cleavages, with these problems only complicating the conduct of interstate commercial activity. The years since this 1992–97 period have been dynamic ones for the economies of Russia and all FSU states. The 1998 Russian financial collapse, for instance, momentarily undermined the Russian Federation's foreign economic relations, but by the end of 2000, nearly all FSU economies were growing, with FSU area trade levels rising accordingly.[50] The strengthening of the Russian economy was central not only to the economic recovery of the region, but to the prospects for more substantial regional commercial linkages. Even the sceptical Uzbek president Islam Karimov publicly linked the improved state of the Russian economy to the prospects for Eurasian economic integration, while Russian politicians and commentators more openly discussed the use of economic pressures to advance regional security and business linkages.[51] We surmise that were more recent, Putin-period, systematic trade data available for an updated analysis, the trends evinced in Tables 1 and 2 would be even stronger.

Conclusion

There is ongoing uncertainty in the reorganising of the post-Soviet space and understandable pressures upon FSU states to structure their relations with the former regional hegemon carefully. The political pluralism which has characterised the FSU complicates Moscow's efforts to reconstruct some semblance of Russia's past leadership position. We have seen contradictory factors at work in the region. On the one hand, there is a mixed – but under-whelming – set of multilateral security-related institutional and policy arrangements which has not proven immediately responsive to Russian security interests. But on the other hand, even in the midst of powerful centrifugal economic and political forces, there are continuing, underlying infrastructural and commercial FSU interconnections, their long-term viability unclear. An important missing element during most of the Yeltsin period was a firm Russian commitment to the creation of a common FSU security and economic space. The ascent of Vladimir Putin, set against the backdrop of an improved domestic economy, may have altered this.

From the onset of his presidency, the FSU area and CIS have been a top foreign policy priority of Putin.[52] This has been signalled in speeches,[53] in numerous trips abroad,[54] in the appointment of key figures to address multi-lateral and bilateral issues in the region,[55] and in the commitment of resources.[56] While granting that Putin went on a foreign policy offensive during his first two years in office, visiting dozens of countries and offering policy initiatives in various areas, immediate high-level attention was given to CIS meetings and arrangements and to bilateral relationships involving such FSU states as Belarus, Ukraine, Kazakhstan and Azerbaijan.[57] Only a month into his presidency, Putin asserted his commitment to a more active CIS, and since then Russia's FSU initiatives could be characterised as multi-faceted and pragmatic.[58] This momentum was not detoured by the September 11 2001 terrorist attacks. Indeed, Putin's regime exhibited considerable creativity and resolve in both its bilateral and multilateral Eurasian relationships, whether in a new engagement of Azerbaijan or in promoting the notion of an FSU 'alliance of gas and oil producers'.[59]

The desire to reverse the seeming Russian irrelevancy to many interna-tional issues, including those in Russia's own Eurasian backyard, has driven the Putin-period Russian actions. A combination of positive and negative incentives has been used, with a more targeted approach that reflects the policy of 'selective engagement' articulated by Russian foreign policy specialists.[60] Thus, the Putin regime has engaged Belarus with loans to support the Belarussian rouble, to restructure its gas debts, and to finance joint industrial programmes; resolved energy debts with Ukraine and Kazakhstan, forgiving sizeable debts for shares in state companies or other concessions; and manipulated Russian troop presence and the promise of future economic deals to pull Eduard Shevardnadze's Georgian government away from outside countries and back towards Russia.

Russia's unilateral FSU efforts have been facilitated by the country's economic upturn, but anxieties over costs reinforce the targeted nature of its initiatives: it has been estimated that direct and indirect subsidies to FSU states still represent 3–4% of Russia's GDP.[61] Thus, not all developments conducive to enhanced integration are championed: while promoting the EEU, the Russian Federation has been cautious in not creating a free trade zone that would be likely to cost the country tens of millions of dollars in transporting energy and other resources.[62] However, as in many policy areas, there are trade-offs here, and not only has the EEU been a useful public platform for countering GUUAM, but it could eventually facilitate the coordination of member states' economic policies and foreign relations.[63]

Tying together the various Putin initiatives, evidence is mounting that Russia will selectively manipulate and augment those linkages and interdependencies that were still in place from the Yeltsin period. It is now building on the CIS organisational shell and consolidating the set of multilateral agreements that had emerged during the CIS's first decade.[64] It has intensively engaged those FSU states that have been traditionally receptive to CIS integration (e.g., Armenia, Belarus, Kazakhstan and Tajikistan), while focusing on perceived common regional threats (e.g., terrorism) to garner support from more reluctant FSU partners (e.g., Azerbaijan, Ukraine and Uzbekistan).[65] It is not surprising that Putin's emphasis on developing rapid-deployment forces and sponsorship of a multistate anti-terrorism centre have found resonance with many CIS members. The heightened American military presence in the FSU, reluctantly agreed to by Moscow, raises new questions about the Eurasian power balance, but it has infused new energy in the Putin government's efforts to consolidate Russia's regional position.[66]

Two years into the Putin presidency, the long-term prospects for revived FSU regional cooperation – and integration – are unclear. Will Putin's government remain committed to the integrating initiatives so far sponsored? Will Russia's economic growth continue and permit the expenditure of the resources needed to consolidate the CIS and at least the half-dozen FSU bilateral relationships targeted? The preferences of other CIS states will no doubt continue to be mixed, but an underlying wariness about a new regional hegemon will confront any Russian action. More than a decade after the Soviet collapse, the long-term regional security implications of Russian power contraction have yet to be determined fully. Uncertainty also surrounds Russia's role in twenty-first-century Eurasia. Developments of the post-Cold War period reveal a constancy in the Russian leadership's commitment to a Eurasian leadership position. The dynamic 1990s and early 2000s may have altered Russian calculations, but its goals remain the same. Only time will tell whether Russia's power resources will be up to its ambitious regional agenda.

Notes

1 Martha Brill Olcott, Anders Aslund and Sherman W. Garnett, *Getting It Wrong:*

Regional Cooperation and the Commonwealth of Independent States (Washington, DC: Carnegie Endowment for International Peace, 1999); and Allen C. Lynch, 'The Realism of Russia's Foreign Policy', *Europe–Asia Studies*, 53:1 (2001), pp. 7–31.

2 Bear F. Braumoeller, 'Deadly Doves: Liberal Nationalism and the Democratic Peace in the Soviet Successor States', *International Studies Quarterly*, 41:3 (1997), pp. 375–402.

3 Ian Bremmer and Alexander Zaslavsky, 'Bush and Putin's Tentative Embrace', *World Policy Journal*, 18:4 (2001–02), pp. 11–17; and Edward Helmore, 'U.S. in Replay of the "Great Game"', *Observer* (20 January 2002), as reprinted in Johnson's Russia List, No. 6032 (21 January 2002), www.cdi.org.

4 Ian Bremmer, 'Russia's Total Security', *World Policy Journal*, 16:2 (1999), pp. 31–9; and Robert Legvold, 'Russia's Unformed Foreign Policy', *Foreign Affairs*, 80:5 (2001), pp. 62–75.

5 Chalmers Johnson, *Blowback: The Costs and Consequences of American Empire* (Empire, NY: Metropolitan Books, 2000).

6 For a discussion of the 'logic' of intergovernmental cooperation and integration in both the European Union and CIS settings, see Helga A. Welsh and John P. Willerton, 'Regional Cooperation and the CIS: West European Lessons and Post-Soviet Experience', *International Politics*, 34:1 (1997), pp. 33–61.

7 For a comprehensive overview, see Richard Sakwa and Mark Webber, 'The Commonwealth of Independent States, 1991–1998: Stagnation and Survival', *Europe–Asia Studies*, 51:3 (1999), pp. 379–415.

8 G. Wesley Johnson (ed.), *Double Impact: France and Africa in the Age of Imperialism*, (Westport, CT: Greenwood Press, 1985).

9 For an overview of Russian calculations during the period June 1990 to August 1991, see Anwara Begum, *Inter-Republican Cooperation of the Russian Republic* (Aldershot: Ashgate, 1997).

10 S. Tsikora, 'Russia and Ukraine: Unity, Force and Resources', *Izvestiya* (20 November 1990).

11 Note Yeltsin's address to the UN, *Rossiiskaya gazeta* (3 February 1992).

12 Igor Sinyakevich, 'The CIS: The Probability of Monetary Reform in Russia', *Nezavisimaya gazeta* (5 January 1993).

13 Emil Pain, 'Can Russia Be a Peacemaker?', *Izvestiya* (29 September 1993).

14 Yeltsin himself stirred up a good deal of controversy with the public comment that Russia should be granted 'special powers' in the FSU; quoted in Vladimir Nadein, 'Predictable Polemics after a Chance Remark', *Izvestiya* (4 March 1993).

15 See Yeltsin's comments as quoted in Sergei Ivanov, '"I Don't Remember Anything Like that Ever Happening Before"', *Kommersant-Daily* (29 March 1997).

16 See comments by Yeltsin and the foreign minister, Kozyrev, in *Izvestiya* (8 October 1993), *New Times*, 4 (1994), and *Rossiiskaya gazeta* (12 January and 12 July 1994).

17 S. Lavrov, 'The CIS Countries at the United Nations', *International Affairs* (Moscow), 43:2 (1997), pp. 7–11.

18 *Izvestiya* (23 November 1993) and *Sovetskaya Rossiya* (12 November 1996). Note that such strong-arm tactics were not unique to Russia. Other FSU states were also willing to leverage their interests by applying economic pressure: both

Turkmenistan and Uzbekistan, for instance, threatened or actually cut off energy deliveries to influence the debt payments of Kazakhstan, Kyrgyzstan and Ukraine.

19 Alex Pravda, 'Foreign Policy', in Stephen White, Alex Pravda and Zvi Gitelman (eds), *Developments in Russian Politics* 5, (Basingstoke: Palgrave, 2001), p. 216.

20 For the text of the Belarussian–Russian unifying charter, see *Rossiiskaya gazeta* (24 May 1997).

21 The costs of this union immediately became clear as external car and vodka producers avoided significant Russian customs charges by entering the Russian market through Belarus; Igor Sinyakevich, 'Ford Enters Russian Market through the "Door" – via Belarus', *Izvestiya* (1 August 1997).

22 Konstantin Zatulin and Andranik Migranyan, 'The CIS after Chisinau', *Sodrushestvo NG*, 1 (1997), pp. 1–2.

23 Konstantin Smirnov, 'Belarusian Ruble Days in Moscow', *Kommersant* (17 January 2001).

24 Taras Kuzio, 'Virtual Foreign Policy in Belarus and Russia', in Jamestown Foundation *Prism*, 7:11, pt 3 (2001), www.jamestown.org.

25 Aleksandr Koretsky and Viktor Yadukha, 'The Prime Minister Takes the President All the Way to Kiev', *Segodnya* (30 May 1997).

26 Igor Sinyakevich, 'Kuchma and Yeltsin Find a Common Language', *Noviye Izvestiya* (28 February 1998).

27 Igor Sinyakevich, 'A Summit that Satisfied Everyone', *Noviye Izvestiya* (3 April 1999).

28 Vyacheslav Shiryayev, 'A Civilized Discussion about Stealing Gas', *Noviye Izvestiya* (19 April 2000).

29 Taras Galyuk, 'USA Ready for Return of Russian Influence in Ukraine', *Nezavisimaya gazeta* (29 December 2001).

30 Welsh and Willerton, 'Regional Cooperation and the CIS', pp. 54–6.

31 Sherman W. Garnett, 'Russia's Illusory Ambitions', *Foreign Affairs*, 76:2 (1997), pp. 61–76.

32 Armenia, Belarus, Georgia, Kazakhstan, Kyrgyzstan, Tajikistan and Russia.

33 Olcott *et al.*, *Getting It Wrong*, pp. 87–94.

34 Bilateral agreements with Moscow by Armenia, Belarus, Georgia, Kazakhstan and Kyrgyzstan.

35 Ilya Bulavinov, 'Marshal Sergeyev is Defense-Capable', *Kommersant* (10 February 2000).

36 James H. Noren and Robin Watson, 'Interrepublican Economic Relations after the Disintegration of the USSR', *Soviet Economy*, 8:2 (1992), pp. 89–109.

37 Lee Kendall Metcalf, 'Regional Economic Integration in the Former Soviet Union', *Political Research Quarterly*, 50:3 (1997), pp. 529–49.

38 Pavel Podlesny, 'Attention Turns to the CIS', *Moscow Times* (27 August 2001).

39 See Solomon W. Polachek, 'Conflict and Trade', *Journal of Conflict Resolution*, 24:1 (1980), pp. 55–78; Brian M. Pollins, 'Conflict, Cooperation, and Commerce: The Effects of International Political Interactions on Bilateral Trade Flows', *American Journal of Political Science*, 33:3 (1989), pp. 737–61; and Brian M. Pollins, 'Does Trade Still Follow the Flag?', *American Political Science Review*, 83:2 (1989), pp. 465–80.

40 The question of causality has not been settled. Mark Gasiorowski and Solomon

W. Polachek, 'Conflict and Interdependence', *Journal of Conflict Resolution*, 26:4 (1982), pp. 709–29, find that 'causality runs largely from trade to conflict' (p. 728). On the other hand, Rafael Reuveny and Heejoon Kang, 'International Trade, Political Conflict/Cooperation, and Granger Causality', *American Journal of Political Science*, 40:3 (1996), pp. 943–70, find that, 'causality between bilateral conflict/cooperation and international trade ... tends to be reciprocal' (p. 943). Theory provides no clear guide in the voluminous literature on the effect of interdependence on conflict.

41 Joanne Gowa, *Allies, Adversaries, and International Trade* (Princeton, NJ: Princeton University Press, 1994); and Joanne Gowa and Edward Mansfield, 'Power, Politics, and International Trade', *American Political Science Review*, 87:2 (1993), pp. 408–20.

42 Semyon Novoprudsky, 'Spatial Imagination', *Izvestiya* (27 February 1999).

43 The 1998 Ukrainian–Turkmen $720-million natural gas contract illustrated a bilateral effort to improve troubled domestic economies while simultaneously loosening dependence on Russia; Vladimir Mikhailov and Georgy Smolnikov, 'Has the Gordian Knot Been Cut?', *Nezavisimaya gazeta* (26 December 1998).

44 On budgetary considerations of the Belarussian–Russian case, see Nikolai Galko, 'Old Budget Is Overturned', *Nezavisimaya gazeta* (23 January 1999).

45 Victor Iwuagwu Oguledo and Craig R. MacPhee, 'Gravity Models: A Reformulation and an Application to Discriminatory Trade Arrangements', *Applied Economics*, 26:2 (1994), pp. 107–20.

46 Sinyakevich, 'Summit that Satisfied Everyone'.

47 Jeffrey H. Bergstrand, 'The Gravity Equation in International Trade: Some Microeconomic Foundations and Empirical Evidence', *Review of Economics and Statistics*, 67:3 (1985), pp. 474–81.

48 The simple form of the gravity model we use is: $M_{ji} = a\, Y_j^{\beta 1}\, Y_i^{\beta 2}\, N_j^{\beta 3}\, N_i^{\beta 4}\, d_{ji}^{\beta 5}\, e_{ji}$. M_{ji} is the flow of trade from country I to country j, Y is each country's income, N is each country's population, d is a vector of all resistance terms, and e_{ji} is a lognormally distributed error term (i.e. $E[\ln e_{ji}] = 0$). Note that this equation can be estimated as a linear model by simply taking the natural log of all terms. The model thus controls for economic size and for proximity. The impact of other potentially determining factors can be estimated by inserting them as part of the resistance term. It should be noted that while the nomenclature of 'resistance' was adopted initially to refer to impediments to trade such as transportation costs as captured by the relative proximity between the two states, the impact of these variables is not precluded from being positive. To estimate the bilateral trade flows between CIS states, we use the simple gravity model equation: $ln\,(Total$ $Trade_{ji}) = a + \beta_1\{ln(Y_j + Yi)\} + \beta_2\{ln(N_j + N_i)\} + \beta3(lnd_{ji}) + \beta_4 CIS + \beta_5 UKRAINE + \beta_6 BELARUS + \beta_7 RUSSIA + e_{ji}$. Total $Trade_{ji}$ is the total trade in current US$ from state I to state j. $Yj + Yi$ is the total GNP, in current US$, of the two states. $Nj + Ni$ is the total population of the two states in millions. dji is the distance in kilometres between the capital cities of the two states. *CIS* is a dummy variable that equals one when both states are members of the CIS. Note that since this equation is derived from the multiplicative gravity model, the actual values used in the estimation are the natural logs (*ln*) of the terms. This presents special difficulties with dealing with dummy variables. We employ the simplest possible method and estimate our dummies as taking on the values of 1 and 0. Thus, if returned to the

original units, our dummy variables have the values of 1 and *e* (the anti-log of 0).

Data and sources for this analysis include: (1) total trade = Exports from state *I* to state *j* + Imports from state *j* to state *I* (nominal US$), taken from International Monetary Fund, *Direction of Trade Statistics* (Washington, DC: IMF, 1998); (2) GNP is nominal in US$ from World Bank, *World Development Indicators on CD-ROM* (1997); (3) mid-year population estimates from International Monetary Fund, *International Financial Statistics*, 51:2 (1998); (4) distance between capital cities is calculated by converting the distance in radians into kilometres. Distance in radians is calculated from the longitude and latitude coordinates of each capital city.

49 These estimates are produced using standard ordinary least squares (OLS) regression. Note that for the year-by-year estimations there is no evidence of any heteroscedastic distribution of the error terms. Nor is there any evidence of autocorrelated disturbances.

50 *Interfax* (29 December 2000), as noted in Johnson's Russia List No. 4717 (31 December, 2000), www.cdi.org.

51 See Igor Torbakov, 'Economic Clout Gives Russia Growing Power in the CIS', www.eurasia.org (4 December 2001), as reported in Johnson's Russia List No. 5582 (5 December 2001), www.cdi.org.

52 Natalya Airapetova, 'CIS Countries Can Expect Some Surprises from Putin', *Nezavisimaya gazeta* (25 January 2000).

53 Beginning with the Moscow CIS Summit, as noted by *Interfax* (25 January 2000).

54 For example, to Azerbaijan, Belarus, Turkmenistan, Ukraine and Uzbekistan.

55 The most notable example being the May 2001 appointment of Viktor Chernomyrdin as ambassador to Ukraine.

56 Elena Chinyaeva, 'Russia in the CIS: The High Costs of Expansion', in Jamestown Foundation, *Prism*, 7:3 (2001), www.jamestown.org.

57 For example, for the renewed commitment to Belarus, see Sergei Vaganov, 'Are We Going to Live in a New Way Now?', *Trud* (18 April 2000); on improved Russian–Kazakh relations, see Armen Khanbabyan, 'Putin and Nazarbayev Reaffirm Warm Relations Between Russia and Kazakhstan', *Nezavisimaya gazeta* (20 June 2000).

58 See the foreign minister, Igor Ivanov's, comments, 'Predictability and Pragmatism', *Izvestiya* (11 April 2000).

59 Robert Cottrell, 'Putin Seeks Eurasian Alliance of Gas Producers', *Financial Times* (22 January 2002), as reported in Johnson's Russia List No. 6034 (22 January 2002), www.cdi.org.

60 Sergei Karaganov, 'The New Foreign Policy', *Moskovskiye novosti* (29 February –6 March, 2000).

61 Podlesny, 'Attention Turns'. For costs involving energy transfers, see Yury Chubchenko, 'Single Natural-Gas Space', *Kommersant* (17 February 2001).

62 Yury Chubchenko, 'Union Disagreement', *Kommersant* (24 May 2000).

63 Meanwhile, less than four years after its creation, GUUAM was weakened by political instability in Ukraine, Georgia's enhanced need for Russian assistance in coping with its secessionist challenges, and the election of Moldovan Communists to control that country's Parliament and presidency.

64 Sergei Blagov, 'CISters are Doing It for Themselves', *Asia Times* (3 January 2002).

65 See Russian Security Council secretary Sergei Ivanov's comments in Konstantin Churganov, 'Russia is Being Pressed, But it Won't be Forced Out', *Rossiiskaya gazeta* (16 March 2000).

66 Boris Volkhonsky, 'The U.S. Tries Walking in the Shoes of the USSR', *Kommersant* (23 January 2002).

11

The Black Sea Economic Cooperation: what contribution to regional security?[1]

Panagiota Manoli

The Black Sea region has been extensively referred to as a bridge, indicating its link with Europe to the West and Asia to the East. As a crossroad of geography, cultures and religions, the Black Sea region presents opportunities for both cooperation and conflict among the region's states. Developments in this area cannot be viewed in isolation, but always in the context of events taking place in Europe and in Central Asia. The Black Sea region is a connecting point with Europe and Central Asia owing to institutional and geopolitical links. This unique geopolitical context suggests that the Black Sea states constitute an interesting paradigm of cooperation and conflict in the international system.

In the early 1990s, the newly emergent states in the Black Sea area arrived at the fundamental understanding that an institutionalisation of their relations at a regional level would do much to promote their security. Eleven countries in the Black Sea region responded to a Turkish initiative to form the BSEC. In Istanbul, at a summit conference, Albania, Armenia, Azerbaijan, Bulgaria, Georgia, Greece, Moldova, Romania, Russia, Turkey and Ukraine signed on 25 June 1992 the Summit Declaration on Black Sea Economic Cooperation, thereby launching a new subregional scheme. Today the organisation, apart from its 11 members, also numbers nine observer states – Tunisia, Egypt, Israel, Poland, the Slovak Republic, Austria, Italy, Germany and France. The Former Yugoslav Republic of Macedonia, the Federal Republic of Yugoslavia, Iran and Uzbekistan are in line for full membership.

The BSEC was not a marriage born of mutual empathy, but an arranged marriage reflecting a confluence of the individual states' common needs, problems and objectives that signalled a new era for the region. It was the first time that 11 countries stretching from the Caspian to the Adriatic adhered to the same institutional framework. As diverse as their individual motivations might have been, the prime objective for joining BSEC was their greater integration into the European and world economies. With its international secretariat in Istanbul, the BSEC provided an agency for opening communication links among neighbouring, newly established states and for upgrading their international stature, particularly *vis-à-vis* the EU. The architects of the BSEC identified economic development as the main pillar of regional security and promoted three objectives: cooperation rather than conflict, regionalism as a step towards global integration, and avoidance of new divisions in Europe.

The BSEC's agenda has mainly restricted itself to functional and economic issues, where consensus is more readily arrived at, and has generally placed hard security issues beyond its scope. It is, however, explicitly mentioned in BSEC's founding documents that the search for security and stability in the region is the main goal and aspiration of the initiative. Principles laid down in the Helsinki Final Act, the Charter of Paris, and the OSCE are basic to the BSEC. Its subregional dimension emerges from its functioning within the framework of the OSCE[2] and, one might also argue, from its dependence on the evolution of the EU.

The BSEC was officially transformed from an initiative into a 'regional economic organisation' on 5 June 1998, when a charter was signed that made it into a formal organisation.[3] The BSEC is neither an economic community along the lines of the EU nor a security alliance like NATO. In addition, its capacity for authoritative decisions over economic and political issues is restricted. It envisages neither the creation of a preferential trading area nor the introduction of a common external tariff. Discussions on the establishment of a free trade area, which led to an initial agreement, were soon dismissed as premature.[4] In turn, any advanced subregional military cooperation still remains out of reach for some BSEC states, since some, like Azerbaijan and Armenia, are still locked in a military confrontation with one another. Although one might argue that it is a nascent 'security community', in the sense that force is rejected in its statutory documents as a way of settling disputes among its members, ongoing military conflicts, even if frozen, indicate something quite different.

If the BSEC provides neither a regional security umbrella nor a constituted 'economic bloc', then what is its *raison d'être?* Essentially, the BSEC is a subregional group that functions as a 'diplomatic community', bringing to the same table the policy-making elites of its 11 member-states. For a decade, elites from the governmental, parliamentary and business sectors, as well as from local administrations, have been regularly meeting to discuss, negotiate and coordinate action around common priority issues. Regional institutions have not only brought together local elites, but have also opened links between them and third party international organisations and actors. Defining security in a comprehensive way, the BSEC has become engaged in disseminating security concerns in fields such as environment, energy and economy.[5]

How has the utility of regional cooperation through the BSEC come about in this new era in terms of security provision? How can we place the BSEC within the broader institutional framework consisting of actors such as the UN, NATO, the OSCE and the EU? What should one reasonably expect from the BSEC? Has it the ability to bring about a positive change in regional security? The foundations of the BSEC's security role lie in its statutory documents and agreements as well as the declarations adopted by its members. Its future development and potential remain hostage to the political will of its members and to the level of recognition accorded it by the international community.

Security mechanisms of the BSEC

Declarations and treaties adopted by the BSEC during its ten years of existence are important tools in identifying and assessing mechanisms for dealing with security issues within the BSEC framework. The BSEC was initiated at a time when the region was already facing serious conflicts and the prospect of new tensions emerging was high. How do the statutory and other documents of the organisation refer to the security situation and the conflict management in the region?

Although the BSEC was established 'to ensure that the Black Sea becomes a sea of peace, stability and prosperity, striving to promote friendly and good-neighbourly relations',[6] the founding declaration, adopted on 25 June 1992, did not include specific security measures to accomplish this main goal. Promotion of economic cooperation received the most attention as the vehicle for attaining prosperity and long-term stability. The Bosphorus Statement, also signed on 25 June 1992 in Istanbul, restated the commitment of the heads of state and government 'to act in a spirit of friendship and good neighbourliness and enhance mutual respect and benefit, cooperation and dialogue in the relations between them'. The Bosphorus Statement deals with the settlement of disputes, emphasising 'the need for the peaceful settlement of all disputes by the means and in accordance with the principles set out in the CSCE documents'.[7] The signatories committed themselves to resisting aggression, violence, terrorism and lawlessness in order to restore peace and justice while relying, as a basis of their common understanding, on the general principles of the UN Charter and Conference on Security and Cooperation in Europe.

The BSEC defines security in a comprehensive way, referring not only to its military dimension, but also to political, economic and social factors. Consequently, in order to achieve the overall goal of stability, the Istanbul Declaration includes actions which constitute a framework for BSEC cooperation in the fields of trade and investment, environment, agriculture, transport, communications, energy, tourism, information, science and technology.[8]

The first specific reference to security concerns, though of a non-traditional nature, appeared in the Bucharest Summit Declaration of 30 June 1995, which stated that the members 'will take coordinated actions by the conclusion of the bilateral agreements, aimed at the struggle with organised crime, drugs sales, illegal transportation of weapons and radioactive materials, acts of terrorism and illegal crossing of borders'.[9] In subsequent declarations, BSEC members steadily expressed their political will to enlarge their partnership from a strictly economic relationship to one undertaking measures in soft security and even more explicit security issues, such as terrorism.[10] That the BSEC was not initially established with the objective of forming a multilateral forum for cooperation on military, defence, peace-keeping or conflict management issues is also reflected in its institutionalisation, which foresees regular meetings of the heads of governments and meetings of the foreign affairs ministers, but not meetings of defence ministers or military staff.

BSEC states are striving to build confidence, familiarity and understanding of each other's positions on international affairs through a system of informal and formal meetings among the leaders, ministers and senior officials of the member-states. All decisions within the organisation are based on consensus, and divisive issues are put aside in order not to hamper the appearance of unity or to impede cooperation in areas where it is feasible. In other words, 'consensus building' has been a byword for establishing the lowest common denominator among member-states. The BSEC's basic principle necessitates that actions taken in the name of the organisation must either contribute to or be neutral towards – and not detract from – the stated and unstated interests of the individual member-states.

Calls for a regional security framework

There have been numerous proposals for a regional security framework. None of the calls, however, has led to formal discussions or to any tangible outcome. In 1996, the Assembly of the Western European Union (WEU) issued a call for security to be incorporated into the existing subregional cooperation structures, including the BSEC. The proposal projected that, in the long term, structures for political and security dialogue would need to be set up in order to ensure systematic headway in developing the stability essential for consolidating economic progress.[11] Although the EU has been a distant voice in Black Sea affairs, it has supported engagement in soft security issues, but has been less encouraging on the inclusion of hard security. The European Commission, in its 1997 report to the Council, suggested that cooperative efforts could constructively focus on the promotion of political dialogue, the strengthening of human rights, democracy and the rule of law, as well as on the reduction of drug trafficking, smuggling and illegal immigration throughout the region.[12] From within the region, stronger calls have been heard, particularly from Georgia and Ukraine. In June 1994, the Ukrainian president, Leonid Kravchuk, proposed seven security measures:

- agreement among the Black Sea basin states on the limitation of large-scale naval exercises in the Black Sea;
- agreement among the Black Sea countries on banning manoeuvres or exercises in the Straits zones and adjacent areas of the Black Sea;
- agreement on advance notifications about the purpose of movement and routes of any formations of assault craft, missile ships and gunboats consisting of more than three craft;
- a memorandum of the BSEC countries on refraining from joint military exercises and manoeuvres in the Black Sea with those states not party to the BSEC, and informing other Black Sea basin countries about the entry of foreign naval ships into territorial waters;
- a declaration on the inviolability and intangibility of the sea frontiers of the coastal countries and on relationships among their naval forces and border-guard detachments;
- a memorandum of the Black Sea countries on the inadmissibility of the use of naval forces, in direct or other form, against each other;
- a declaration of the Black Sea basin countries on the refusal to provide their territories for any aggressive or subversive acts carried out against other Black Sea countries.[13]

Within the same framework, President Eduard Shevardnadze of Georgia has regularly argued in favour of a 'Peaceful Caucasus Initiative' that would involve the BSEC. At the 1992 Istanbul Summit he had suggested the establishment of a Council of Defence and Foreign Ministers to tackle subregional crises, a proposal that found little support.[14] On 17 November 1999, on the eve of the OSCE's Istanbul Summit, he once more proposed an enhanced BSEC and called for greater balance between the interrelated economic, political and security issues facing the BSEC member-states:

> Perhaps the time is ripe for BSEC to strike an appropriate balance between economic cooperation and cooperation on regional security, and determine its place within the family of the other regional alliances and intergovernmental organisation in the new European architecture of the 21st century. These issues are increasingly relevant and BSEC' s ultimate success depends on them ... you will perhaps concur that an increasing threat to the regional stability prompts us to think in this direction as well.[15]

At the same time, four leaders in the region – Heydar Aliev (Azerbaijan), Robert Kocharian (Armenia), Eduard Shevardnadze (Georgia) and Suleyman Demirel (Turkey) – supported the development of some kind of stability or security pact for the Caucasus. Following up on this proposal, the Centre for European Policy Studies in Brussels drafted a Stability Pact for the

Caucasus. Elaborated by Michael Emerson, it proposed that, in order to upgrade its effectiveness, the BSEC could enlarge its activities in the field of politics and security, be renamed the Black Sea–Caucasus Cooperation (BSC), and sponsor meetings of a wider political forum, the Black Sea–Caucasus–Caspian Political Forum (BSCC). Thus, the BSC members would be joined by the Caspian states and also by the United States to discuss the broader political concerns of the region.[16] The inclusion of the United States in the BSEC framework, although welcomed by most of the countries in the region, has generated strong opposition as well.[17]

Neither of the other 'leading' countries in the BSEC (Russia and Greece) has, however, been actively asking for an active security role for the organisation. These states have clearly refrained from creating a regional security complex in the area, preferring in practice either bilateralism (as in the case of Russia) or broader multilateralism (as in the case of Greece). Concurrently, a main concern for an active BSEC security role stems from the suspicion with which several BSEC states view an enhanced role for Russia (or Turkey) within the organisation. Instead, these states prefer frameworks where an EU or American presence is guaranteed. Most of them presume that the BSEC's future depends upon whether the EU, the United States and international organisations such as the OSCE will become engaged in BSEC affairs, thereby increasing its credibility and effectiveness while relaxing the concern held by many of its members that the BSEC might evolve into an organisation not recognised by the EU or NATO.

Dealing with soft security politics in a zone of hard security concerns

Traditional security issues have by no means lost their relevance. In fact, following the end of the Cold War, they have increased in importance in the region. There are ongoing or frozen conflicts involving Transdniestria, Abkhazia, Nagorno-Karabakh, South Ossetia and Chechnya. The Black Sea region also harbours the potential for other conflicts generated by long-standing animosities, territorial disputes, military rivalries, ethnic tensions, the presence of foreign military forces, minority issues and mutual suspicion. Moreover, the region is vulnerable to the security threats associated with organised crime, drug trafficking and corruption, which grow out of the endemic economic hardship, social inequality and civil unrest in the area.[18]

The internal weakness of most BSEC countries in transition and their vulnerability to outside pressures, as well as their inadequate or absent integration into new security frameworks, have intensified the overall climate of regional insecurity. These states are at different stages of the political and economic transition towards democratic societies and market economies; they face concurrently an often antagonistic external environment. The main domestic barrier to the peaceful and effective settlement of disputes lies in ineffective state institutions and leaderships that are either unwilling or unable to impose the rule of law. Moreover, a number of states have incomplete control over their territory or population.

In the post-Cold War era, there is growing recognition of the need for conflict prevention and conflict management mechanisms to cope with the challenges posed by economic and soft security concerns. Subregional groupings like the BSEC that emerged in Eurasia during the 1990s, although dedicated to mainly economic and developmental goals, have assumed implicit security and conflict prevention dimensions. They have sought to establish a normative and legal framework that governs interstate relations and establishes regional policy priorities, both of which establish the basis for the relaxation of security concerns.

The BSEC has a political and security dimension derived from the institutionalisation of economic relations, which has both a normative and a political dimension.[19] Subregional organisations might lack the ability to mediate interstate conflicts, but they have the competence to respond to 'soft' security challenges. Alyson Bailes's 'security spectrum', which distinguishes between 'existential' and 'soft' security levels, is a useful analytical tool for understanding the levels of the BSEC's security engagement.[20] The organisation acts as a 'diplomatic community' with three dimensions: interovernmental, interparliamentary (Parliamentary Assembly of the BSEC), and business (the BSEC Business Council). It contributes to regional identity building by increasing solidarity, opening up lines of communication, and increasing mutual knowledge (the 'existential' level). Policy elites from the levels of government, parliament, business and local authorities meet regularly. Biannual meetings take place at the level of foreign ministers and frequently at that of experts within working groups. Parliamentarians regularly meet at biannual general assemblies and committee meetings on economic, political and social affairs. The BSEC has also granted observer status to other European assemblies – the Assembly of the OSCE, the Assembly of the Council of Europe, and the European Parliament – which helps fulfil the goal of involving international organisations more closely in the region. Although the actual power of the interparliamentary dimension in influencing the decisions taken by the BSEC Council is limited, interparliamentary diplomacy has a role to play in the regional task of building democratic institutions. It was the Assembly of the BSEC, for example, that placed issues such as trafficking in people, migration, organised crime and social rights on the regional agenda.

The BSEC has thus kept open channels of dialogue that could be important for emergency situations, fostered the accumulation of shared knowledge, and contributed to confidence building among its members.[21] It aims to undertake projects and identify issues which provide the opportunity for increasing confidence and reduce the risk of conflict. However, BSEC interventions are always in non-military issues. Interventions in the fields of energy, transport and communications, trade and banking have produced the realisation of concrete projects and the concluding of agreements, action plans and memoranda of understanding. Improving economic conditions in participating countries, establishing an integrated infrastructure network, and supporting measures for the protection of the environment are the main areas where the BSEC tries to engender cooperation.[22]

The BSEC has taken concerted action in the non-traditional but explicit security issues of organised crime, terrorism, drugs and illegal migration, which pose a common threat for all the member-states. Specific initiatives, including a police liaison centre and a task force on money laundering, are currently under discussion. Initiatives on cooperation in emergency situations, crisis management and soft security (organised crime, trafficking, terrorism) all point to the BSEC's interest in addressing the elements of the soft security agenda and in carving out a security competence.

Combating organised crime and terrorism was the main concern of the BSEC interior ministers beginning in 1996.[23] At the Yerevan meeting in October 1996, the interior ministers produced a joint statement that marked the launching of interaction between law-enforcement agencies in combating organised crime, terrorism, trafficking of drugs, illicit trade and illegal migration. At the next meeting, held in Istanbul in October 1997, the ministers agreed to establish a joint front and common institutions of cooperation in the sphere of combating crime,[24] followed by a subsequent agreement in October 1998.[25] In the aftermath of September 11 2001, and in response to the urgent need for implementation of the BSEC Agreement on Cooperation in Combating Crime, in Particular its Organised Forms, an additional protocol was agreed upon that envisaged the establishment of a central network of liaison officers on combating crime. This protocol was designed to provide for a speedy regional response in urgent cases and to inform members of transnational crime trends in the region. The agreement covers acts of terrorism, corruption, smuggling, trafficking in people and weapons, economic crime, ecological crime, high-tech crime, trade in human organs, kidnaping, maritime crime, and illegal trafficking in vehicles.

The BSEC Economic Agenda for the Future, adopted by the Council of Ministers of Foreign Affairs in Moscow in April 2001, established a set of short- and long-term security priorities for BSEC. The agenda governs the organisation's activities in the security realm and makes explicit reference to soft security measures within the framework of multilateral economic cooperation. The BSEC agreed to develop policies for three categories of the soft security agenda:

- *National anti-corruption:* the member-states agreed to build on existing programmes and create new ones, and to develop the legislation, institutions and practices needed to combat corruption.
- *Ethics infrastructure:* the member-states acknowledged the need for a more explicit political commitment, a stronger legal framework, better

accountability measures, and a workable code of conduct.
* *International action:* the member states agreed to joint international
  action by drawing on the advice and assistance of Transparency
  International.[26]

Cooperation in emergency situations became another field of successful
engagement with the April 1998 signing of an 'Agreement on Collaboration
in Emergency Assistance and Emergency Response to Natural and Man-
Made Disasters'. The agreement covers cases of extraordinary natural or
technological disasters which require a collective response and are beyond
the ability of individual states to cope with alone. While this category of
agreement is not specifically related to security, it does generate the externality of increasing confidence building within the region.

A central concern of the BSEC is to promote collaboration with international organisations, on the premise that further institutionalisation of
regional affairs increases stability, makes interstate behaviour more
predictable, and binds national policies around broader, common political
objectives. The BSEC and its Parliamentary Assembly have acted as channels
through which regional and international institutions, particularly the UN,
the OSCE and the Council of Europe, have been engaged in the area. Outside
the BSEC framework, the Agreement on the Establishment of the Black Sea
Naval Cooperation Task Group, signed on 2 April 2001, made an important
first step towards the institutionalisation of naval cooperation among all
littoral states on the Black Sea. The agreement is intended to be an on-call
force – christened BlackSeaFor – composed of naval units from the participating states (Bulgaria, Georgia, Romania, Russia, Turkey, Ukraine).[27] The
purpose of BlackSeaFor is to foster cooperation in search and rescue operations, mine clearing operations and environmental activities, and to organise goodwill visits among the Black Sea navies. Although all six signatory
states of the BlackSeaFor participate in the BSEC, most of the members
preferred none the less to pursue that initiative outside the BSEC framework.

The relationship between the BSEC and security initially seems tenuous.
It is increasingly evident that the BSEC, like any other subregional group in
Europe, has an implicit security function. Since the BSEC's geographic delineation includes areas with interstate and civil conflicts, the only way for it to
survive is a 'desecuritisation' of relations within the group, by building cooperation around seemingly unrelated areas, and by undertaking confidence-
building measures which will have the cumulative effect of helping its
members stabilise the regional environment.[28]

Constraints on the BSEC's security role

The difficulties attending the BSEC's aspiration to play a role in the peaceful
settlement of disputes in the region is underscored by the European

Commission's acknowledgement that the ability of the BSEC to bring together representatives of all Black Sea states is itself a notable achievement.[29] In fact, neither the states of the region nor the international community have requested the BSEC to undertake an active role in arms control issues or direct involvement in conflict management crises. It would be hard for such a heterogeneous group of neighbouring states with no formal competence for conflict management, no shared military resources, and no large economic sticks or carrots to undertake such a role.[30]

The primarily economy-oriented mandate and relevant competencies of the BSEC have conditioned its security potential. As a regional economic organisation, it has developed no mechanisms or competencies in the 'hard' security field. In general, one of the most significant shortcomings of the BSEC has been the lack of implementation mechanisms in all areas of its competence. Security expertise, adequate resources and international experience are three other features that the BSEC lacks. At the same time, outstanding territorial and maritime jurisdictional disputes have been the chief obstacle to formal multilateral security cooperation. The divergent regional interests of the individual BSEC states have resulted in the absence of a clear sense of regional interest and a common perception of threat.

Since the region's actual geographic delimitation is not clear, the scope and the area of intervention are also unclear. The large number and the diversity of BSEC member-states, although enriching the organisation in terms of its plurality and resources, generate problems on drafting common 'region-wide' policies. Fishing rights are a case on point. There have been several cases of 'hot incidents' regarding fishing zones in the Black Sea, but the signing of a multilateral agreement has been delayed, because there is no consensus yet as to whether such an agreement should engage only the Black Sea coastal countries or all BSEC members.

The BSEC is both too small and too large to assume hard security roles. It is too small in the sense that it cannot call on the resources of the western powers or extend a credible defence guarantee to its members; it is too large in that its diverse membership hinders effective coordination. Subregional organisations, in general, do not have the military or economic leverage to meet the necessary conditions for an effective security organisation.[31]

The BSEC's role has been likewise undermined by the low degree of member-state commitment to cooperation within the institution. Its weak political voice results from the fact that all of the member-states prefer other foreign and security fora to the BSEC for meeting their security objectives.[32] Some BSEC members therefore place greater priority on pursuing their foreign policy objectives in the region by other means.[33] At least one of the major players, Russia, displays a lack of interest in using multilateral institutions in the area. It has not revealed any enthusiasm for building a Caucasian or Black Sea regional community. However, states from the region formed other smaller groups, such as GUUAM, in an effort to counterbalance Russian influence and in response to their particular security concerns. Historically rooted animosities and distrust have undermined close security cooperation and weakened the commitment to a common front against new security challenges, including terrorism and organised crime.[34]

The fear of being dominated by larger neighbours, such as Russia or Turkey, has been another undermining factor. BSEC members are reluctant to establish a strong regional security framework in which large countries from within the region – often seen as a part of the region's security problem – might prevail. States have chosen to place their security concerns within broader security fora like the OSCE, where the weight of larger states, particularly of Russia, can be balanced by the presence of other powers.

Finally, there is no functional interface between the BSEC and other organisations with security and political functions such as the OSCE, the EU, and NATO. Consequently, even where the BSEC could play a constructive role in regional projects such as civil society building, limitations have been placed on its potential role. The BSEC has also failed to function as the conduit for member-state cooperation with other organisations and international financial institutions. Bulgaria and Romania, for example, have cooperated on soft security issues and undertaken common actions as part of their pre-accession strategies for NATO, but that collaboration does not extend to the BSEC. None the less, the failure of close collaboration between international organisations and the BSEC should not be laid at the latter's door. The BSEC has been eager to integrate the region with the rest of Europe and to become a partner in the EU processes. Towards that goal, the BSEC has proposed the institutionalisation of its affairs with the EU through a Platform of Cooperation, while the BSEC Assembly has unilaterally provided the European Parliament with observer status. The EU response to these initiatives has varied between the vague and the negative. Notwithstanding BSEC deficiencies, the EU's reluctance to engage the BSEC might be rooted in insufficient knowledge in EU policy-making elites of BSEC's actual role and functions; or perhaps, as a locally initiated project, the BSEC lacks the international recognition that it would attract if it were an initiative sponsored by Brussels or Washington.

Further engagement: why and how?

The relative strategic equilibrium of the Cold War has been replaced by a relative strategic vacuum. The subsequent instability of the Black Sea–Eurasia region matters profoundly to the world for several reasons.[35] First, regional instability permits the operation and growth of terrorist movements that have not only local but also global ramifications. Second, and relatedly, the surge of illicit narcotics trade throughout the region also provides a major source of funding for these groups. Third, the Caspian Sea is an emerging oil-producing region that requires unimpeded access to western (and Asian) markets. Finally, regional conflicts have the potential of developing into major power confrontations that cannot but affect the security of Europe and beyond.

Regional cooperation plays a large role in ameliorating security conditions, particularly now that one witnesses a higher salience of non-traditional security threats – environmental, economic and societal – which have regional dimensions and implications.[36] How can subregional institutions like the BSEC assume an operational security role? First, they must cultivate cooperative attitudes, integrate regional economic and political regimes into the global system, and increase dialogue among peoples of different cultures and religions. Importantly, a subregional organisation such as the BSEC, which functions as a political, economic and cultural bridge between Europe and Central Asia, should receive additional external support for its activities. Subregionalism best serves stability by closing the political, economic and social gaps between western and Eurasian states that pose a barrier to greater cohesion and solidarity.

The BSEC's operation as a 'diplomatic community' generates two indirect, positive effects for interstate relations in the region. First, the overall security environment is improved because the BSEC keeps open the channels of dialogue; and second, it recasts challenges and threats as a common concern in the interest of enhancing a sense of regionalism. The international community long ago recognised that subregional initiatives contribute to promoting regional security and stability through political dialogue and shared economic development.[37] Though weak in military power, subregional organisations can become relatively strong in diplomatic power or in economic activities.[38]

Most subregional economic initiatives in Eurasia, which support sustainable models of development and growth, promote self-confidence and encourage greater self-reliance in matters of security. What appears as economic subregionalism is, in fact, driven by political, military or cultural considerations.[39] It thus addresses domestic sources of insecurity resulting from economic inequality, poverty and economic exclusion, while soothing the unease with which countries of different cultural backgrounds face each other. Major threats to security and stability are increasingly understood by regional elites as originating from within the region itself and reflect the destabilising effects of poor economic and political performance.

What constructive forms of interaction can be developed between the BSEC and other, larger organisations? To date, the BSEC approach has not dealt directly with local conflicts; if anything, it has dealt with them by putting them aside. Direct involvement of the BSEC in high security issues, such as the demilitarisation or denuclearisation of the region, cannot be expected or encouraged in the short or medium term. Subregional groups within the OSCE contribute to the overall institutional structure of the security space covered by the OSCE.[40] They are devoted to security in this broader sense, but are not specifically or directly engaged in the military aspects. Instead, these subregional institutions concentrate on policies that promote regional and domestic stability and address the non-military aspects of security: financial and technical support for the transition to the market and democracy, economic development, a stable energy supply, environmental cooperation and the networking of civil societies. Subregional groups thus consolidate the OSCE model of security building by offering a means for the dissemination and adoption of the norms and standards of the OSCE, the Council of Europe and the EU. Subregional institutions cannot, however, compensate for the denial of the benefits attending EU and NATO membership.[41]

An important undertaking of the BSEC is reducing intra-regional tensions by creating and sponsoring a process of community building. By encouraging the involvement of actors other than state ones (NGOs, business people, local authorities), subregional institutions cultivate a bottom-up approach to conflict prevention and management and adhere to a 'pre-emptive' diplomacy. The BSEC should be assisted in its attempts to sustain the evolution of democratic civil societies in the region, control unwanted migratory flows, ameliorate the sources of conflict attending the soft security agenda (trafficking, organised crime, terrorism), and foster cooperation on economic development and environmental cooperation. Constructive engagement of subregional institutions like the BSEC in these fields produces appreciable value added and facilitates crisis prevention, conflict containment and post-settlement reconstruction.[42] The main instrument of the BSEC for crisis prevention is diplomatic (and potentially economic), and thus its dialogue channels could assist 'proximity talks' as a mode of interaction.[43] A division of labour between the BSEC and other institutions, particularly the UN, the OSCE and NATO's PfP, for the purposes of the regional verification of agreements and monitoring of conflicts could also be established.[44] At the same time, the BSEC's diplomatic power might be deployed to contain conflict through its influence within the framework of UN debates and actions. The links of communication and confidence already existing among policy-making elites in the area could be used to forestall conflict situations and prevent the outbreak of hostilities or other forms of disruptive behaviour. The deepening of institutional ties between the BSEC and the EU, NATO, the OSCE and specialised UN agencies could assist in the formulation of clear economic objectives for the region towards the supplementary goal of conflict prevention and management. The BSEC process of region building could also lead to the redefinition of the identity, interests and capacities of its member-states, which would, in turn, help create conditions for a system of institutionalised negotiation or conflict resolution that would enhance regional security and stability.

The area where the BSEC can make a positive contribution is in post-conflict rehabilitation of conflict zones. The area covered by BSEC states is still characterised by ongoing or frozen conflicts, but the BSEC's agenda is not so ambitious as to include resolution of these conflicts. The BSEC acknowledges the comparative advantage of other organisations long practised in the art of crisis management, particularly the OSCE and the UN. The BSEC could prove an effective mediator and manager in the post-settlement period when there is the need for financial assistance to reconstruct destroyed housing stock and economic infrastructure, as well as re-establishing normalised flows of goods, services and people. The BSEC is well equipped to sponsor rehabilitation programmes for those areas.[45]

The BSEC's effectiveness is as contingent upon the support of the international community as it is upon the efforts and will of its members. As part of the Eurasian security architecture, the BSEC cannot be seen as a viable alternative to any larger European organisation. Its potential for contributing to regional security is located in its ability to bring together diverse groups of states in a cooperative framework and to tackle specific elements of the soft security agenda. At the same time, within the context of NATO and EU enlargement, it sustains cooperation between NATO/EU members, those seeking NATO/EU membership, and those states remaining aloof or excluded from the enlargement processes.

The long-term political aim of BSEC members is an institutionalisation of relations with the EU. That shared political goal very often becomes the only common ground of discussions held within the BSEC framework. EU support for subregional actors such as the BSEC is crucial, because it sends an important political signal to states within the region, testifying to the legitimacy of the subregional group and reassuring them that subregional cooperation is a step towards further integration with the world and European structures. The EU presence in the region, and especially the development of modes of practical BSEC–EU interaction, acquires a strong security dimension for the accompanying stabilising effects.

A subregional organisation cannot fulfil its role if certain internal and external conditions are not present. The recognition of its role by the states from within the region as well as by external powers is decisive for the realisation of the BSEC's security potential. Intra-BSEC solidarity depends heavily on the unifying effect of common threat perception, which, though weak, has mainly evolved around issues of soft security. It has now become increasingly obvious that the fight against organised crime in all its forms is a priority security concern for all countries in the region and beyond. The determination of the Black Sea Eurasian countries to cooperate on common policies meeting the soft security agenda has increased over time.

Regarding the internal requirements for a successful and effective BSEC, the most important objectives are strengthening institutional functions and enhancing the legitimacy of its member-states. Conflicts and insecurity surface in areas of 'weak' or 'failed' states where the vacuum of state authority permits the deployment of destabilising actors. Weak states and fragmented societies constitute the main factors of instability; well-functioning states remain the main actors for the provision of security. In the absence of the latter, a necessary condition for interstate cooperation on security matters is seriously impaired.

The future of the BSEC as a security actor is hostage to a number of developments largely outside its immediate control.[46] First, an enhanced role for the BSEC is contingent upon successful economic cooperation. Without economic growth, the political stability necessary for sustained cooperation in security affairs is unlikely to materialise. Second, the political instability in the Eurasian region and the ongoing conflicts create conditions conducive to the emergence of criminal groups and the growth of organised crime. Either development, left unchecked, would impede the development of market economies in the region, weaken the evolution of a democratic civil society, and debilitate state institutions. Third, the readiness of the international organisations (and the great powers) to integrate the BSEC into their plans of action for the region will be decisive for the organisation's future. In the absence of external legitimisation, the BSEC will be less likely to foster security cooperation in the Black Sea region, a key security zone along the borders of Europe.

Conclusion

Eurasian security has come to the forefront after several years of neglect owing to the Balkan conflicts, which monopolised international interest and great power resources for much of the 1990s. Eurasia suffers from pervasive misrule and accompanying economic difficulties, and thus a security approach for the region should have a broad, comprehensive perspective. Subregional organisations have their own multidimensional security potential to be exploited by the international community in its search for appropriate instruments to address the security challenges originating in Eurasia. The BSEC, a formal economic institution, has already served security in the region by keeping communication channels open and bringing policy-making elites to the same negotiating table. It has established regional regimes in the domains of economy, infrastructure and the environment. Region building, *per se*, has a security dimension, because it increases societal stability, contributes to the process of confidence building, makes state preferences more transparent, and facilitates the exchange of information by policy-making elites. Security and peace are promoted through the BSEC approach, which combines the two basic tasks of confidence building among peoples and strengthening cooperation between governments. The BSEC's geographic delimitation straddles Europe and Asia. It forms one nexus linking together their security. A constructive mode of collaboration by the international community with the BSEC would have long-term stabilising effects, and it would indicate to the states of the area that cooperative attitudes, first of all towards their immediate neighbours, have added value for security. In an era when globalisation has not only changed the economic and social domains, but also altered the preconditions of security and made territorial state borders very porous, the constructive reliance upon subregional institutions like the BSEC, which provide stability mechanisms spanning sovereign jurisdictions, should be encouraged and supported by the broader international community.

Notes

1 The views expressed are the author's own and should not be regarded as a statement of the Secretariat of the Parliamentary Assembly of the BSEC.
2 Subregional integration is defined as 'the construction of institutional structures to combine the interests of a group of countries within a wider region'. William Wallace, 'Regionalism in Europe: Model or Exception', in Louise Fawcett and Andrew Hurrel (eds), *Regionalism in World Politics, Regional Organization and International Order* (New York: Oxford University Press, 1997), p. 202.
3 For the 'Charter of the Organisation of the Black Sea Economic Cooperation' and all founding documents, see BSEC *Statutory Documents* (Istanbul: BSEC PERMIS, 2001).
4 The 'Declaration of Intention on the Creation of a Zone of Free Trade of BSEC' was approved by the Istanbul Meeting of Ministers of Foreign Affairs on 7 February 1997.
5 This approach to the problem of security reflects the approach found in Barry Buzan, *People, States and Fear: An Agenda for International Security Studies in the Post-Cold War Era*, second edn (Boulder CO: Lynne Rienner, 1991).
6 Article 8, 'Summit Declaration of the BSEC', Istanbul, 25 June 1992, in BSEC, *BSEC Handbook of Documents, I*, (Istanbul: BSEC PERMIS, 1995), p. 4.
7 'Bosphorus Statement', adopted on 25 June 1992, in BSEC, *Handbook I*, pp. 9–10.
8 Article 8, p. 4.
9 'Bucharest Statement' adopted on 30 June 1995, in BSEC, *Handbook I*, p. 17.
10 See 'Moscow Declaration' adopted on 25 October 1996 by the Ministers of Foreign Affairs, in BSEC, *BSEC Handbook of Documents, II* (Istanbul: BSEC PERMIS, 1996), p. 7.
11 Assembly of the WEU, *Parliamentary Cooperation in the Black Sea Area*, Rapporteur Sir John Hunt, Doc. 1544 (Paris: WEU, 4 November 1996), p. 9.
12 Commission of the European Communities, *Regional Cooperation in the Black Sea Area: State of Play, Perspectives for EU Action Encouraging its Further Development*, COM(97), 597 final (Brussels: EC, 1997), pp. 8–9.
13 Assembly of the WEU, *Parliamentary Cooperation*, p. 11.
14 Plamen Pantev, 'Security Cooperation in the Black Sea Basin', in Tunç Aybak (ed.), *Politics of the Black Sea: Dynamics of Cooperation and Conflict* (London and New York: I. B. Tauris, 2001), pp. 123–4.
15 Remarks by Eduard Shevardnadze, president of Georgia, at the Informal Summit of the BSEC, 17 November 1999.
16 Michael Emerson, *A Stability Pact for the Caucasus* (Brussels: Centre for European Policy Studies, 2000), p. 12.

17 *Ibid.*
18 Louise I. Shelley, 'Organised Crime and Corruption: Security Threats', in David W. P. Lewis and Gilles Lepesant (eds), *What Security for Which Europe? Case Studies from the Baltic to the Black Sea*, (New York: Peter Lang, 1999), pp. 149–68.
19 Pantev, 'Security Cooperation', p. 121. Also Ercan Özer, 'The Black Sea Economic Cooperation and Regional Security', *Perceptions*, 2:3 (1997), pp. 76–106.
20 Alyson J. K. Bailes, 'The Role of Subregional Cooperation in Post-Cold War Europe: Integration, Security, and Democracy', in Andrew Cottey (ed.), *Subregional Cooperation in the New Europe: Building Security, Prosperity and Solidarity from the Barents to the Black Sea* (London: Macmillan, 1999), pp. 170–1.
21 Nicolae Micu, 'Black Sea Economic Co-operation (BSEC) as a Confidence-Building Measure', *Perceptions*, 1:4 (1996–97), www.gov.tr/grupa/percept/i4/14–5.htm.
22 Another important institution is the Black Sea Trade and Development Bank, which has been functioning since 1998 and is based in Thessaloniki, Greece. Apart from promoting economic cooperation, the bank functions as an agent of structural reform and facilitator of integration.
23 E. N. Borisenko, A. P. Kononenko and I. V. Semenenko, *Black Sea Economic Cooperation: From Regional Initiative to International Organisation* (Istanbul: UZMAN, 1998), pp. 139–42.
24 'Joint Statement' adopted at the Meeting of the Ministers of Internal Affairs of the BSEC Participating States; and 'Joint Declaration' adopted at the Second Meeting of the Ministers of Internal Affairs of the BSEC Participating States, in BSEC, *BSEC Handbook of Documents, III* (Istanbul: BSEC PERMIS, 1998), pp. 139–42, 148–9.
25 'Agreement Among the Governments of the Black Sea Economic Cooperation Participating States on Cooperation in Combating Crime, in Particular in its Organised Forms' (Kerkyra, 2 October 1998).
26 BSEC, *BSEC Economic Agenda for the Future: Towards a More Consolidated, Effective and Viable Partnership* (Istanbul: BSEC PERMIS, ICBSS, October 2001).
27 'Agreement on the Establishment of the Black Sea Naval Cooperation Task Group', www.blackseafor.org.
28 Bailes, 'Role of Subregional Cooperation', p. 165.
29 Commission of the European Communities, *Regional Cooperation*, p. 4.
30 Bailes, 'Role of Subregional Cooperation', p. 167.
31 Ian Bremmer and Alyson J. K. Bailes, 'Subregionalism in the Newly Independent States', *International Affairs*, 74:1 (1998), pp. 131–47, esp. p. 133.
32 Pantev, 'Security Cooperation', p. 120.
33 Commission of the European Communities, *Regional Cooperation*, p. 4.
34 See the conference report of the Black Sea Strategy Group, *Coping with New Security Threats in the Black Sea Region* (Kiev: EastWest Institute, 2002), p. 3.
35 For the significance of the Black Sea region, see Yannis Valinakis, 'The Black Sea Region: Challenges and Opportunities for Europe', *Chaillot Paper 36* (Paris: Institute for Security Studies of WEU, 1999).
36 For the regionalising logic of the new security – economic, environmental, societal – threats, see Barry Buzan, 'The Logic of Regional Security in the Post-Cold War World', in Björn Hettne, András Inotai and Osvaldo Sunkel (eds), *The New Regionalism and the Future of Security and Development, 4* (New York: St Martin's Press in association with UNU/WIDER, 2000), pp. 26–50.

37 Assembly of the WEU, *Parliamentary Cooperation*, p. 4.
38 Muthiah Alagappa, 'Regionalism and Conflict Management: A Framework for Analysis', *Review of International Studies*, 21:4 (1995), pp. 359–87, esp. p. 378.
39 Buzan, 'Logic of regional security', p. 21.
40 'Charter for European Security' (Istanbul: OSCE, November 1999), para. 13. For the OSCE's role in this context, see chapter 8 by P. Terrence Hopmann in this volume.
41 K. Mottola, 'Security in-between Regionalism and Subregionalism in the OSCE security model', paper presented at the 3rd Pan-European International Relations Conference and Joint Meeting with the International Studies Association, Vienna, 16–19 September 1998, p. 9; and Bremmer and Bailes, 'Subregionalism'.
42 Bailes, 'Role of Subregional Cooperation', p. 167.
43 Bremmer and Bailes, 'Subregionalism', p. 145.
44 Pantev, 'Security Cooperation', p. 123.
45 Michael Emerson and Marius Vahl, *Europe's Black Sea Dimension: Model European Regionalism, Prêt à Porter* (Brussels: Centre for European Policy Studies, 2001), p. 12.
46 George Pirinski, 'BSEC: A New Agenda '21?', *Journal of Southeast European and Black Sea Studies*, 1:3 (2001), pp. 174–8, esp. p. 178.

12

The EU and Eurasia:
a bounded security role in
a greater Europe

Simon Serfaty

Entering the twentieth century, the most important strategic location in the world was said to be a 'pivot area' that consisted of the northern and interior portion of the Eurasian continent, 'where the rivers flow either to the icebound Arctic Ocean or inward to salt seas and salt lakes having no oceanic outlets.'[1] So it was viewed then, and so it is often viewed now as other 'Great Games' are being staged in or around this same 'pivot area' for the never-ending struggle among or against great powers.

Notwithstanding the significance of the area, the EU has little involvement with 'Eurasia' as compared to the extensive relations it has developed with other parts of the world. Going west, the EU and the United States are forming an 'ever closer union' of their own – a Euro-Atlantic community that would complete a vision that was born out of the ruins of two world wars half-way into the past century. Moving east, the EU is extending this vision to enough new members to make the continent west of Russia 'whole and free' – while cautiously progressing with a special bilateral relationship with Russia as a power in Europe that need not be, and cannot become, a power within the Union. Going south, the empires have come home and past EU dreams of becoming a power in the Middle East have resulted in the fear that too many immigrants are making of the EU a Middle Eastern power – a condition that reinforces the Union's intention of making the Mediterranean the continent's final geographic boundary (notwithstanding its historic presence in a series of islands that would include Malta and Cyprus) while keeping Turkey separate from its institutions.

By comparison, the EU's presence in Eurasia is elusive. For one, it is diluted by the very nature of a 'region' that escapes any reliable definition: thus, while Halford J. Mackinder remained faithful to his concept of a 'pivot area', he redefined it periodically throughout his life, expanding its reach farther east and south.[2] Moreover, the area is so diverse as to present the EU with challenges that exceed the limits of what its institutions can do.

Politically, the EU lacks a common foreign and security policy, and none is likely to emerge any time soon. Economically, the Union's attention is elsewhere as it attends to the consequences of its enlargement and other dimensions of a heavy parochial agenda. As a result, outside Russia and Turkey, whatever influence is exerted by the EU in Eurasia results mainly from the interests of individual member-states rather than from the presence of the institutions to which they belong. After the events of September 11 2001, however, and in the context of an expanded war on terrorism, this may cease to be true as 'Eurasia' includes or touches upon a number of pivot countries, including Pakistan and Afghanistan, where the EU will be asked by its members, as well as by the United States, to play a separate, distinctive and even vital role.[3]

End game?

By any standard, the EU does not qualify as a sovereign state, either as a matter of fact (in its territory, population, government and army) or as a state of mind (in its loyalty, values, identity and history). Yet, not only does the EU matter but also, for some of the issues that seem to matter most, it often matters more than its members. Moving in an increasingly integrated space – peaceful, affluent, democratic and de-ideologised – the states of Europe are playing out an ambitious end game: widen in order to deepen, deepen in order to widen, and reform in order to do both.[4]

Deepening is Euro-speak for doing more. It has to do with increasing institutional cooperation in more and more substantive areas, thereby leaving less room for the exercise of national sovereignty. Because each new initiative often sets the stage for the initiative that follows, there seems to be no end to the process and, accordingly, for most of the past 50 years few attempts have been made to define that end point before it is reached. *Widening* is Euro-speak for bringing more members in the community – from six to nine to ten to 12 to 15, and possibly twice as many by 2010. Yet, enlargement is not open-ended and its limits – part geographical, part cultural and part organisational – are real even as they remain unstated.[5] Finally, *reforming* the institutions has to do with devising new ways whereby an expanding institutional discipline – the *acquis communautaire* – can be effectively imposed on the community.[6] Predictably, the more the process unfolds and the more institutional reforms are needed through intergovernmental conferences (IGCs) held to modify the original treaties – as will have been the case on three occasions during the period 1996–2004.

This reorganisation of Europe's political space is historically awesome. Yet because the process remains very erratic, moving from setbacks to *relance*, many continue to dismiss it. That will puzzle future historians. When dealing with contemporary Europe and its future role as security actor, particularly outside Europe proper, it is best to think retroactively – what used to be once upon a time and has been achieved over time, rather than what is and is being attempted at a given time. Thinking in time helps gain the perspective needed to follow Europe's revival during the second half of the twentieth century when, with America's encouragement, its mosaic of nation-states gained unparalleled cohesion and stability as a union of member-states.

Jean Monnet, who viewed the 1957 Rome Treaties as a feeble and 'rather vague' idea, would be astounded.[7] Can the young member-states of the EU be the old great powers of Europe that celebrated the horrific deaths of tens of millions in the name of a mythical white man's burden, an elusive *mission civilisatrice*, a constrained *Kultur*, or self-appointed and barbaric Soviet commissars? Living in an increasingly integrated and civil space, the new Europeans show an identity that is increasingly common. Over the years, there has emerged a community of people living in a collage of regions whose shared characteristics overcome national stereotypes. Forget the clichés: with cultures increasingly compatible, attitudes have become complementary. Now, the 'ideal' European is found most convincingly as a composite of what the idealised German, French, Spaniard, Italian and Englishman used to be – enhanced by the cultural colours brought by the defunct overseas empires, and completed by the US influence that has spread throughout much of the continent.

Even as Europeans gain a better sense of the reality *communautaire* they form, they fail to understand how their emerging community serves them, and why. Not surprisingly, that creates new tensions with institutions that often seem to proceed 'as if' they knew better than the states they serve. 'The concept of "as if"', wrote Timothy Ash, 'is a subjective, idealistic self-definition in which the idea takes absolute precedence over reality and consciousness determines being.'[8] For the EU, the concept means treating 'Europe' as if it holds the same legitimacy as each of its members, even though their citizens view it as a cage within which their democratic institutions are imprisoned and their national identity is diluted. The agenda could not be any more parochial. For the citizens to accept a recycling of their cherished nation-state within an ill-defined union of member-states, the European institutions will have to do more in such areas as jobs, income distribution, ageing populations and inadequately funded pension funds, immigration flows, education, national cohesion, political leadership and much else. Not 'as if' but 'what if' the EU could save the nation-states, once again, from their inability to attend to issues that cannot be resolved individually as effectively as collectively.[9]

On September 11 2001 an unpredictable 'what if' entered the transatlantic and Eurasian mix within which the EU was to play out its end game. History need not unfold further to conclude that America's loss of its territorial invulnerability, assumed to be inviolable, will impact not only on the United States and its vision of, and role in, the world, but also on every region and, within each region, every country too. With all nations asked to choose sides – 'with us or against us', insisted President George W. Bush on 20 September – alliances and adversary relations will be tested in ways that are likely to change them significantly, for the much better or the much worse. With the EU countries open to catastrophic, terror-ridden scenarios developed south of the Mediterranean, new 'civilisational' hostilities could seriously impact on their relations with the Greater Europe that lies outside the EU's institutional boundaries, including Russia as well as Turkey and its immediate neighbours in the Caucasus and Caspian region – all institutional orphans that receive limited attention from the EU.

On the whole, however, the end game that began in the latter part of the 1990s will still be nearing completion at the end of this decade. This means that by that time, Europe will have progressively become: larger, with 25 members or more, but excluding, under any conceivable circumstances, Turkey, Russia and any former Soviet republic except the Baltic countries; deeper, with a functioning euro zone comprised of at least all current 15 EU countries, including Great Britain; more globally engaged, with an increasingly common (but still incomplete) foreign policy that would reflect the improved cohesion of EU countries, but with none of the political will required for evoking yet a common defence policy; somewhat stronger, with some early elements of a common security policy in place, including institutions but also minimal capabilities for rapid deployment in and beyond Europe; and more united as a reborn superpower, though not as an emerging superstate.

Going west: an ever closer union

After World War II and throughout the Cold War, America's embrace of the idea of Europe was never unconditional. Nor, for that matter, did it ever need to be. Instead, the US commitment to a united and strong Europe relied on criteria of political, economic and societal convergence that would help the countries of Europe act more like the United States, even if they could not quite 'be' the United States. But these were also criteria of institutional convergence that would enable an emerging European Community to join the United States in a community of action where the values and the interests shared across the Atlantic would be translated into common policies. In other words, an ever more united and stronger Europe would become inseparable from the United States, even as it remained separate from America.[10]

During the formative Cold War phase of Europe's construction, US apprehensions were significant but also comprehensible. Keeping the Communists out of coalition governments in NATO countries was a matter of common sense. With hindsight, the passions aroused over US opposition to Euro-communism, in Italy and elsewhere, are baffling. Whatever else was said, Communist participation in allied governments would have adversely affected NATO cohesion. Sustaining the US dollar as the Euro-Atlantic currency of choice was also compelling. As was shown during the monetary storms of the 1970s, an erratic dollar rattled more than the sole US economy. Preserving the US control of the nuclear deterrent should not have been a matter for serious debate either: who else? Even assuming that de Gaulle had a visionary sense of the future, being right 25 years too early would also mean having been wrong for 25 years too many. And so the discord went – never so far, however, that any country in Europe withdrew from the alliance, and never so disruptive that the United States might wish to derail the unfolding process in Europe.[11]

Early in the 2000s, US concerns over the conclusive phase of the European construction are different. Centrist republics in Europe can hardly raise fears comparable to those raised by political changes during the Cold War. The 'foreign national parties' of yesteryear have become 'European national parties' as they enter into domestic coalitions that barely move from centre left to centre right. As Europe expands to the east, criteria of membership are comparable to the criteria that were implicitly outlined earlier for the Euro-Atlantic community, including democratic structures, market economy and the ability to compete. For 50 years, the United States remodelled the countries of western Europe to its image, and now it is their turn to refashion eastern Europe to that new image.

Some ambivalence remains, however. A united Europe whose strength would rest ultimately on the joint pillars of its single currency and a common security and defence policy could be viewed either as a counterweight or as a counterpart of American leadership and power. The distinction is real. The defining image of a counterweight is adversarial, as the 'weight' to 'counter' would be primarily, if not exclusively, that of the United States.[12] Fears of such a counter have to do with the assumption that Europe's follower-ship must be absolute lest America's leadership be weakened. As the image gains focus, the euro emerges as a challenger, even a threat, to the dollar – a global reserve currency whose economic clout would make it an effective *force de frappe* aimed at deflating or reversing US influence everywhere. A common security, foreign and (eventually) defence policy would provide this counterweight with capabilities that might confirm the rise of Europe as an option to the United States in areas where American leadership was traditionally tolerated for lack of available alternatives. The additional risk raised by such emerging military capabilities would not be that they might be used in spite of the United States and NATO. The risk would be that the 'authorised' use of an 'autonomous' force would be so ineffective (or premature) as to force subsequently an American involvement that the United States might not have considered otherwise. In this case, far from being a counterweight, 'Europe' and its alleged new power would have proven to be a counterfeit.[13]

Standing in exaggerated opposition to the counterweight view of Europe's future is a more united, larger and stronger Europe acting as a counterpart to the United States.[14] The driving assumption behind this view is that what has been happening in Europe over the past 50 years has been generally good for America, and that more integration would be just as good (and certainly better than any alternative). Admittedly, the rise of a strong euro as a global currency could harm a dollar that has provided well for Europe's (and America's) affluence, and an autonomous Europe could hamper a US leadership that has served well Europe's (and America's) security. Yet, while differences between the two sides of the Atlantic remain – geopolitical, economic and cultural – these have been narrowing significantly as America becomes more European, and Europe more American. In sum, more integration in Europe need not mean less America in an integrated Europe.

The political, economic, strategic and even cultural indivisibility of the Euro-Atlantic space will be sorely tested in the early 2000s. Predictably, an America targeted by 'evildoers' intent on turning back the clock of their history, as well as that of other nations, a thousand years will not be satisfied with half-hearted support. The magnitude of the killing – approximating the official total of the Revolutionary War or of Pearl Harbor's 'day of infamy' – made the peaceful resolution of this 'act of war' neither possible nor desirable. This shared threat was also promptly perceived in Europe, where heads of state and government quickly understood their own vulnerability. *'Ich bin ein New-Yorker'* – this was Europe's time to respond to these events with tones of solidarity voiced in the name of their own interests as well as on America's behalf. Coming days after the unprecedented NATO decision to view the attack against New York and Washington as an action covered by Article 5 of the 1949 Washington Treaty, the EU pledge of 'unlimited solidarity' for the campaign against the 'barbaric acts' of September 11 provided the United States with a powerful reminder that even a nation without peers needs the comfort of its allies. To paraphrase John F. Kennedy again, entering the new century, it is Europe's turn to ask not what America can do for the Old World but what the Old World must do with America.[15]

Bigger is safer

After World War II, the division of Europe was not preordained. Rather, the United States envisioned a whole and united Europe that would rely on the Grand Alliance, including the Soviet Union, to achieve a lasting reconciliation with the defeated states, including Germany. Sensitive to the conflicts that had followed the end of the previous world war, the Truman administration reasoned that Europe's instabilities would be best overcome within an integrated, democratic and affluent continental space. In June 1947, the American offer of Marshall aid was extended to the east, but Moscow's refusal was imposed on neighbouring countries that were to start a 'community' of their own a few years later. As the Cold War was unfolding, the Atlantic idea, which was a European idea, helped overcome resistance to a

European construction that the United States was more determined to pursue than the Europeans themselves.[16]

Entering the 1990s, the end of the Cold War briefly appeared to threaten both ideas and both institutions. By then, however, Europe and America's earlier choices had become irreversible. Now, talks of dissolution of NATO (in the United States) or withdrawal from 'Europe' (for any of its members) had become meaningless. Instead, enlargement to the east quickly became the favoured option that would move NATO but also the EU beyond their Cold War areas so that neither could be moved out of business. In 1995, Europe's fourth enlargement – to Austria, Finland and Sweden – involved nearly all the European states that had chosen to be, or were compelled to remain, neutral during the Cold War. In 1999, NATO's fourth enlargement to the Czech Republic, Hungary and Poland involved three of the four countries in Central Europe that had previously constituted the dividing line between the east and the west.

EU enlargement is a vital dimension of Europe's future and a central dimension of an evolving Euro-Atlantic security partnership in the twenty-first century. First, a larger EU is the most effective way to extend the democratic stability of western Europe to the continent. What else is there? The transformation of Europe's hard core – France, Germany and Italy – is a case in point: it is within a united Europe that France ended its wars of the republics, Italy began to complete its unification, and Germany exhausted its appetite for living space. Examples of domestic upheavals within the European community have been few and have become fewer. At the margins of Europe, Ireland first, then Spain and Portugal, and Greece next, also gained unprecedented democratic stability and affluence thanks, in part at least, to the advantages of EU membership: economic gains, financial transfers, political centrism and western legitimacy. Finally, domestic challenges to stability mounted by ideological or separatist groups could be all the more successful as the EU progressively helped contain the risks that the governments' reaction might raise for civil liberties that would have otherwise been left unprotected.

A sense of failure resulting from unfulfilled promises of enlargement would be destabilising. The EU timetables for enlargement must be robust and credible, and deadlines that serve short-term political interests at home but cannot be met within the EU – or are not met because of these interests – are self-defeating. In the 1990s, too many target dates for enlargement were postponed when the prerequisite of institutional reform within the EU imposed criteria on member-states even more difficult to meet than the criteria for membership faced by applicant countries. But, unlike the case with NATO, the benefits of EU membership are as quantifiable as their costs, and a failure to make membership work after it has been granted would be no less significant than a failure to grant it. After the Cold War the countries of central and eastern Europe endured many years of economic pain and turbulence, even under conditions of growth, as the need to prepare for the *acquis communautaire* denied the generous peace dividends expected by the people. Now, these sacrifices must be justified not only with the fact of membership but also with its rewards – meaning, rewards of economic affluence and democratic stability. A decade after the end of the Cold War, these rewards remain far short of public expectations.[17]

Bidding for NATO membership does not help bids for EU membership, but achieving one does help the other. Admittedly, because both institutions are distinct, the two processes of enlargement should remain separate. Yet, a parallel enlargement of both institutions would enable them to work together more effectively than under conditions that keep European NATO states that are not EU members away from EU initiatives, and EU states that are not NATO members away from NATO initiatives. Such convergence occurred during the Cold War, when the European Economic Community grew from six to 12 – and NATO from 12 to 16 members. By 1986, only one of the new European Community states (Ireland) had failed to join NATO as well, and only three of the 14 NATO European countries were not European Community members, with only Turkey wishing otherwise (unlike Norway and Iceland). After the Cold War, the gap widened again: the three neutral states that joined the EU in 1995 did not seek NATO membership, and none of the three countries that joined NATO in 1999 were in the EU although all were included in the short list of EU applicants.

A strategy of dual enlargement would keep the two processes of enlargement separate, but it would recognise that EU and NATO decisions are not separable as the two institutions best equipped to serve as primary guarantors of the new European security order.[18] To achieve this goal, each institution should also reach out to European states that already belong to the other. Thus, by 2005–7, most European members of an enlarged NATO are likely to be in the EU, while most members of an enlarged EU will probably have joined NATO, thus extending the boundaries of a Greater Europe to the Baltic region, central Europe and Slovenia. By that time, too, the reorganisation of a common Euro-Atlantic space may begin to cover the former neutral states that objected to NATO membership, including Austria (and even, in the not-too-distant future, Sweden and Finland), as well as persistent Eurosceptics that stood away from the EU (including Norway). Thus, the convergence between NATO and EU membership would have been restored in the east and the south, thereby building new common ground for complementary strategies in these areas. NATO does not command the wide variety of diplomatic and commercial tools available to the EU to influence the decisions that might lead to unwanted military actions. The EU does not command the decisive type of capabilities available to NATO to shape events after these decisions have been made. For both NATO and the EU, dual enlargement is a vital dimension of a western strategy for the unfinished security business in and beyond Europe.

With NATO and the United States thus standing on each sideline of the playing field, the transatlantic dimensions of the EU's end game are clearly drawn. Entering the twenty-first century, America has a relationship with Europe that is no longer reversible. It may not be, and not wish to become, a European power, but it is, and is bound to remain, a power in Europe. Such a conclusion is not an invitation to debate America's membership in the EU, but it is a plea to debate the consequences of America's status as a non-member member–state within the EU. In short, a vital but carefully hidden dimension of EU enlargement has to do with the structure of US relations with the EU, as well as with the nature of EU–NATO relations.

Going east: smaller is better

Farther to the east, it is politically ironic that the disintegration of the Soviet Union initially moved Moscow and its former republics farther away from the Europe that Mikhail Gorbachev hoped to lease as a common home. At least the Soviet Union had an ideology that many in Europe were seemingly prepared to endorse for a while. But it also had a history inherited from a Russian state whose steadfast expansion to the west sought to define a territorial niche – 'a safe and productive location', according to Robert Legvold – on a continent that Dostoevsky and Tolstoy understood much better than Marx, Lenin and Stalin.[19] Now, nothing is left of the Soviet Union except a leadership that has more to do with the remnants of the amputated Communist empire it inherited by default than with *la grande Russie* of an earlier Europe.

Throughout the Cold War, the Kremlin never viewed 'Europe' on its own terms. Rather, an emerging European community was misrepresented as a sort of NATO without America's (nuclear) teeth – too tempting for Moscow to ignore but not strong enough to fear. Accordingly, Soviet policies towards the then-European Community were policies towards the United States, whose periodic tensions with one or more EU states provided opportunities – usually illusive – to drive a wedge between the two sides of the Atlantic. After the Cold War, however, a sense of neglect and even harassment by the United States progressively sharpened Moscow's interest in Europe and its union. As Stephen Cohen observed at the time, 'By 2000, some 81 per cent [of Russians] believed that US policy in general was anti-Russian and even pro-Western Russians thought a "reverse iron curtain" was being imposed on the country's borders.'[20] In July 2000, a newly elected president, Vladimir Putin, readily approved a 'Foreign Policy Concept of the Russian Federation' that identified the EU as Russia's second highest priority – after the CIS, but before any other part of the world, including the United States and China. Confirmed in Putin's state-of-Russia message in April 2001, this new Russian vision was offered as a direct response to the EU's earlier Common Strategy on Russia – the first of its kind on both accounts, form ('common strategy') and substance (Russia).[21] In October 2001, the EU–Russia summit tasked the High Level Group on Common European Economic Space, a joint group formed earlier that year, to elaborate a concept for closer bilateral economic ties over a 15-month period and in ways that seemed to parallel the EU's approach to creating a single market. With Russia's primary interest thus moving towards the EU, and with the EU responding in kind, Moscow's interest in privileged ties with individual European countries – especially France and Germany – has acquired a double significance: not only on their own merits but also in terms of their role in, and influence over, European integration.[22]

The consequences of Russia's belated discovery of the EU should not be exaggerated, however. Their relations are complicated by a tenacious idea of Russia's place in Europe – an idea that has defied the realities of geography, withstood the trials of history, adjusted to repeated waves of authoritarian governance, and never integrated those convictions that some rulers occasionally sought to import from other countries. Tim McDaniel has described this idea as the certainty that Russia has a distinctive cultural and historical tradition that sets it apart from the rest of Europe and guarantees its future as a great power.[23] Not surprisingly, the problem with this idea of Russia – *la grande Russie* and *la Russie éternelle* – is that the Russian state can no longer support it, the Russian people can no longer endure it, and Europe can no longer afford it.

Russia is too close to ignore, too big to integrate, too unstable to rattle, and too nuclear to offend: neither the United States nor the states of Europe could afford for long to neglect the risks of disintegration within Russia and its related spillovers elsewhere. Yet, while tensions between the petty realities of what Russia is and the grand illusions that shape its self-image remain, they have become less urgent because Russia can no longer have the sort of universal ambitions that still characterised Russian policies during their most recent Soviet phase. Even Moscow's regional aspirations are illusive: the 300 million Muslims systematically antagonised by Russia since the Cold War, the 1.3 billion Chinese whom Russia repeatedly offended after World War II, and the hundreds of millions of neighbours that Russians have openly harassed throughout history are poised for geopolitical revenge.[24] The conclusion for Russia is all too obvious. Isolation is not an option, and the best of all available choices is a closer relationship with its former adversaries in the West, individually but also with the institutions to which they belong or hope to join. That is well understood by Putin, whose attempt to bring Russia deeper into the EU need not clash with his post-9/11 bid for a special relationship with the United States as a non-member member-state of the military organisation, NATO, that was initially designed to contain the Russian empire.

Russia's territorial intimacy with Europe is reinforced as enlargement brings the EU and NATO closer to, and even into, Russian territory through the enclave of Kaliningrad, where Moscow's demands for special transit rights will have to be addressed by the time the Baltic countries became EU members. Admittedly, Russia was from the start a main feature of NATO enlargement, if only because of an implicit need to accommodate its objections when NATO moved into central Europe in 1999, and, after that, prepared its entry into former Soviet territory – before the 'wars of 9/11' seemed to marginalise that decision even before it was to be announced at the NATO Prague summit in November 2002. But even then, EU countries too had to show sensitivity about the impact of their own decisions on Moscow, a feat initially less complex than for NATO because there could be no ambiguity over a Russian membership in the EU, which could not be an option either then or for the predictable future.

Short of opening the doors of either institution, NATO and EU members are somehow learning to live cooperatively and lastingly with Russia. A Janus-like Russian face that smiles at one and frowns at the other will not work because a frowning Russia, wherever it looks, is likely to scare even the side at which it is smiling. Admittedly, the security questions raised after the events of September 11 made of Russia a most valuable and capable ally – one whose resources, institutions and experience would suit especially well the security needs faced in and beyond Afghanistan. Yet, a separate grand bargain with the fallen superpower in search of a mission and an institutional home would have dire consequences for both NATO and the EU. With regard to the former, an ever-closer bilateral relationship between the United States and Russia would introduce new ambiguities within and about NATO, where the EU allies (with the possible exception of Britain) would fall at the margins of US interests. That in turn would redirect the EU efforts towards a Common Security and Defence Identity that would be asserted within or in spite of NATO, leaving Britain torn between the aspirations of its prime minister, Tony Blair, across the Atlantic and his ambitions across the Channel.

Going south: farther is safer

Passion was the glue for the collective 'We' of the nation – the passion that kept the few different from (and better than) the many who were to be kept away across territorial and ideological lines. Notwithstanding the erosion of much of that passion, some of its darker sides linger, especially to the south. Thus, in June 1955, the choice of Messina as the site of Europe's *relance* after the French defeat of the European Defence Community was ironic. Messina was the small Italian port where the Christian fleets had paused before going to battle with the Turkish fleet, whose destruction in Lesanto kept the Infidels away.[25] Nearly five hundred years later, and half-a-century after Messina, Europe's Christian 'We' still aims at a rigid separation from the Muslim 'They': the farther, the safer.

That may change, but not yet. For Europeans whose loyalty is evolving from the nation-state to the institution to which it belongs, the related question of identity is best answered with a recognisable sense of a plausible 'They' whose leaders must be feared and kept at a distance. Lacking that threat, it may be tempting to turn against something (the post-World War II idea of Europe or a post-Cold War idea of America) or someone (the elusive foreigner or the intrusive Iman). Populist calls to arms follow readily: these are the *déjà entendus* of yesteryear – close the borders and protect the sacred patrimony from intruders that must be denied access or worse. This is a Cartesian logic turned inside out – I am, therefore you are not. Each affirms its specificity in order to escape the other's – 'foreign, different, if not barbarian, fundamentalist or fanatic' are words that can define both Europe's worst vision of Islam and Islam's worst vision of the West.[26] In sum, there is little debate where enlargement ends: at the border of the Eurasian countries that Moscow used to control, and across the Mediterranean where individual EU countries used to find the size and the resources they lacked on the continent.

As EU boundaries move in the direction of Malta and Cyprus, an ever more populous and religious Middle East is feared as a dagger pointed at the soul of an older and depopulated Europe. Admittedly, Turkey and its neighbours in the Caucasus and Caspian region are hardly part of the Middle East. Yet a cultural self-definition of the EU pushes them away from the European landmass and conditions the debate surrounding Turkey and its meagre prospects for EU membership, notwithstanding the vague promises extended in December 2002. Indeed, if Turkey were given a role in Europe commensurate with its size, power and potential, the EU would be transformed into a power in the Middle East. But that is unlikely. While Turkey's bid for membership is thus stalled in the maze of institutional reforms that will make access negotiations even more tedious and inconclusive after enlargement to the east is completed, the millions of immigrants who have overcome the increasingly higher legal and physical ramparts raised on their way into Europe are transforming the EU into a Middle Eastern power.

The Euro-Atlantic dialogue about Turkey and its place in Europe points to an ironic reversal of roles between an America that thinks in geopolitical terms and a Europe that responds with semi-formulated cultural or ethnic arguments. Geography, as well as history, explains Europe's (and America's) position. Turkey is a pivot state for nearly every issue of importance to the United States (and its EU allies) on the Eurasian continent, including but not limited to the needed transit routes for Central Asian oil and gas.[27] For the wars of 9/11, it is one of America's two most significant NATO allies (with Britain) – and, accordingly, one whose dependability ought to be reinforced with the secular rewards of democratic affluence expected from EU membership. In the American view, therefore, EU enlargement to Turkey would make NATO stronger as its borders are extended to Syria, Iraq and Iran, as well as the Caspian states. Indeed, according to some who worry about alleged anti-American sentiments in the new Europe, America's most reliable European allies are non-EU countries that include Turkey but also Russia.[28]

That view is not shared in Europe, where Turkey is still feared as an unwanted community partner – an alien and even hostile neighbour that would make the EU weaker by threatening the institution's internal balance, especially but not exclusively culturally. Yet with a large and growing range of EU activities and projects dependent on some kind of consultation with, or cooperation from, Turkish ministries and agencies in order to operate or develop effectively, there is no escape from closer ties. In short, with prospects for Turkey's membership in the EU dim to non-existent for the balance of the present decade and beyond, their dialogue should focus more explicitly on the best ways to strengthen Turkey's European-ness within the EU with cooperative projects that would weaken that country's own concern over the influence of an anti-Turkish, pro-Greek sentiment among EU members.[29]

The tensions faced in building a multicultural community within the EU, and separately within each of its members, serve as reminders of the obstacles facing its extension to Eurasian states and former colonial dependencies in the Greater Middle East about which the EU and its members show a considerable interest, but which they have no intention of including in their institutions at any time in the foreseeable future. Pretending otherwise can only arouse self-defeating expectations among Europe's neighbours, and worsen Europe's own concerns about them. Most generally, regions that remain politically diffuse and elusive can only afford or generate a security structure with Europe and with the United States that remains invisible.[30] Thus, more realistic than a broad Mediterranean community is the limited free trade area envisioned by the Barcelona framework as the centrepiece of an architecture that relies on performance-linked financial support and even new institutional linkages for dialogue, security and otherwise. After September 11, the case for a free trade area to which the United States might be associated was strengthened further. Non-state groups and even regimes that advocate terror will not be defeated, let alone pre-empted, by the use of overwhelming military power alone. After the war has been won militarily, it still needs to be ended politically: reconciliation demands reconstruction, and reconstruction will be especially needed if these wars spread further to a distraught and hopeless populace among adversaries and allies alike. The logic applies to the totality of the Greater Middle East, going from North Africa to the Persian Gulf, but it also applies to the newly independent states of the Caucasus and Caspian region – with the latter countries grossly neglected by the EU and most of its members despite a geopolitical significance that was vital long before September 11.

While NATO will remain the security institution of choice for the foreseeable future, it is not a full service institution – no more and possibly even less than the EU. Soft security issues that impact on stability can be addressed most effectively by the EU, with the direct support of its members and with occasional assistance from the United States and even NATO. Conversely, hard security issues are best managed by the United States, within or outside NATO, whose members should be entitled to a right of first refusal when their support is sought, and within or outside the EU. This is not a recipe for an ill-defined 'multilateralism *à la carte*' or an artificial division of labour: both sets of issues are separable but they cannot be separated, and, accordingly, so are policies that address them. A neglect of soft security issues would exacerbate issues of hard security, while the neglect of hard security issues would stall issues of development and reconstruction.

In the Greater Middle East more than anywhere else, EU countries hold and respond to different priorities and vulnerabilities that stand in the way of common policies among them, let alone between them and the United States. Now as before, *laissez-les faire* is not an option. The region is just too important (energy supplies), reckless (terrorism), dangerous (four major wars), unstable (*fin de régimes*), expensive (for keeping the peace and waging war) and intrusive (because of the domestic spillovers of instability and war in the area) to be abandoned to the goodwill and capabilities of others. Yet, on the whole, differences within the EU have been getting smaller, and initiatives based on specific national interests now embody a European policy rather than the interests of one EU country only. As shown in 2002, over President Bush's denunciation of a so-called 'axis of terror', but also over Israeli prime minister Ariel Sharon's attacks against a so-called 'coalition of terror', such convergence could not be seen as readily between Europe and the United States. Indeed, the reverse may prove to be true, and the compatibility of US and EU views for the region will be sorely tested in coming years.

Going global

During the Cold War, the Atlantic idea helped develop a community of values that protected its members from military aggression. Simultaneously, the idea of Europe also helped develop a community of interests that could protect its members from war with each other. Both ideas were complementary as neither could have been launched and blossomed without the other. The Atlantic idea and the organisation that embodied it helped keep the peace, but the idea of Europe and the institutions to which it gave birth helped do away with the very idea of war. Neither the peace of the bullies nor the peace of the braves, the peace achieved by the EU is a peace of contentment and assimilation that was initially guaranteed by NATO. No gain, however construed, could compensate the 'winners' for the losses that would result from a war between EU countries, whatever its origin. In truth, within the EU, there is no threat of a return to past conflicts: in the 1990s, post-Cold War conflicts in Europe all took place in countries that were not eligible for membership any time soon, notably those in the Balkans and the former Soviet republics.[31]

While the EU, unlike NATO, cannot protect its members or its neighbours from external aggression, it can help keep peace between them, within and outside the European continent. In several primary areas of conflict in Europe, including the Balkans, credible prospects for membership can encourage moderation: arguably, some of the horror that plagued the former Yugoslavia in the 1990s might have been avoided had the EU been involved earlier. While no country in southeastern Europe, with the exception of Slovenia, can realistically expect to enter the EU before 2010, every country in southeastern Europe should still be able to view the EU as part of its future. The process is not open-ended, however, and the geographic 'E' of the EU may prove more restrictive than the historic 'North Atlantic' definition of NATO. Yet, short of membership the EU can still play a useful role in helping its non-EU neighbours by acting more like a bilateral donor than an international financial institution.[32]

While the institutional and budgetary consequences of enlargement will continue to limit such a role for the years to come, the EU is none the less making substantial contributions to the management of soft security issues at its extended boundaries. Thus, at the January 2002 conference held in Tokyo in the context of the war in Afghanistan, the EU (both the Commission and the member-states) pledged a total of 2.3 billion euros for the period 2002–06, amounting to 45 per cent of the total pledges made in Tokyo. Concerned with a spillover of the war onto the European continent, the EU also made substantial commitments for Pakistan, including aid and preferential trade treatment extended to textiles, and for Central Asia it doubled its allocations.[33] In future years, more will be expected from the EU, especially for the Arab–Israeli conflict, where a pronounced pro-Arab bias often leaves the EU at odds with the United States, and in the Persian Gulf, where the United States and most EU members continue to hold different views on the political rehabilitation of both Iran and Iraq. But for the EU to respond to these lofty expectations, its members will first need to agree over the boundaries of a common foreign policy that is still debated not only among them but also between the institutions that represent them.

As to traditional security issues, there should be no misunderstanding. For many years to come, significant capability gaps and interest divergences among EU countries themselves will continue to stand in the way of coordinated, let alone common, EU action. Predictably, these differences are even sharper, and getting wider, in a Euro-Atlantic context – between the United States and the states of Europe within NATO, and even between a US-led 'NATO at 20' (*cum* Russia) and the EU from which both the United States and Russia are excluded. Indeed, in 2001–02, the military campaign in Afghanistan pointed to a new American doctrine of strategic relevance that provided for 'mutually assured recrimination' across the Atlantic. Because large 'coalitions of the willing' might confuse or dilute the mission, as had been shown during the 1999 war in Kosovo, credible offers of usable capabilities from willing coalition partners were mostly ignored or dismissed as unnecessary. With the transatlantic 'capabilities gap' scheduled to grow dramatically in coming years, the military 'need' for allies may, therefore, be questioned increasingly in the United States. When recognised within or outside NATO, such a need will be determined by the unavailability of US capabilities (for lack of interest or lack of will) or by the availability of new allies (on grounds of geographic location or political convenience) more than by the capabilities of traditional European allies.

Yet the security agenda for the twenty-first century is an agenda *tous azimuts* of traditional and new security issues. This agenda will demand large coalitions of countries, including but hardly limited to NATO countries, that are not only willing but also capable of administering the full range of national power, hard and soft. None of the global wars waged in the twentieth century is likely to serve as a model for what President George W. Bush dubbed the 'first war of the twenty-first century'. To each mission its own coalition, with all coalitions assembled into a pyramidal structure that would keep the few national powers at the top still dependent on the many countries and even institutions grouped at the wider bottom. How these coalitions are managed – and how they perform – may well determine the future of NATO and the conditions under which the EU will evolve as a security institution of primary or complementary choice for its members. The goal for NATO and the EU, as well as for their respective member-states, is not to do everything together but to be sure that together they all do everything that is needed for attending to the security of a whole and free Euro-Atlantic area.

Notes

1 Halford J. Mackinder first presented his thesis in January 1904. See Arthur Hall, 'Mackinder and the Course of Events', *Annals of the Association of American Geographers*, 45:2 (1955), p. 109.

2 Mackinder's evolution is discussed in detail by Hall, 'Mackinder', pp. 109–26.

3 'There is no need to throw out regional peculiarities altogether', writes Charles King in an excellent review essay, but 'the real challenge is to recast what counts as the geographic area (or, more likely, areas)'. Eurasia, adds King, 'will be meaningful in the future only if it seriously admits Turkey, Iran, and perhaps Pakistan and Afghanistan into the mix'. Charles King, 'Post-Postcommunism: Transition, Comparison, and the End of "Eastern Europe"', *World Politics*, 53:1 (2000), pp. 143–72.

4 For a brief statement on the nature of this end game, see my 'Reflections on European Unification', *Responsive Community*, 11:3 (2001), pp. 4–7. A longer discussion appears in my 'Europe 2007: From Nation-States to Member States',

Washington Quarterly, 23:4 (2000), pp. 15–29.

5 These limits suggest that countries that were not conducting access negotiations in 2002 are not likely to enter the EU over the next 15 years if ever – including especially Russia and all former Soviet Republics except the Baltic countries. Exceptions include countries that have declined or opposed membership thus far (Norway and Switzerland) and countries in the former Yugoslavia (besides Slovenia) that could gain membership in the early 2010s.

6 Andrew Moravcsik, 'Europe's Integration at Century's End', in Andrew Moravcsik (ed.), *Centralization or Fragmentation? Europe Facing the Challenges of Deepening, Diversity, and Democracy* (New York: Council on Foreign Relations, 1998), pp. 1–58.

7 Jean Monnet, *Memoirs* (Garden City, NY: Doubleday, 1978), p. 403. 'I have never doubted', adds Monnet, 'that one day this process will lead us to the United States of Europe; but I see no point in trying to imagine today what political form it will take ... No one can say.' *Ibid.*, pp. 523–4.

8 Timothy Garton Ash, *The Uses of Adversity: Essays on the Fate of Central Europe* (New York: Random House, 1989), p. 106.

9 Admittedly, a utilitarian form of legitimacy is a double-edged sword that cuts both ways. As the EU is viewed as an effective producer of gains for its members, its legitimacy grows, and so does public support for, or indifference to, further institutional deepening. Conversely, as the effectiveness of the EU decreases, its members can readily turn to its institutions to explain their own failures and erode the legitimacy of the EU institutions.

10 This theme is developed at greater length in my *Stay the Course: European Unity and Atlantic Solidarity* (New York: Praeger, 1997).

11 Return, for example, to the 'limited war' waged between France and the United States in the mid-1960s over NATO, including President Johnson's dismissal of any response to de Gaulle that might disrupt the 'natural' amity between the two countries and, by implication, further disrupt relations between the United States and its European allies. Frank Costigliola, 'LBJ, Germany, and the "End of the Cold War"', in Warren I. Cohen and Nancy Bernkopf Tucker (eds), *Lyndon Johnson Confronts the World* (New York: Cambridge University Press, 1994), p. 195.

12 For examples of this view, see Peter Rodman, *Drifting Apart? Trends in US–European Relations* (Washington, DC: Nixon Center, 1999); and John Bolton, 'European Common Foreign, Security, and Defense Policies: Implications for the United States and the Atlantic Alliance', *Hearings*, House Committee on International Relations, 106th Congress, First Session, 10 November 1999, pp. 65–78.

13 Whether in 1917 or in 1941, but also most recently in the Balkans in 1995, the use of US military power in Europe aimed at wars that the countries of Europe started or joined but failed to end on their own. With regard to Bosnia, Richard Holbrooke has written that the war could only be ended in Dayton after, 'finally, we told the Serbs that henceforth the United States and NATO, not the U.N., would decide if they were in compliance'. See Richard Holbrooke, *To End a War* (New York: Random House, 1998), p. 157.

14 Charles Kupchan, 'In Defence of Europe's Defence: An American Perspective', *Survival*, 42:2 (2000), pp. 16–32; also my testimonies, 'European Common

Foreign, Security, and Defense Policies', *Hearings*, House Committee on International Relations, 106th Congress, First Session, 10 November 1999, pp. 94–104, and 'U.S.–European Relationship: Opportunities and Challenges', *Hearings*, Subcommittee on Europe of the House Committee on International Relations, 107th Congress, First Session, 25 April 2001, pp. 8–16.

15 See my 'The Wars of 9/11', *International Spectator*, 36:4 (2001), pp. 5–11, and 'The New Normalcy', *Washington Quarterly*, 25:2 (2002), pp. 209–19; also, Antony Blinken and Simon Serfaty, 'Regional Strategies – Europe', in Kurt M. Campbell and Michèle A. Flournoy (principal authors), *To Prevail: An American Strategy for the Campaign Against Terrorism* (Washington, DC: CSIS Press, 2001), pp. 211–21.

16 For an especially enlightening – and beautifully written – account of the US postwar debates about Europe and its future, see John L. Harper, *American Visions of Europe* (Cambridge: Cambridge University Press, 1994).

17 As noted by Charles Gati in 2002, the 'sense of confusion and ambivalence' in the ten countries of central and eastern Europe is best reflected in the fact that their publics 'have failed to re-elect any of their governments since 1989'. Charles Gati, 'All that NATO Can Be', *National Interest*, 68 (2002), p. 81.

18 James Sperling, 'Two Tiers or Two Speeds? Constructing a Stable European Security Order', in James Sperling (ed.), *Two Tiers or Two Speeds? The European Security Order and the Enlargement of the European Union and NATO* (Manchester: Manchester University Press, 1999), p. 186.

19 See Robert Legvold, 'The Three Russias', in Robert A. Pastor (ed.), *A Century's Journey* (New York: Basic Books, 2000), p. 190.

20 Stephen Cohen, *Failed Crusade: America and the Tragedy of Post-Communist Russia* (New York and London: Norton, 2000), p. 33.

21 'Common strategies to be implemented by the Union in areas where the Member States have important interests in common' were mandated by the 1997 Amsterdam Treaty. Approved in June 1999, the Common Strategy on Russia was first dismissed by Moscow as a 'simplified register of policy already carried out by the EU'. None the less, the choice of Russia as the first target of these common strategies in 1998–99, Russia's subsequent response in 2000–01, and the initial EU–Russia summit held in Moscow in May 2001 confirm the end of the inertia that had characterised EU–Russian relations. Hiski Haukkala and Sergei Medveded (eds), *The EU Common Strategy on Russia: Learning the Grammar of the CFSP* (Helsinki: Ulkopoliittinen instituutti; Bonn: Institut für Europäische Politik, 2000).

22 More on this in my 'A Euro-Atlantic Ostpolitik', *Orbis*, 45:4 (2001), pp. 597–607.

23 Tim McDaniel, *The Agony of the Russian Idea* (Princeton, NJ: Princeton University Press, 1996).

24 Zbigniew Brzezinski, *The Geostrategic Triad: Living with China, Europe, and Russia* (Washington, DC: Center for Strategic and International Studies, 2001), pp. 55ff.

25 Luigi Barzini, *The Europeans* (New York: Penguin, 1983), p. 55.

26 Tariq Ramadan, *To Be a European Muslim* (Markfield and Lancaster: Islamic Foundation, 1999), p. 1.

27 F. Stephen Larrabee, 'U.S. and European Policy toward Turkey and the Caspian Basin', in Robert D. Blackwill and Michael Stürmer (eds), *Allies Divided: Transatlantic Policies in the Greater Middle East* (Cambridge, MA.: MIT Press, 1997), p. 144.

28 Jeffrey Gedmin, 'The Alliance is Doomed', *Washington Post* (20 May 2002).

29 David Blanchard, *Turkey and the European Union* (London: Centre for European Reform, 1998), pp. 40–3.

30 See my 'Europe, The Mediterranean, and the Middle East', *Joint Force Quarterly*, 24 (2000), pp. 56–62; and George Joffé, 'The Euro-Mediterranean Partnership: Two Years After Barcelona', *Middle East Program Briefing* (London: Royal Institute for International Affairs, May 1998).

31 John Mearsheimer thinks otherwise. 'Almost every European state, including the United Kingdom and France, still harbors deep-seated, albeit muted, fears that a Germany unchecked by American power might behave aggressively'. Driven by the inescapable logic of 'offensive realism', EU countries remain driven by the imperative 'to be the hegemon – that is, the only great power in the system'. Indeed, for the EU, as well as for NATO, 'there is little evidence that [it] can compel member states to act against [its] strategic interests'. Applied to Europe, this theoretical reading of past and recent history (involving, for example, great power relations in the Balkans in the 1910s and the 1990s) is intellectually challenging but factually misleading and analytically flawed. John J. Mearsheimer, *The Tragedy of Great Power Politics* (New York: W. W. Norton, 2001), pp. 2, 364.

32 Esther Bremmer, 'Redefining European Security? Insights from United States, European Union, and German Assistance to the Russian Federation, 1991–2000', *AICGS/DAAD Working Paper* (Washington, DC: AICGS, 2002).

33 'The European Union and Afghanistan', issued by the EU Presidency with the European Commission Delegation, Washington, DC, May 2002.

IV
Conclusion

13

Reflections on Eurasian security

David P. Calleo

It seems an especially appropriate moment for American scholars to consider the long-term issues of Eurasian security. At this time, of course, it is not easy to have a long-term vision of anything. Since the atrocities of September 11 2001, the world seems to have changed for us in fundamental ways. Old trends, therefore, may no longer apply.

It is not true, however, that the hatred of the United States that exploded on September 11 began on that same day. Indeed, even among our closest allies, there has been serious opposition to the role that we have often seemed to assume for ourselves since the end of the Cold War – the role of global hegemon and of the world's only superpower. It is particularly important that we not mistake the profound sympathy that we have received from our friends around the world as unconditional support for a forceful new assertion of that hegemony. Global hegemony is probably not the real direction of things in the world – not before September 11 and not thereafter. Most probably, the real direction is towards a more plural world order with several great powers. That has been, I suspect, the general drift in Eurasia over the past ten years and it will not now change.

Europe's postwar retreat

Thirty years ago it was fashionable to observe that Europe was only a regional power, whereas the United States was a global power. When Americans talked about being 'global', they meant the Far East. Our attention was focused there because American diplomacy was about to play its 'China card', its greatest coup of the Cold War. By exploiting the breach between China and the Soviets, the US hoped to rein in both. The Asian pressure on Russia did seem to stabilise and prolong détente in Europe at least – a situation that encouraged the germination of Gorbachev's reforms and undermined the Soviet system. Thus, the 'global' United States seemed able to determine the fate of Europe through the Far East.[1] Europe, being merely regional, had little role in the Asian game that held the key to Europe's own destiny. Hence our patronising view of the time.

It was rather disingenuous to fault Europeans for lacking interest in Asia. It was also rather indelicate, given America's fervent enthusiasm for 'decolonisation' after World War II – that is to say, for the ejection of the Europeans from their old empires. Many Europeans, mindful of this history, watched the American discomfiture in Vietnam with more than a touch of *Schadenfreude*. In any event, European states were not uninterested in Asia; they simply had few cards to play there. The geopolitical hands dealt at the end of World War II left Europe devastated and truncated, menaced by a huge Soviet military force planted in the middle of a divided Germany. Security depended heavily on the Americans. Europeans lacked the geopolitical leisure or resources for a big independent role in Asia. With the Americans occupying and protecting Japan, East Asia's postwar political climate was set by its own Cold War – by the antipathies between the United States, China and Russia. China, isolated and paranoid, was left to the domestic preoccupations of its Revolution.

America triumphant

The end of the Cold War saw this postwar geopolitical situation radically changed. All parties – the United States, Russia, China and Europe – were dealt new geopolitical hands. The United States, the obvious victor of the Cold War, began the new era as the only superpower in an increasingly integrated global system. Remarkable American growth in the 1990s reinforced the sense of American predominance. Of course, the United States may never have been as strong as it seemed in the 1990s. Today, we are painfully aware of our physical vulnerability. But signs of our economic weaknesses have been visible for a long time. We have, for example, had a huge external deficit for several decades. That deficit reflects a long-standing habit: the American economy absorbs more than it yields; it consumes and invests more than it produces. The difference is the habitual external deficit and it has to be financed, one way or another, by Europe and Japan. In other words, America's high growth and high standard of living are borrowed, in part, from the rest of the world. Financing this deficit has generally been easy, thanks not least to the international role of the dollar. But European Monetary Union (EMU), with its emerging euro, creates an international alternative to the dollar.[2] As a result, it is not at all unlikely that the cost of our deficits will grow more and more burdensome to us. Nevertheless, it will not be easy to reduce the deficit very substantially. It will require cutting consumption or cutting investment – probably both. Cutting consumption means lowering America's standard of living, cutting investment means lowering its rate of growth and technological advancement. Reducing our external deficit will not be pleasant for the rest of the world, either. Asia's trade surplus is the counterpart to America's current-account deficit. At a time when Asia is suffering from many signs of overproduction, a drastic reduction of the American deficit spells deep trouble for many Asian economies, perhaps including China.

Russia demoted

If the end of the Cold War left America triumphant, Russia's new geopolitical hand seemed a terrible demotion. America's economic problems, real or hypothetical, seem minor by comparison with those of Russia. Indeed, the abrupt economic decline following the collapse of the Soviet Union is one of the major economic catastrophes of modern history. Amazingly, Russia is now one of the poorest countries of the world. Nevertheless, it was the Russians themselves who dismantled the Soviet construction and their long-term prospects are probably much better for having done so. Russia has gained a fresh chance to develop its own version of a constitutional state and a market-based economy. The country still has its vast economic potential. Perhaps it is slowly acquiring a stable and competent government. In any event, it is liberated from its diplomatic isolation of the Cold War, particularly vis-à-vis Europe. Arguably, its long-term geopolitical position is thereby greatly improved.

Europe released

Europe's new hand seems a less ambiguous improvement. Europe no longer faces the Soviet threat with its accompanying need for American protection. Instead, Europe is restored to its pan-European space, including Russia. Western Europe's states, led by France and Germany, have reacted by accelerating their integration into the EU, while broadening its scope and membership. Hence the EMU, the Common Foreign and Security Policy (CFSP), the European Security and Defence Policy (ESDP), the attempts to reform NATO through the European Security and Defence Identity (ESDI), the negotiations with prospective new EU members in central and eastern Europe, along with the struggle to recast the EU's constitution. In effect, the EU seems determined to make itself the dominant institution in the new pan-Europe.[3] Europe's big ambitions leave it rather vulnerable. Completing the European Union on a pan-European scale will require, at the very least, a long period of digestion and internal preoccupation. Too rapid an expansion risks making the whole system ungovernable. Still, the EU has tested and resilient institutions; its leading countries retain a strong geopolitical consciousness. It should not surprise anybody if, in our new century, Europe is once more a major force in Eurasia and around the world – a major global power.

China unbound

China, too, has a new hand. Since 1978, its growth has been very rapid. Its GDP is already the second in the world; its per capita income, however, is still extremely low, which suggests that rapid growth should continue.[4] Like Russia, China is no longer isolated diplomatically. To be sure, it faces severe short-term problems – uncompetitive state firms, a precarious banking system, poorly developed fiscal institutions. Beyond are deeper questions about China's place in a global system. Nevertheless, so far China's government has managed the contradictions of its evolving system with great skill, even if Tiananmen Square suggests what happens when problems spin out of control.

A more plural world order

Looking at the geopolitical positions of the United States, Russia, Europe and China since the end of the Cold War, all four have reason to believe that their basic situations have improved. Three are deeply preoccupied with developing new national or regional prospects. Only one, the United States, has the resources and geopolitical leisure to be a major presence in the regions of all the others, a presence that seems likely to swell with America's new preoccupation with international terrorism. Nevertheless, given the favourable long-term prospects of the others, the global system seems unlikely to remain unipolar. The post-Cold War prospects of Europe, Russia and China point to a more plural global system, perhaps still highly integrated but not dominated by any single power. To work, such a system will require a high degree of multilateral cooperation. But that cooperation will depend not only on the wisdom and goodwill of statesmen and publics, but also on the degree to which the four centres of power – and perhaps others – develop interests and expectations that can be reconciled. It is frequently said that our present world is looking more and more like the world in 1900. As in 1900, the world system faces the problem of how to accommodate rapidly rising powers. Then, it was a question of appeasing Germany and Japan and, of course, the power that was really rising, the United States. And, as is often said, the failure of Britain, France, Germany and Russia to make room for one another led to two world wars and the mutual ruination of Britain and Europe together. In retrospect, considering how much was destroyed, we tend to believe that the great powers of 1900 ought to have been able to accommodate each other, and we fault them for failing.

But what about our own future? How easy will it be for today's four big powers to live together on an integrated planet? Obviously, this is a huge question. Let me explore two aspects of it. First, can the United States – still bemused by its unipolar vision – react successfully to a more plural world? And second, can a plural system absorb the rise of newly powerful poor states, in particular China?

American global policy in a plural world system

In the 1990s, only the United States had an active foreign policy beyond its own sphere. But that American foreign policy in the 1990s, even though informed by a rather hubristic self-consciousness about being the world's only superpower, had no great organising theme – other than shoring up the global economy and furthering American economic and financial interests within it. Otherwise, the Clinton administration's foreign policy can best be described as a sort of low-grade imperialism – meddling everywhere, often to prevent local horrors, as in Somalia or Haiti, but without much conviction and with a paralysing aversion to casualties. In principle, the president favoured a stronger, more self-sufficient Europe, and gave ritual support to the ambitious European goals of Maastricht. But, as time went on, the Clinton administration adopted a more aggressive view of international relations, a view promoted by 'peace theorists' equating 'perpetual peace' with the spread of American hegemony. With Congress in the hands of the Republicans, the Clinton administration felt constrained to make many concessions to the prejudices of the unilateralist right.

A decisive change in European policy came when the president decided to press for NATO enlargement in 1994. American policy began to reaffirm NATO's role as the manager of European security, and America's role as NATO's hegemonic leader. As the European intervention in Bosnia faltered, the United States came to the rescue. Thereafter, American rhetoric was much less diffident about reaffirming American primacy in Europe.[5] After Bosnia came NATO's intervention in Kosovo, this time with Americans firmly in charge from the start. Meanwhile NATO enlargement took on an open-ended character. In 1999, Poland, the Czech Republic and Hungary were the first to be admitted, but the United States made clear that the next round might well include at least one of the Baltic states and that Ukraine could not be ruled out. In its early days, the new Bush administration sharpened the unilateralist tone of America's European diplomacy. Its favourite project, National Missile Defense, implied destabilising the existing regime of nuclear deterrence, while renewing Europe's military and technological subordination to the United States.

This direction of American policy did not sit well with the EU's ambitious plans to assert its own primacy over the new pan-European space. Early in the 1990s, Europeans put on the table their project for a European Security and Defence Identity, designed to make NATO less hegemonic. The idea was to transform NATO's traditional integrated and pyramidal framework, with a designated enemy and an American commander at the top, into a looser structure that would rely on ad hoc coalitions for specific purposes. But, as the Europeans discovered painfully in Bosnia, they first needed to create EU institutions to coordinate common security and defence policies among themselves. Ultimately, they needed to create effective military forces of their own. By now, the Europeans have undertaken to build a rapid reaction force and have made considerable progress towards consolidating and rationalising their defence industries, an important step in building support for more defence spending.

It is still far too early to judge Europe's reaction to the Bush administration's American campaign against international terrorism. The atrocious attacks on New York and Washington triggered a strong outpouring of sympathy for the United States. But whether this powerful current of sympathy will also restore Europe's traditional subordination within NATO seems doubtful. In the short run, much will depend on how the Americans conduct their anti-terrorist campaign. The wider and deeper the effort, the greater the need for allies, and the more those allies will weigh on American policies. A good part of European enthusiasm for joining the American 'crusade' can be traced to apprehension over what the Americans will do unless checked by their allies. Most European governments feel the Americans have consistently mismanaged their relations with Israel and the Palestinians, Iran and even Iraq. Europeans, who feel themselves far more vulnerable to Muslim fanaticism, are unlikely to entrust their security to an unchecked American hegemon. Nor are Europeans likely to tolerate intense American presence in their domestic security arrangements. This does not mean that Americans and Europeans will no longer remain allies. But the trend towards a more balanced and autonomous transatlantic relationship seems unlikely to be reversed.

Russia's reaction

US policies that irritated the Europeans in the 1990s infuriated the Russians. Arguably, NATO's first enlargement – to Poland, the Czech Republic and Hungary – was not very significant to the Russians. They seemed less interested in blocking the enlargement than in extracting as many concessions from it as possible. Similarly, the Russians did not so much oppose the Kosovo intervention as insist upon joining it, and thus limiting American action. But the second enlargement of NATO, particularly its extension to the Baltic states, is a much more serious assault on Russian strategic interests.

One Russian option was to oppose enlargement vociferously and thereby perhaps persuade the Europeans to stall it. The other was, as before, to accept the enlargement but to extract concessions. But what concessions would be adequate for so serious a deterioration of Russia's strategic position as NATO in the Baltics or American forces deployed in Central Asia? Perhaps the most obvious way out is to have the Russians themselves join NATO, in one fashion or another, thereby transforming it from an implicitly anti-Russian alliance into a pan-European security system. The creation of the NATO–Russian Council in May 2002 seems to be a step in that direction.

NATO may now become a more potent version of the OSCE, with elaborate military staffs and great prestige. Full Russian membership in the future would almost certainly mean the end of NATO's traditional hierarchical structure dominated by an American SACEUR. The alliance would be most likely to move towards the flexible, ad hoc structures proposed by the French. In reality, this has already been NATO's pattern during the various Balkan interventions, where NATO's forces are a *de facto* coalition, directed by a 'Contact Group' of the major participants, with the Russians among them.[6]

Arguably, NATO's fate ultimately depends upon its not becoming a serious obstacle to European–Russian cooperation. This cooperation, of course, is still in its infancy. Nevertheless, NATO enlargement clearly can threaten its further development. Having Russia as an at least *de facto* member of NATO – as a result of NATO's own ambition to expand – would be a highly ironical outcome. Geopolitically, such a step would end the explicit western alliance against Russia. Europeans, left without any formal American protectorate, should logically accelerate the building of their own structures for collective defence. More European–Russian military cooperation might also seem a logical step as the way to control European problems in the Balkans, and possibly also Russian problems in the Caucasus and Central Asia. Russia, in short, is getting ready to play its European card.

US policy towards China

American policy in the 1990s had been abrasive not only towards Europe and Russia but also towards China. The Chinese have grown acutely sensitive to signs of a growing American taste for interventionism. They have been uneasy about NATO's excursions into Central Asia through PfP and highly critical of NATO's role in the Balkans. They are also among the most vociferous critics of NATO enlargement. They take a dim view of American enthusiasm for the Dalai Lama. Most of all, they are angry and fearful over the shift in US policy towards Taiwan. And they see Bush's National Missile Defense as designed primarily to neutralise China's deterrent, a project revealing that American strategic planners believe a major confrontation with China is inevitable and are fast preparing for it. If the United States soon grows heavily engaged militarily in Afghanistan and Central Asia generally, Chinese apprehensions are unlikely to diminish. It will be difficult for the Chinese to avoid thinking of American counter-terrorism as a new version of hegemonic imperialism. This judgement will be still more difficult to avoid in so far as the United States refuses to conduct its campaign through the UN Security Council, where China has a veto.

Eurasian reactions

Antagonising China and Russia at the same time has had a not unpredictable consequence: the two have moved closer together. Both have started promoting together a new organisation of Eurasian states.[7] A China card is being played again, but this time by Russia rather than the United States. Official American analysts apparently have decided, *a priori*, that such a development cannot occur. The inherent conflict between declining Russia, endowed with Siberia's energy, and fast-growing China, hungry for it, is supposedly too great for a durable alliance between the two. This judgement may seriously underestimate the capacity of the Russians and Chinese for rational behaviour. Russia, after all, needs to develop the potential of Siberia and needs to sell its products to someone. Why not to China – soon the world's biggest economy and probably for a long time among its fastest growing? Given the dangers, Russia would not want to see a real confrontation between the United States and China. But continuing tension would increasingly tie down the Americans and allow Russia to bargain for concessions in the West.

The other key element in Russia's grand strategy is a closer relationship with western Europe. Given Europe's need for Russia's resources and taste for collaborative rather then confrontational diplomacy, a Russian–EU entente seems not at all unlikely. This should not mean a definitive break between the EU and the United States. But it would tend to detach the EU from any aggressive anti-Russian policies from the United States that do not seem in Europe's interest. Without European support, or at least acquiescence, it would be more difficult for the United States to continue such policies.

A developing European relationship with China would complete the Eurasian geopolitical revolution. It is difficult to imagine Europe playing a heavy and direct military role in Asia, except by refusing to support the enthusiasms of the United States. But Europe already has enormous economic interests in Asia generally. America's huge current account deficit already depends heavily on European support to finance it. Since Europeans could expect to profit from peace but not from war, they would presumably use their influence to dampen aggressive military enthusiasm on all sides. Having the Europeans present in the region should inhibit the tendency of Americans and Chinese to demonise each other and polarise relations.

Geopolitical realignment?

In summary, four great power centres have been active in the nascent post-Cold War Eurasian system – the United States, the EU, Russia and China. All were dealt new geopolitical hands. Everyone's cards seemed to promise a bright future. For the short term, the US cards seemed far and away the best.

Gradually, the United States began to play the unipolar game that went with its cards. 'Peace theory' and 'globalisation' provided the ideological cover. The United States began to find itself everywhere opposing the ambitions of others in their own spheres. As a result, the United States has, little by little, been building a global consensus against itself. The world's other three great powers have begun to see the United States as a sort of rogue hegemon, increasingly self-centred, unilateral and inconvenient to their own regional ambitions. Not surprisingly, they have begun moving closer to each other. American diplomacy is thus provoking a pan-Eurasian coalition – as a way for the rest of the global system to balance and contain the superpower.

Is this a threat to our interests? It depends on whether we define our interest as being the global hegemon – struggling to frustrate the rise of the others. If we do not, if instead we work to create a genuine multilateral system, one that leaves generous room for the aspirations of the others, it is difficult to see how this pluralist trend in Eurasia threatens our vital interests. Our assets remain huge, our ties to each of the others intimate. We can no doubt remain pre-eminent for a long time but will have to evolve a less bombastic style and vainglorious notion of our role. This is perhaps not the worst outcome for the post-Cold War system, or indeed for the United States itself. Ideally, it will provide a global Treaty of Westphalia, without first having to go through a Thirty Years War.

Accommodating the newly powerful poor

Considering the possibilities of coexistence in a pluralist system necessarily brings up my second question, raised at the chapter's outset: can a concert of mostly very rich states find a place for a newly powerful but still very poor China? The global conflict between rich and poor states is hardly a new topic. But we have developed a rather abstract way of talking about it. We note that 60 per cent of the world's people live in 'poor countries', those with a per capita income of less than $2,900. We also note that rich westernised states, with incomes averaging $20,000 to $30,000 per capita and higher, make up only 15 per cent of the world's population. But our abstract category, 'poor countries', blurs a critical geopolitical distinction. Among these poor countries are China and India. Indeed, their populations together constitute roughly two thirds of the world's poor and two and a half times the population of all the rich states combined. China alone has 21 per cent of the world's population, India 17 per cent. Nothing in the long history of humanity leads us to presuppose that China and India must be poor, and Europe and America rich. Indeed, even as late as the eighteenth century China's growth and living standards were, in many respects, comparable to those in Europe. China's decline came as the nineteenth century progressed.[8] In recent years, China has started growing very rapidly.[9] In an OECD study of China's likely growth pattern from 1995 to 2015, written by Angus Maddison, a leading analyst of comparative economic history, China's GDP is forecast to overtake the American by 2015. But the same projections foresee a Chinese per capita income in 2015 of still only $6,398 (adjusted for purchasing power) as opposed to $30,268 for the United States; $25,533 for Japan; $23,199 for '32 advanced capitalist countries'; and $3,120 for India.[10] In other words, even when China's national GDP equals the American, US per capita income is expected to remain five times greater than China's and ten times greater than India's. China will thus be a rich state but with a poor population.

Having China among the world's economic and military giants will, in itself, empower a large proportion of the world's poor. And the superpower status that seems quite near for China is not unimaginable later for India. Both states have nuclear weapons and an already impressive scientific infrastructure that could grow formidably with the vast new wealth their national economies are expected to generate. Both countries enrol substantial parts of their populations in first-class educational systems. Under the circumstances, demands to reduce the global income gap are likely to grow more insistent. Even those who are complacent about the inequality of wealth will be compelled to pay attention to the narrowing gap of power.

World redistribution?

Would a major global redistribution be a bad thing? The answer, from a western point of view, depends on whether more equality is brought by a zero-sum allocation – the poor taking from the rich – or by growth – where the rich stay rich but the poor get richer too. Zero-sum redistribution can happen when highly competitive industries in poor countries destroy industries in advanced countries and leave many people jobless. Some of that has been occurring over the past half century, with the rise of Japan or the various smaller Asian 'tigers'. Western labourers have faced very considerable competition and displacement. But, as Asian wages have risen sharply, new markets have been created and new industries and services have sprung up in the West. [11] The resulting production is more efficient worldwide and the benefits to the West have, we say, greatly outweighed the costs.

China, however, is much poorer per capita than Japan and the Asian tigers.[12] It is also several times more populous than all of them together. Thanks to China's radically low income per capita and radically high population growth, even very modest per capita growth in China requires very large aggregate growth. To fulfil Maddison's projection and equal the US GDP by 2015, China will have to triple its GDP of 1995. Even so, its per capita income is then expected to be equivalent to only one fifth of the American. But in achieving this goal, over two decades, China's new growth will alone equal the whole size of the American economy of 1995.[13] If growth on such a scale is achieved by taking wealth away from others, the consequences will be very unpleasant for those who are the losers. But even if China's growth is achieved entirely by expanding the world's collective GDP, expansion on such a scale will constitute enormous new pressure on the price of raw materials – oil being the obvious example.[14] And the vastly increased energy use implicit in China's growth cannot help but have a serious impact on environmental conditions – all the more because China relies heavily on coal.[15] In short, accommodating China, let alone India, will be a big problem for the world as a whole and, of course, for China itself. Compared to this huge Malthusian problem that we seem bound to face, the challenges of 1900 – accommodating imperial Germany and the United States – seem relatively minor.

Nevertheless, it would be unwise to forget that the great wars of modern times have been among the most rich and highly developed countries. Today's intensely competitive free trade leads to a high commercial tension among the rich states. All struggle to find specialisations in high technology and finance that will permit their outsized standards of living to be sustained. Governments are deeply involved. Industrial espionage intensifies and trade disputes grow increasingly acerbic. As China's competition weighs more and more heavily on all advanced countries, the competition among them can only increase.

In short, no one should be too optimistic about the prospects for resolving peacefully the intractable conflicts of interest among powerful states, rich or poor, that seem clearly foreseeable in the new century. It will help greatly, of course, if technology continues coming to the rescue. Malthusian crises have been predicted regularly over the past two centuries, but have been avoided, as stunning technological mutations have repeatedly changed the parameters of economic possibilities. Cultural change is another way to adjust. Perhaps China can find a better model for itself than simply aping the consumerism of western societies. And perhaps western societies themselves can find a better way to sustain their democratic legitimacy than the expectation of ever growing consumption.

The most promising geopolitical framework

Would a reborn Westphalian system for Eurasia be a better framework for managing these grand questions than the hegemonic model imagined by American triumphalists? I would argue yes. The experience of the 1990s does not suggest that the unipolar vision brings out the best qualities of American statecraft. The general thrust of American diplomacy, admittedly only languid until now, has been to oppose Europe, Russia and China together. This does not seem a helpful direction. Acton's dictum about power corrupting may even apply, it seems, to the United States.

A self-consciously plural system is perhaps more promising. Given the realities of modern warfare, if the great problems of the future are to be addressed successfully, they must be addressed in a collaborative rather than a confrontational fashion. No one country has the political, economic and military resources, let alone the moral imagination, by itself, to manage the great problems looming in our world. A unipolar vision of the world thus seems inherently unstable. It creates a single target for all the frustrations inevitable in a rapidly changing world. Instead of promoting a generalised sense of responsibility for world order, the unipolar vision encourages free-riding and opportunism. In such a world, self-righteous confrontation is all too easy.

Westerners will, for example, be inclined to complain bitterly as a rapidly growing China notably degrades the world's environment. Chinese will have every reason to answer: 'Who are you in America – with your colossal waste of energy – to complain about our pollution?'[16] If China were Korea, that might be an adequate answer. But China is already a great power in the world. In due course, it will be greater still. Great powers have a particular responsibility for dealing with the world's problems. In the coming genera-tions, they must find a way together to ease modern societies into a world order that is sustainable – politically, economically, environmentally, culturally and morally. If they, or rather we, try to resolve our differences by force, we run a very high risk of repeating the fate of the world system of 1910. To avoid such an outcome requires a new concert of mutual respect and responsibility. Ideally, a self-conscious plural system in pan-Eurasia would be more conducive to such a concert.

Successfully rebalancing the West and building a collaborative system with Russia, China, Europe and America probably requires more wisdom and skill from the world's leaders than we have any reason to expect. But Europe, having suffered so much from its own selfish divisions and come such a long way in learning to control them, may now have something special to teach the rest of the world. We can hope that a stronger Europe can settle its differences with America, that it can embrace Russia and help it to find a worthy new version of itself. And we can hope that the pan-Eurasian system that follows can find an honoured place for China, at long last restor-ing itself as a great force in the world. We can hope that all the great powers of our time can together find the moral imagination to redefine their social and economic ideals to suit a more equal world. If the human experiment is to continue, the world's great civilisations must find a way to concert their ideals and forces. As scholars, we have a not inconsiderable responsibility to imagine and promote this concert.

Notes

1 Playing the China card also favoured reform in China. By 1978, China was launched on its great attempt to reconcile itself with capitalism and to enter the world economy.

2 For my own extended discussion, see David P. Calleo, 'Strategic Implications of

the Euro', *Survival*, 41:1 (1999), pp. 5–19.

3 For my own extended analysis of Europe's ambitions and prospects, see David P. Calleo, *Rethinking Europe's Future* (Princeton, NJ: Princeton University Press, 2001).

4 Using a standard based on purchasing power parity. Otherwise, based on current exchange rates, it is seventh – after the United States, Japan, Germany, France, Italy and the United Kingdom. See World Bank statistics, at www.worldbank.org/data/databytopic/keyrefs.html. For growth projections see Angus Maddison, *Chinese Economic Performance in the Long Run* (Paris: OECD, 1998), p. 97.

5 In his recollections of the Bosnia negotiations in 1995 and 1996, Richard Holbrooke argues that the Bosnian tragedy and the resulting Dayton accords marked a shift in US foreign policy. It became, in his words, 'more assertive, more muscular'. Richard Holbrooke, *To End a War* (New York: Random House, 1998), p. 359. This, in his view, was in large degree a reaction to the failure of the Europeans to deal with a major crisis in their own backyard: 'While both the U.S. and the EU initially viewed the Balkan wars as a European problem, the Europeans chose not to take a strong stand, restricting themselves to dispatching U.N. "peacekeepers" to a country where there was no peace to keep, and withholding from them the means and the authority to stop the fighting'. *Ibid.*, p. xv.

6 In 1994, the Contact Group was established among the five major powers involved – the United States, Russia, Germany, France and the United Kingdom – thereby reducing the cumbersome decision-making processes characteristic of the EU, NATO and the UN. Creating the Group reflected a western desire to accommodate Russia in its perceived sphere of influence in the Balkans and in the light of already strained relations over NATO enlargement. The actual work of the Contact Group reflected a deepening of the NATO–Russia working relationship. While the success of the Contact Group's proceedings (and more specifically Russia's unsuccessful attempt to restrain the Bosnian Serbs) was ambivalent, it did lay the groundwork for substantial cooperation in implementing the peace agreement in Bosnia. Nevertheless, the West and Russia continued to see distinct geopolitical interests in the Balkans. For the creation of the Contact Group see David Owen, *Balkan Odyssey* (New York: Harcourt Brace, 1995), pp. 275–8. For a critical appraisal of the role of the Contact Group in the Balkan conflicts and in NATO–Russia collaboration, see Carsten Giersch, 'Multilateral Conflict Regulation: The Case of Kosovo', *Weatherhead Center for International Affairs Working Paper No. 00–04* (Cambridge, MA: Harvard University, August 2000).

7 By an agreement signed on 15 June 2001, the heads of state of Russia, China and four Central Asian republics established the SCO. This organisation will work to promote political, military and intelligence cooperation among the six signatory countries. In theory, the SCO has impressive resources. It covers approximately 1.5 billion people, has access to a large contingent of strategic and tactical nuclear weapons, and combines conventional forces of over 3.6 million soldiers. Mongolia, Turkmenistan and Iran are supposedly ready to join the organisation soon. In addition, China would like to see Pakistan join, whereas the Russians promote the entry of India. The creation of the SCO was followed by the signature of a cooperation treaty between Russia and China on 15 July, aimed at improving military and political cooperation between the two countries and at promoting a 'new international order'.

  8 Maddison, *Chinese Economic Performance*, Chs 1 and 2.
  9 *Ibid.*, pp. 14, 19.
10 *Ibid.*, p. 97 (adjusted for purchasing power parity). Maddison's projection, where China surpasses the US GDP in 2015, assumes an average per capita growth rate of only 4.5 per cent. The IMF figures for overall real growth, adjusted for population growth, show China's real GDP growth per capita since 1995 to have been as follows: 9.6 per cent (1996), 8.8 per cent (1997), 7.8 per cent (1998), 7.1 per cent (1999). IMF estimates are 7.5 per cent (2000) and 7.3 per cent (2001). For the unadjusted real GDP growth figures, see IMF, *World Economic Outlook* (Washington, DC: IMF, October 2000), p. 22. Of course, these projections also assume that China will be able to manage the structural flaws of its current economic system, in particular a reform of the highly volatile and unstable banking system as well as an effective reorganisation (and privatisation) of inefficient and oftentimes corrupt state-owned companies.
11 Japan, Hong Kong and Singapore have surpassed western per capita income levels. Most of the Asian 'little tigers', however, have a GDP per capita that is still low by western standards, even if several times greater than in China or India. But Asia's tigers have comparatively small populations. Even Japan, with 126 million people, is smaller than France and Germany put together.
12 In 1999, for example, Chinese per capita income, adjusted for purchasing power, was 14.9 per cent that of Japan, 47.1 per cent that of Malaysia, 22.7 per cent that of Korea and only 11.5 per cent that of the U.S. See World Bank, www.worldbank.org/data/databytopic/keyrefs.html. China's population of 1.267 billion probably still exceeds India's (see World Bank, *World Development Indicators Database* (16 July 2001), www.worldbank.org). China's birth rate and natural population growth rate have decreased spectacularly – from 33.43 per cent and 25.83 per cent in 1970 to 15.23 per cent and 8.77 per cent in 1999. Nevertheless, China's population is still growing at a rapid pace (see China Population Information and Research Center, *White Paper China's Population and Development in the 21st Century*, Internet edition (2001), www.cpirc. org.cn/whitepaper.htm).
13 According to Maddison's data and data projections, the US GDP in 1995 was $6,150 billion. Chinese GDP in 1995 was $3,196 billion. The projected Chinese GDP for 2015 is $9,406 billion (figures in 1990 US$). Maddison, *Chinese Economic Performance*, p. 97.
14 Indeed, from 1980 to 1997, China's energy use was up by one third. By 1997, China had become an oil importer. See International Energy Agency, *Energy Balances: Non-OECD Countries* (Paris: IEA, 2000). Overall, China's energy use is expected to grow exponentially. Consumption of fuels is likely to quadruple by 2015. The continuously rising demand indicates daily oil imports of 8.6 million barrels by the same year. Total energy consumption is likely to redouble by 2006 from a 1996 base, and again by 2015. See Verne W. Louse and Ian McCreary, 'China's Energy: A Forecast to 2015', *Los Alamos National Laboratory International Economics Reports LA-UR-96–2972* (Los Alamos, NM: Los Alamos National Laboratory, 1996).
15 China's use of coal as a source of energy has increased exponentially and this trend is likely to continue in the foreseeable future. At the moment, China's per capita pollution is small by comparison with that of the US (see n. 16 below). Nevertheless,

experts predict that by the year 2025, China will emit more carbon dioxide and sulphur dioxide (products from coal burning) than the United States, Japan and Canada combined. For consequent concerns about the environment, see Louse and McCreary, 'China's Energy', pp.1–9, as well as World Resources Institute, *A Guide to the Global Environment 1994–95* (Washington, DC: World Resources Institute, 1995). China's future pollution would contribute substantially to climate change (see World Resources Institute, *The Environment and China: Climate Change*, Internet edition (2001), www.wri.org/china/climate.htm).

16 Between 1971 and 1998, China's per capita emission of CO_2 has more than doubled, from 1.02 to 2.30 tons. US per capita emissions of CO_2 actually decreased, but remained at a very high level (having fallen from 20.7 to 20.1 tons per capita). International Energy Agency Data Services (2001), www.iea.org.

Select bibliography

Abashin, S. and V. Bushkov, *Sotsial'naya napryazhennost i mezhnatsional'nye Konflikty v severnykh raionah Tadjikistana*, Document 24 (Moscow: IEA, 1991).

Adler, Emanuel and Michael Barnett (eds), *Security Communities* (Cambridge: Cambridge University Press, 1998).

Agadjanian, Alexander, 'Revising Pandora's Gifts: Religious and National Identity in the Post-Soviet Societal Fabric', *Europe–Asia Studies*, 53:3 (2001), pp. 473–89.

Akbarzededeh, Shahram, 'National Identity and Political Legitimacy in Turkmenistan', *National Papers*, 27:2 (1999), pp. 271–90.

Akiner, Shirin, 'Conflict, Stability and Development in Central Asia', in C. J. Dick (ed.), *Instabilities in Post-Communist Europe* (Portsmouth: Carmichael and Sweet, 1996).

Alagappa, Muthiah, 'Regionalism and Conflict Management: A Framework for Analysis', *Review of International Studies*, 21:4 (1995), pp. 359–87.

Allison, Roy, 'Central Asia: A Region in the Making', paper presented at the conference on Central Asia in a New Security Context, Swedish Institute of International Affairs, Stockholm, 2–3 September 1999.

Allison, Roy and Lena Johnson (eds), *Central Asian Security: The New International Context* (Washington, DC: Brookings Institution, 2001).

Allworth, Edward, 'History and Group Identity in Central Asia', in Graham Smith, Edward Allworth and Vivien Law (eds), *Nation-Building in the Post-Soviet Borderlands: The Politics of National Identities* (Cambridge: Cambridge University Press, 1998).

Altstadt, Audrey, 'Azerbaijan's Struggle Toward Democracy', in Karen Dawisha and Bruce Parrott (eds), *Conflict, Cleavage, and Change in Central Asia and the Caucasus* (Cambridge: Cambridge University Press, 1997).

Anderson, Benedict, *Imagined Communities: Reflections on the Origin and Spread of Nationalism* (Norfolk: Thetford, 1983).

Anderson, Benedict, *Imagined Communities: Reflections on the Origin and Spread of Nationalism*, rev. edn (New York: Verso, 1991).

Andrews-Speed, Philip and Sergei Vinogradov, 'China's Involvement in Central Asian Petroleum: Convergent or Divergent Interests?', *Asian Survey*, 40:2 (2000), pp. 377–97.

Anon., *Agenda: A Global Survey* (Tokyo: Japan Center for International Exchange, 1998).

Arbatov, Aleksei, *Rossiiskaia natsionalnaia ideia i vneshniaia politika* (Moscow: Moscow Social Science Foundation, 1998).

Arquilla, John and David Ronfeldt, *Networks and Netwars* (Santa Monica: Rand Corporation, 2001).

Ash, Timothy Garton, *The Uses of Adversity: Essays on the Fate of Central Europe* (New York: Random House, 1989).

Assembly of the WEU, *Parliamentary Cooperation in the Black Sea Area*, Rapporteur Sir John Hunt, Doc. 1544 (Paris: WEU, 4 November 1996).

Axelrod, Robert and Robert O. Keohane, 'Achieving Cooperation under Anarchy: Strategies and Institutions', in David Baldwin (ed.), *Neorealism and Neoliberalism: The Contemporary Debate* (New York: Columbia University Press, 1996).

Baev, Pavel, *Russia's Policies in the Caucasus* (London: Royal Institute of International Affairs, 1997).

Bailes, Alyson J. K., 'The Role of Subregional Cooperation in Post-Cold War Europe: Integration, Security, and Democracy', in Andrew Cottey (ed.), *Subregional Cooperation in the New Europe: Building Security, Prosperity and Solidarity from the Barents to the Black Sea* (London: Macmillan, 1999).

Barber, Benjamin R., *Jihad Versus McWorld* (New York: Ballantine, 1996).

Barnett, Michael, 'Sovereignty, Nationalism, and Regional Order in the Arab State System', *International Organization*, 49:3 (1995), pp. 479–510.

Barth, Fredrik, 'Introduction', in Fredrik Barth (ed.), *Ethnic Groups and Boundaries: The Social Organization of Cultural Difference* (Boston: Little, Brown, 1969).

Barzini, Luigi, *The Europeans* (New York: Penguin, 1983).

Bayart, Jean-François, Stephen Ellis and Béatrice Hibou, *The Criminalization of the State in Africa* (Bloomington: Indiana University Press, 1999).

Bedford, Daniel, 'International Water Management in the Aral Sea', *Water International*, 21 (1996), pp. 63–9.

Begum, Anwara, *Inter-Republican Cooperation of the Russian Republic* (Aldershot: Ashgate, 1997).

Bergstrand, Jeffrey H., 'The Gravity Equation in International Trade: Some Microeconomic Foundations and Empirical Evidence', *Review of Economics and Statistics*, 67:3 (1985), pp. 474–81.

Bhatty, Robin and Rachel Bronson, 'NATO's Mixed Signals in the Caucasus and Central Asia', *Survival*, 42:3 (2000), pp. 129–45.

Black Sea Strategy Group, *Coping with New Security Threats in the Black Sea Region* (Kiev: EastWest Institute, 2002).

Blanchard, David, *Turkey and the European Union* (London: Centre for European Reform, 1998).

Blank, Stephen, *Energy, Economics, and Security in Central Asia: Russia and its Rivals* (Carlisle Barracks, PA: US Army War College, 1995).

Blank, Stephen, 'Partners in Discord Only', *Orbis*, 44:4 (2000), pp. 557–71.

Blank, Stephen, *U.S. Military Engagement with Transcaucasia and Central Asia* (Carlisle Barracks, PA: US Army War College, Strategic Studies Institute, June 2000).

Blank, Stephen, 'Towards Geostrategic Realignment in Central Asia', *Central Asia-Caucasus Analysts* (Washington, DC: Central Asia-Caucasus Institute, Johns Hopkins University, 10 October 2001).

Blank, Stephen, 'The United States and Central Asia', in Roy Allison and Lena Jonson (eds), *Central Asian Security: The New International Context* (Washington, DC: Brookings Institution, 2001).

Blinken, Antony and Simon Serfaty, 'Regional Strategies – Europe', in Kurt M. Campbell and Michèle A. Flournoy (principal authors), *To Prevail: An American Strategy for the Campaign Against Terrorism* (Washington, DC: CSIS Press, 2001).

Bode, Denise A., 'Energy Shortage in Energy-Rich America: Why?', *Heritage Lectures* (Washington, DC: Heritage Foundation, 16 November 2000).

Bolton, John, 'European Common Foreign, Security, and Defense Policies: Implications for the United States and the Atlantic Alliance', *Hearings*, House Committee on International Relations, 106th Congress, First Session, 10 November 1999, pp. 65–78.

Borisenko, E. N., A. P. Kononenko and I. V. Semenenko, *Black Sea Economic Cooperation: From Regional Initiative to International Organisation* (Istanbul: UZMAN, 1998).

Brailsford, H. N., *Macedonia: Its Races and their Future* (London: Methuen, 1906).

Braumoeller, Bear F., 'Deadly Doves: Liberal Nationalism and the Democratic Peace in the Soviet Successor States', *International Studies Quarterly*, 41:3 (1997), pp. 375–402.

Bremmer, Esther, 'Redefining European Security? Insights from United States, European Union, and German Assistance to the Russian Federation, 1991–2000', *AICGS/DAAD Working Paper* (Washington, DC: AICGS, 2002).

Bremmer, Ian, 'Russia's Total Security', *World Policy Journal*, 16:2 (1999), pp. 31–9.

Bremmer, Ian and Alyson J. K. Bailes, 'Subregionalism in the Newly Independent States', *International Affairs*, 74:1 (1998), pp. 131–47.

Bremmer, Ian and Alexander Zaslavsky, 'Bush and Putin's Tentative Embrace', *World Policy Journal*, 18:4 (2001–02), pp. 11–17.

Bronson, Rachel, 'NATO's Expanding Presence in the Caucasus and Central Asia', in Stephen Blank (ed.), *NATO After Enlargement: New Challenges, New Missions, New Forces* (Carlisle Barracks, PA: Strategic Studies Institute, US Army War College, 1998), pp. 229–54.

Brown, Michael E., 'The Causes and Regional Dimensions of Internal Conflict', in Michael E. Brown (ed.), *The International Dimensions of Internal Conflict* (Cambridge, MA: Center for Science and International Affairs, 1996), pp. 571–602.

Brown, Michael E., 'Internal Conflict and International Action', in Michael E. Brown (ed.), *The International Dimensions of Internal Conflict* (Cambridge, MA: Center for Science and International Affairs, 1996), pp. 603–28.

Brubaker, Rogers, *Nationalism Reframed: Nationhood and the National Question in the New Europe* (Cambridge: Cambridge University Press, 1996).

Brzezinski, Zbigniew, *The Grand Chessboard: American Primacy and its Geostrategic Imperatives* (New York: Basic Books, 1997).

Brzezinski, Zbigniew, *The Geostrategic Triad: Living with China, Europe, and Russia* (Washington, DC: Center for Strategic and International Studies, 2001).

BSEC (Black Sea Economic Cooperation), *BSEC Handbook of Documents, I* (Istanbul: BSEC PERMIS, 1995).

BSEC, *BSEC Handbook of Documents, II* (Istanbul: BSEC PERMIS, 1996).

BSEC, *BSEC Handbook of Documents, III* (Istanbul: BSEC PERMIS, 1998).

BSEC, *BSEC Economic Agenda for the Future: Towards a More Consolidated, Effective and Viable Partnership* (Istanbul: BSEC PERMIS, ICBSS, 2001).

BSEC, *Statutory Documents* (Istanbul: BSEC PERMIS, 2001).

Burles, Mark, *Chinese Policy Toward Russia and the Central Asian Republics* (Santa Monica: Rand Corporation, 1999).

Buzan, Barry, *People, States and Fear: An Agenda for International Security Studies in the Post-Cold War Era*, second edn (Boulder, CO: Lynne Rienner, 1991).

Buzan, Barry, 'The Logic of Regional Security in the Post-Cold War World', in Björn Hettne, András Inotai and Osvaldo Sunkel (eds), *The New Regionalism and the Future of Security and Development*, 4 (New York: St Martin's Press in association with UNU/WIDER, 2000).

Buzan, Barry, Ole Wæver and Jaap de Wilde, *Security: A New Framework for Analysis* (Boulder, CO: Lynne Rienner, 1998).

Calleo, David P., 'Strategic Implications of the Euro', *Survival*, 41:1 (1999), pp. 5–19.

Calleo, David P., *Rethinking Europe's Future* (Princeton, NJ: Princeton University Press, 2001).

Campbell, David, *Writing Security: United States Foreign Policy and the Politics of Identity*, rev. edn (Minneapolis: University of Minnesota Press, 1998).

Carrere d'Encausse, Hélène, *Islam and the Russian Empire: Reform and Revolution in Central Asia* (London: I. B. Tauris, 1988).

Carter, Ashton B., William J. Perry and John D. Steinbruner, *A New Concept of Cooperative Security* (Washington, DC: Brookings Institution, 1992).

Center for Foreign Policy and Analysis, *Shanghai Cooperation Organization* (Almaty: Center for Foreign Policy and Analysis, 2001).

Chayes, Abram and Antonia Handler Chayes (eds), *Preventing Conflict in the Post-Communist World* (Washington, DC: Brookings Institution, 1996).

Checkel, Jeffrey T., 'The Constructivist Turn in International Relations Theory', *World Politics*, 50:2 (1998), pp. 324–48.

Chinn, Jeff, 'Moldovans: Searching for Identity', *Problems of Post-Communism*, 44:3 (1997), pp. 43–52.

Christensen, Thomas J., 'Posing Problems without Catching Up: China's Rise and Challenges for U.S. Security Policy', *International Security*, 25:4 (2001), pp. 5–40.

Christensen, Thomas J. and Jack Snyder, 'Chain Gangs and Passed Bucks: Predicting Alliance Patterns in Multipolarity', *International Organization*, 44:2 (1990), pp. 137–69.

Cohen, Ariel, 'The New "Great Game": Pipeline Politics in Eurasia', *Eurasian Studies*, 3:1 (1996), pp. 2–15.

Cohen, Stephen, *Failed Crusade: America and the Tragedy of Post-Communist Russia* (New York and London: Norton, 2000).

Commission of the European Communities, *Regional Cooperation in the Black Sea Area: State of Play, Perspectives for EU Action Encouraging its Further Development*, COM(97), 597 final (Brussels: EC, 1997).

Coon, Charli, 'National Security Demands More Diverse Energy Supplies', *Executive Memorandum* (Washington, DC: Heritage Foundation, 15 September 2001).

Coon, Charli and James Phillips, 'Strengthening National Energy Security by Reducing Dependence on Imported Oil', *Backgrounder* (Washington, DC: Heritage Foundation, 24 April 2002).

Cordesman, Anthony H., *The US Government View of Energy Development in the*

Caspian, Central Asia, and Iran (Washington, DC: Center for Strategic and International Studies, 2000).

Cornell, Svante, *Small Nations and Great Powers: A Study of Ethnopolitical Conflict in the Caucasus* (Richmond: Curzon Press, 2001).

Cortell, Andrew and James Davis, 'How Do International Institutions Matter? The Domestic Impact of International Rules and Norms', *International Studies Quarterly*, 40:4 (1996), pp. 451–78.

Costigliola, Frank, 'LBJ, Germany, and the "End of the Cold War"', in Warren I. Cohen and Nancy Bernkopf Tucker (eds), *Lyndon Johnson Confronts the World* (New York: Cambridge University Press, 1994).

Cronin, Bruce, *Community Under Anarchy: Transnational Identity and the Evolution of Cooperation* (New York: Columbia University Press, 1999).

Crowther, William, 'Moldova: Caught Between Nation and Empire', in Ian Bremmer and Ray Taras (eds), *New States, New Politics: Building the Post-Soviet Nations* (Cambridge: Cambridge University Press, 1997).

Cutler, Robert M., 'The Key West Conference on Nagorno-Karabakh: Preparing Peace in the South Caucacus?', *A Global Affairs Commentary*, Foreign Policy in Focus, 4 October 2001.

Cutler, Robert M., 'Cozying up to Karimov?', *A Global Affairs Commentary*, Foreign Policy in Focus, 4 October 2001.

Cutler, Robert M., 'Central Asian Energy and Security in Light of the Afghanistan Crisis', *Central Asia-Caucasus Analysts* (Washington, DC: Central Asia-Caucasus Institute, Johns Hopkins University, 10 October 2001).

Cutler, Robert M., 'Islamic Militancy in Central Asia: What is to Be Done?', *A Global Affairs Commentary*, Foreign Policy in Focus, 19 October 2001.

Cutler, Robert M., 'U.S. Intervention in Afghanistan: Implications for Central Asia', *A Global Affairs Commentary*, Foreign Policy in Focus, 21 November 2001.

Daugherty, William H., 'System Management and the Endurance of the Concert of Europe', in Jack Snyder and Robert Jervis (eds), *Coping with Complexity in the International System* (Boulder, CO: Westview Press, 1993).

Dekmejian, R. Hrair, 'Islamic Revival: Catalysts, Categories, and Consequences', in Shireen Hunter (ed.), *The Politics of Islamic Revivalism: Diversity and Unity* (Bloomington: Indiana University Press, 1988).

Department of Energy, *International Energy Outlook, 1999* (Washington, DC: GPO, 1999).

Department of Energy, *New Energy Policy Report* (Washington, DC: GPO, May 2001).

Deutsch, Karl W. *et al.*, *Political Community and the North Atlantic Area: International Organizations in the Light of Historical Experience* (Princeton, NJ: Princeton University Press, 1953).

Dimitrijevic, Nenad (ed.), *Managing Multiethnic Local Communities in the Countries of the Former Yugoslavia* (Budapest: Open Society Institute, 2000).

Downs, Erica Strecker, *China's Quest for Energy Security* (Santa Monica: Rand Corporation, 2000).

Downs, George W. (ed.), *Collective Security Beyond the Cold War* (Ann Arbor: University of Michigan Press, 1994).

Dudwick, Nora, 'Armenia: The Nation Awakes', in Ian Bremmer and Ray Taras (eds), *Problems in the Soviet Successor States* (Cambridge: Cambridge University Press, 1993).

Dudwick, Nora, 'The Cultural Construction of Political Violence in Armenia and Azerbaijan', *Problems of Post-Communism*, 42:4 (1995), pp. 18–20.

Duffield, John, 'NATO's Functions after the Cold War', *Political Science Quarterly*, 109:5 (1994–95), pp. 763–87.

Duffield, John, 'Transatlantic Relations after the Cold War: Theory, Evidence, and the Future', *International Studies Perspectives*, 2:1 (2001), pp. 93–115.

Dunlop, John, *Russia Confronts Chechnya: Roots of a Separatist Conflict* (New York: Cambridge University Press, 1998).

Economist Intelligence Unit, *Uzbekistan Country Profile 2001* (London: EIU, 2001).

Emerson, Michael, *A Stability Pact for the Caucasus* (Brussels: Centre for European Policy Studies, 2000).

Emerson, Michael and Marius Vahl, *Europe's Black Sea Dimension: Model European Regionalism, Prêt à Porter* (Brussels: Centre for European Policy Studies, 2001).

Fearon, James D. and David D. Laitin, 'Explaining Interethnic Cooperation', *American Political Science Review*, 90:4 (1996), pp. 715–35.

Finnemore, Martha and Kathryn Sikkink, 'International Norm Dyamics and Political Change', *International Organization*, 52:4 (1998), pp. 887–917.

Forsythe, Rosemarie, 'The Politics of Oil in the Caucasus and Central Asia', *Adelphi Paper 300* (Oxford: Oxford University Press for the International Institute for Strategic Studies, 1996).

Gagnon, V. P., 'Ethnic Nationalism and International Conflict: The Case of Serbia', *International Security*, 19:3 (1994/95), pp. 130–66.

Garnett, Sherman W., 'Russia's Illusory Ambitions', *Foreign Affairs*, 76:2 (1997), pp. 61–76.

Garnett, Sherman W., 'The United States and the Caspian Basin', in Sherman W. Garnett, Alexander Rahr and Koji Watanabe (eds), *The New Central Asia: In Search of Stability. A Report to the Trilateral Commission, 54* (New York: Trilateral Commission, 2000).

Garnett, Sherman W. and Rachel Lebenson, 'Ukraine Joins the Fray', *Problems of Post-Communism*, 45:6 (1998), pp. 22–33.

Garnett, Sherman W., Alexander Rahr and Koji Watanabe (eds), *The New Central Asia: In Search of Stability. A Report to the Trilateral Commission, 54* (New York: Trilateral Commission, 2000).

Gasiorowski, Mark and Solomon W. Polachek, 'Conflict and Interdependence', *Journal of Conflict Resolution*, 26:4 (1982), pp. 709–29.

Gati, Charles, 'All that NATO Can Be', *National Interest*, 68 (2002), p. 81.

Giersch, Carsten, 'Multilateral Conflict Regulation: The Case of Kosovo', *Weatherhead Center for International Affairs Working Paper No. 00–04* Cambridge, MA: Harvard University, 2000).

Gilpin, Robert, *War and Change in World Politics* (Cambridge: Cambridge University Press, 1981).

Glaser, Charles L., 'Why NATO is Still Best: Future Security Arrangements for Europe', *International Security*, 18:1 (1993), pp. 5–50.

Glaser, Charles L., 'Realists as Optimists: Cooperation as Self-Help', in Michael E. Brown *et al.* (eds), *Theories of War and Peace: An International Security Reader* (Cambridge, MA: MIT Press, 1998).

Glaser, Charles L. and Chaim Kaufmann, 'What is the Offense-Defense Balance and How Can We Measure It?', *International Security*, 22:1 (1998), pp. 44–82.

Gleason, Gregory, *The Central Asian States: Discovering Independence* (Boulder, CO: Westview Press, 1997).

Gleditsch, Nils, 'Armed Conflict and the Environment: A Critique of the Literature', *Journal of Peace Research*, 35:3 (1998), pp. 381–400.

Glenny, Misha, *The Fall of Yugoslavia: The Third Balkan War*, 3rd rev. edn (London: Penguin, 1996).

Goertz, Gary, *Contexts of International Politics* (Cambridge: Cambridge University Press, 1994).

Goldgeier, James M., *Not Whether But When: The U.S. Decision to Enlarge NATO* (Washington, DC: Brookings Institution, 1999).

Goldgeier, James M. and Michael McFaul, 'A Tale of Two Worlds: Core and Periphery in the Post-Cold War Era', *International Organization*, 46:2 (1992), pp. 467–91.

Goldman, Z., 'Environmentalism and Nationalism: An Unlikely Twist in an Unlikely Direction', in John Massey Stewart (ed.), *The Soviet Environment: Problems, Policies and Politics* (Cambridge: Cambridge University Press, 1992).

Gowa, Joanne, 'Bipolarity, Multipolarity, and Free Trade', *American Political Science Review*, 83:4 (1989), pp. 1245–56.

Gowa, Joanne, *Ballots and Bullets: The Elusive Democratic Peace* (Princeton, NJ: Princeton University Press, 1999).

Gowa, Joanne, *Allies, Adversaries, and International Trade* (Princeton, NJ: Princeton University Press, 1994).

Gowa, Joanne and Edward Mansfield, 'Power, Politics, and International Trade', *American Political Science Review*, 87:2 (1993), pp. 408–20.

Grieco, Joseph, 'Anarchy and the Limits of Cooperation: A Realist Critique of the Newest Liberal Institutionalism', *International Organization*, 42:3 (1988), pp. 485–507.

Gurr, Ted and Michael Haxton, 'The Gagauz of Moldova: Settling an Ethnonational Rebellion', in Ted Gurr (ed.), *Peoples Versus States: Minorities at Risk in the New Century* (Washington, DC: United States Institute of Peace, 2000).

Gvosdev, Nikolas, 'The New Party Card? Orthodoxy and the Search for Post-Soviet Russian Identity', *Problems of Post-Communism*, 47:6 (2000), pp. 29–38.

Hale, Henry, 'Integration and Independence in the Caspian Basin', *SAIS Review*, 19:1 (1999), pp. 163–89.

Hall, Arthur, 'Mackinder and the Course of Events', *Annals of the Association of American Geographers*, 45:2 (1955), p. 109.

Hampton, Mary N., 'NATO, Germany, and the United States: Creating Positive Identity in Trans-Atlantia', *Security Studies*, 8:2 (1998/99), pp. 235–69.

Hampton, Mary N. and James Sperling, 'Positive/Negative Identity: Germany and the Euro-Atlantic Communities', *Journal of European Integration*, 24:4 (2002), pp. 281–302.

Hanrieder, Wolfram F., 'Dissolving International Politics: Reflections on the Nation-State', *American Political Science Review*, 72:4 (1978), pp. 1276–87.

Harper, John L., *American Visions of Europe* (Cambridge: Cambridge University Press, 1994).

Haukkala, Hiski and Sergei Medveded (eds), *The EU Common Strategy on Russia: Learning the Grammar of the CFSP* (Helsinki: Ulkopoliittinen instituutti; Bonn: Institut für Europäische Politik, 2000).

Herz, John H., 'The Rise and Demise of the Territorial State', *World Politics*, 9:4 (1957), pp. 473–93.

Hewitt, George, 'Abkhazia, Georgia and the Circassians (NW Caucasus),' *Central Asian Survey*, 18:4 (1999), pp. 463–500.

Hill, Fiona, *Russia's Tinderbox: Conflict in the North Caucasus and its Implications for the Future of the Russian Federation* (Cambridge, MA: Harvard University, JFK School of Government, Strengthening Democratic Institutions Project, September 1995).

Hill, Fiona, 'The Caucasus and Central Asia', *Policy Brief No. 80* (Washington, DC: Brookings Institution, May 2001).

Hill, Fiona and Regine Spector, 'The Caspian Basin and Asian Energy Markets', *Conference Report No. 8* (Washington, DC: Brookings Institution, September 2001).

Hoffman, Bruce, *Inside Terrorism* (London: Indigo, 1999).

Hoffman, Bruce, 'Terrorism Trends and Prospects', in Ian Lesser *et al.*, *Countering the New Terrorism* (Santa Monica: Rand Corporation, 1999).

Hoffmann, Stanley, *Primacy or World Order* (New York: McGraw-Hill, 1978).

Hoffmann, Stanley, *World Disorders: Troubled Peace in the Post-Cold War Era* (Lanham, MD: Rowman and Littlefield, 1998).

Holbrooke, Richard, *To End a War* (New York: Random House, 1998).

Holm-Hansen, Jorn, 'Political Integration in Kazakhstan', in Pal Kolsto (ed.), *Nation-Building and Ethnic Integration in Post-Soviet Societies* (Boulder, CO: Westview Press, 1999).

Holsti, Kalevi J., *Peace and War: Armed Conflicts and International Order, 1648–1989* (Cambridge: Cambridge University Press, 1991).

Homer-Dixon, Thomas, 'Environmental Scarcities and Violent Conflict: Evidence from Cases', *International Security*, 19:1 (1994), pp. 5–40.

Hopf, Ted, 'The Promise of Constructivism in International Relations Theory', *International Security*, 23:1 (1998), pp. 171–200.

Hopf, Ted, *Social Construction of International Politics: Identities and Foreign Policies, Moscow, 1955 and 1999* (Ithaca, NY: Cornell University Press, 2002).

Hopmann, P. Terrence, *Building Security in Post-Cold War Eurasia: The OSCE and U.S. Foreign Policy* (Washington, DC: United States Institute of Peace, Peaceworks No. 39, 1999).

Hopmann, P. Terrence, 'The Organization for Security and Cooperation in Europe: Its Contribution to Conflict Prevention and Resolution', in Paul C. Stern and Daniel Druckman (eds), *International Conflict Resolution After the Cold War* (Washington, DC: National Academy Press, 2000).

Horowitz, Donald, *A Democratic South Africa?: Constitutional Engineering in a Divided Society* (Berkeley, CA: University of California Press, 1991).

Horsman, Stuart, 'Security Issues Facing the Newly Independent States of Central Asia: The Cases of Kazakhstan and Uzbekistan', PhD dissertation, University of Sheffield, 1999.

Horsman, Stuart, 'Water, Security and Development in Central Asia', in EBRD (ed.) *The Next Ten Years: Mapping the Challenges* (London: EBRD, 2001).

Howard, Glen E., 'NATO and the Caucasus: The Caspian Axis', in Stephen Blank (ed.), *NATO After Enlargement: New Challenges, New Missions, New Forces* (Carlisle Barracks, PA: Strategic Studies Institute, US Army War College, 1998).

Hsue Chuntu and Xing Guangcheng (eds), *Zhongguo yu Zhongya* (*China and Central Asia*), (Beijing: Shehuikexue chubanshe, 1999).

Hunter, Shireen, 'Azerbaijan: Search for Identity', in Ian Bremmer and Ray Taras (eds), *Nations and Politics in the Soviet Successor States* (Cambridge: Cambridge University Press, 1983).

Hunter, Shireen, *Central Asia Since Independence* (Washington, DC: Center for Strategic and International Studies, 1995).

Huntington, Samuel, *The Clash of Civilizations and the Remaking of World Order* (New York: Simon and Schuster, 1996).

Hyde-Price, Adrian, *European Security beyond the Cold War: Four Scenarios for the Year 2010* (London: Sage, 1991).

Inayatullah, Naeem and David Blaney, 'Knowing Encounters: Beyond Parochialism in International Relations History', in Yosef Lapid and Friedrich Kratchowil (eds), *The Return of Culture and Identity in IR Theory* (Boulder, CO: Lynne Rienner, 1996).

International Energy Agency, *World Energy Outlook* (Vienna: IEA, 1999).

International Energy Agency, *Energy Balances: Non-OECD Countries* (IEA, 2000).

International Institute for Strategic Studies, *The Military Balance: 2001–2002* (London: International Institute for Strategic Studies, 2001).

International Institute for Strategic Studies, *Strategic Survey: 2000–2001* (London: International Institute for Strategic Studies, 2001).

International Monetary Fund, *Direction of Trade Statistics* (Washington, DC: IMF, 1998).

International Monetary Fund, *International Financial Statistics*, 51:2 (1998).

International Monetary Fund, *World Economic Outlook* (Washington, DC: IMF, October 2000.

International Organization for Migration, *CIS Migration Report* (Geneva: IOM, 1997).

Jervis, Robert, *Perception and Misperception in International Politics* (Princeton, NJ: Princeton University Press, 1976).

Jervis, Robert, 'Cooperation under the Security Dilemma', *World Politics*, 30:2 (1978), pp. 167–214.

Jervis, Robert, 'Theories of War in an Era of Leading Power Peace', *American Political Science Review*, 96:1 (2002), pp. 1–14.

Joffé, George, 'The Euro-Mediterranean Partnership: Two Years After Barcelona', *Middle East Program Briefing* (London: Royal Institute for International Affairs, May 1998).

Johnson, Chalmers, *Blowback: The Costs and Consequences of American Empire* (Empire, NY: Metropolitan Books, 2000).

Johnson, G. Wesley (ed.), *Double Impact: France and Africa in the Age of Imperialism* (Westport, CT: Greenwood Press, 1985).

Johnson, Lena and Roy Allison, 'Central Asian Security: Internal and External Dynamics', in Roy Allison and Lena Johnson (eds), *Central Asian Security: The New International Context* (Washington, DC: Brookings Institution, 2001).

Kalicki, Jan H., 'Caspian Energy at the Crossroads', *Foreign Affairs*, 80:5 (2001), pp. 120–35.

Kamrava, Mehran, 'State-Building in Azerbaijan: The Search for Consolidation', *Middle East Journal*, 55:2 (2001), pp. 216–37.

Kaplan, Robert D., *Balkan Ghosts: A Journey Through History* (New York: Random House, 1993).

Katzenstein, Peter (ed.), *The Culture of National Security: Norms and Identity in World Politics* (New York: Columbia University Press, 1996).

Kaufman, Stuart, 'Spiraling to Ethnic War: Elites, Masses and Moscow in Moldova's Civil War', *International Security*, 21:2 (1996), pp. 108–38.

Kaufman, Stuart J., *Modern Hatreds: The Symbolic Politics of Ethnic War* (Ithaca, NY: Cornell University Press, 2001).

Kaufmann, Chaim, 'Possible and Impossible Solutions to Ethnic Wars', *International Security*, 20:4 (1996), pp. 136–75.

Kaufmann, Chaim, 'When All Else Fails', *International Security*, 23:2 (1998), pp. 120–56.

Kay, Sean, *NATO and the Future of European Security* (Lanham, MD: Rowman and Littlefield, 1998).

Kay, Sean, 'NATO's Open Door: Geostrategic Priorities and the Impact of the European Union', *Security Dialogue*, 32:2 (2001), pp. 201–16.

Kelleher, Catherine M., *The Future of European Security: An Interim Assessment* (Washington, DC: Brookings Institution, 1995).

Keohane, Robert O., *After Hegemony: Cooperation and Discord in the World Political Economy* (Princeton, NJ: Princeton University Press, 1984).

Keohane, Robert O., *International Institutions and State Power* (Boulder, CO: Westview Press, 1989).

Keohane, Robert O., 'Governance in a Partially Globalized World', *American Political Science Review*, 95:1 (2001), pp. 1–13.

Keohane, Robert O., Joseph S. Nye and Stanley Hoffman (eds), *After the Cold War: International Institutions and State Strategies in Europe, 1989–1991* (Cambridge, MA: Harvard University Press, 1994).

King, Charles, 'Post-Postcommunism: Transition, Comparison, and the End of "Eastern Europe"', *World Politics*, 53:1 (2000), pp. 143–72.

Kissinger, Henry, *Diplomacy* (New York: Simon and Schuster, 1994).

Klötzli, Stefan, *The Water and Soil Crisis in Central Asia: A Source for Future Conflicts?*, ENCOP *Occasional Paper No.11* (Zurich: Center for Security Policy and Conflict Research; Berne: Swiss Peace Foundation, May 1994).

Kolsto, Pal, 'Bipolar Societies?', in Pal Kolsto (ed.), *Nation-Building and Ethnic Integration in Post-Soviet Societies* (Boulder, CO: Westview Press, 1999).

Koremenos, Barbara, Charles Lipson and Duncan Snidal, 'The Rational Design of International Institutions', *International Organization*, 55:4 (2001), pp. 761–99.

Koremenos, Barbara, Charles Lipson and Duncan Snidal (eds), *The Rational Design of International Institutions*, special issue of *International Organization*, 55:4 (2001).

Kowert, Paul and Jeffrey Legro, 'Norms, Identity, and their Limits: A Theoretical Reprise', in Peter Katzenstein (ed.), *The Culture of National Security: Norms and Identity in World Politics* (New York: Columbia University Press, 1996).

Kramer, Mark, 'Neorealism, Nuclear Proliferation, and East-Central European Strategies', in Ethan B. Kapstein and Michael Mastanduno (eds), *Unipolar Politics: Realism and State Strategies After the Cold War* (New York: Columbia University Press, 1999).

Kupchan, Charles, 'The Case for Collective Security', in George Downs (ed.), *Collective Security After the Cold War* (Ann Arbor: University of Michigan Press, 1994).

Kupchan, Charles, 'Strategic Visions', *World Policy Journal*, 11:1 (1994), pp. 112–22.

Kupchan, Charles, 'In Defence of Europe's Defence: An American Perspective', *Survival*, 42:2 (2000), pp. 16–32.

Kupchan, Charles and Clifford Kupchan, 'The Promise of Collective Security', *International Security*, 20:1 (1995), pp. 52–61.

Kuzio, Taras (ed.), *Contemporary Ukraine: Dynamics of Post-Soviet Transformation* (Armonk, NY, and London: M. E. Sharpe, 1998).

Kuzio, Taras, 'Promoting Geopolitical Pluralism in the CIS: GUUAM and Western Foreign Policy', *Problems of Post-Communism*, 47:3 (2000), pp. 25–35.

Kydd, Andrew, 'Sheep in Sheep's Clothing: Why Security Seekers Do Not Fight Each Other', *Security Studies*, 7:1 (1997), pp. 114–55.

Kydd, Andrew, 'Trust, Reassurance, and Cooperation', *International Organization*, 54:2 (2000), pp. 325–57.

Lake, Anthony, *Six Nightmares* (Boston: Little, Brown, 2000).

Lake, David and Donald Rothchild, 'Containing Fear: The Origins and Management of Ethnic Conflict', *International Security*, 21:2 (1996), pp. 41–75.

Lampton, David M., 'Cycles, Process, Constraints, and Opportunities in U.S.–China Relations', paper presented at the Conference on Post-APEC China–US Relations, Shanghai Institute of International Studies, 3–4 September 2001, Shanghai.

Lampton, David M., 'Small Mercies: China and America after 9/11', *National Interest*, 66 (2001/02), pp. 106–13.

Laqueur, Walter, *The New Terrorism*, (New York: Oxford University Press, 1999).

Larrabee, F. Stephen, 'U.S. and European Policy toward Turkey and the Caspian Basin', in Robert D. Blackwill and Michael Stürmer (eds), *Allies Divided: Transatlantic Policies in the Greater Middle East*, (Cambridge, MA: MIT Press, 1997).

Lavrov, S., 'The CIS Countries at the United Nations', *International Affairs* (Moscow), 43:2 (1997), pp. 7–11.

Lederach, John Paul, *Building Peace: Sustainable Reconciliation in Divided Societies* (Washington, DC: US Institute of Peace, 1997).

Legvold, Robert, 'The Three Russias', in Robert A. Pastor (ed.), *A Century's Journey* (New York: Basic Books, 2000).

Legvold, Robert, 'Russia's Unformed Foreign Policy', *Foreign Affairs*, 80:5 (2001), pp. 62–75.

Lesser, Ian, *et al.*, *Countering the New Terrorism* (Santa Monica: Rand Corporation, 1999).

Li Zhisheng, 'Zhongguo de Nengyuan Weiji' ('China's Energy Crisis'), in Li Ming (ed.), *Zhongguo de Weiji (Xia)* (*The Crisis of China II*) (Beijing: Gaige chubanshe, 1998).

Lieven, Anatol, *Chechnya: Tombstone of Russian Power* (New Haven, CT: Yale University Press, 1998).

Lieven, Anatol, 'The (Not So) Great Game', *National Interest*, 58 (1999–2000), pp. 69–81.

Lijphart, Arendt, *Democracy in Plural Societies: A Comparative Exploration* (New Haven, CT: Yale University Press, 1977).

Liu Hong Xuan (ed.), *Zhongguo Mulin Shi: Zhongguo yu Zhoubian Guanxi Shi* (*The History of China's Relations with its Neighbouring States*) (Beijing: Shijiezhishi chubanshe, 2002).

Loriaux, Michael, 'Realism and Reconciliation: France, Germany, and the European Union', in Ethan B. Kapstein and Michael Mastanduno (eds), *Unipolar Politics: Realism and State Strategies After the Cold War* (New York: Columbia University Press, 1999).

Louse, Verne W. and Ian McCreary, 'China's Energy: A Forecast to 2015', *Los Alamos National Laboratory International Economics Reports LA-UR-96-2972* (Los Alamos, NM: Los Alamos National Laboratory, 1996).

Luong, Pauline Jones and Erika Weinthal, 'New Friends, New Fears in Central Asia', *Foreign Affairs*, 81:2 (2002), pp. 61–70.

Lynch, Allen C., 'The Realism of Russia's Foreign Policy', *Europe–Asia Studies*, 53:1 (2001), pp. 7–31.

Lynch, Dov, 'Euro-Asian Conflicts and Peacekeeping Dilemmas', in Yelena Kalyuzhnova and Dov Lynch (eds), *The Euro-Asian World: A Period of Transition* (New York: St Martin's Press, 2000).

MacFarlane, Neil, 'Realism and Russian Strategy after the Collapse of the USSR', in Ethan B. Kapstein and Michael Mastanduno (eds), *Unipolar Politics: Realism and State Strategies after the Cold War* (New York: Columbia University Press, 1999), pp. 218–60.

Mackinder, Halford, 'The Geographical Pivot of History', *Geographical Journal*, 23:4 (1904), pp. 421–44.

Maddison, Angus, *Chinese Economic Performance in the Long Run* (Paris: OECD, 1998).

Malashenko, Aleksei, 'Russian Nationalism and Islam', in Michael Waller, Bruno Coppieters and Alexei Malashenko (eds), *Conflicting Loyalties and the State in Post-Soviet Eurasia* (Moscow: Institute of Oriental Studies, Russian Academy of Sciences, 1998).

Malik, Hafeez (ed.), *Central Asia: Its Strategic Importance and Future Prospects* (New York: St Martin's Press, 1994).

Mann, Michael, 'The Autonomous Power of the State', in Marvin Olsen and Martin Marger (eds), *Power in Modern Societies* (Boulder, CO: Westview Press, 1993).

March, James G. and Johan P. Olsen, 'The Institutional Dynamics of International Political Orders', *International Organization*, 52:4 (1998), pp. 943–69.

Mark, David, 'Eurasia Letter: Russia and the New Transcaucasus', *Foreign Policy*, 105 (1996/97), pp. 141–59.

Martin, Lisa, 'Interests, Power and Multilateralism', *International Organization*, 46:4 (1992), pp. 765–92.

Martin, Lisa, 'The Rational State Choice', in John Gerard Ruggie (ed.), *Multilateralism Matters: The Theory and Praxis of an Institutional Form* (New York: Columbia University Press, 1993).

Martin, Lisa L. and Beth A. Simmons, 'Theories and Empirical Studies of International Institutions', *International Organization*, 52:4 (1998), pp. 729–57.

Mastanduno, Michael, 'Economics and Security in Statecraft and Scholarship', *International Organization*, 52:4 (1998), pp. 825–54.

McCalla, Robert, 'NATO's Persistence after the Cold War', *International Organization*, 50:3 (1996), pp. 445–75.

McDaniel, Tim, *The Agony of the Russian Idea* (Princeton, NJ: Princeton University Press, 1996).

McFaul, Michael, 'State Power, Constitutional Change, and the Politics of Privatization in Russia', *World Politics*, 47:2 (1995), pp. 210–43.

Mearsheimer, John J., 'The False Promise of International Institutions', *International Security*, 19: 3 (1994–95), pp. 5–49.

Mearsheimer, John J., *The Tragedy of Great Power Politics* (New York: W. W. Norton, 2001).

Medvedev, Sergei, 'Former Soviet Union', in Paul B. Stares (ed.), *The New Security: A Global Survey* (Tokyo: Japan Center for International Exchange, 1998).

Mendelson, Sarah, 'The Putin Path', *Problems of Post-Communism*, 47:5 (2000), pp. 3–12.

Menon, Rajon, 'In the Shadow of the Bear: Security in Post-Soviet Central Asia', *International Security*, 20:1 (1995), pp. 161–3.

Metcalf, Lee Kendall, 'Regional Economic Integration in the Former Soviet Union', *Political Research Quarterly*, 50:3 (1997), pp. 529–49.

Miall, Hugh, *Shaping a New European Order* (New York: Council of Foreign Affairs for the Royal Institute of International Affairs, 1994).

Micklin, Phillip, 'The Water Crisis in Soviet Central Asia', in P. Pryde (ed.), *Environmental Management in the Soviet Union* (Cambridge: Cambridge University Press, 1991).

Micklin, Phillip, 'The Aral Sea Crisis: An Introduction to the Special Edition', *Post-Soviet Geography*, 33:5 (1992), pp. 269–82.

Micklin, Phillip, 'Regional and International Responses to the Aral Crisis', *Post-Soviet Geography and Economics*, 39:1 (1998), pp. 399–416.

Micklin, Phillip, *Managing Water in Central Asia* (London: Royal Institute of International Affairs, 2000).

Migdal, Joel, *Strong Societies and Weak States: State–Society Relations and State Capabilities in the Third World* (Princeton, NJ: Princeton University Press, 1988).

Mittelman, James H., *The Globalization Syndrome: Transformation and Resistance* (Princeton, NJ: Princeton University Press, 2000).

Molander, Roger *et al.*, *Strategic Information Warfare* (Santa Monica: Rand Corporation, 1996).

Molchanov, Mikhail, 'Post-Communist Nationalism as a Power Resource: A Russia–Ukraine Comparison', *Nationalities Papers*, 28:2 (2000), pp. 263–89.

Monaghan, Peter, 'Does International Relations Reflect a Bias in Favor of the U.S.?', *Chronicle of Higher Education*, 24 September 1999, pp. A20–1.

Monnet, Jean, *Memoirs* (Garden City, NY: Doubleday, 1978).

Moravcsik, Andrew, 'Europe's Integration at Century's End', in Andrew Moravcsik (ed.), *Centralization or Fragmentation? Europe Facing the Challenges of Deepening, Diversity, and Democracy* (New York: Council on Foreign Relations, 1998).

Morgan, Patrick M., 'Multilateralism and Security: Prospects in Europe', in John Gerard Ruggie (ed.), *Multilateralism Matters: The Theory and Praxis of an Institutional Form* (New York: Columbia University Press, 1993).

Moroney, Jennifer, 'Frontier Dynamics and Ukraine's Ties to the West', *Problems of Post-Communism*, 48:2 (2001), pp. 15–25.

Morrow, James D., Randolph M. Siverson and Tressa E. Tabares, 'The Political Determinants of International Trade: The Major Powers, 1907–1990', *American Political Science Review*, 92:3 (1998), pp. 649–61.

Morse, Edward L. and James Richard, 'The Battle for Energy Dominance', *Foreign Affairs*, 81:2 (2002), pp. 16–31.

Most, Benjamin A. and Harvey Starr, 'Diffusion, Reinforcement, Geopolitics, and the Spread of War', *American Political Science Review*, 74:4 (1980), pp. 932–46.

Mottola, K., 'Security in-between Regionalism and Subregionalism in the OSCE Security Model', paper presented in the 3rd Pan-European International Relations Conference and Joint Meeting with the International Studies Association, Vienna,

16–19 September 1998.

Motyl, Alexander and Bohdan Krawchenko, 'Ukraine: From Empire to Statehood', in Ian Bremmer and Ray Taras (eds), *New States, New Politics: Building the Post-Soviet Nations* (Cambridge: Cambridge University Press, 1997).

Naff, Thomas and Ruth Matson (eds), *Water in the Middle East: Conflict or Cooperation?* (Boulder, CO: Westview Press, 1984).

Neklessa, Aleksandr, 'Konets tsivilizatsii, ili zigzag istorii', *Znamia*, 1:3 (1998), pp. 165–79.

Nelson, Daniel N., 'Post-Communist Insecurity', *Problems of Post-Communism*, 47:5 (2000), pp. 31–7.

Ni Weidong, Li Zheng and Xue Yuan, 'National Energy Futures Analysis and Energy Security Perspective in China', paper presented at Strategic Thinking on the Energy Issue in the 10th Five-Year Plan (FYP) Workshop on East Asia Energy Futures, Beijing, June 2000.

Nolan, Janne (ed.), *Global Engagement: Cooperation and Security in the 21st Century* (Washington, DC: Brookings Institution, 1994).

Noren, James H. and Robin Watson, 'Interrepublican Economic Relations after the Disintegration of the USSR', *Soviet Economy*, 8:2 (1992), pp. 89–109.

Oguledo, Victor Iwuagwu and Craig R. MacPhee, 'Gravity Models: A Reformulation and an Application to Discriminatory Trade Arrangements', *Applied Economics*, 26:2 (1994), pp. 107–20.

O'Hara, Sarah, 'Managing Central Asia's Water Resources: Prospects for the 21st Century', ICREES Seminar on Environmental Issues in Central Asia, University of Nottingham, 9 December 1998.

O'Hara, Sarah, 'Water and Conflict in Central Asia', in Andrew Dobson and Jeffery Stanyer (eds), *Contemporary Political Studies 1998* (Nottingham: University of Nottingham, 1998).

Olcott, Martha, 'Nation Building and Ethnicity', in Roman Szporluk (ed.), *National Identity and Ethnicity in Russia and the New States of Eurasia* (New York: M. E. Sharpe, 1994).

Olcott, Martha, 'Nursultan Nazarbaev and the Balancing Act of State Building in Kazakhstan', in Timothy Colton and Robert Tucker (eds), *Patterns in Post-Soviet Leadership* (Boulder, CO: Westview Press, 1995).

Olcott, Martha, 'National Consolidation', *Harvard International Review*, 22:1 (2000), pp. 50–5.

Olcott, Martha Brill, Anders Aslund and Sherman W. Garnett, *Getting it Wrong: Regional Cooperation and the Commonwealth of Independent States* (Washington, DC: Carnegie Endowment for International Peace, 1999).

Omrod, Jane, 'The North Caucasus: Confederation in Conflict', in Ian Bremmer and Ray Taras (eds), *New States, New Politics: Building the Post-Soviet Nations* (Cambridge: Cambridge University Press, 1997).

OSCE (Organisation for Security and Cooperation in Europe), *The OSCE Handbook* (Vienna: OSCE, 1999).

Osgood, Robert Endicott, *Ideals and Self-Interest in American Foreign Policy* (Chicago: University of Chicago Press, 1952).

Owen, David, *Balkan Odyssey* (New York: Harcourt Brace, 1995).

Özer, Ercan, 'The Black Sea Economic Cooperation and Regional Security', *Perceptions*, 2:3 (1997), pp. 76–106.

Pain, Emil, 'Contagious Ethnic Conflicts and Border Disputes along Russia's Southern Flank', in Graham Smith, Edward Allworth and Vivien Law (eds), *Nation Building in the Post-Soviet Borderlands: The Politics of National Identities* (Cambridge: Cambridge University Press, 1998).

Pan Zhiping (ed.), *Minzu Zijue, Haishi Minzu Fenlie: Minzu he Dangdai Minzu Fenlie Zhuyi* (*Ethnic Sovereignty or Ethnic Separatism*) (Urumuchi: Xinjiangremin chubanshe, 1999).

Pantev, Plamen, 'Security Cooperation in the Black Sea Basin', in Tunç Aybak (ed.), *Politics of the Black Sea: Dynamics of Cooperation and Conflict* (London and New York: I. B. Tauris, 2001).

Pasicolan, Paolo, 'Strengthening the U.S.–Philippine Alliance for Fighting Terrorism', *Executive Memorandum* (Washington, DC: Heritage Foundation, 13 May 2002).

Peck, Connie, *Sustainable Peace: The Role of the UN and Regional Organizations in Preventing Conflict* (Lanham, MD: Rowman and Littlefield, 1998).

Petersen, D. J., *Troubled Lands: The Legacy of Soviet Environmental Destruction* (Boulder, CO: Westview Press, 1993).

Peterson, John and Hugh Ward, 'Coalitional Instability and the New Multidimensional Politics of Security: A Rational Choice Argument for US–EC Cooperation', *European Journal of International Relations*, 1:1 (1995), pp. 131–56.

Piirainen, Timo, 'The Fall of an Empire, the Birth of a Nation: Perceptions of the New Russian National Identity', in Chris Chulos and Timo Piirainen (eds), *The Fall of an Empire, the Birth of a Nation: National Identities in Russia* (Burlington, VT: Ashgate, 2000).

Pirinski, George, 'BSEC: A New Agenda '21?,' *Journal of Southeast European and Black Sea Studies*, 1:3 (2001), pp. 174–8.

Piscatori, James P. (ed.), *Islam in the Political Process*, (Cambridge: Royal Institute for International Affairs/Cambridge University Press, 1983).

Plokhy, Serhii, 'The Ghosts of Pereyaslav: Russo-Ukrainian Historical Debates in the Post-Soviet Era', *Europe–Asia Studies*, 53:3 (2001), pp. 489–506.

Polachek, Solomon W., 'Conflict and Trade', *Journal of Conflict Resolution*, 24:1 (1980), pp. 55–78.

Pollins, Brian M., 'Conflict, Cooperation, and Commerce: The Effects of International Political Interactions on Bilateral Trade Flows', *American Journal of Political Science*, 33:3 (1989), pp. 737–61.

Pollins, Brian M., 'Does Trade Still Follow the Flag?', *American Political Science Review*, 83:2 (1989), pp. 465–80.

Posen, Barry R., *The Sources of Military Doctrine* (Ithaca, NY: Cornell University Press, 1984).

Posen, Barry R., 'The Security Dilemma and Ethnic Conflict', *Survival*, 35:1 (1993), pp. 27–47.

Powell, Robert, 'Absolute and Relative Gains in International Relations Theory', *American Political Science Review*, 85:4 (1991), pp. 1303–20.

Pravda, Alex, 'Foreign Policy', in Stephen White, Alex Pravda and Zvi Gitelman (eds), *Developments in Russian Politics 5* (Basingstoke: Palgrave, 2001).

Prazauskas, Algimantas, 'The Influence of Ethnicity on the Foreign Policies of the Western Littoral States', in Roman Szporluk (ed.), *National Identity and Ethnicity in Russia and the New States of Eurasia* (New York: M. E. Sharpe, 1994).

Ramadan, Tariq, *To Be a European Muslim* (Markfield and Lancaster: Islamic Foundation, 1999).

Reno, William, *Warlord Politics and African States* (Boulder, CO: Lynne Rienner, 1998).

Report of the National Energy Policy Development Group, *National Energy Policy: Reliable, Affordable, and Environmentally Sound Energy for America's Future* (Washington, DC: GPO, May 2001).

Reuveny, Rafael and Heejoon Kang, 'International Trade, Political Conflict/Cooperation, and Granger Causality', *American Journal of Political Science*, 40:3 (1996), pp. 943–70.

Rodman, Peter, *Drifting Apart? Trends in US–European Relations* (Washington, DC: Nixon Center, 1999).

Roeder, Phillip, 'Soviet Federalism and Ethnic Mobilization', *World Politics*, 43:2 (1991), pp. 196–232.

Ro'i, Yacoov, 'Central Asia Riots and Disturbances, 1989–90: Causes and Context', *Central Asian Survey*, 10:3 (1991), pp. 21–54.

Rose, Gideon, 'Neoclassical Realism and Theories of Foreign Policy', *World Politics*, 51:1 (1998), pp. 144–72.

Rosecrance, Richard, *Action and Reaction in World Politics: International Systems in Perspective* (Boston: Little, Brown, 1963).

Rosenau, James N., *Turbulence in World Politics* (Princeton, NJ: Princeton University Press, 1990).

Rosenau, James N., *Along the Domestic–Foreign Frontier: Exploring Governance in a Turbulent World* (Cambridge: Cambridge University Press, 1997).

Rosenau, James N. and Ernst-Otto Czempiel (eds), *Governance Without Government: Order and Change in World Politics* (Cambridge: Cambridge University Press, 1992).

Rothchild, Donald, *Managing Ethnic Conflict in Africa: Pressures and Incentives for Cooperation* (Washington, DC: Brookings Institution, 1997).

Roy, Olivier, 'Islam in Tajikistan', *Project on Open Society in Central Eurasia, Occasional Paper No. 1* (New York: Open Society Institute, 1996).

Roy, Olivier, *The New Central Asia: The Creation of Nations* (New York: New York University Press, 2000).

Ruggie, John Gerard, 'Continuity and Transformation in the World Polity: Toward a Neo-Realist Synthesis', in Robert O. Keohane (ed.), *Neorealism and its Critics* (New York: Columbia University Press, 1986).

Ruggie, John Gerard (ed.), *Multilateralism Matters: The Theory and Praxis of an Institutional Form* (New York: Columbia University Press, 1993).

Russett, Bruce M. and John Oneal, *Triangulating Peace: Democracy, Interdependence and International Organizations* (New York: Norton, 2001).

Ryan, Stephen, *Ethnic Conflict and International Relations* (Aldershot: Dartmouth, 1990).

Rywkin, Michael, *Moscow's Muslim Challenge: Soviet Central Asia* (New York: M. E. Sharpe, 1982).

Sakwa, Richard and Mark Webber, 'The Commonwealth of Independent States, 1991–1998: Stagnation and Survival', *Europe–Asia Studies*, 51:3 (1999), pp. 379–415.

Sarsembayev, Azamat, 'Imagined Communities: Kazak Nationalism and

Kazakification in the 1990s', *Central Asian Survey*, 18:3 (1999), pp. 319–47.

Sarty, Leigh, 'Environmental Security After Communism: The Debate', in J. DeBardeleben and J. Hannigan (eds), *Environmental Security and Quality after Communism: Eastern Europe and the Soviet Successor States* (Boulder, CO: Westview Press, 1995).

Schatz, Edward, 'The Politics of Multiple Identities: Lineage and Ethnicity in Kazakhstan', *Europe–Asia Studies*, 52:3 (2000), pp. 489–506.

Schroeder, Paul W., 'The Transformation of Political Thinking: 1787–1848', in Jack Snyder and Robert Jervis (eds), *Coping with Complexity in the International System* (Boulder, CO: Westview Press, 1993).

Schweller, Randall L., *Deadly Imbalances: Tripolarity and Hitler's Strategy of World Conquest* (New York: Columbia University Press, 1998).

Schweller, Randall L., 'Neorealism's Status Quo Bias: What Security Dilemma?,' *Security Studies*, 5:3 (1996), pp. 90–121.

Schweller, Randall L., 'Bandwagoning for Profit: Bringing the Revisionist State Back In', *International Security*, 19:1 (1994), pp. 72–107.

Seidelmann, Reimund, 'NATO's Enlargement as a Policy of Lost Opportunities', *Journal of European Integration*, 20:2–3 (1997), pp. 233–45.

Serfaty, Simon, *Stay the Course: European Unity and Atlantic Solidarity* (New York: Praeger, 1997).

Serfaty, Simon, 'European Common Foreign, Security, and Defense Policies', *Hearings*, House Committee on International Relations, 106th Congress, First Session, 10 November 1999.

Serfaty, Simon, 'Europe 2007: From Nation-States to Member States', *Washington Quarterly*, 23:4 (2000), pp. 15–29.

Serfaty, Simon, 'Europe, the Mediterranean, and the Middle East', *Joint Force Quarterly*, 24 (2000), pp. 56–62.

Serfaty, Simon, 'A Euro-Atlantic Ostpolitik', *Orbis*, 45:4 (2001), pp. 597–607.

Serfaty, Simon, 'Reflections on European Unification', *Responsive Community*, 11:3 (2001), pp. 4–7.

Serfaty, Simon, 'U.S.–European Relationship: Opportunities and Challenges', *Hearings*, Subcommittee on Europe of the House Committee on International Relations, 107th Congress, First Session, 25 April 2001.

Serfaty, Simon, 'The Wars of 9/11', *International Spectator*, 36:4 (2001), pp. 5–11.

Serfaty, Simon, 'The New Normalcy', *Washington Quarterly*, 25:2 (2002), pp. 209–19.

Sharp, Jane M. O., 'Dayton Report Card', *International Security*, 22:3 (1997/98), pp. 101–37.

Shelley, Louise I., 'Organised Crime and Corruption: Security Threats', in David W. P. Lewis and Gilles Lepesant (eds), *What Security for Which Europe? Case Studies from the Baltic to the Black Sea* (New York: Peter Lang, 1999).

Shi Zulin and Xu Yugao, 'The Impact of China's Accession to the World Trade Organization on China's Energy Sector', paper presented at Strategic Thinking on the Energy Issue in the 10th Five-Year Plan (FYP) Workshop on East Asia Energy Futures, Beijing, China, June 2000.

Shlapentokh, Vladimir, Roman Levita and Mikhail Loiberg, *From Submission to Rebellion: The Provinces Versus the Center in Russia* (Boulder, CO: Westview Press, 1997).

Shnirelman, Viktor, 'National Identity and Myths of Ethnogenesis in Transcaucasia', in Graham Smith, Edward Allworth and Vivien Law (eds), *Nation Building in the Post-Soviet Borderlands: The Politics of National Identities* (Cambridge: Cambridge University Press, 1998).

Silber, Laura and Allen Little, *Yugoslavia: Death of a Nation*, rev. edn (New York: Penguin, 1997).

Singer, Max and Aaron Wildavsky, *The Real World Order: Zones of Peace, Zones of Turmoil* (Chatham, NJ: Chatham House, 1996).

Siverson, Randolph M. and Harvey Starr, 'Opportunity, Willingness, and the Diffusion of War', *American Political Science Review*, 84:1 (March 1990), pp. 47–67.

Slezkine, Yuri, 'The USSR as Communal Apartment, or How a Socialist State Promoted Ethnic Particularism', *Slavic Review*, 53:2 (1994), pp. 414–53.

Smith, Anthony D., *The Ethnic Origins of Nations* (Oxford: Blackwell, 1986).

Smith, David R., 'Environmental Security and Shared Water Resources in Post-Soviet Central Asia', *Post-Soviet Geography*, 36:6 (1995), pp. 351–70.

Smith, Graham, 'Post Colonialism and Borderland Identities', in Graham Smith, Edward Allworth and Vivien Law (eds), *Nation-Building in the Post-Soviet Borderlands: The Politics of National Identities* (Cambridge: Cambridge University Press, 1998).

Smith, Graham, *The Post-Soviet States: Mapping the Politics of Transition* (New York: Oxford University Press, 1999).

Smith, Michael, 'The European Union and a Changing Europe: Establishing the Boundaries of Order', *Journal of Common Market Studies*, 34:1 (1996), pp. 5–27.

Snidal, Duncan, 'Relative Gains and the Pattern of International Cooperation', *American Political Science Review*, 85:3 (September 1991), pp. 701–26.

Snyder, Craig A., 'Regional Security Structures', in Craig A. Snyder (ed.), *Contemporary Security and Strategy* (London: Macmillan, 1999).

Snyder, Glenn H., 'The Security Dilemma in Alliance Politics', *World Politics*, 36:4 (1985), pp. 461–96.

Snyder, Glenn H., 'Alliances, Balance and Stability', *International Organization*, 45:1 (1991), pp. 121–42.

Snyder, Jack, *From Voting to Violence: Democratization and Nationalist Conflict* (New York: W. W. Norton, 2000).

Snyder, Jack and Robert Jervis, 'Civil War and the Security Dilemma', in Barbara Walter and Jack Snyder (eds), *Civil Wars, Insecurity, and Intervention* (New York: Columbia University Press, 1999).

Sokolsky, Richard and Tanya Charlick-Paley, *NATO and Caspian Security: A Mission Too Far?* (Santa Monica: Rand Corporation, 1999).

Spector, Regine A., 'The Caspian Basin and Asian Energy Market', *Background Paper* (Washington, DC: Brookings Institution, 24 May 2001).

Sperling, James, 'Two Tiers or Two Speeds? Constructing a Stable European Security Order', in James Sperling (ed.), *Two Tiers or Two Speeds? The European Security Order and the Enlargement of the European Union and NATO* (Manchester: Manchester University Press, 1999).

Sperling, James (ed.), *Two Tiers or Two Speeds? The European Security Order and the Enlargement of the European Union and NATO* (Manchester: Manchester University Press, 1999).

Sperling, James, 'The United States: Strategic Vision or Tactical Planning?,' in Martin Smith and Graham Timmins (eds), *Uncertain Europe* (London: Routledge, 2001).

Sperling, James and Emil Kirchner, *Recasting the European Order: Security Architectures and Economic Cooperation* (Manchester: Manchester University Press, 1997).

Sperling, James and Emil Kirchner, 'The Security Architectures and Institutional Features of Post-1989 Europe', *Journal of European Public Policy*, 42:2 (1997), pp. 155–70.

Sperling, James and Emil Kirchner, 'Economic Security and the Problem of Cooperation in Post Cold War Europe', *Review of International Studies*, 24:2 (1998), pp. 221–37.

Spero, Joshua B., 'Enhancing Great Powers: Medium Size State Impact on Regional Security Cooperation', manuscript.

Spruyt, Hendrik and Laurent Ruseckas, 'Economics and Energy in the South: Liberal Expectations Versus Likely Realities', in Rajan Menon, Yuri Fyodorov and Ghia Nodia (eds), *Russia, the Caucasus, and Central Asia: The 21st Century Security Environment* (Armonk, NY: M. E. Sharpe, 1999).

Starr, S. Frederick (ed.), *The Legacy of History in Russia and the New States of Eurasia* (Armonk, NY: M. E. Sharpe, 1994).

Starr, S. Frederick, 'Making Eurasia Stable', *Foreign Affairs*, 75:1 (1996), pp. 80–92.

Stein, Arthur, *Why Nations Cooperate* (Ithaca, NY: Cornell University Press, 1993).

Stepanenko, Victor and Sergei Sorokopud, 'The Construction of National Identity: A Case Study of the Ukraine', in Christopher Williams and Thanasis Sfikas (eds), *Ethnicity and Nationalism in Russia, the CIS and the Baltic States* (Brookfield, VT: Ashgate, 1999).

Stoner-Weiss, Kathryn, 'Wither the State? The Regional Sources of Russia's Post-Soviet Governance Crisis', paper prepared for the 2000 Annual Meeting of the American Political Science Association, Washington, DC, 31 August–3 September 2000.

Strange, Susan, '*Cave! Hic Dragones*: A Critique of Regime Analysis', *International Organization*, 36:2 (1982), pp. 479–96.

Suleymanov, Elin, 'Azerbaijan, Azerbaijanis and the Search for Identity', *Analysis of Current Events*, 13:1 (2001), pp. 3–6.

Suny, Ronald, *Looking Toward Ararat: Armenia in Modern History* (Bloomington: Indiana University Press, 1993).

Suny, Ronald, *The Revenge of the Past: Nationalism, Revolution, and the Collapse of the Soviet Union* (Stanford, CA: Stanford University Press, 1993).

Suny, Ronald, 'Provisional Stabilities: The Politics of Identities in Post-Soviet Eurasia', *International Security*, 24:3 (1999/2000), pp. 139–79.

Swanstro, Niklas and Svante E. Cornell, 'China's Trepidation in Afghanistan', *Central Asia Caucasus Analysts* (Washington, DC: Central Asia Caucasus Institute, Johns Hopkins University, 10 October 2001).

Swietochowski, Tadeusz, *Russia and Azerbaijan: A Borderland in Transition* (New York: Columbia University Press, 1995).

Swietochowski, Tadeusz, 'Azerbaijan: Perspectives from the Crossroads', *Central Asian Survey*, 18:4 (1999), pp. 419–35.

Talbott, Strobe, 'A Farewell to Flashman: American Policy in the Caucasus and Central Asia', address at the Johns Hopkins School of Advanced International

Studies, Washington DC, *U.S. Department of State Dispatch*, 8:7 (1997), pp. 10–13.

Taliaferro, Jeffrey W., 'Security Seeking under Anarchy: Defensive Realism Revisited', *International Security*, 25:3 (2000/1), pp. 128–61.

Tang, Frank C. and Fereidun Fesharaki, 'China: Evolving Oil Trade Patterns and Prospects to 2000', *Natural Resources Forum*, 19:1 (1995), pp. 47–58.

Tang Shiping, 'Economic Integration in Central Asia: The Russian and Chinese Relationship', *Asian Survey*, 40:2 (2000), pp. 360–76.

Taylor, Brian D., 'Commentary on Moldova', in Alexei Arbatov, (ed.), *Managing Conflict in the Former Soviet Union* (Cambridge, MA: MIT Press, 1997).

Tilly, Charles, 'War Making and State Making as Organized Crime', in Peter B. Evans, Dietrich Rueschemeyer and Theda Skocpol (eds), *Bringing the State Back In* (Cambridge: Cambridge University Press, 1985).

Tishkov, Valery, *Ethnicity, Nationalism and Conflict in and after the Soviet Union: The Mind Aflame* (London: Sage, 1997).

Tolz, Vera, 'Forging the Nation: National Identity and Nation Building in Post-Communist Russia', *Europe–Asia Studies*, 50:6 (1998), pp. 993–1022.

Troush, Sergei, 'China's Changing Oil Strategy and its Foreign Policy Implications', *CNAP Working Paper* (Washington, DC: Brookings Institution, 1999).

Tuminez, Astrid, *Russian Nationalism since 1856: Ideology and the Making of Foreign Policy* (Lanham, MD: Rowman and Littlefield, 2000).

US Department of Defense, *United States Security Strategy for Europe and NATO* (Washington, DC: GPO, 1995).

US Department of Defense, *Partnership for Peace* (Washington, DC: GPO, 1996).

Valinakis, Yannis, 'The Black Sea Region: Challenges and Opportunities for Europe', *Chaillot Paper 36* (Paris: Institute for Security Studies of WEU, 1999).

Van Evera, Steven, 'Offense, Defense, and the Causes of War', *International Security*, 15:3 (1990–91), pp. 33–40.

Viega da Cuhna, Luis, 'The Aral Sea Crisis: A Great Challenge in Transboundary Water Resources Management', NATO Advanced Research Workshop on Transboundary Water Resources Management: Technical and Institutional Issues, Skopelos, May 1994.

Volkov, Vadim, 'Violent Entrepreneurship in Post-Communist Russia', *Europe–Asia Studies*, 51:5 (1999), pp. 741–54.

Wæver, Ole, Barry Buzan, Morten Kelstrup and Pierre Lemaitre, *Identity, Migration and the New Security Agenda in Europe* (London: Pinter, 1993).

Wallace, William, 'Regionalism in Europe: Model or Exception', in Louise Fawcett and Andrew Hurrel (eds), *Regionalism in World Politics, Regional Organization and International Order* (New York: Oxford University Press, 1997).

Wallander, Celeste A., 'Institutional Assets and Adaptability: NATO after the Cold War', *International Organization*, 54:4 (2000), pp. 705–36.

Walt, Stephen, *The Origins of Alliances* (Ithaca, NY: Cornell University Press, 1987).

Walter, Barbara F., 'The Critical Barrier to Civil War Settlement', *International Organization*, 51:3 (1997), pp. 335–64.

Waltz, Kenneth N., *Theory of International Politics* (New York: Random House, 1978).

Wang Qingyi, 'Zhongguo de Nengyuan Weiji' ('China's Energy Crisis),' in Li Ming (ed.), *Zhongguo de Weiji (Xia) (The Crisis of China II)* (Beijing: Gaige chubanshe, 1998).

Wang Zhiyi and Pan Zhiping, 'Lishi Huigu: Zhongya de Dongdang he Xinjiang de

Wending' ('History Recollection: Turbulence in Central Asia and Stability of Xinjiang'), in Pan Zhiping (ed.), *Minzu Zijue, Haishi Minzu Fenlie: Minzu he Dangdai Minzu Fenlie Zhuyi (Ethnic Sovereignty or Ethnic Separatism)* (Urumuchi: Xinjiangrenmin chubanshe, 1999).

Webber, Mark, 'Security Governance and the "Excluded" States of Central and Eastern Europe', in Andrew Cottey and Derek Averre (eds), *Ten Years after 1989: New Security Challenges in Central and Eastern Europe* (Manchester: Manchester University Press, 2002).

Weinthal, Erica, 'Making Waves: Third Parties and International Mediation in the Aral Sea Basin', in Melanie Greenberg, John Barton and Margaret McGuiness (eds), *Words over War: Mediation and Arbitration to Prevent Deadly Conflict* (Lanham, MD: Rowman and Littlefield, 2000).

Weisbrode, Kenneth, *Central Eurasia: Prize or Quicksand? Contending Views of Instability in Karabakh, Ferghana and Afghanistan* (London: International Institute for Strategic Studies, 2001).

Welsh, Helga A. and John P. Willerton, 'Regional Cooperation and the CIS: West European Lessons and Post-Soviet Experience', *International Politics*, 34:1 (1997), pp. 33–61.

Wendt, Alexander, 'Anarchy is What States Make of It: The Social Construction of Power Politics', *International Organization*, 46:2 (1992), pp. 391–425.

Wendt, Alexander, 'Collective Identity Formation and the International State', *American Political Science Review*, 88:2 (1994), pp. 384–96.

Wendt, Alexander, *Social Theory of International Politics* (Cambridge: Cambridge University Press, 1999).

Wheeler, Gregory, *The Modern History of Central Asia* (London: Weidenfeld and Nicolson, 1964).

Williams, Nick, 'Partnership for Peace: Permanent Fixture or Declining Asset?', in Philip H. Gordon (ed.), *NATO's Transformation: The Changing Shape of the Atlantic Alliance* (Lanham, MD: Rowman and Littlefield, 1997).

Williamson, Joel E. and Jennifer D. P. Moroney, 'Security Cooperation Pays Off: A Lesson from the Afghan War', *Current Defense Analyses*, 3 (2002), pp. 1–3.

Wilson, Andrew, 'National History and National Identity in Ukraine and Belarus', in Graham Smith, Edward Allworth and Vivien Law (eds), *Nation-Building in the Post-Soviet Borderlands: The Politics of National Identities* (Cambridge: Cambridge University Press, 1998).

Wilson, Andrew, 'Redefining Ethnic and Linguistic Boundaries in Ukraine: Indigenes, Settlers, and Russophone Ukrainians', in Graham Smith, Edward Allworth and Vivien Law (eds), *Nation-Building in Post-Soviet Borderlands: The Politics of National Identities* (Cambridge: Cambridge University Press, 1998).

Wittfogel, Karl, *Oriental Despotism: A Comparative Study of Total Power* (New Haven, CT: Yale University Press, 1957).

Wolfers, Arnold, *Discord and Collaboration: Essays on International Politics* (Baltimore, MD: Johns Hopkins University Press, 1962).

World Bank, *World Development Indicators on CD-ROM* (Washington, DC: World Bank, 1997).

World Resources Institute, *A Guide to the Global Environment 1994–95* (Washington, DC: World Resources Institute, 1995).

Xing Guancheng, 'China and Central Asia: Towards a New Relationship', in Zhang

Yongjin and Ronben Azizian (eds), *Ethnic Challenges Beyond Borders: Chinese and Russian Perspectives on the Central Asian Conundrum* (New York: St Martin's Press, 1998).

Xing Guancheng, 'China and Central Asia', in Roy Allison and Lena Johnson (eds), *Central Asian Security: The New International Context* (Washington, DC: Brookings Institution, 2001).

Yost, David S., *NATO Transformed: The Alliance's New Roles in International Security* (Washington, DC: US Institute of Peace Press, 1998).

Young, Oran R., 'The Effectiveness of International Institutions: Hard Cases and Critical Variables', in James N. Rosenau and Ernst-Otto Czempiel (eds), *Governance without Government: Order and Change in World Politics* (Cambridge: Cambridge University Press, 1992).

Young, Oran R., *International Governance: Protecting the Environment in a Stateless Society* (Ithaca, NY: Cornell University Press, 1994).

Young, Oran R., *Governance in World Affairs* (Ithaca, NY: Cornell University Press, 1999).

Zacher, Mark W., 'The Territorial Integrity Norm: International Boundaries and the Use of Force', *International Organization*, 55:2 (2001), pp. 215–50.

Zevelev, Igor, 'The Russian Quest for a National Identity: Implications for Security in Eurasia', in Sharyl Cross *et al.* (eds), *Global Security Beyond the Millennium: American and Russian Perspectives* (New York: St Martin's Press, 1999).

Zhang Wenmu, *Zhongguo Xin Shiji Anquan Zhanlue* (*China's Security Strategy in the New Century*) (Jinan: Shandongremin chubanshe, 2000).

Zhang Yongjin and Rouben Azizian (eds.), *Ethnic Challenges Beyond Borders: Chinese and Russian Perspective of the Central Asian Conundrum* (New York: St Martin's Press, 1998).

Zheng Yu (ed.), *Dulianti Shinian: Xianzhuang, Wenti, Qianjing 1991–2000* (*The Ten Years of the CIS: Present Situation, Problems and Prospects 1991–2001*) (Beijing: Shijie chubanshe, 2002).

Zhongguo Xiandai Guoji Guanxi Yanjiusuo (China Contemporary International Relations Institute), *Guoji Zhanlue yu Anquan Xinshi Pinggu 2001/2002* (*International Strategic and Security Review 2001/2002*) (Beijing: Shishi chubanshe, 2002).

Zhongguo Xiandai Guoji Guanxi Yanjiusuo (China Contemporary International Relations Institute) (ed.), *Shanghai Hezuo Zuzhi: Xin Anquanguan yu Xin Jizhi* (*Shanghai Cooperation Organisation: New Security Perceptions and System*) (Beijing: Shishi chubanshe, 2002).

Zhou Fengqi, *Prospect of Petroleum and Natural Gas Supply and Demand in China and in the World by 2010 and by 2020* (Beijing: Energy Resources Institute, State Development Planning Commission, November 1998).

Zviagelskaia, Irina and Vitali Naumkin, 'Non-Traditional Threats, Challenges, and Risks in the Former Soviet South', in Graham Smith, Edward Allworth and Vivien Law (eds), *Nation-Building in the Post-Soviet Borderlands: The Politics of National Identities* (Cambridge: Cambridge University Press, 1998).

Index